LOVE MANGA
LET US KNOW WHAT YOU THINK!

DETROIT PUBLIC LIBRARY

W9-DEK-268

OUR MANGA SURVEY IS NOW
AVAILABLE ONLINE. PLEASE VISIT:
VIZ.COM/MANGASURVEY

HELP US MAKE THE MANGA
YOU LOVE BETTER!

VIZ
MEDIA

FULLMETAL ALCHEMIST © Hiromu Arakawa/SQUARE ENIX. INUYASHA © 1997 Rumiko TAKAHASHI/Shogakukan Inc.
NAOKI URASAWA'S MONSTER © 1995 Naoki URASAWA Studio Nuts/Shogakukan Inc. ZATCH BELL! © 2001 Makoto RAIKU/Shogakukan Inc.

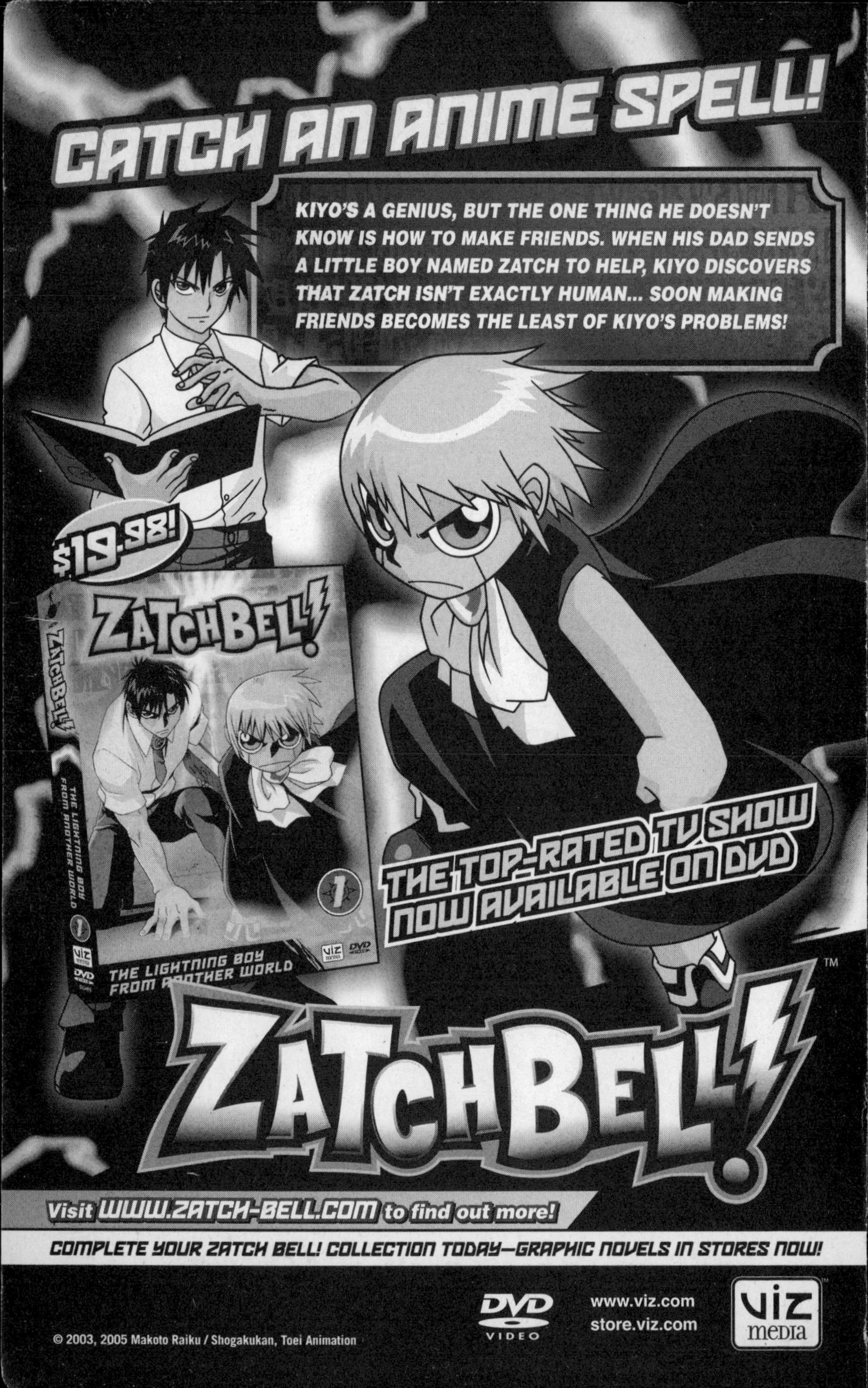
CATCH AN ANIME SPELL!
KIYO'S A GENIUS, BUT THE ONE THING HE DOESN'T KNOW IS HOW TO MAKE FRIENDS. WHEN HIS DAD SENDS A LITTLE BOY NAMED ZATCH TO HELP, KIYO DISCOVERS THAT ZATCH ISN'T EXACTLY HUMAN... SOON MAKING FRIENDS BECOMES THE LEAST OF KIYO'S PROBLEMS!
$19.98!
ZATCH BELL!
THE LIGHTNING BOY FROM ANOTHER WORLD
THE TOP-RATED TV SHOW NOW AVAILABLE ON DVD
ZATCH BELL!™
Visit WWW.ZATCH-BELL.COM to find out more!
COMPLETE YOUR ZATCH BELL! COLLECTION TODAY—GRAPHIC NOVELS IN STORES NOW!
DVD VIDEO
www.viz.com
store.viz.com
VIZ MEDIA
© 2003, 2005 Makoto Raiku / Shogakukan, Toei Animation

STORY AND ART BY

MAKOTO RAIKU

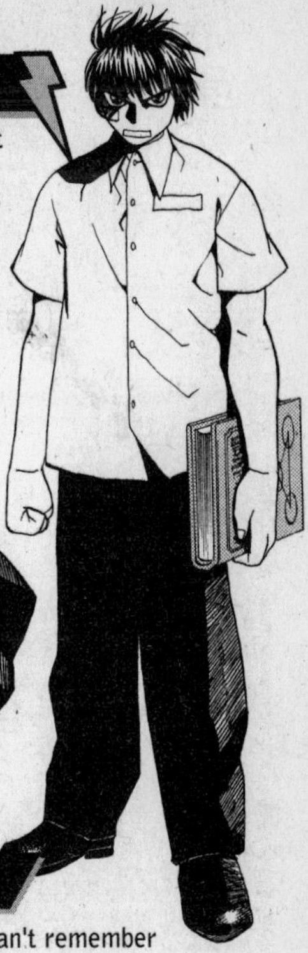

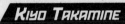

Kiyo Takamine

A cool junior high student with a genius intellect. The day he met Zatch, he became the owner of the "Red Book"—and started growing up.

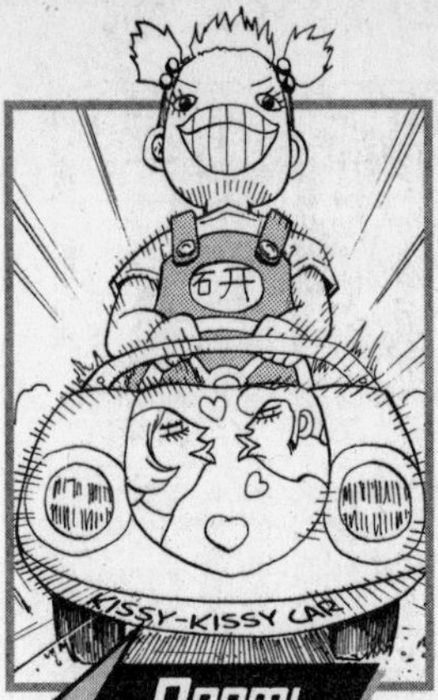
KISSY-KISSY CAR

Naomi

A girl who picks on Zatch. But what does that character on her shirt say?

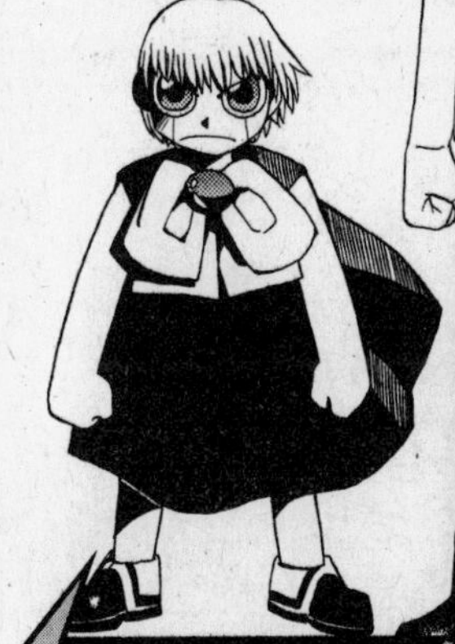

Zatch Bell

A mamodo child who can't remember his past. When Kiyo holds the "Red Book" and reads a spell, electric shocks shoot from Zatch's mouth.

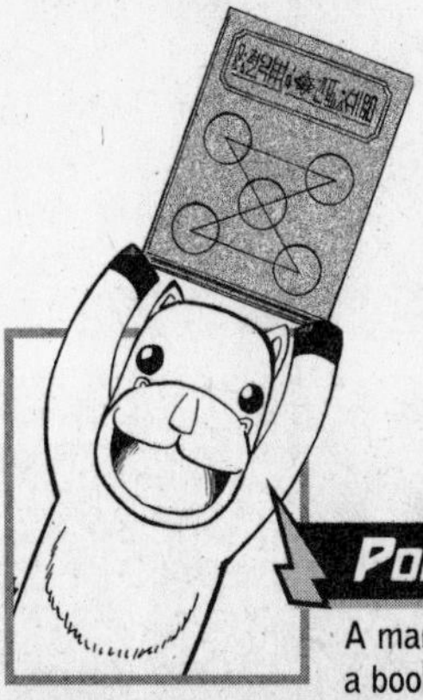

Ponygon

A mamodo without a book owner.

Kiyo's classmates

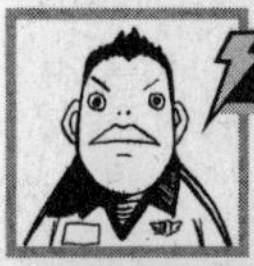

Iwashima

A funny guy.

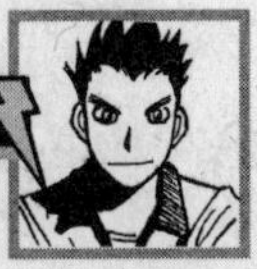

Yamanaka

On the baseball team.

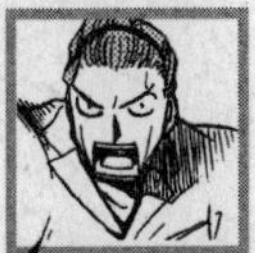

Kane

A bully.

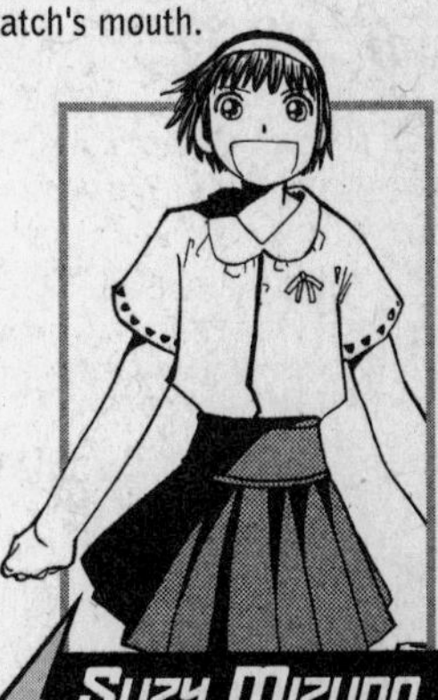

Suzy Mizuno

A classmate who likes Kiyo—and trouble!

ZATCH'S PAST OPPONENTS

| Kolulu | Sugino | Gofure | Brago | Reycom |

| Maruss | Robnos | Kanchomé | Eshros | Fein |

| | | | Kikuropu | Baltro |

THE STORY THUS FAR

Kiyo is a junior high student who's so intelligent that he's bored by life and doesn't even go to school. Kiyo's father sends him an amazing child named Zatch as a birthday present. When Kiyo holds the "Red Book" (which only Kiyo can read) and reads a spell, Zatch displays various powers. Zatch is one of 100 mamodo children chosen to fight in a battle which will determine who is king of the mamodo world for the next 1,000 years. The bond between Zatch and Kiyo deepens as they're forced to fight for their own survival.

Zatch and Kiyo visit England, where Zatch's look-alike has been spotted. After surviving another difficult match with the mamodo, they reunite with Kiyo's father, who had been kidnapped. Having regained part of his lost memory, Zatch and Kiyo return to Japan safely...along with Ponygon...

ZATCHBELL! 7

CONTENTS

LEVEL.58 **WHAT HAPPENED TO SUZY?** 7

LEVEL.59 **THE MAN OF FREEDOM** 25

LEVEL.60 **UNLIMITED POWER** 49

LEVEL.61 **KIYO'S STRENGTH** 67

LEVEL.62 **THE MOST POWERFUL SPELL** 85

LEVEL.63 **THE BATTLE IN THE PARK** 103

LEVEL.64 **THE MASTERPIECE** 121

LEVEL.65 **DANNY'S POWER** 139

LEVEL.66 **MISSION ACCOMPLISHED** 157

LEVEL 58:
What Happened to Suzy?

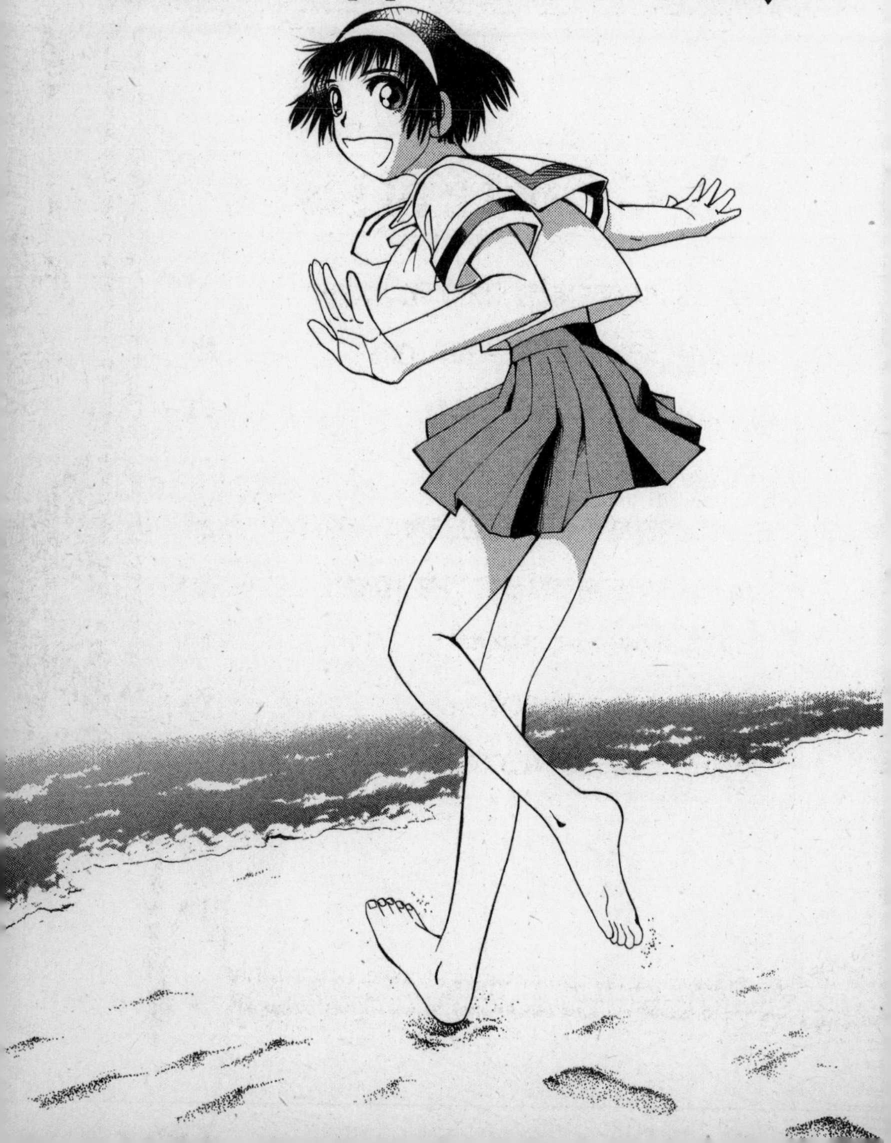

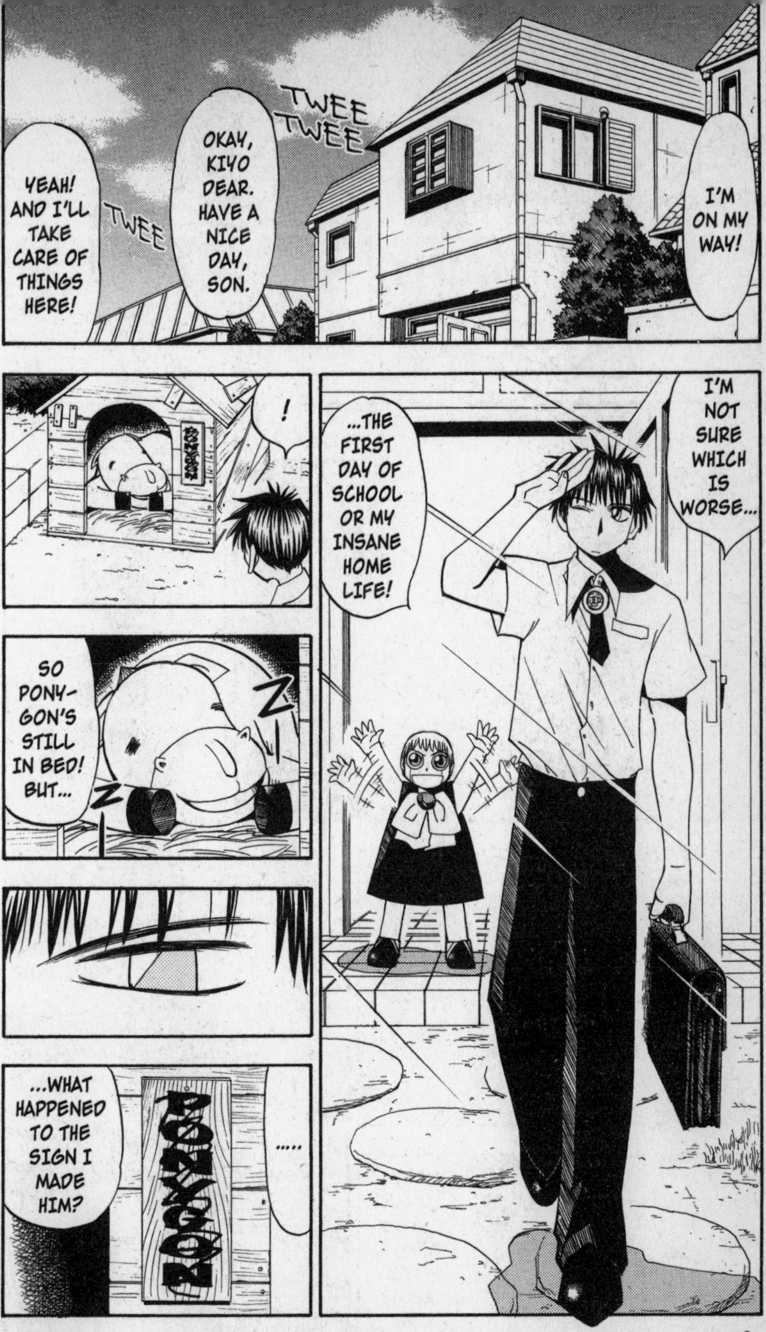
I'M ON MY WAY!
TWEE TWEE
OKAY, KIYO DEAR. HAVE A NICE DAY, SON.
TWEE
YEAH! AND I'LL TAKE CARE OF THINGS HERE!
I'M NOT SURE WHICH IS WORSE...
...THE FIRST DAY OF SCHOOL OR MY INSANE HOME LIFE!
!
SO PONYGON'S STILL IN BED! BUT...
Z
Z
.....
...WHAT HAPPENED TO THE SIGN I MADE HIM?

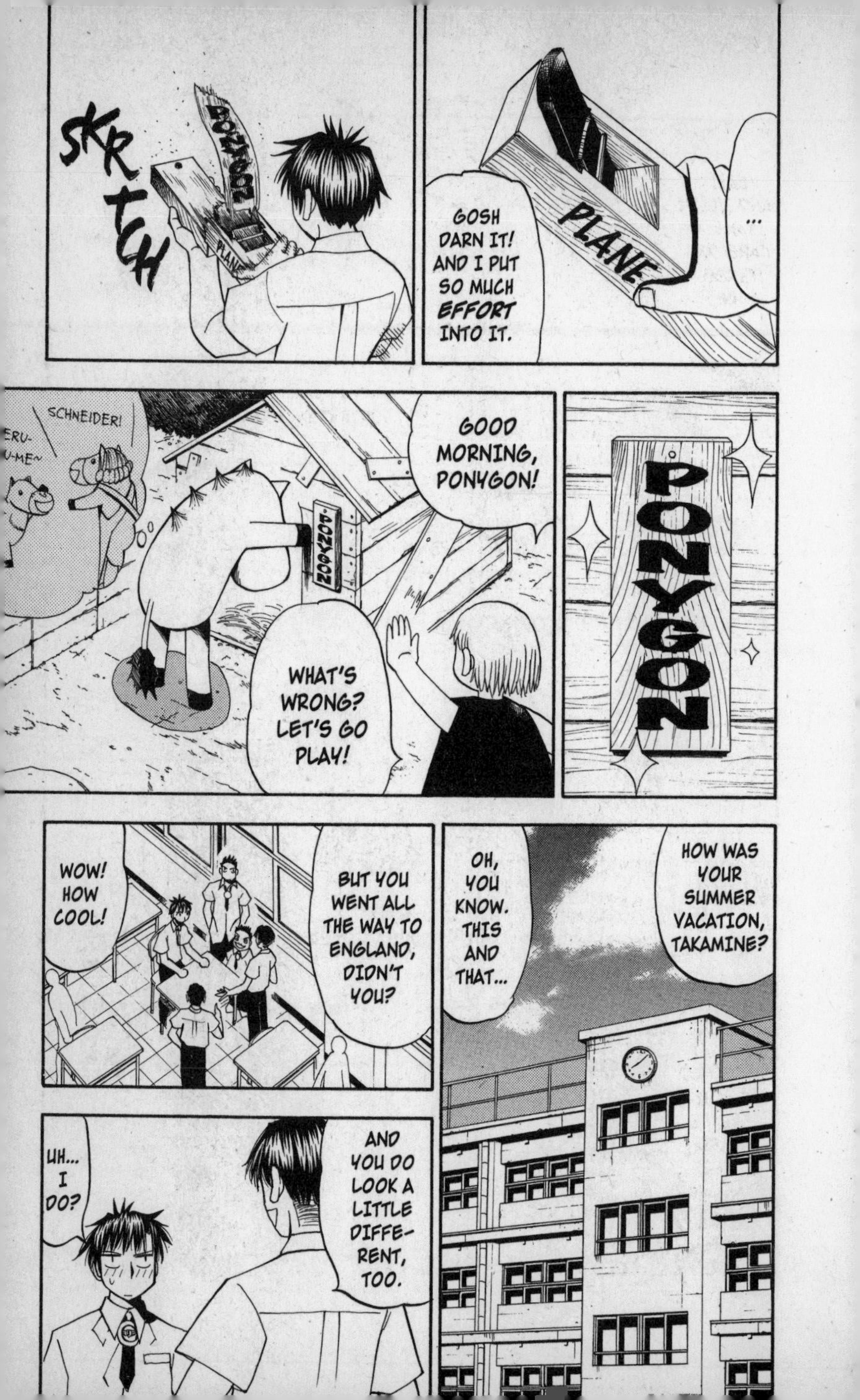
...
PLANE
GOSH DARN IT! AND I PUT SO MUCH EFFORT INTO IT.
SKRTCH
PONYGON
PLANE
PONYGON
GOOD MORNING, PONYGON!
PONYGON
WHAT'S WRONG? LET'S GO PLAY!
SCHNEIDER!
HOW WAS YOUR SUMMER VACATION, TAKAMINE?
OH, YOU KNOW. THIS AND THAT...
BUT YOU WENT ALL THE WAY TO ENGLAND, DIDN'T YOU?
WOW! HOW COOL!
AND YOU DO LOOK A LITTLE DIFFERENT, TOO.
UH... I DO?

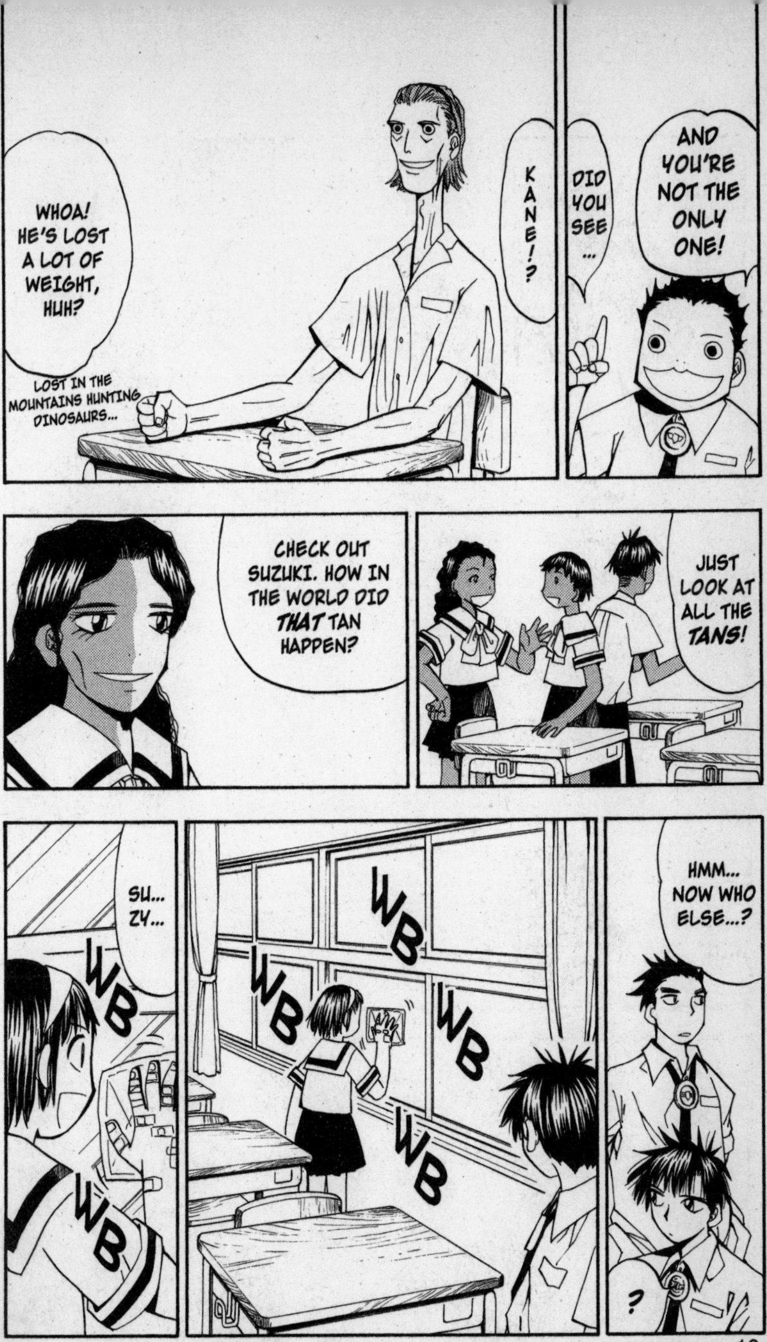
AND YOU'RE NOT THE ONLY ONE!
DID YOU SEE ...
KANE!?
WHOA! HE'S LOST A LOT OF WEIGHT, HUH?
LOST IN THE MOUNTAINS HUNTING DINOSAURS...
JUST LOOK AT ALL THE *TANS!*
CHECK OUT SUZUKI. HOW IN THE WORLD DID *THAT* TAN HAPPEN?
HMM... NOW WHO ELSE...?
?
WB
WB
WB
WB
SU... ZY...
WB
WB

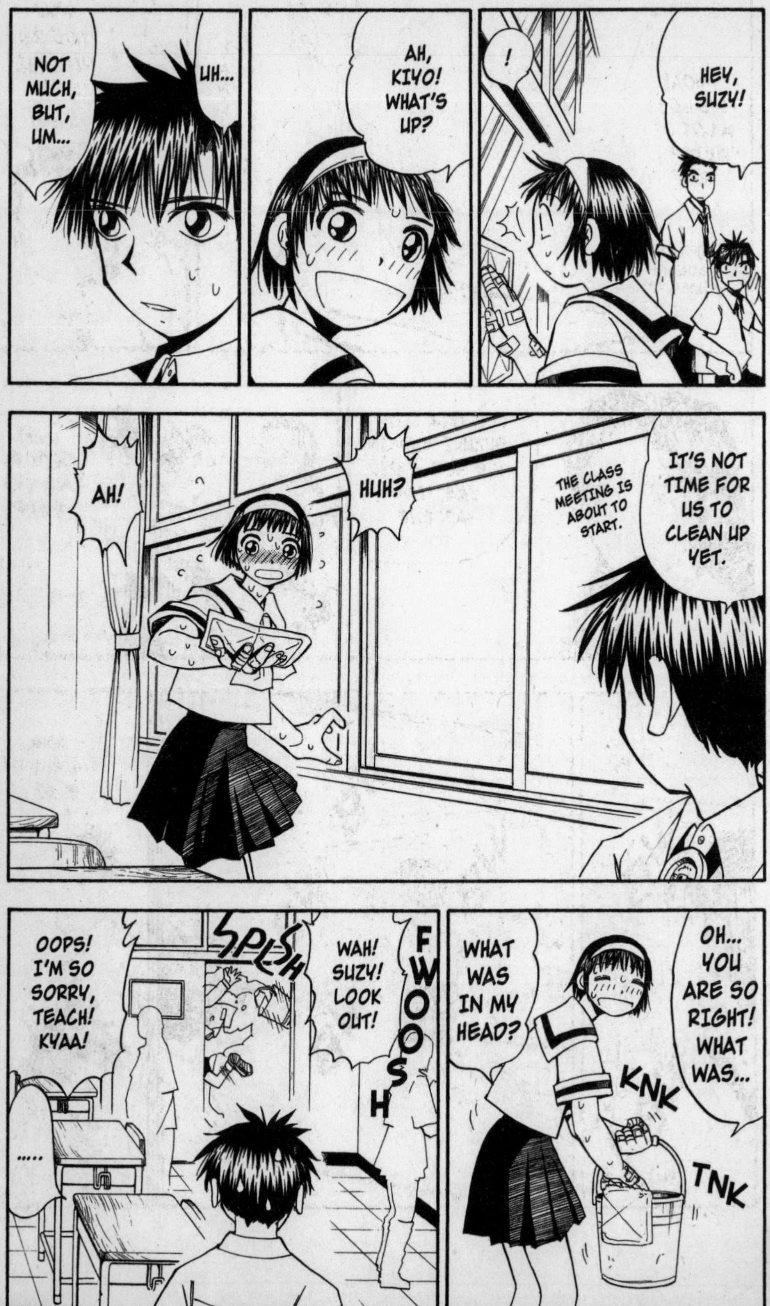
HEY, SUZY!
!
AH, KIYO! WHAT'S UP?
UH...
NOT MUCH, BUT, UM...
IT'S NOT TIME FOR US TO CLEAN UP YET.
THE CLASS MEETING IS ABOUT TO START.
HUH?
AH!
OH... YOU ARE SO RIGHT! WHAT WAS...
KNK
TNK
WHAT WAS IN MY HEAD?
FWOOOSH
WAH! SUZY! LOOK OUT!
SPLSH
OOPS! I'M SO SORRY, TEACH! KYAA!
.....

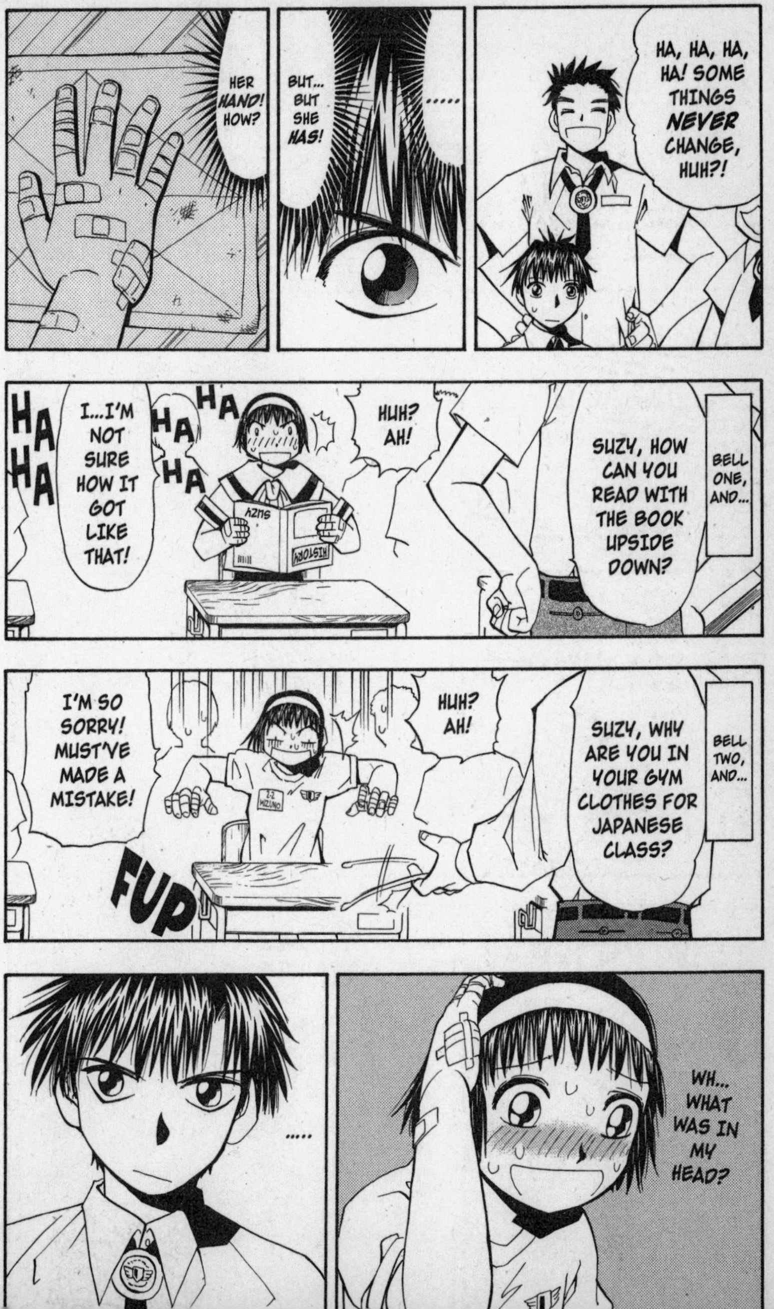
HA, HA, HA, HA! SOME THINGS NEVER CHANGE, HUH?!
.....
BUT... BUT SHE HAS!
HER HAND! HOW?
BELL ONE, AND...
SUZY, HOW CAN YOU READ WITH THE BOOK UPSIDE DOWN?
HUH? AH!
HA HA HA
HA
I...I'M NOT SURE HOW IT GOT LIKE THAT!
HA HA HA
BELL TWO, AND...
SUZY, WHY ARE YOU IN YOUR GYM CLOTHES FOR JAPANESE CLASS?
HUH? AH!
I'M SO SORRY! MUST'VE MADE A MISTAKE!
FUP
WH... WHAT WAS IN MY HEAD?
.....

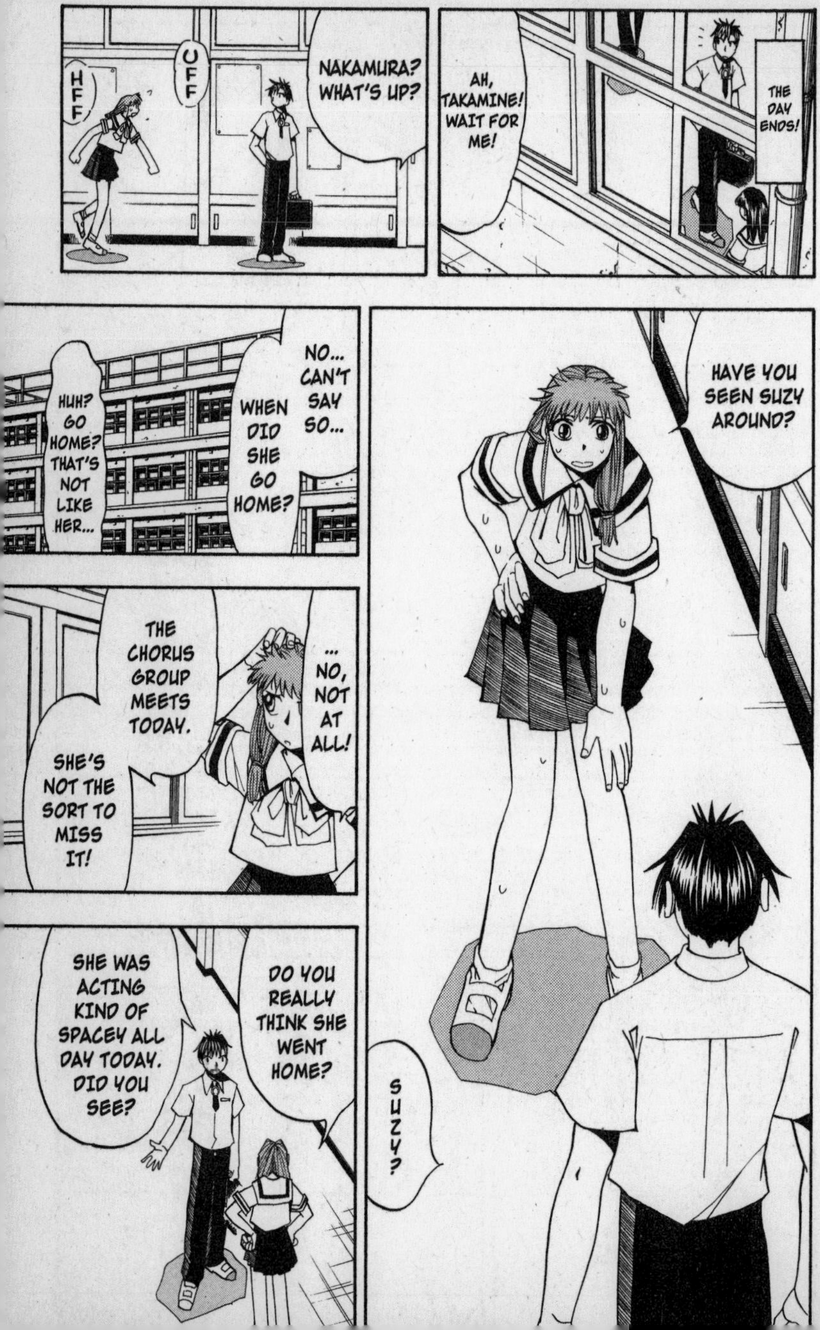
THE DAY ENDS!
AH, TAKAMINE! WAIT FOR ME!
NAKAMURA? WHAT'S UP?
UFF
HFF
HAVE YOU SEEN SUZY AROUND?
SUZY?
NO... CAN'T SAY SO...
WHEN DID SHE GO HOME?
HUH? GO HOME? THAT'S NOT LIKE HER...
... NO, NOT AT ALL!
THE CHORUS GROUP MEETS TODAY.
SHE'S NOT THE SORT TO MISS IT!
DO YOU REALLY THINK SHE WENT HOME?
SHE WAS ACTING KIND OF SPACEY ALL DAY TODAY. DID YOU SEE?

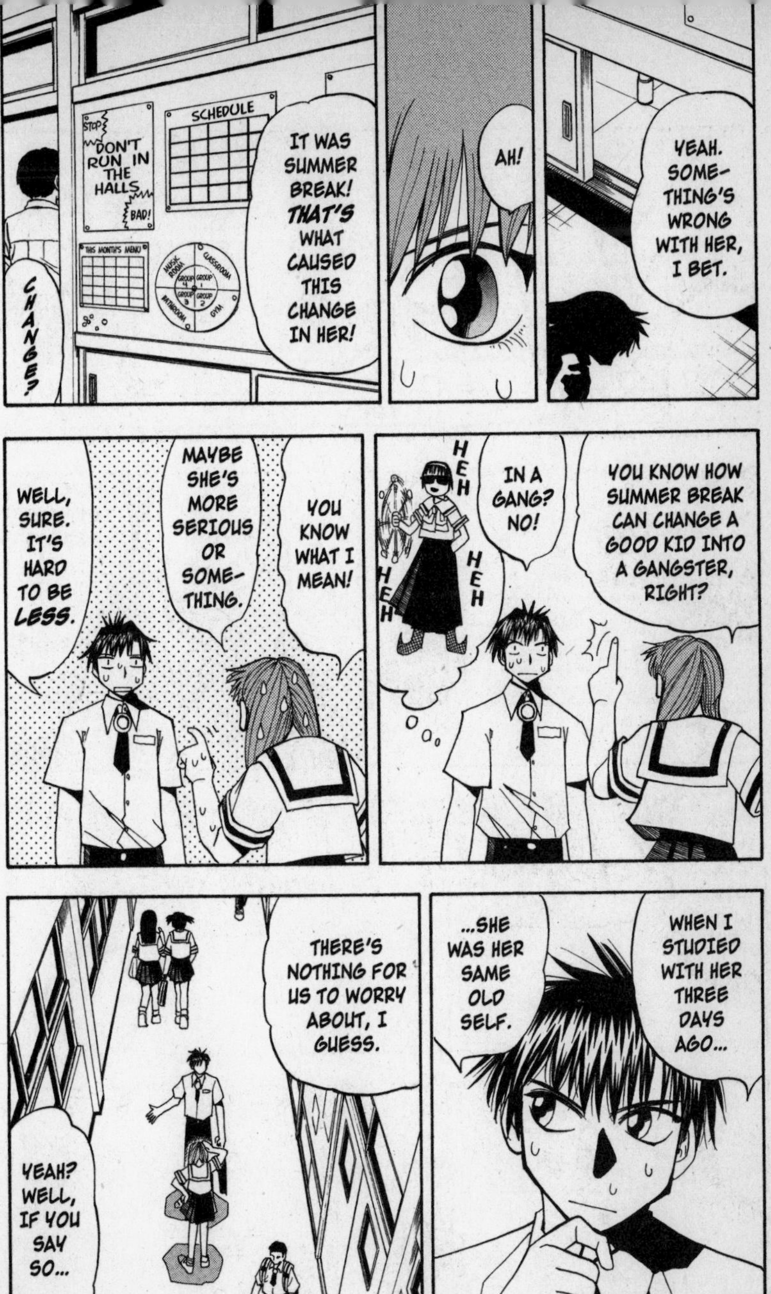
YEAH. SOME-THING'S WRONG WITH HER, I BET.
AH!
IT WAS SUMMER BREAK! THAT'S WHAT CAUSED THIS CHANGE IN HER!
SCHEDULE
STOP DON'T RUN IN THE HALLS BAD!
THIS MONTH'S MENU
CHANGE?
YOU KNOW HOW SUMMER BREAK CAN CHANGE A GOOD KID INTO A GANGSTER, RIGHT?
IN A GANG? NO!
HEH HEH HEH
YOU KNOW WHAT I MEAN!
MAYBE SHE'S MORE SERIOUS OR SOME-THING.
WELL, SURE. IT'S HARD TO BE LESS.
WHEN I STUDIED WITH HER THREE DAYS AGO...
...SHE WAS HER SAME OLD SELF.
THERE'S NOTHING FOR US TO WORRY ABOUT, I GUESS.
YEAH? WELL, IF YOU SAY SO...

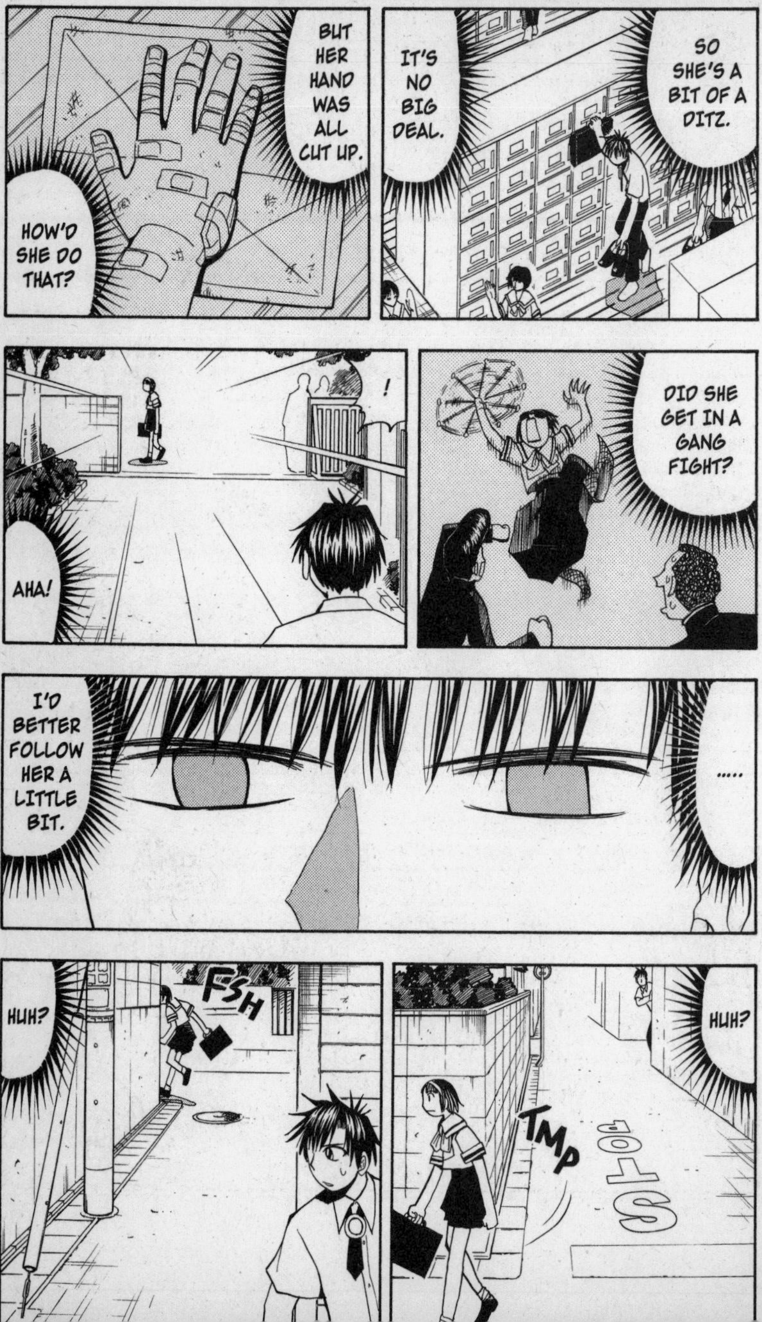
SO SHE'S A BIT OF A DITZ.
IT'S NO BIG DEAL.
BUT HER HAND WAS ALL CUT UP.
HOW'D SHE DO THAT?
DID SHE GET IN A GANG FIGHT?
!
AHA!
.....
I'D BETTER FOLLOW HER A LITTLE BIT.
HUH?
TMP
STOP
HUH?
FSH

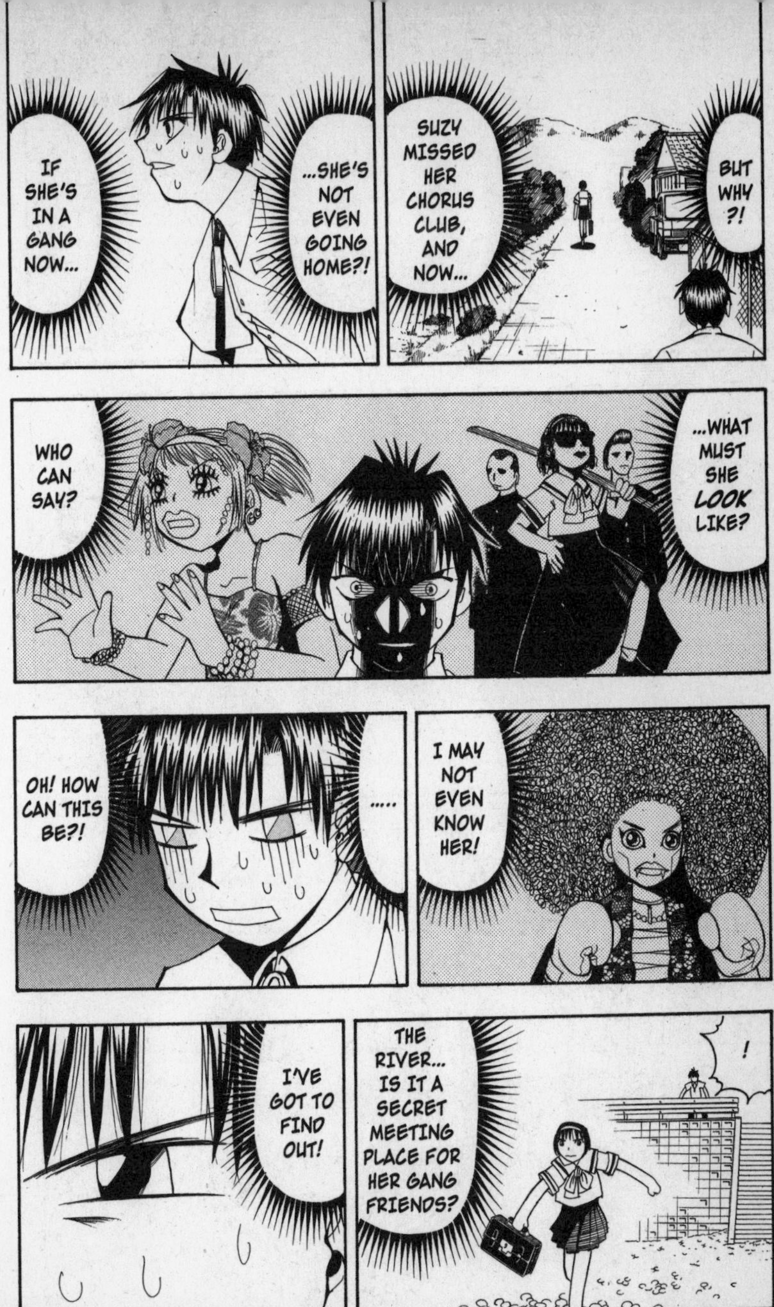
BUT WHY?!
SUZY MISSED HER CHORUS CLUB, AND NOW...
...SHE'S NOT EVEN GOING HOME?!
IF SHE'S IN A GANG NOW...
...WHAT MUST SHE LOOK LIKE?
WHO CAN SAY?
I MAY NOT EVEN KNOW HER!
.....
OH! HOW CAN THIS BE?!
!
THE RIVER... IS IT A SECRET MEETING PLACE FOR HER GANG FRIENDS?
I'VE GOT TO FIND OUT!

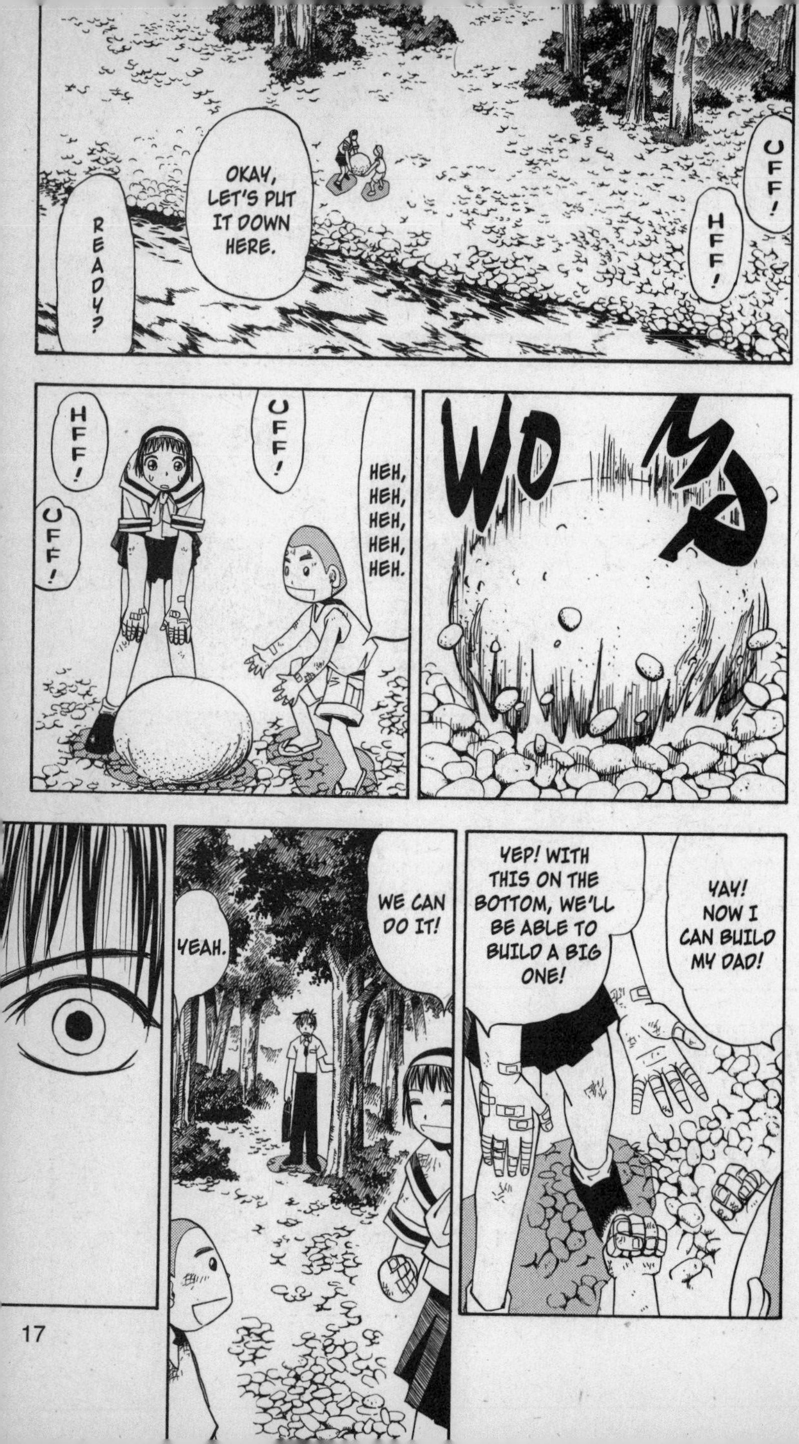
UFF!
HFF!
OKAY, LET'S PUT IT DOWN HERE.
READY?
WOMP
HEH, HEH, HEH, HEH, HEH.
UFF!
HFF!
UFF!
YAY! NOW I CAN BUILD MY DAD!
YEP! WITH THIS ON THE BOTTOM, WE'LL BE ABLE TO BUILD A BIG ONE!
WE CAN DO IT!
YEAH.

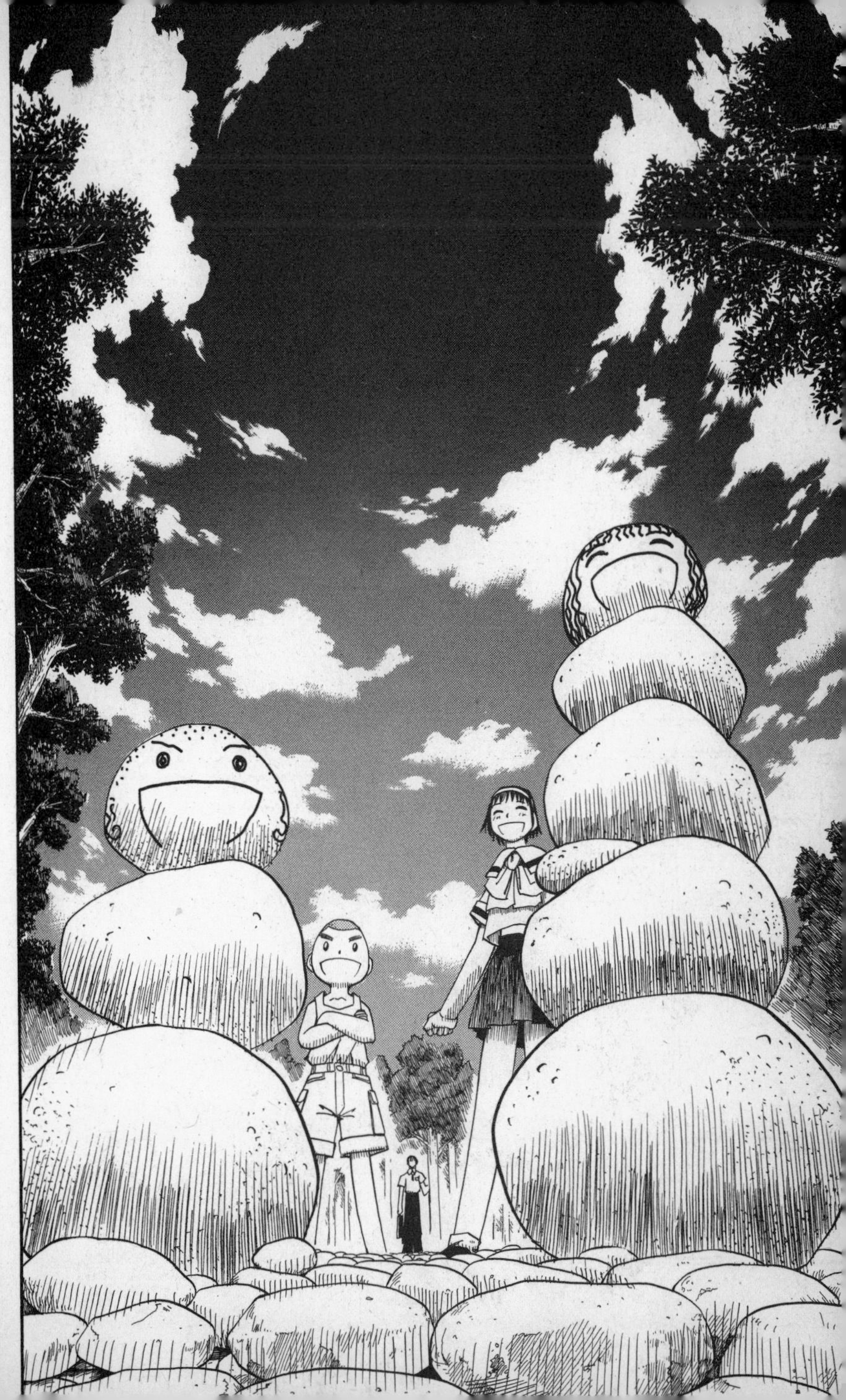

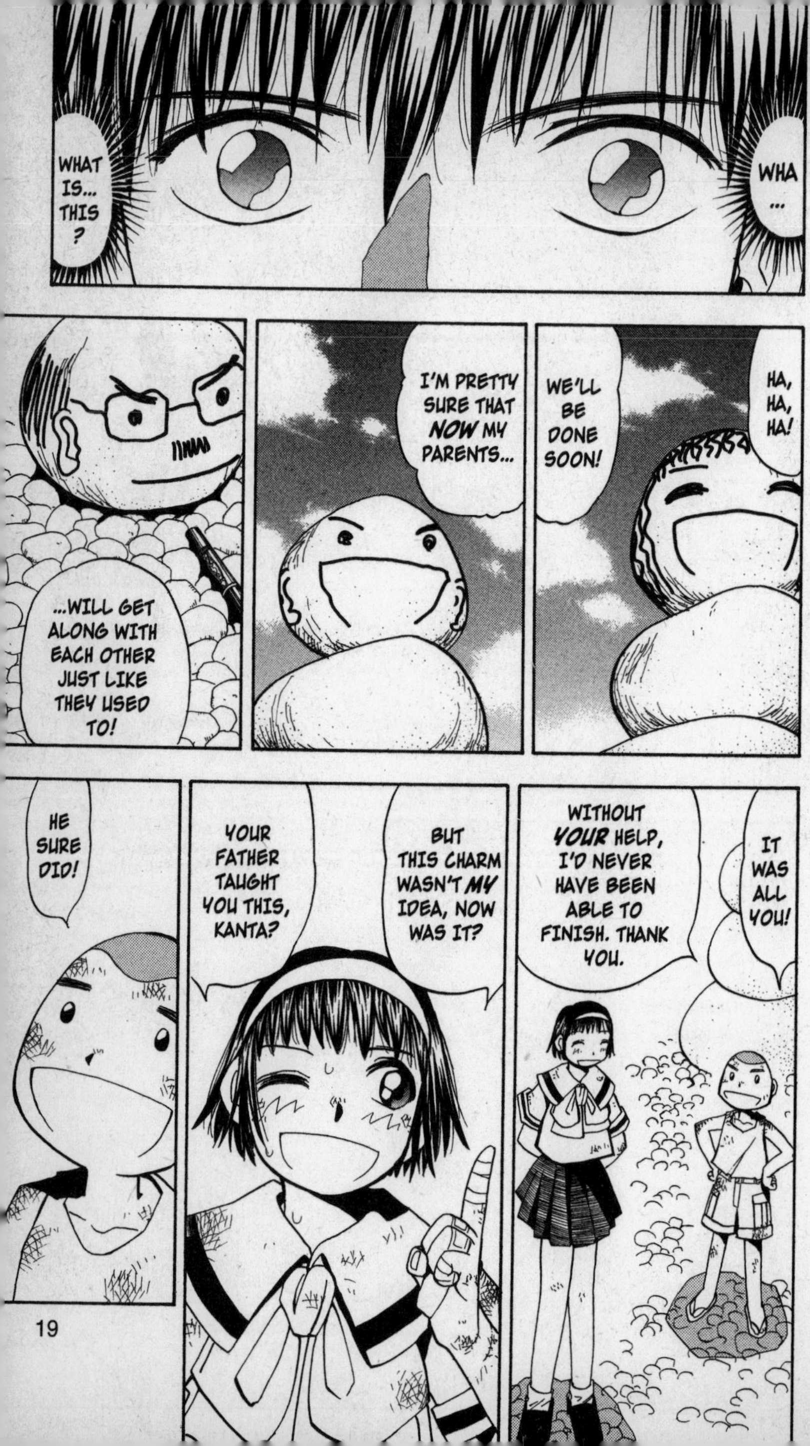
WHA...
WHAT IS... THIS?
HA, HA, HA!
WE'LL BE DONE SOON!
I'M PRETTY SURE THAT NOW MY PARENTS...
...WILL GET ALONG WITH EACH OTHER JUST LIKE THEY USED TO!
IT WAS ALL YOU!
WITHOUT YOUR HELP, I'D NEVER HAVE BEEN ABLE TO FINISH. THANK YOU.
BUT THIS CHARM WASN'T MY IDEA, NOW WAS IT?
YOUR FATHER TAUGHT YOU THIS, KANTA?
HE SURE DID!

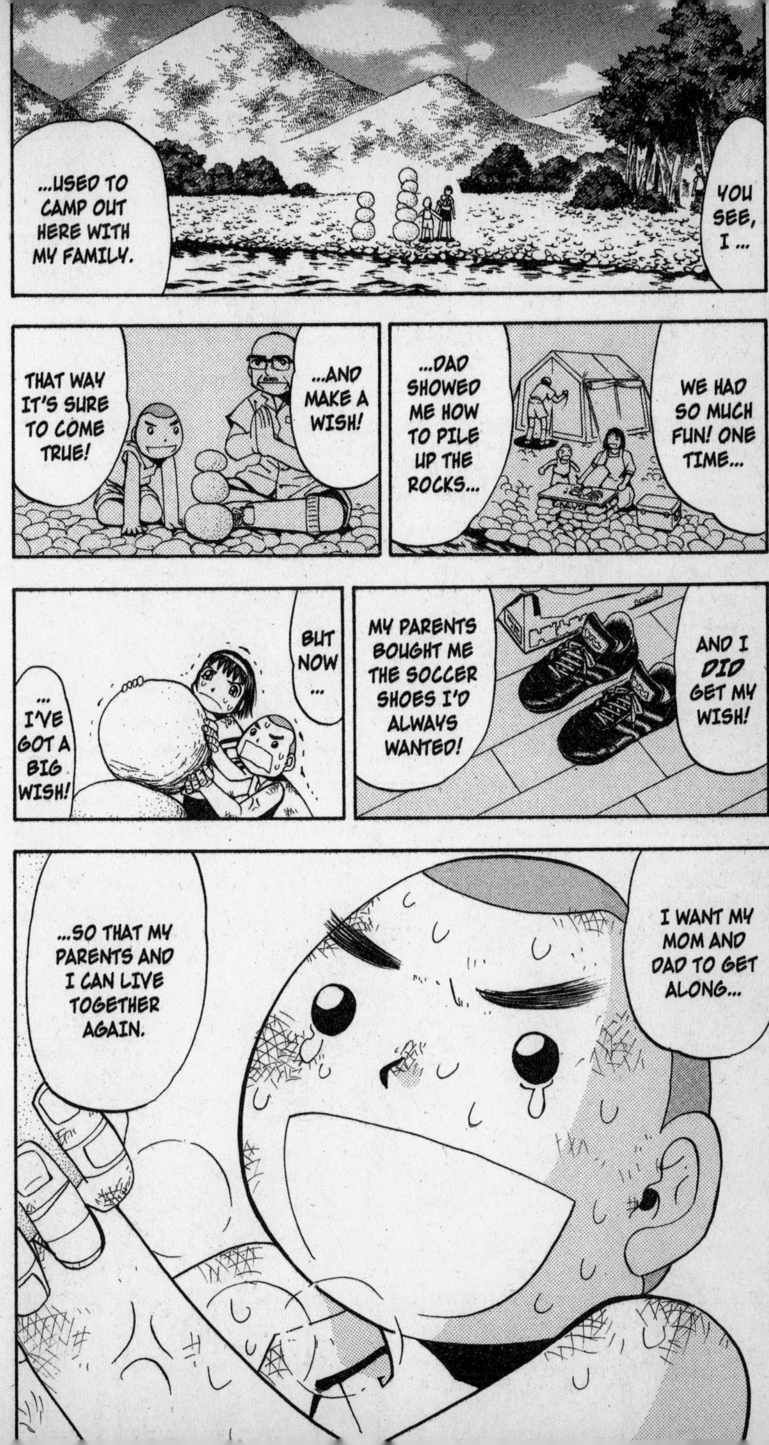
YOU SEE, I ...
...USED TO CAMP OUT HERE WITH MY FAMILY.
WE HAD SO MUCH FUN! ONE TIME...
...DAD SHOWED ME HOW TO PILE UP THE ROCKS...
...AND MAKE A WISH!
THAT WAY IT'S SURE TO COME TRUE!
AND I DID GET MY WISH!
MY PARENTS BOUGHT ME THE SOCCER SHOES I'D ALWAYS WANTED!
BUT NOW ...
... I'VE GOT A BIG WISH!
I WANT MY MOM AND DAD TO GET ALONG...
...SO THAT MY PARENTS AND I CAN LIVE TOGETHER AGAIN.

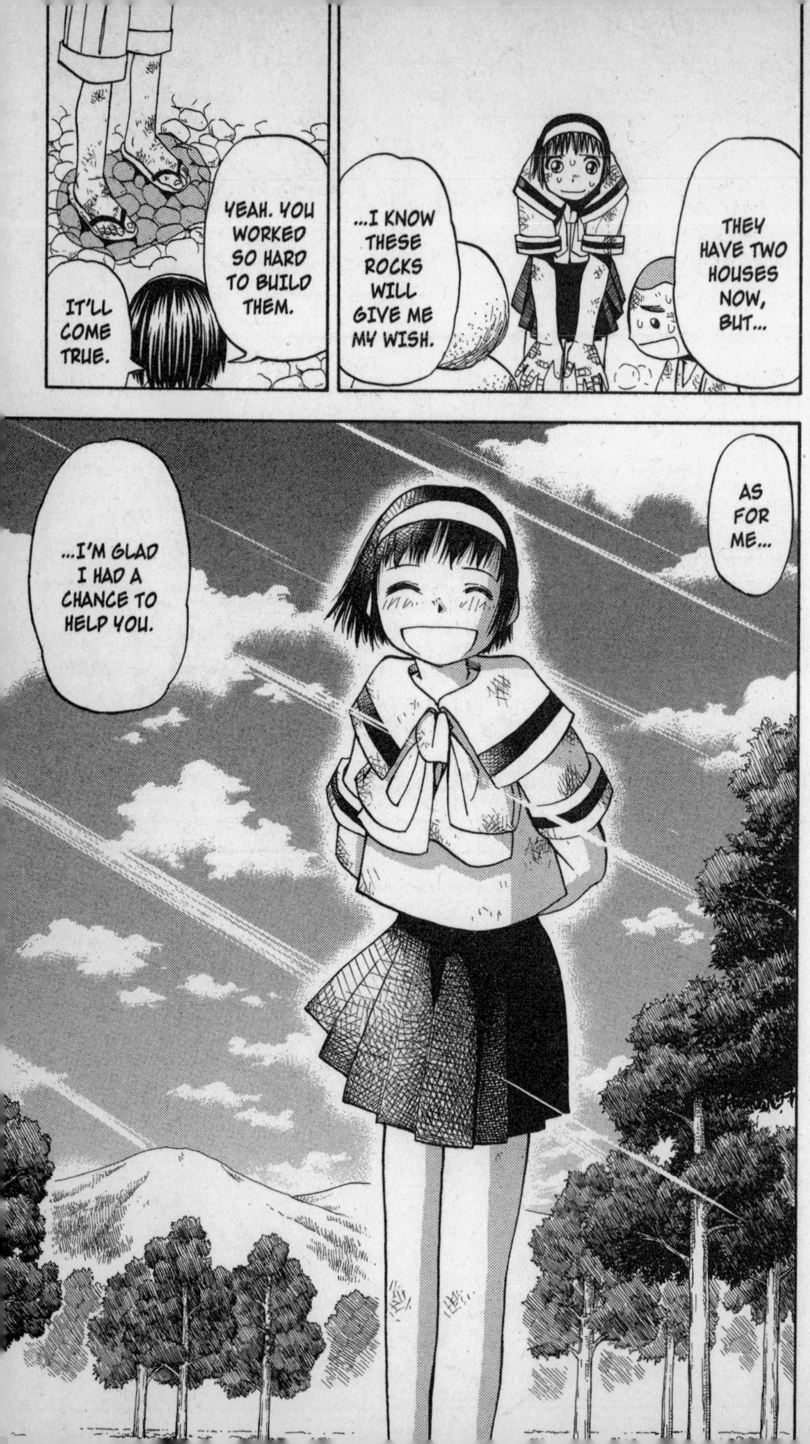
THEY HAVE TWO HOUSES NOW, BUT...
...I KNOW THESE ROCKS WILL GIVE ME MY WISH.
YEAH. YOU WORKED SO HARD TO BUILD THEM.
IT'LL COME TRUE.
AS FOR ME...
...I'M GLAD I HAD A CHANCE TO HELP YOU.

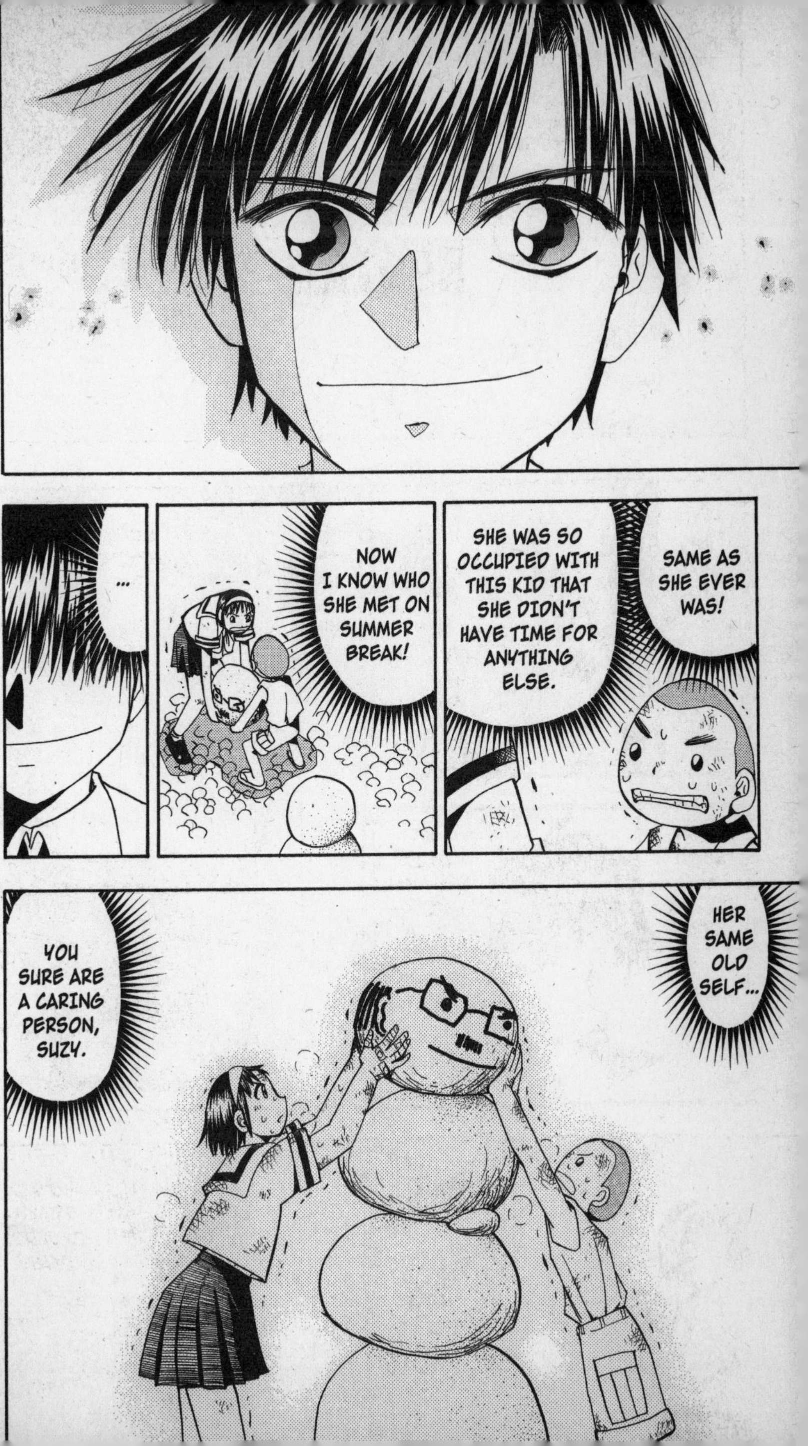
SAME AS SHE EVER WAS!
SHE WAS SO OCCUPIED WITH THIS KID THAT SHE DIDN'T HAVE TIME FOR ANYTHING ELSE.
NOW I KNOW WHO SHE MET ON SUMMER BREAK!
...
HER SAME OLD SELF...
YOU SURE ARE A CARING PERSON, SUZY.

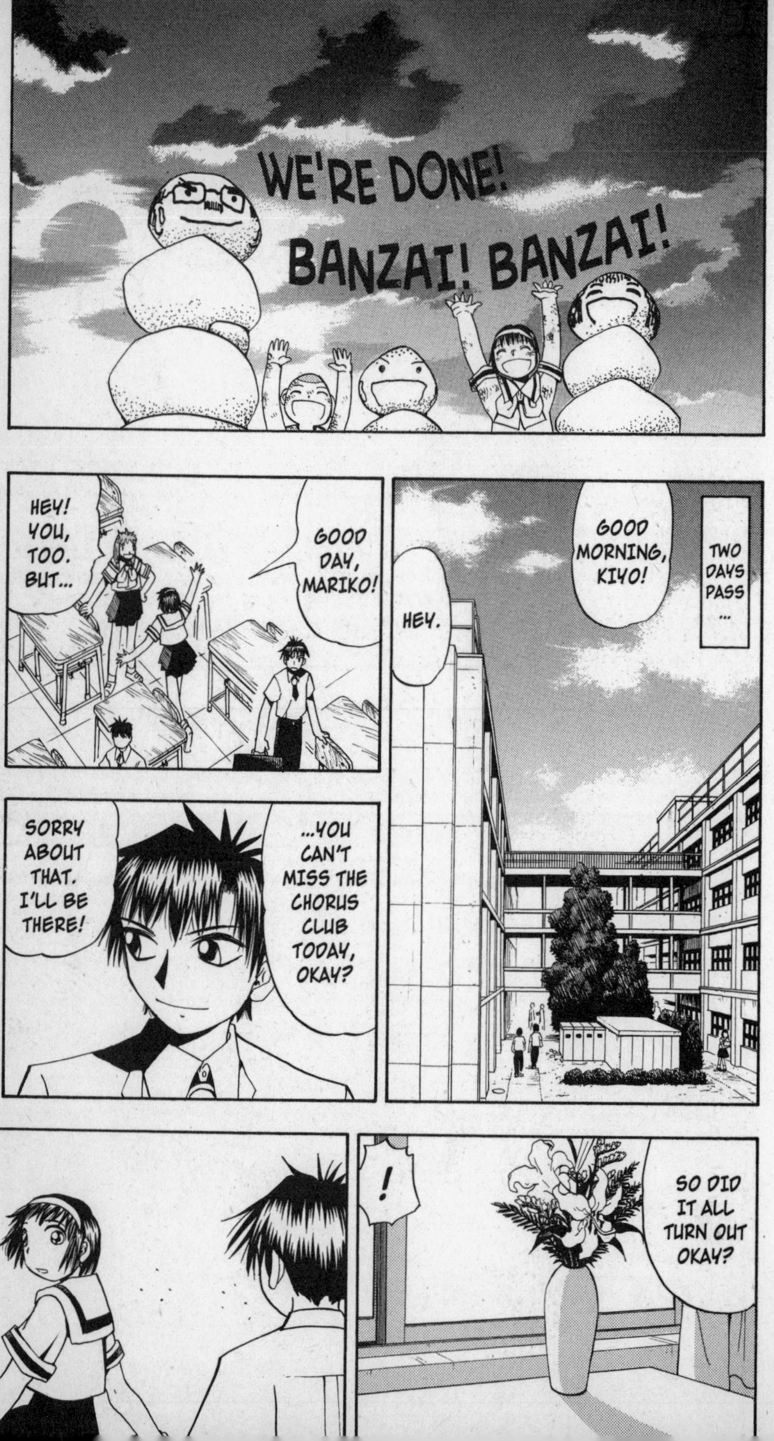
WE'RE DONE!
BANZAI! BANZAI!
TWO DAYS PASS ...
GOOD MORNING, KIYO!
HEY.
GOOD DAY, MARIKO!
HEY! YOU, TOO. BUT...
...YOU CAN'T MISS THE CHORUS CLUB TODAY, OKAY?
SORRY ABOUT THAT. I'LL BE THERE!
SO DID IT ALL TURN OUT OKAY?
!

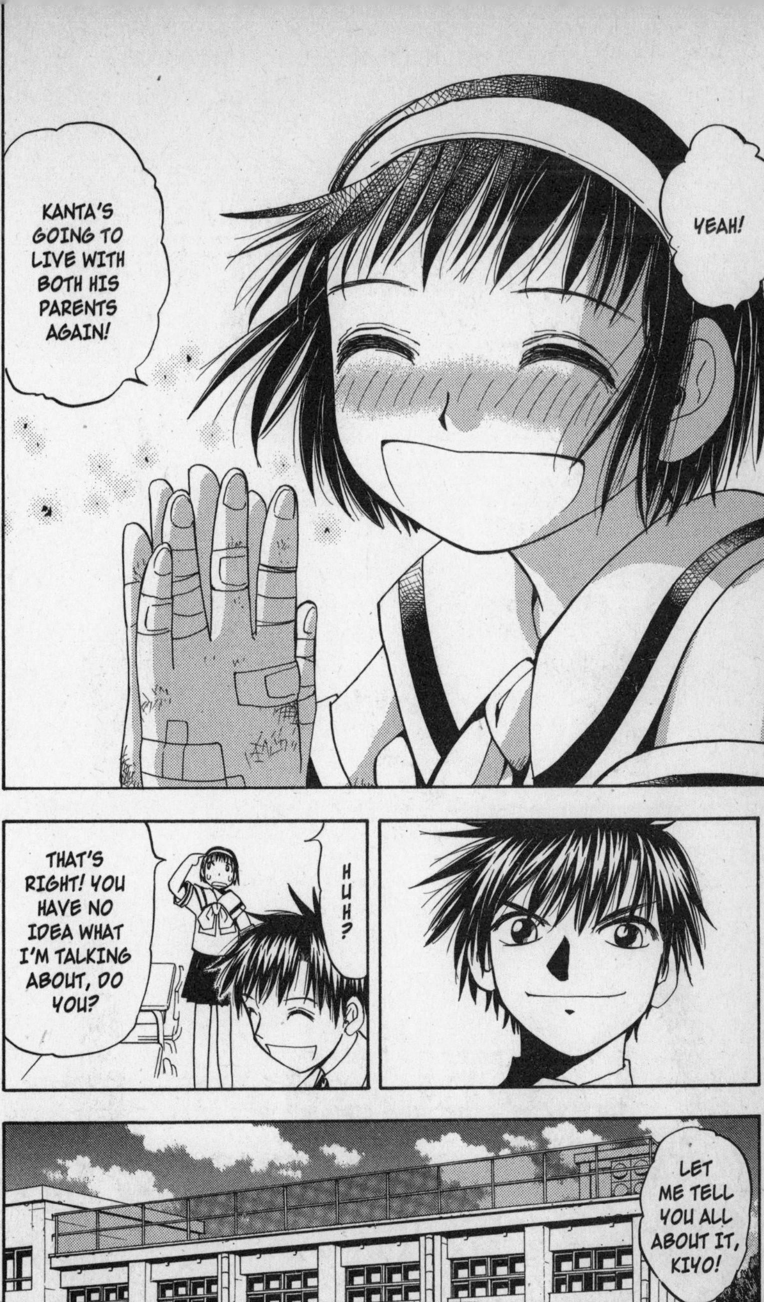
YEAH!
KANTA'S GOING TO LIVE WITH BOTH HIS PARENTS AGAIN!
HUH?
THAT'S RIGHT! YOU HAVE NO IDEA WHAT I'M TALKING ABOUT, DO YOU?
LET ME TELL YOU ALL ABOUT IT, KIYO!

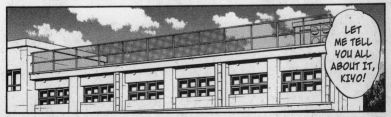

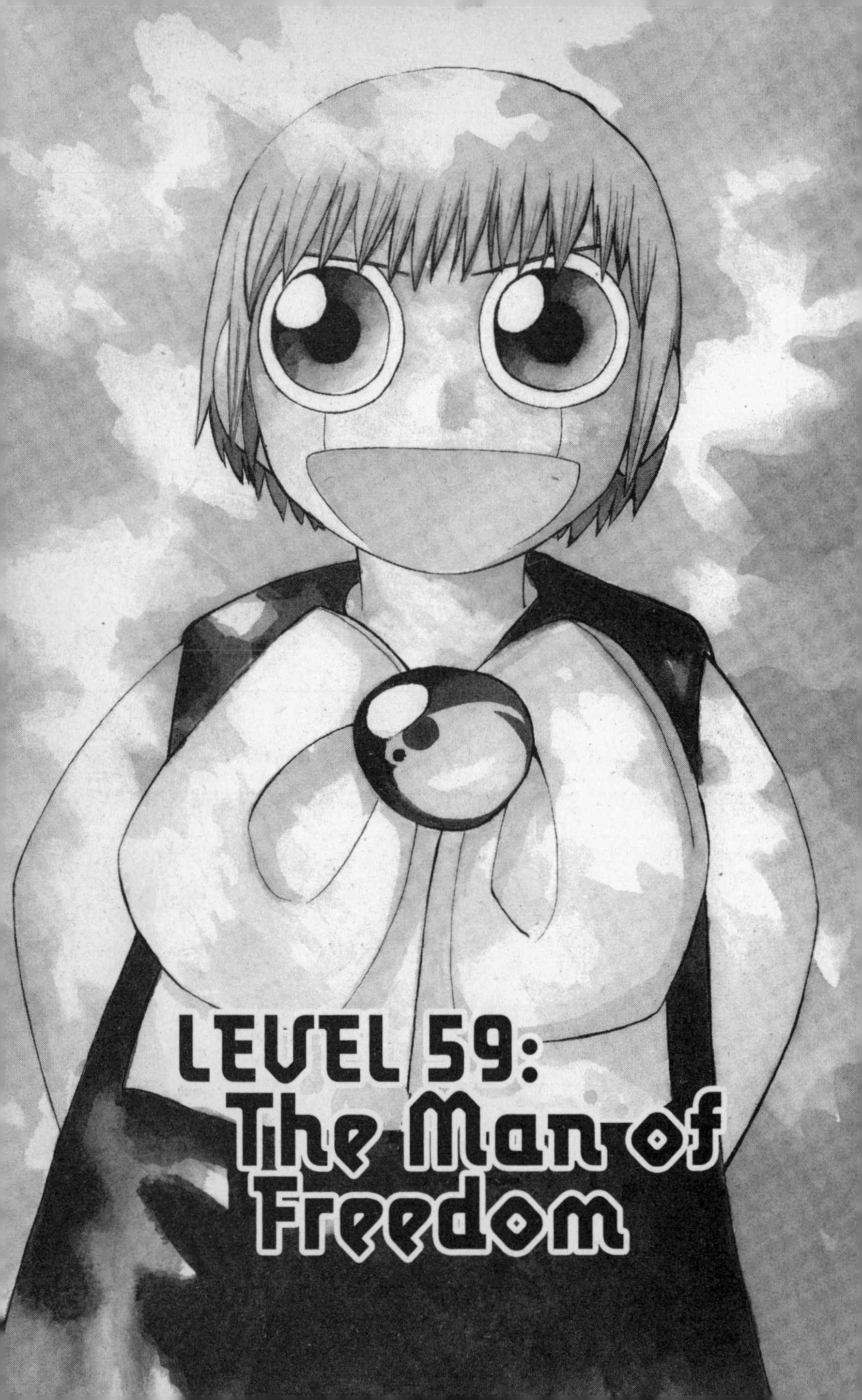
LEVEL 59:
The Man of
Freedom

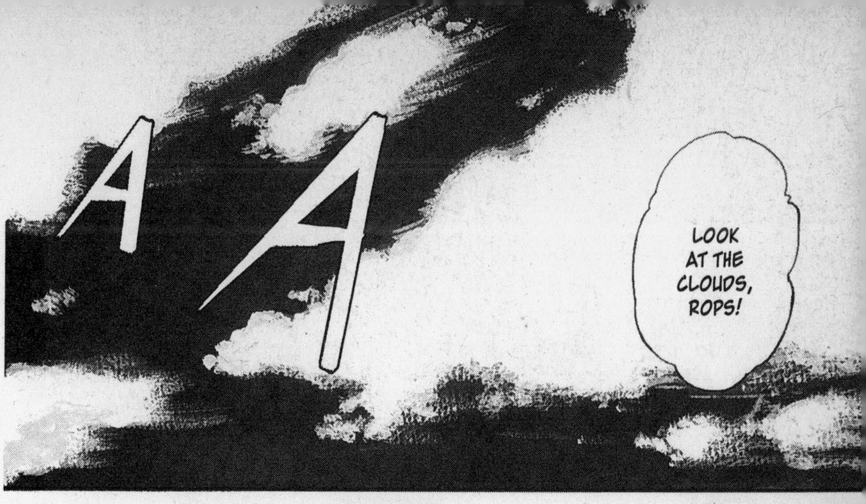
LOOK AT THE CLOUDS, ROPS!
A A

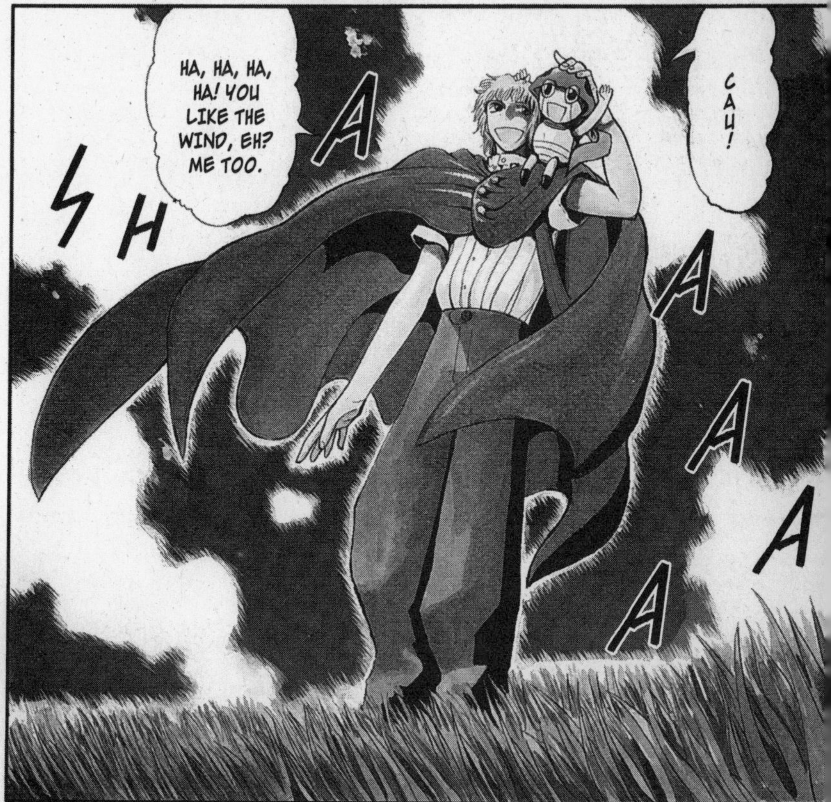
CAW!
HA, HA, HA, HA! YOU LIKE THE WIND, EH? ME TOO.
A
SH
AAAAA

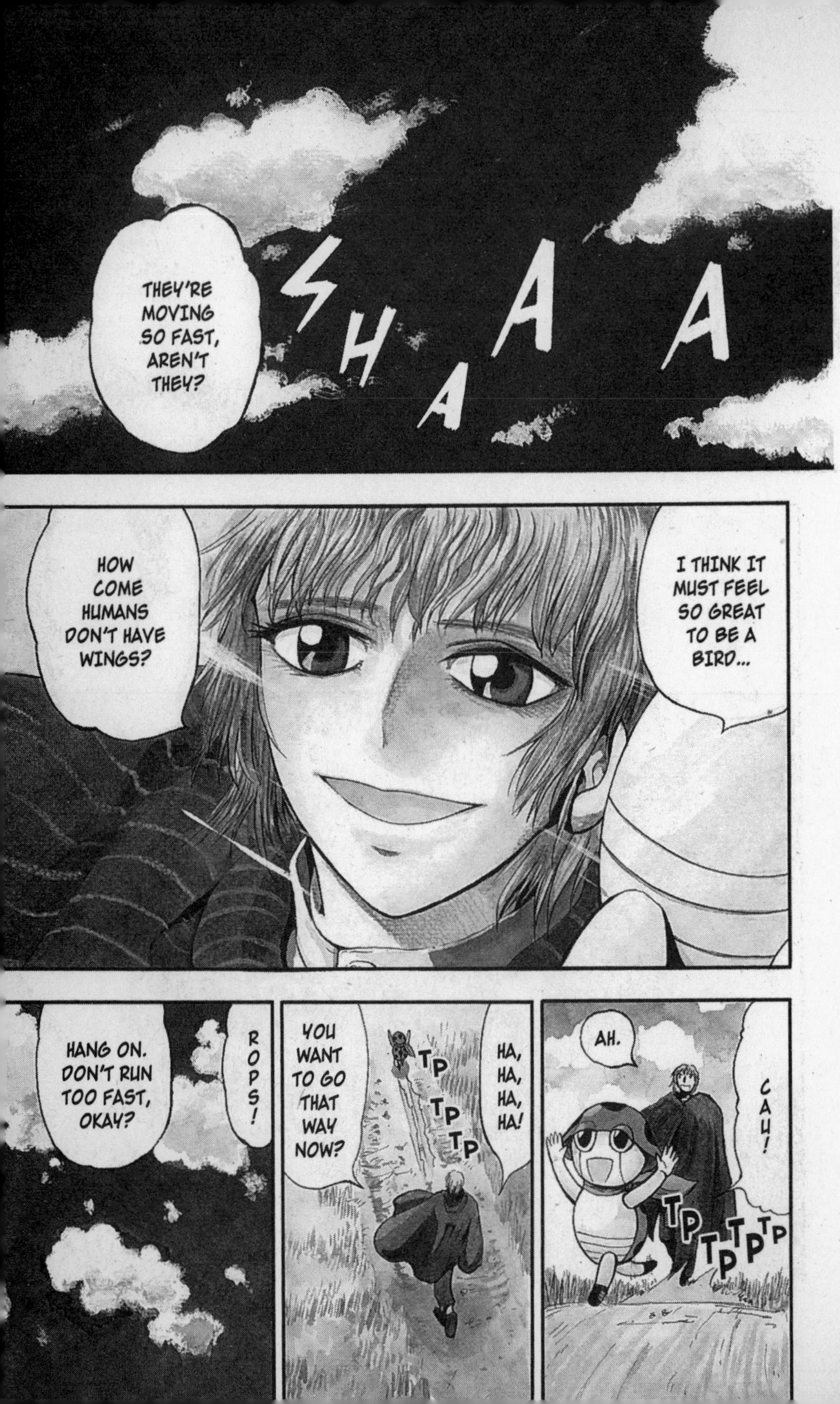
SHAAAA
THEY'RE MOVING SO FAST, AREN'T THEY?
I THINK IT MUST FEEL SO GREAT TO BE A BIRD...
HOW COME HUMANS DON'T HAVE WINGS?
CAU!
AH.
TPTPTPTP
HA, HA, HA, HA!
YOU WANT TO GO THAT WAY NOW?
TP TPTP
ROPS!
HANG ON. DON'T RUN TOO FAST, OKAY?

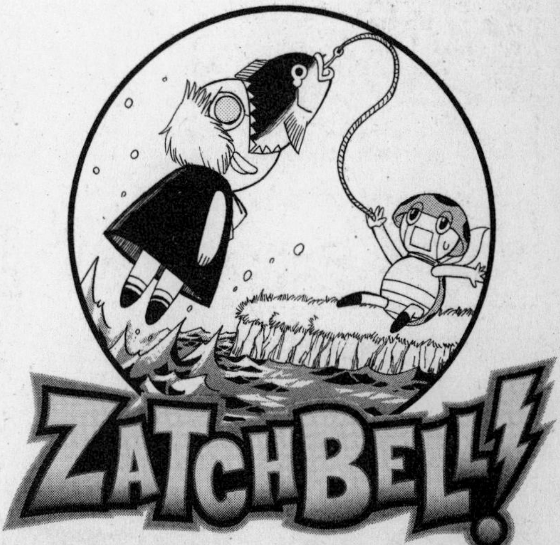
ZATCHBELL!

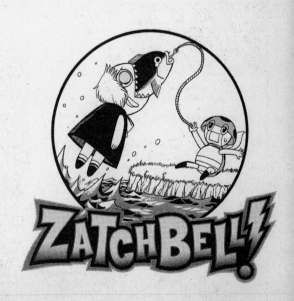

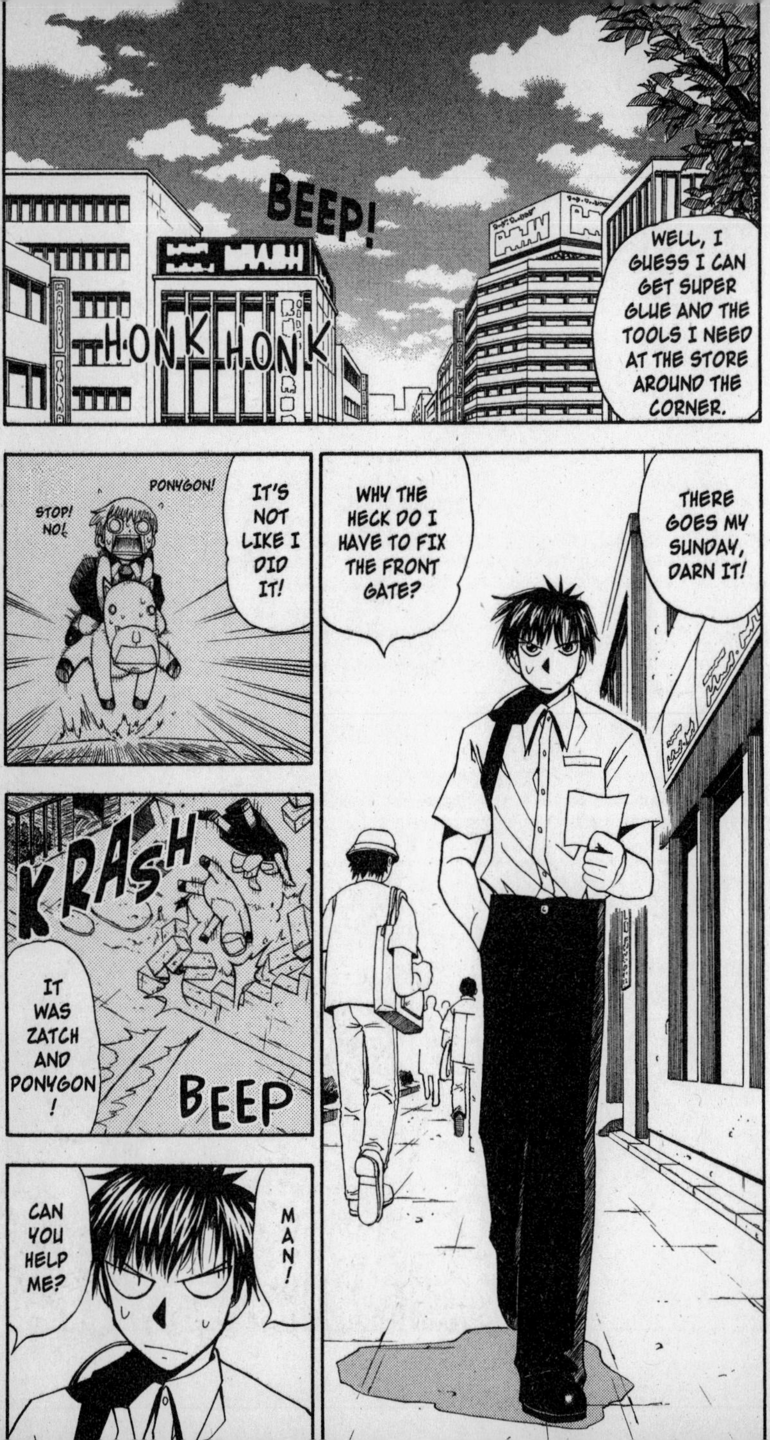
BEEP!
WELL, I GUESS I CAN GET SUPER GLUE AND THE TOOLS I NEED AT THE STORE AROUND THE CORNER.
HONK HONK
THERE GOES MY SUNDAY, DARN IT!
WHY THE HECK DO I HAVE TO FIX THE FRONT GATE?
IT'S NOT LIKE I DID IT!
PONYGON!
STOP! NO!
KRASH
IT WAS ZATCH AND PONYGON!
BEEP
MAN!
CAN YOU HELP ME?

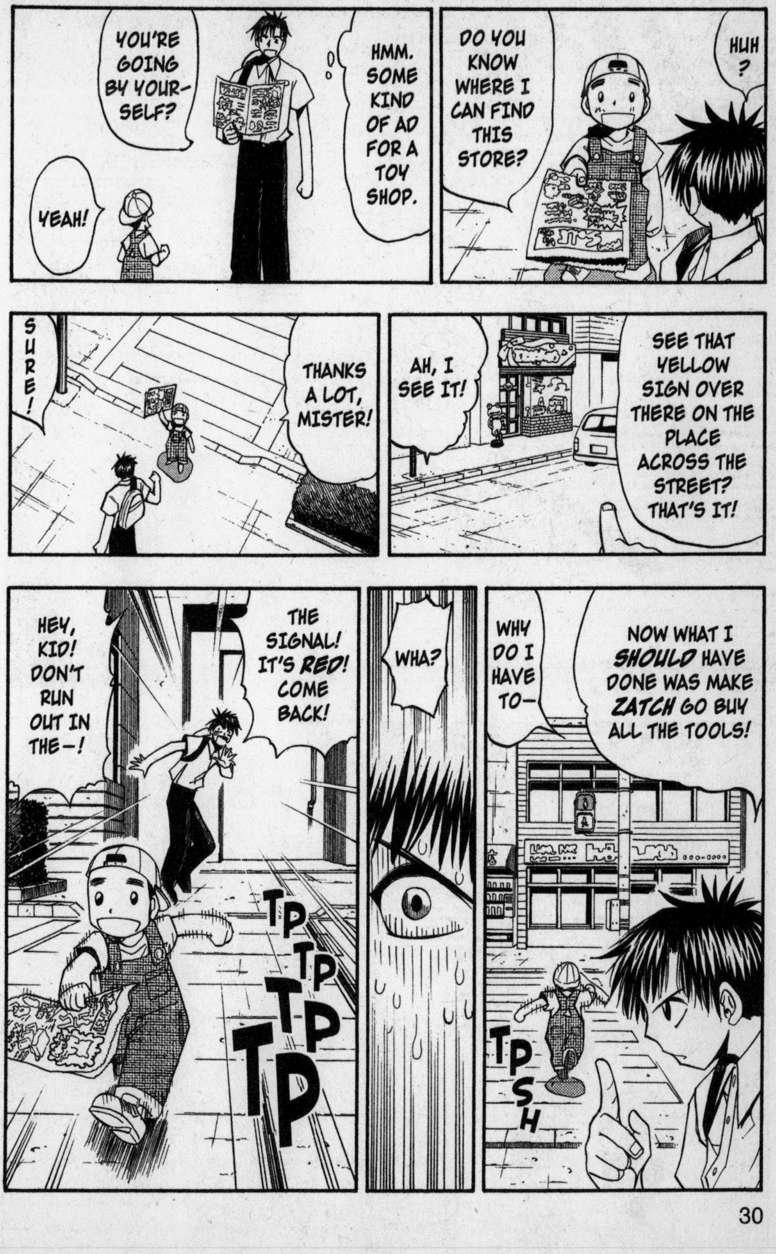
HUH?
DO YOU KNOW WHERE I CAN FIND THIS STORE?
HMM. SOME KIND OF AD FOR A TOY SHOP.
YOU'RE GOING BY YOURSELF?
YEAH!
SEE THAT YELLOW SIGN OVER THERE ON THE PLACE ACROSS THE STREET? THAT'S IT!
AH, I SEE IT!
THANKS A LOT, MISTER!
SURE!
NOW WHAT I *SHOULD* HAVE DONE WAS MAKE *ZATCH* GO BUY ALL THE TOOLS!
WHY DO I HAVE TO—
TPSH
WHA?
THE SIGNAL! IT'S *RED!* COME BACK!
HEY, KID! DON'T RUN OUT IN THE—!
TP TP TP TP TP

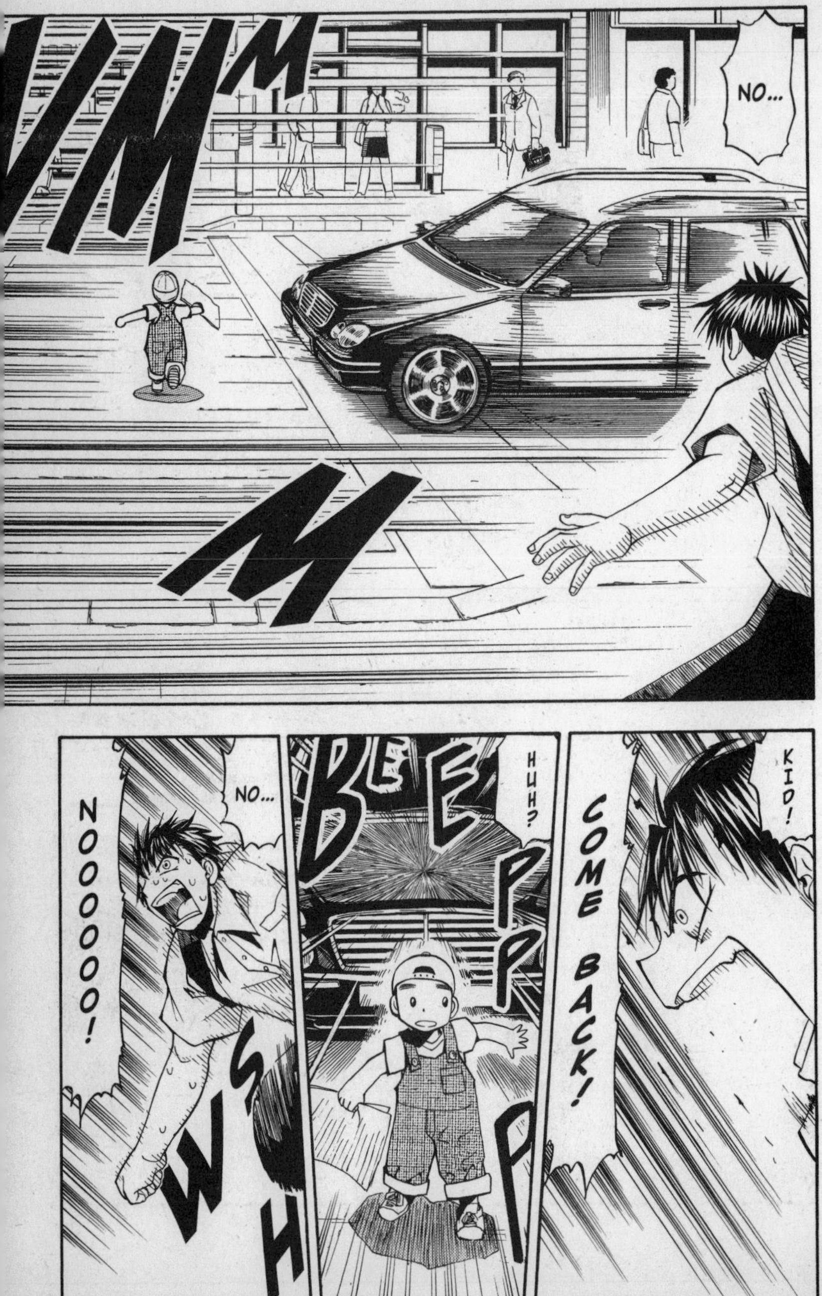
VMMM
M
NO...
KID!
COME BACK!
HUH?
BEEPP
P
NO...
NOOOOOOO!
WSH

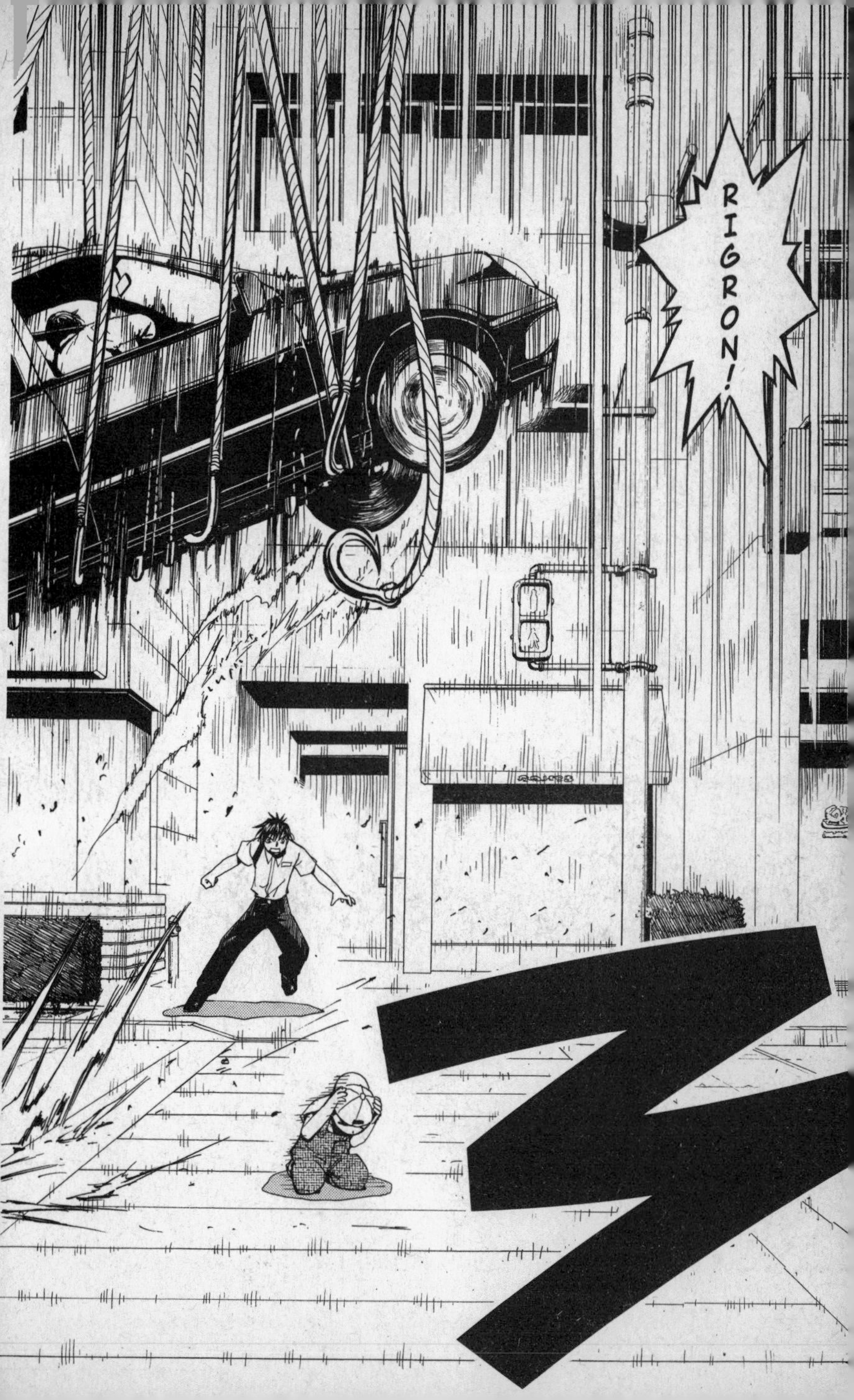
RIGRON!

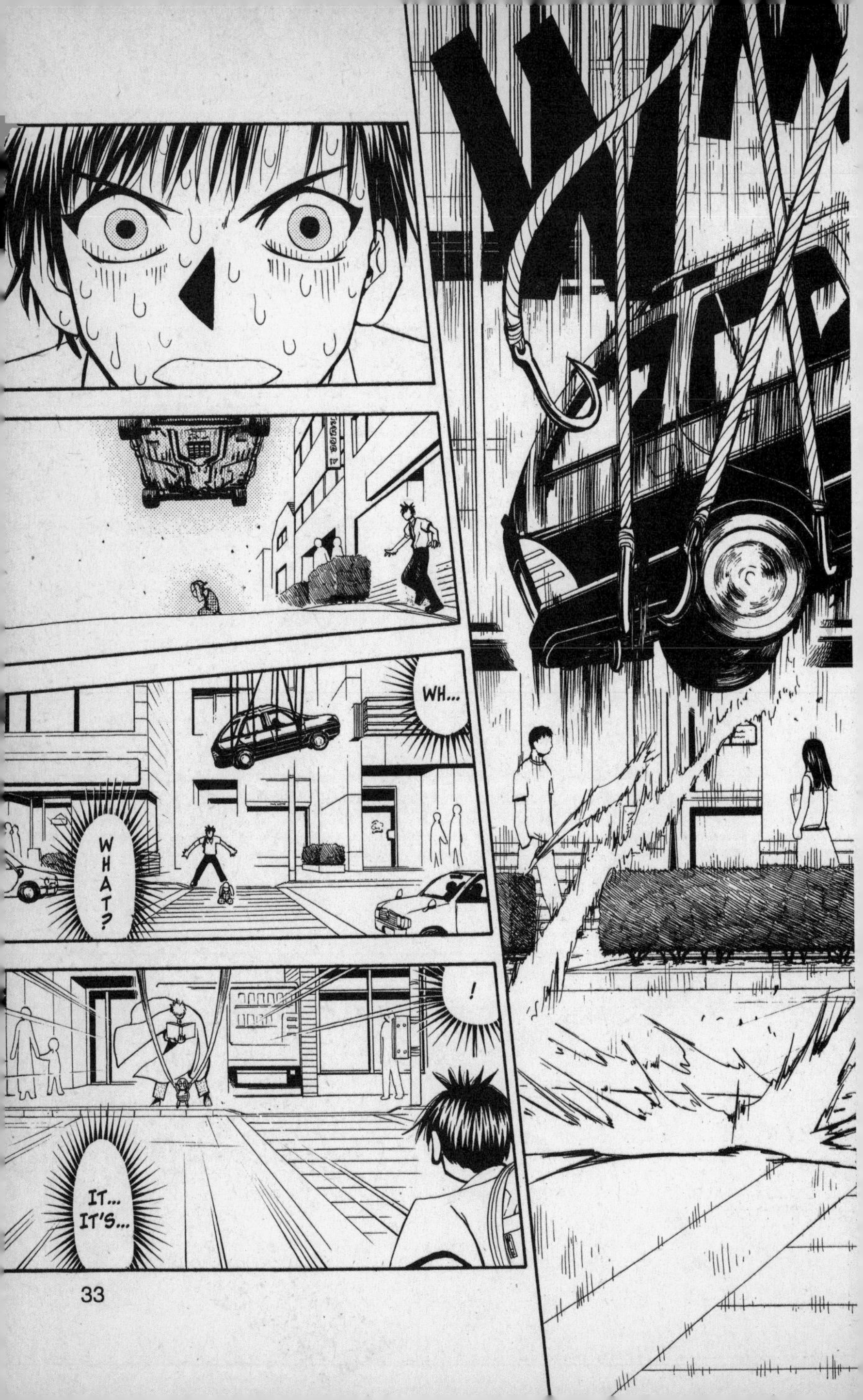
WH...
WHAT?
!
IT... IT'S...

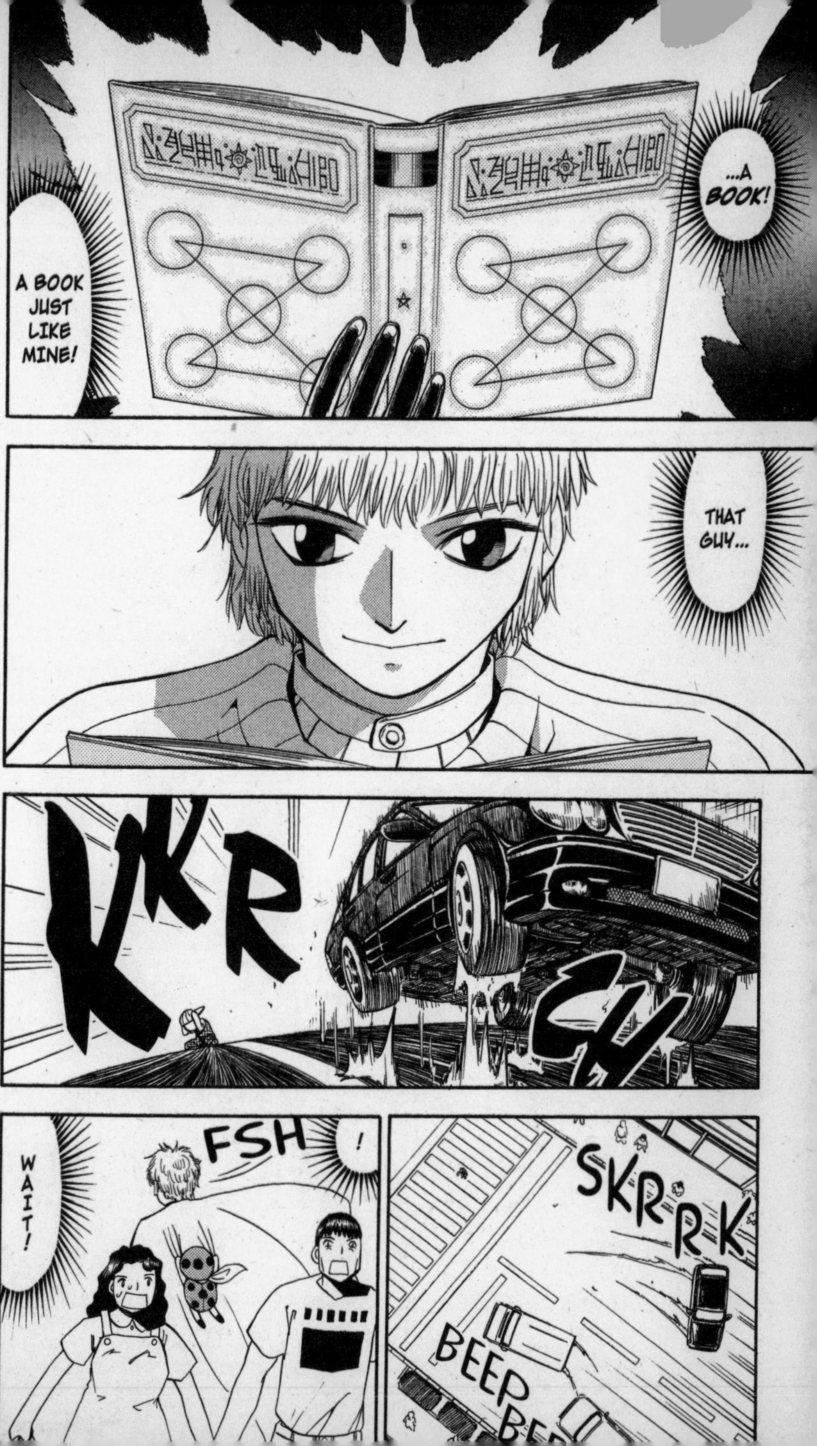
...A BOOK!
A BOOK JUST LIKE MINE!
THAT GUY...
KKRCH
SKRRK
BEEP
!
FSH
WAIT!

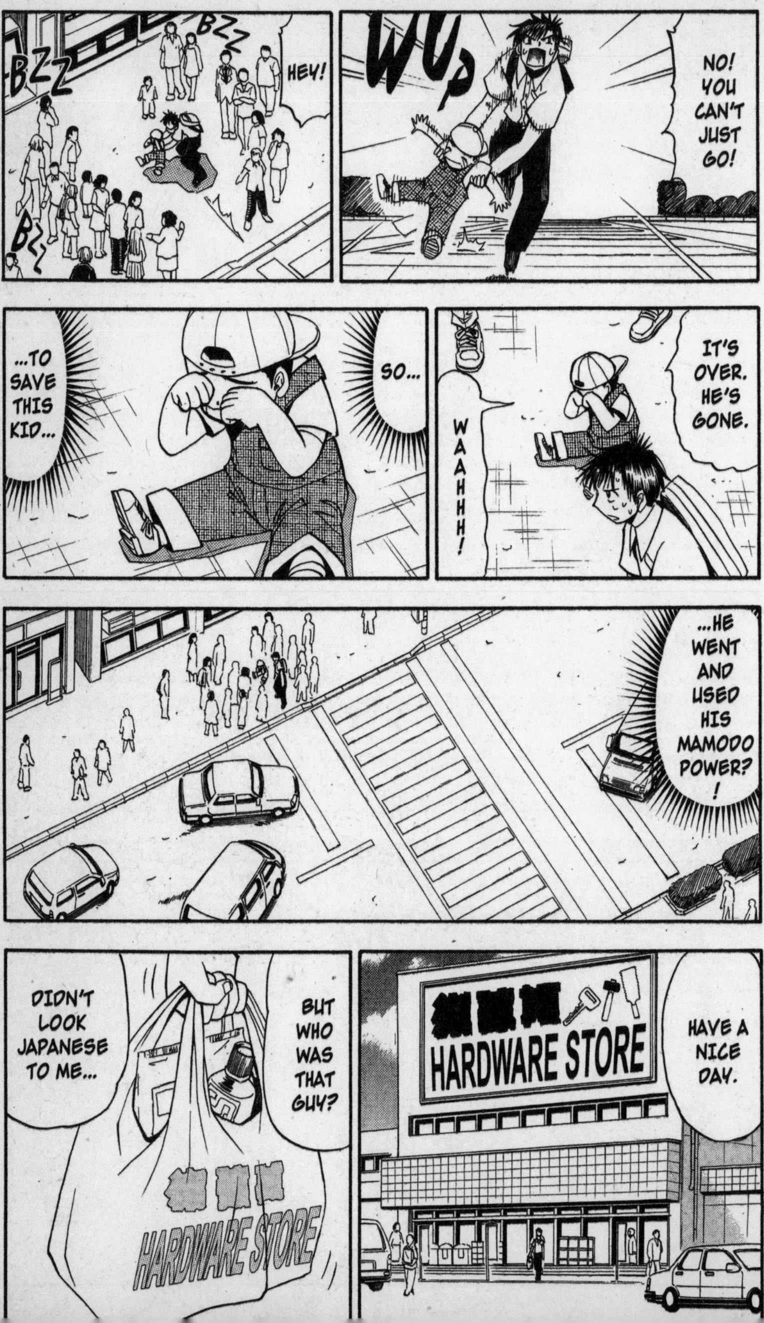
WUP
NO! YOU CAN'T JUST GO!
BZZ
BZZ
BZZ
HEY!
IT'S OVER. HE'S GONE.
WAAHHH!
SO...
...TO SAVE THIS KID...
...HE WENT AND USED HIS MAMODO POWER?!
HARDWARE STORE
HAVE A NICE DAY.
BUT WHO WAS THAT GUY?
DIDN'T LOOK JAPANESE TO ME...
HARDWARE STORE

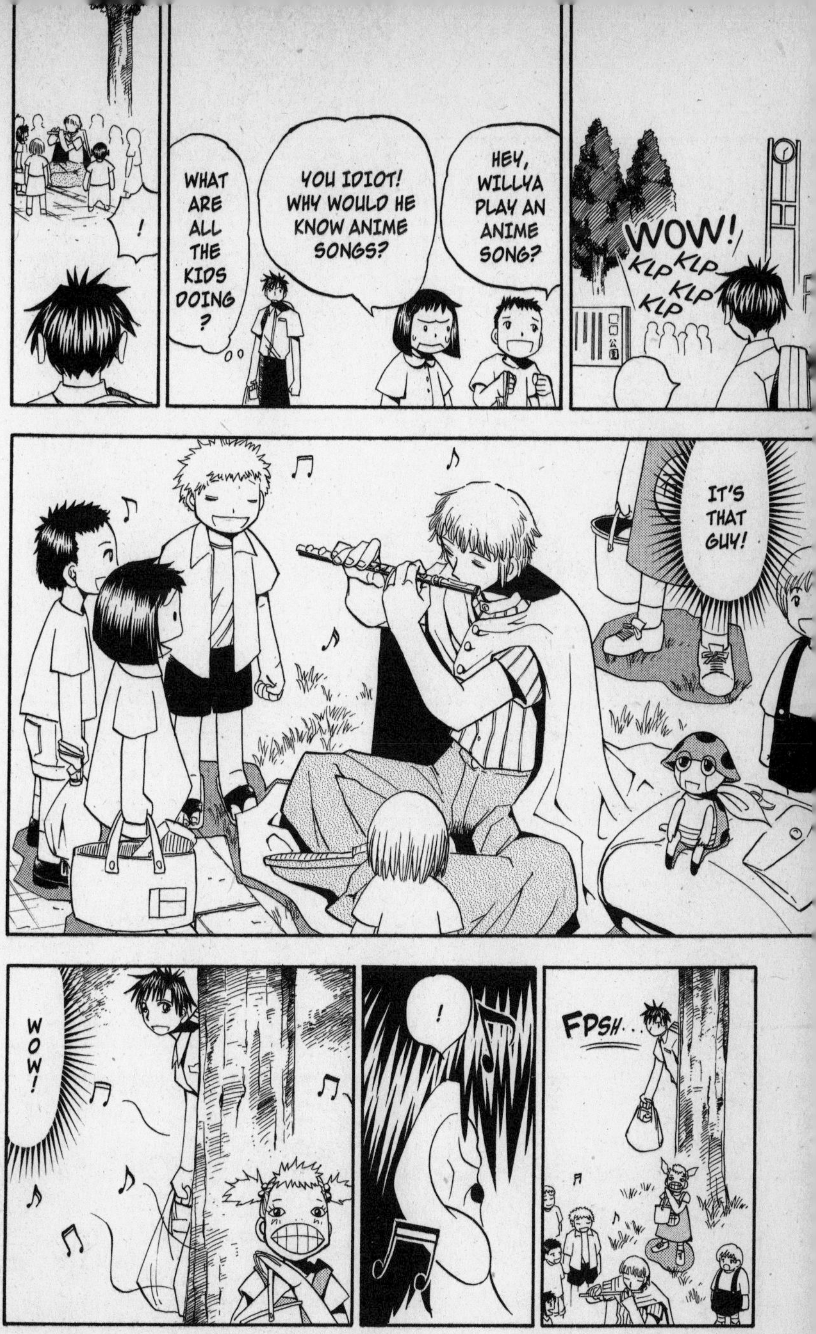
WOW!
KLP KLP KLP KLP
HEY, WILLYA PLAY AN ANIME SONG?
YOU IDIOT! WHY WOULD HE KNOW ANIME SONGS?
WHAT ARE ALL THE KIDS DOING?
!
IT'S THAT GUY!
FPSH...
!
WOW!

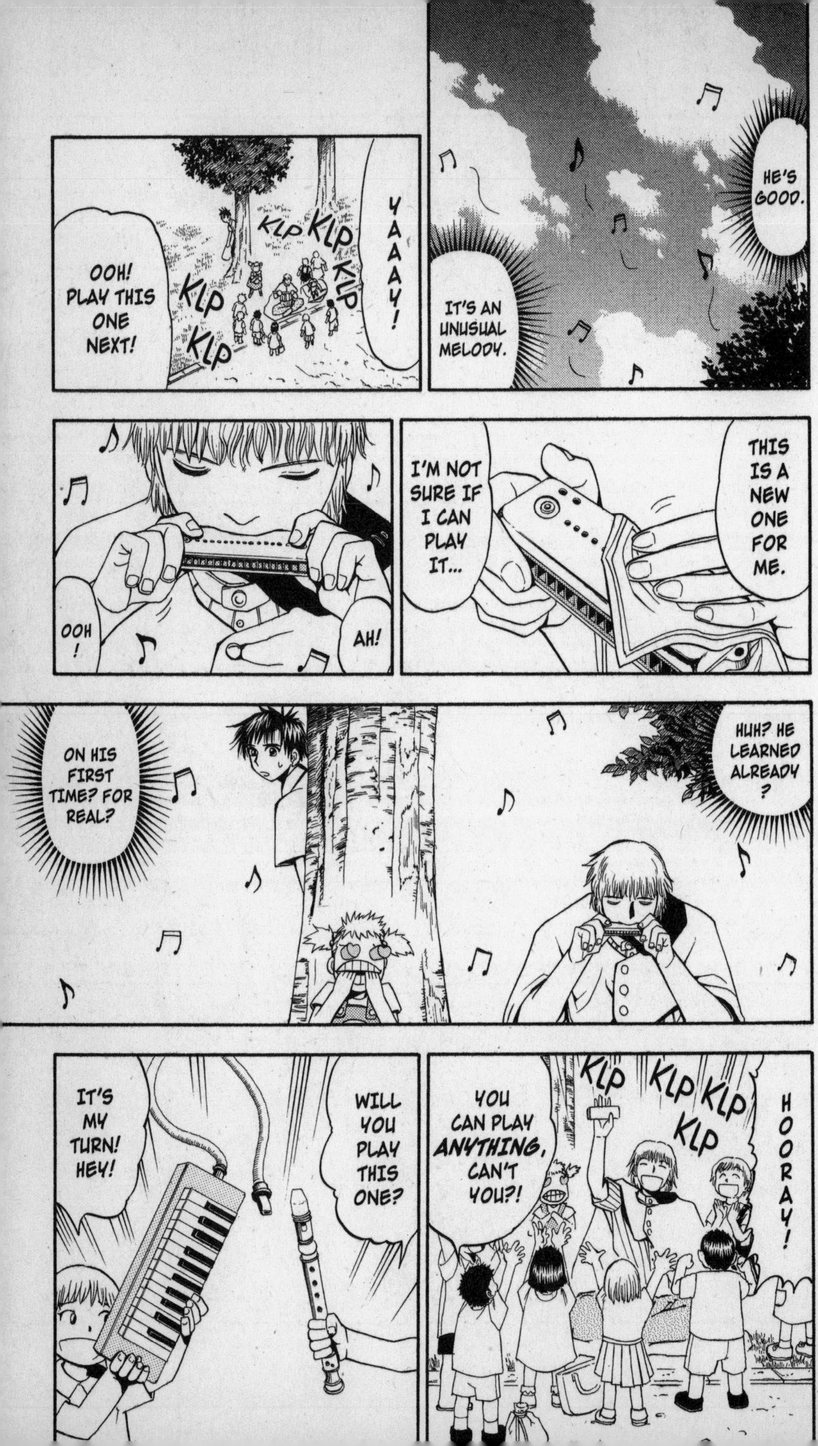
HE'S GOOD.
IT'S AN UNUSUAL MELODY.
YAAAAY!
KLP KLP KLP
KLP
KLP KLP
OOH! PLAY THIS ONE NEXT!
THIS IS A NEW ONE FOR ME.
I'M NOT SURE IF I CAN PLAY IT...
AH!
OOH!
HUH? HE LEARNED ALREADY?
ON HIS FIRST TIME? FOR REAL?
HOORAY!
KLP KLP KLP KLP
YOU CAN PLAY ANYTHING, CAN'T YOU?!
WILL YOU PLAY THIS ONE?
IT'S MY TURN! HEY!

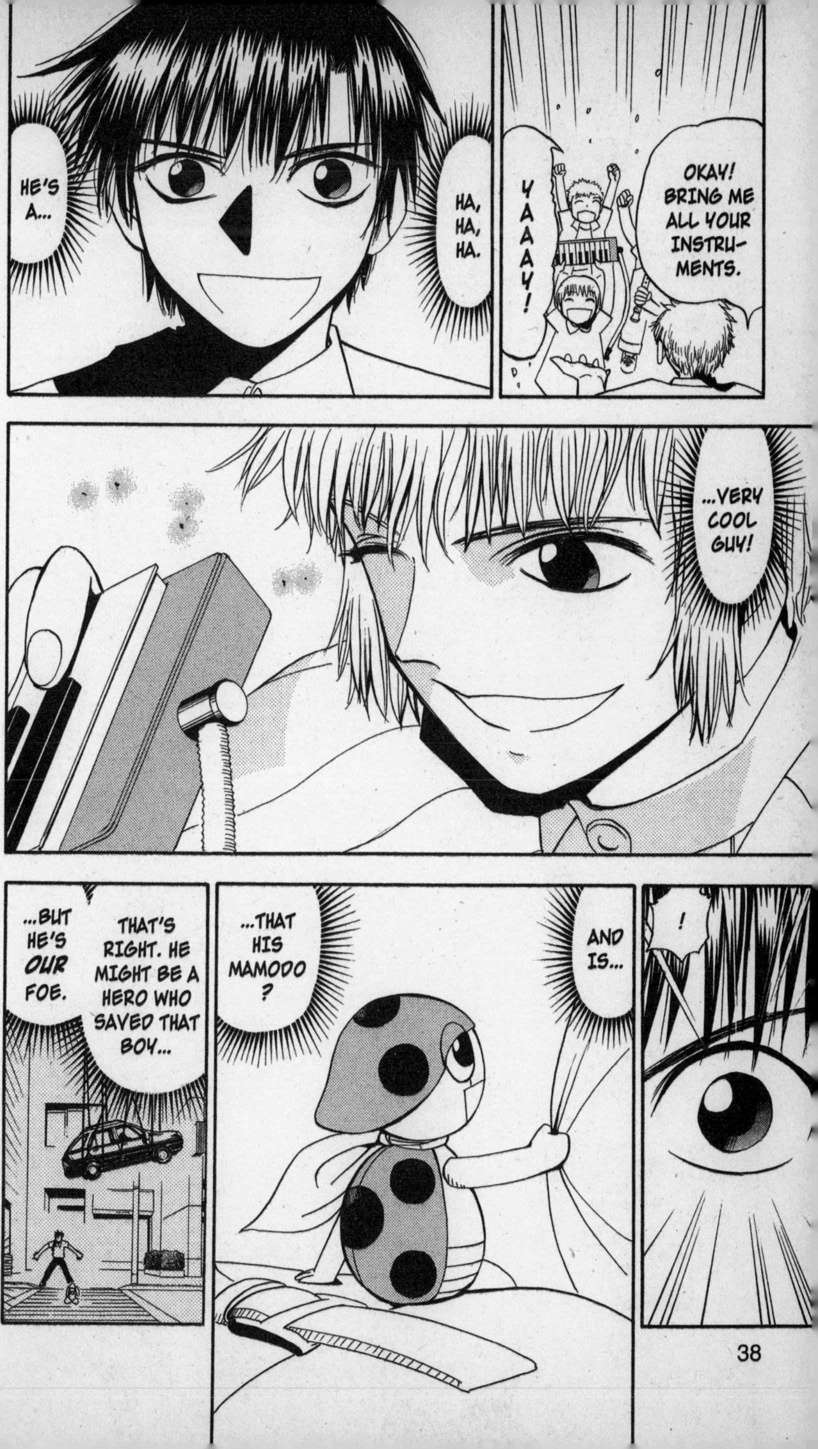
OKAY! BRING ME ALL YOUR INSTRU- MENTS.
YAAAAY!
HA, HA, HA.
HE'S A...
...VERY COOL GUY!
!
AND IS...
...THAT HIS MAMODO?
THAT'S RIGHT. HE MIGHT BE A HERO WHO SAVED THAT BOY...
...BUT HE'S OUR FOE.

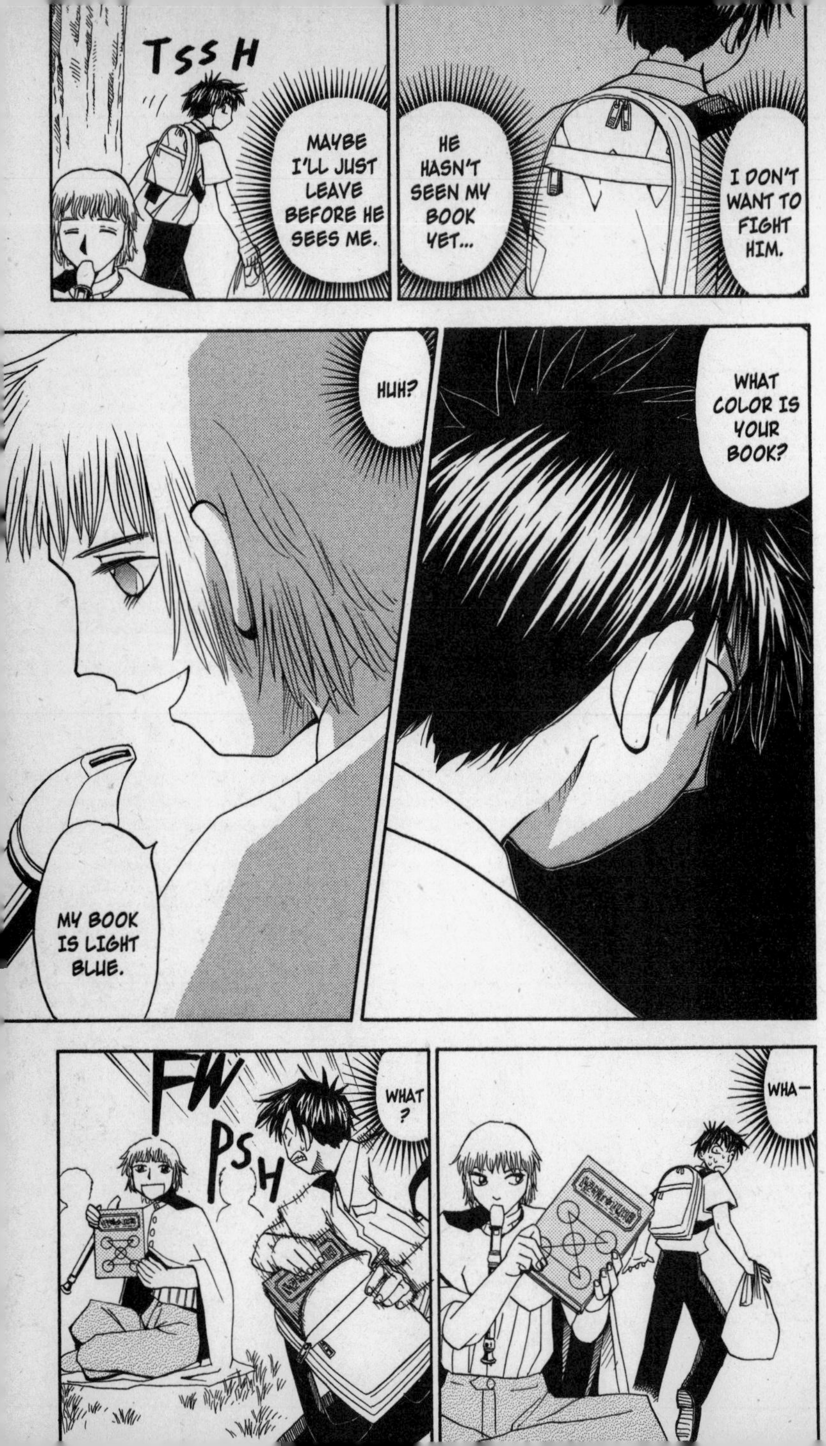
I DON'T WANT TO FIGHT HIM.
HE HASN'T SEEN MY BOOK YET...
TSSH
MAYBE I'LL JUST LEAVE BEFORE HE SEES ME.
WHAT COLOR IS YOUR BOOK?
HUH?
MY BOOK IS LIGHT BLUE.
WHA-
WHAT ?
FWPSH

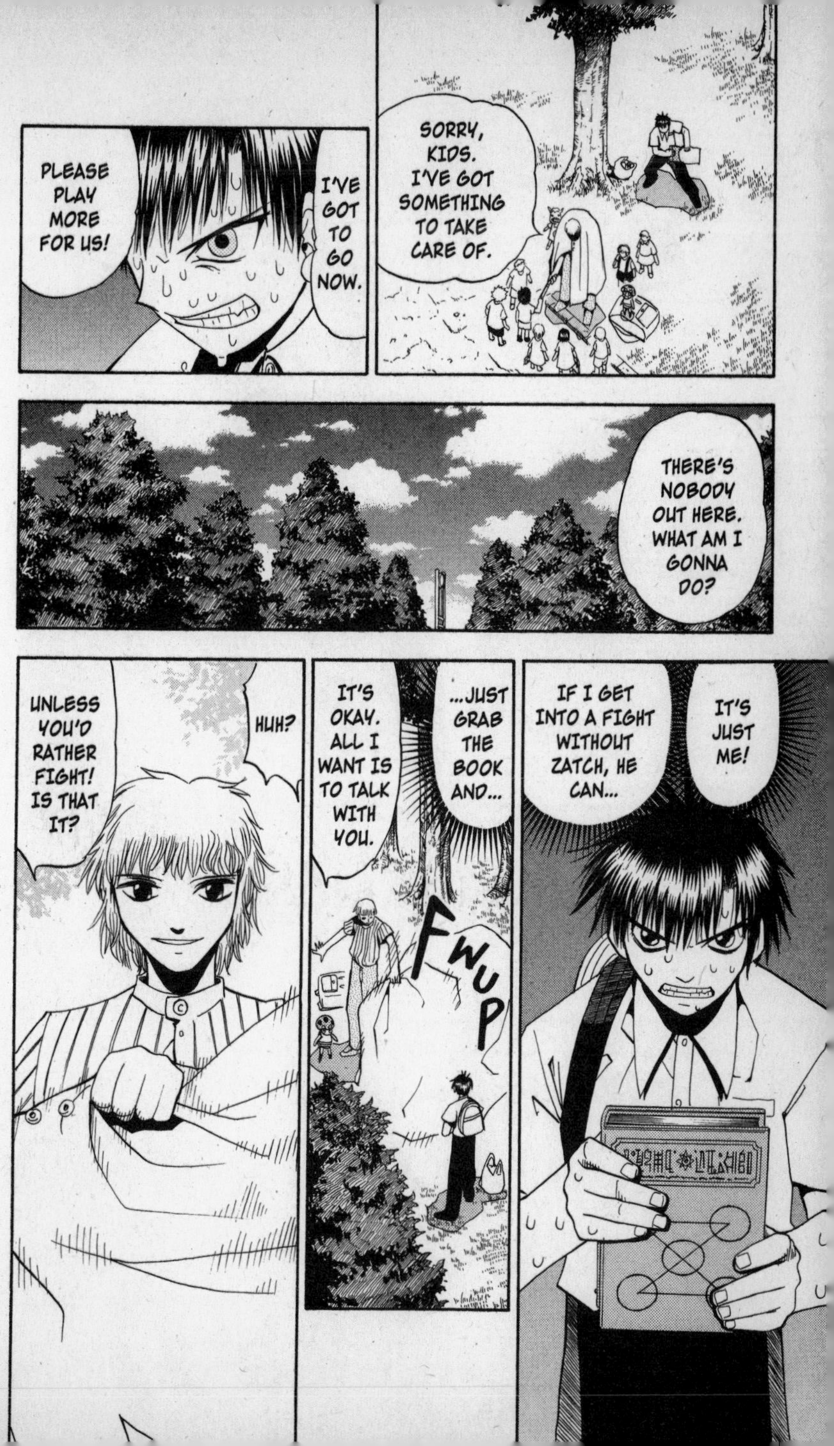
SORRY, KIDS. I'VE GOT SOMETHING TO TAKE CARE OF.
I'VE GOT TO GO NOW.
PLEASE PLAY MORE FOR US!
THERE'S NOBODY OUT HERE. WHAT AM I GONNA DO?
IT'S JUST ME!
IF I GET INTO A FIGHT WITHOUT ZATCH, HE CAN...
...JUST GRAB THE BOOK AND...
IT'S OKAY. ALL I WANT IS TO TALK WITH YOU.
FWUP
HUH?
UNLESS YOU'D RATHER FIGHT! IS THAT IT?

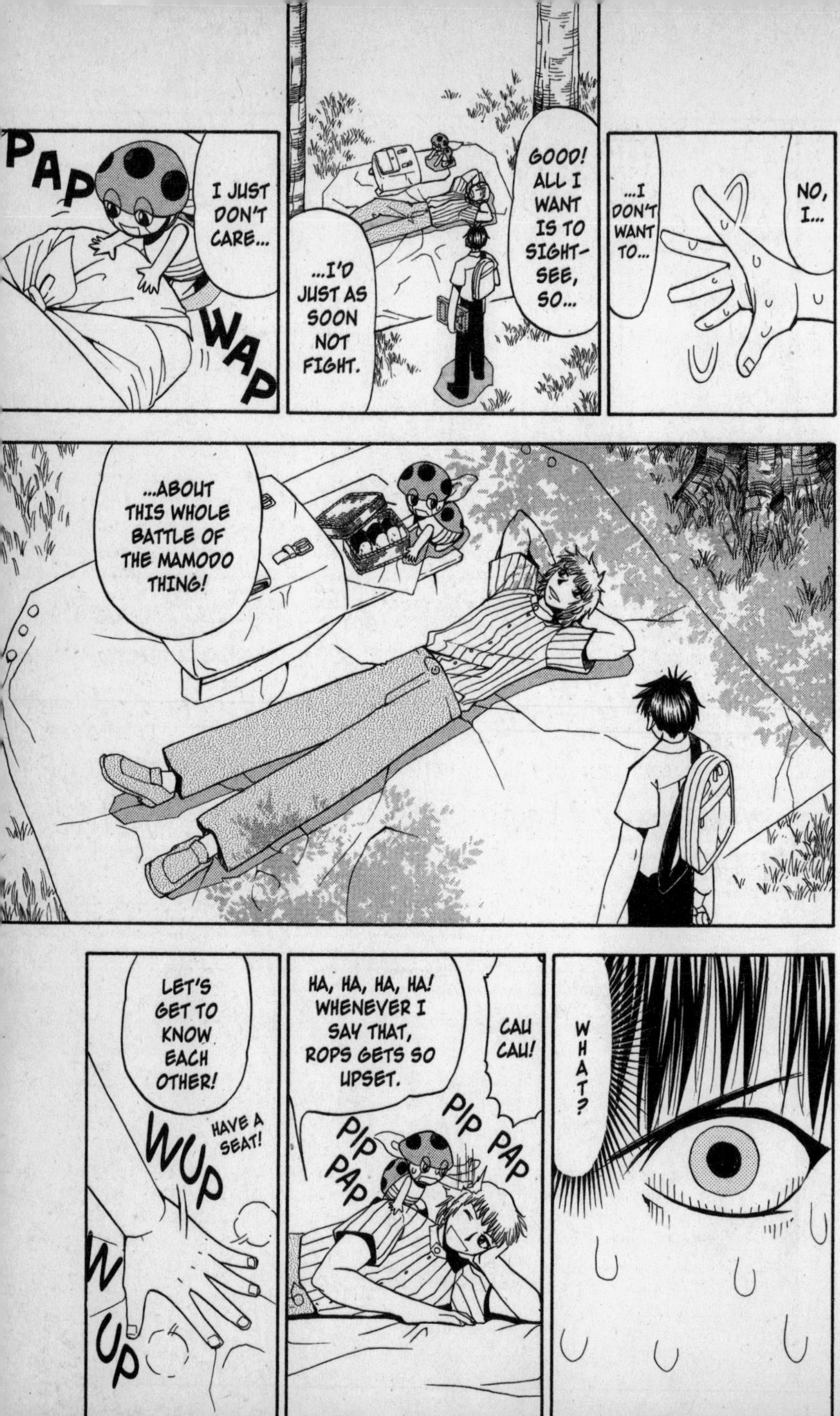
NO, I...
...I DON'T WANT TO...
GOOD! ALL I WANT IS TO SIGHT-SEE, SO...
...I'D JUST AS SOON NOT FIGHT.
I JUST DON'T CARE...
PAP
WAP
...ABOUT THIS WHOLE BATTLE OF THE MAMODO THING!
WHAT?
CAU CAU!
HA, HA, HA, HA! WHENEVER I SAY THAT, ROPS GETS SO UPSET.
PIP PAP
PIP PAP
LET'S GET TO KNOW EACH OTHER!
HAVE A SEAT!
WUP
WUP

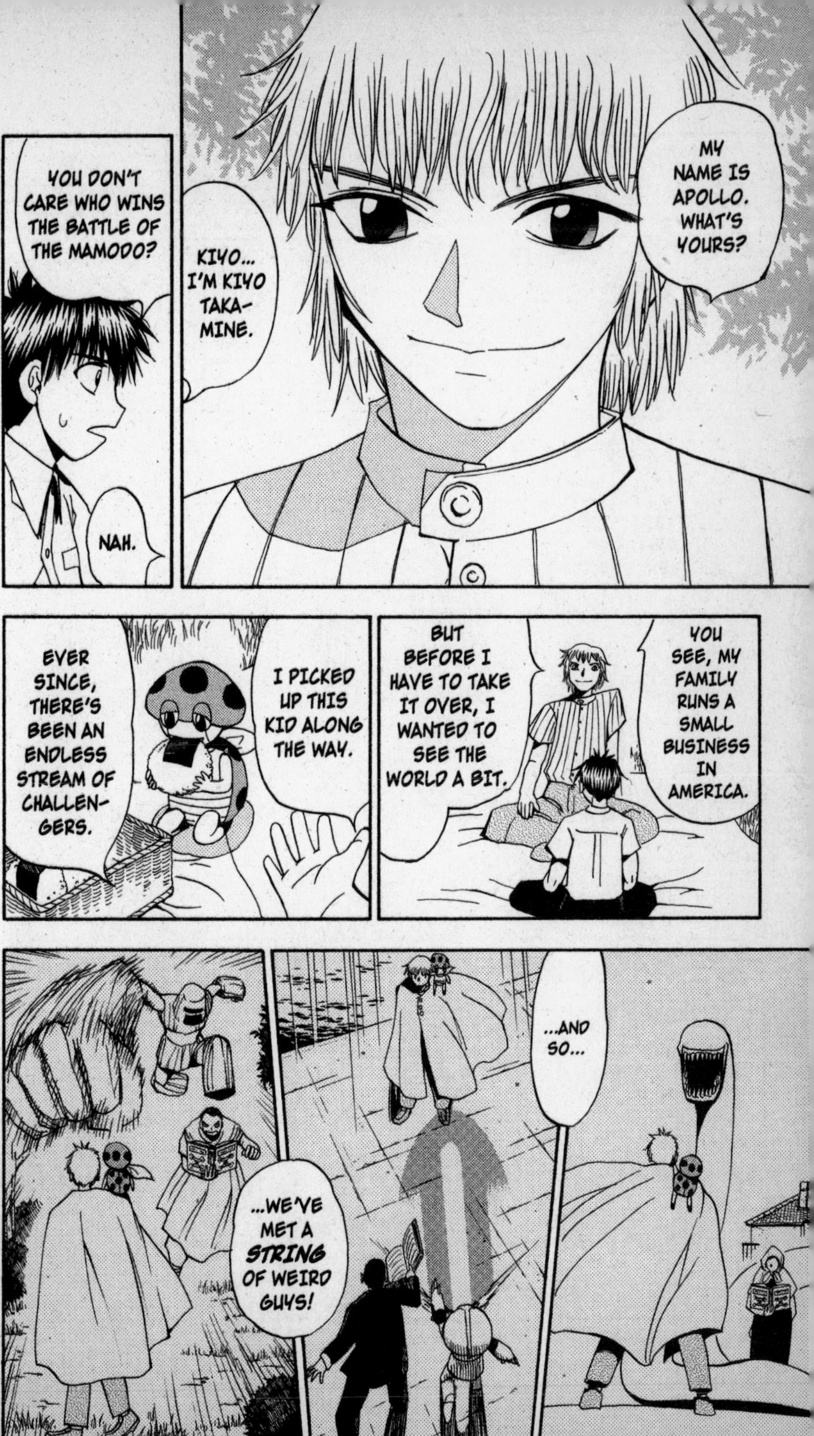
MY NAME IS APOLLO. WHAT'S YOURS?
KIYO... I'M KIYO TAKAMINE.
YOU DON'T CARE WHO WINS THE BATTLE OF THE MAMODO?
NAH.
YOU SEE, MY FAMILY RUNS A SMALL BUSINESS IN AMERICA.
BUT BEFORE I HAVE TO TAKE IT OVER, I WANTED TO SEE THE WORLD A BIT.
I PICKED UP THIS KID ALONG THE WAY.
EVER SINCE, THERE'S BEEN AN ENDLESS STREAM OF CHALLENGERS.
...AND SO...
...WE'VE MET A STRING OF WEIRD GUYS!

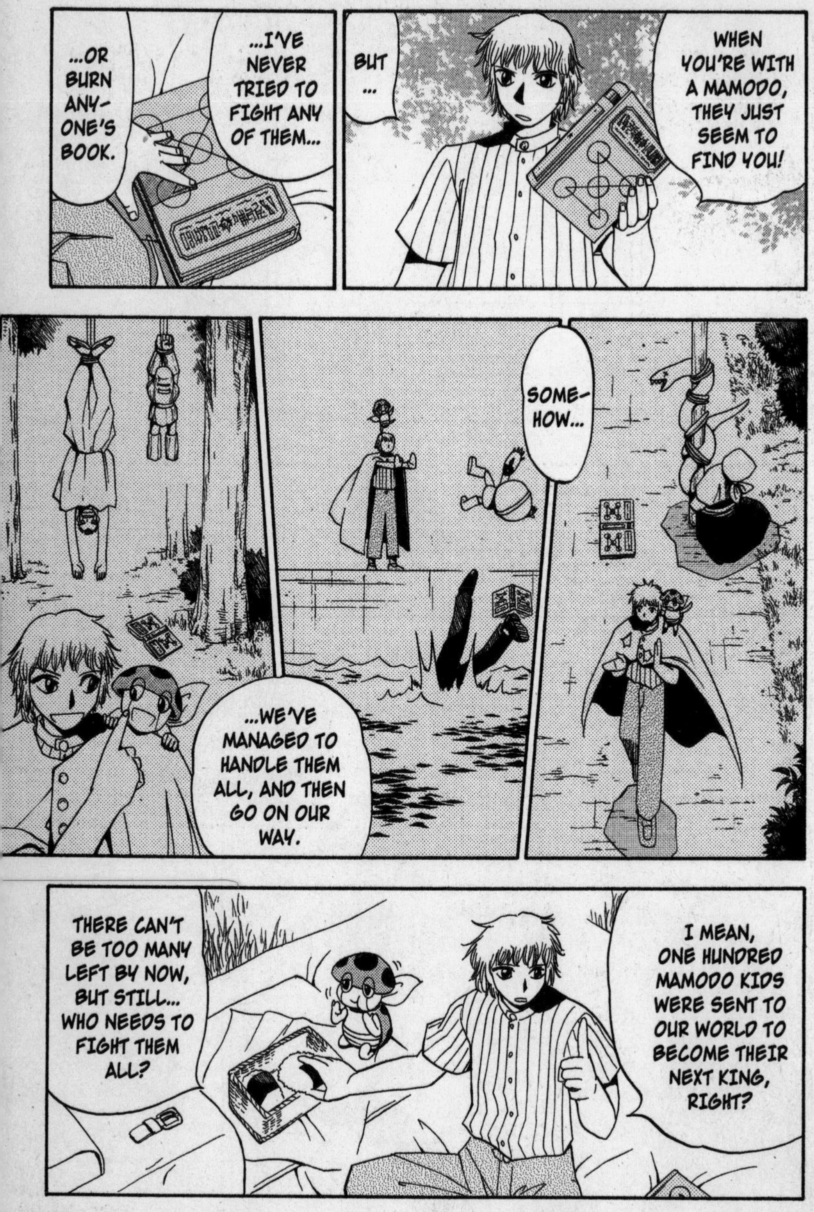
WHEN YOU'RE WITH A MAMODO, THEY JUST SEEM TO FIND YOU!
BUT ...
...I'VE NEVER TRIED TO FIGHT ANY OF THEM...
...OR BURN ANY-ONE'S BOOK.
SOME-HOW...
...WE'VE MANAGED TO HANDLE THEM ALL, AND THEN GO ON OUR WAY.
I MEAN, ONE HUNDRED MAMODO KIDS WERE SENT TO OUR WORLD TO BECOME THEIR NEXT KING, RIGHT?
THERE CAN'T BE TOO MANY LEFT BY NOW, BUT STILL... WHO NEEDS TO FIGHT THEM ALL?

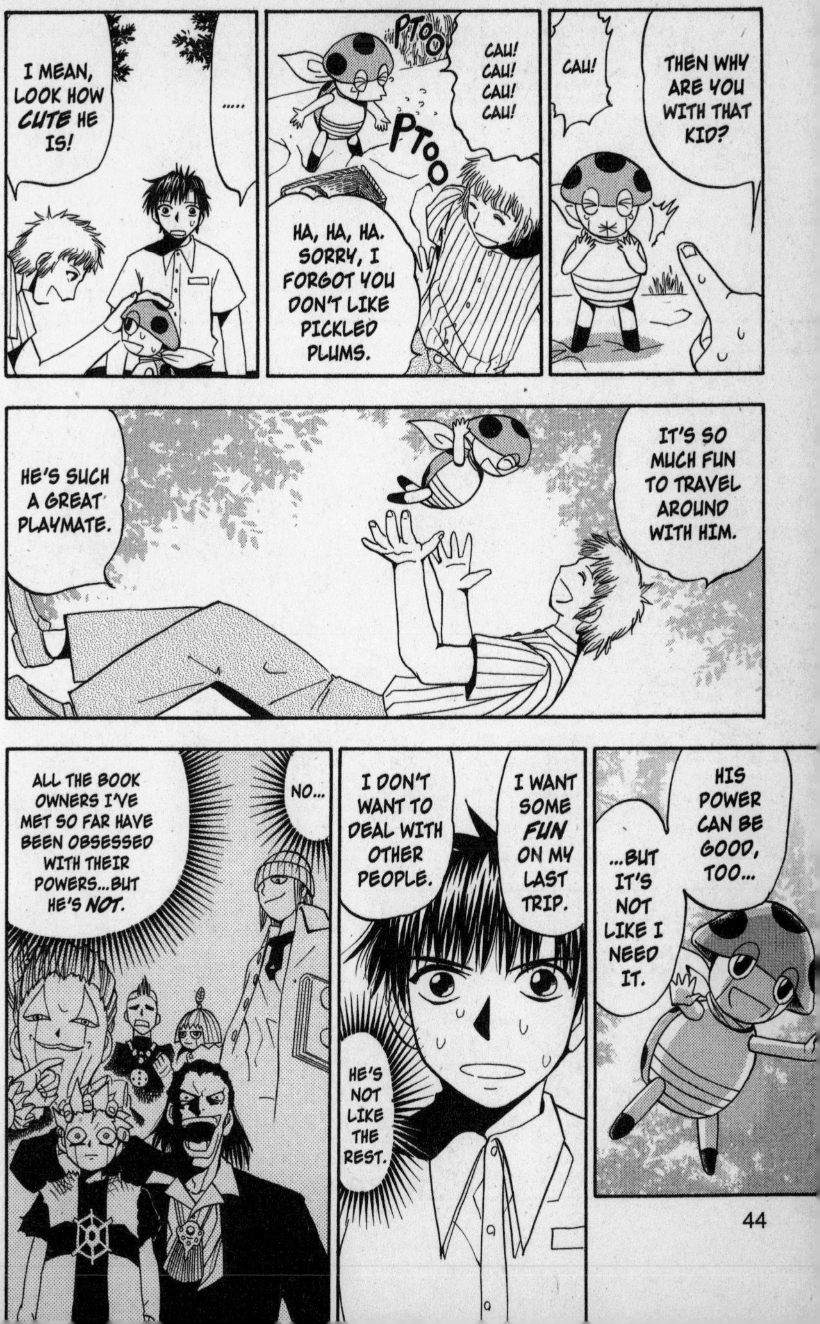
THEN WHY ARE YOU WITH THAT KID?
CAU!
CAU! CAU! CAU! CAU!
PTOO
PTOO
HA, HA, HA. SORRY, I FORGOT YOU DON'T LIKE PICKLED PLUMS.
.....
I MEAN, LOOK HOW CUTE HE IS!
IT'S SO MUCH FUN TO TRAVEL AROUND WITH HIM.
HE'S SUCH A GREAT PLAYMATE.
HIS POWER CAN BE GOOD, TOO...
...BUT IT'S NOT LIKE I NEED IT.
I WANT SOME FUN ON MY LAST TRIP.
I DON'T WANT TO DEAL WITH OTHER PEOPLE.
HE'S NOT LIKE THE REST.
NO...
ALL THE BOOK OWNERS I'VE MET SO FAR HAVE BEEN OBSESSED WITH THEIR POWERS...BUT HE'S NOT.

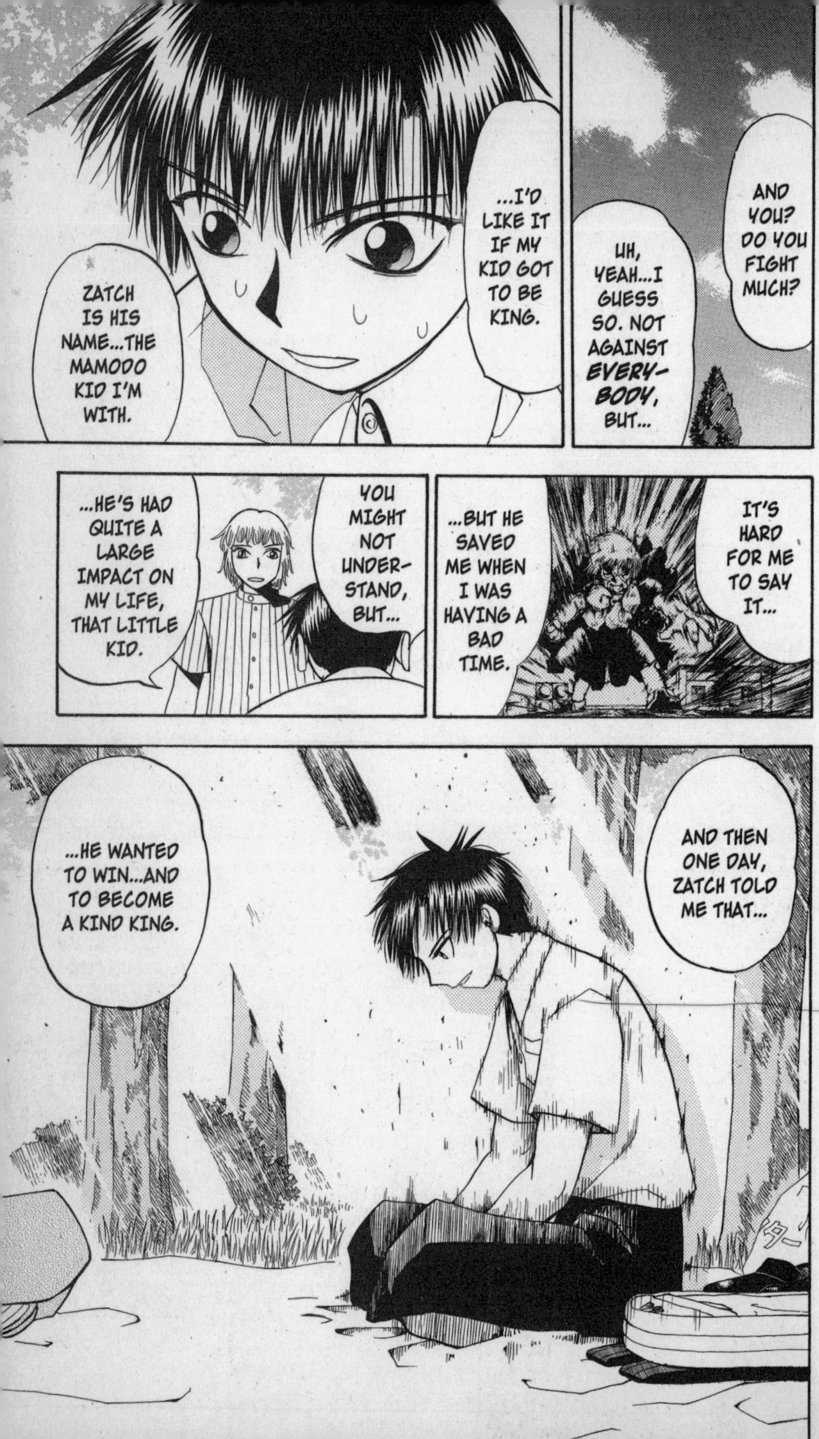
AND YOU? DO YOU FIGHT MUCH?
UH, YEAH...I GUESS SO. NOT AGAINST EVERY-BODY, BUT...
...I'D LIKE IT IF MY KID GOT TO BE KING.
ZATCH IS HIS NAME...THE MAMODO KID I'M WITH.
IT'S HARD FOR ME TO SAY IT...
...BUT HE SAVED ME WHEN I WAS HAVING A BAD TIME.
YOU MIGHT NOT UNDER-STAND, BUT...
...HE'S HAD QUITE A LARGE IMPACT ON MY LIFE, THAT LITTLE KID.
AND THEN ONE DAY, ZATCH TOLD ME THAT...
...HE WANTED TO WIN...AND TO BECOME A KIND KING.

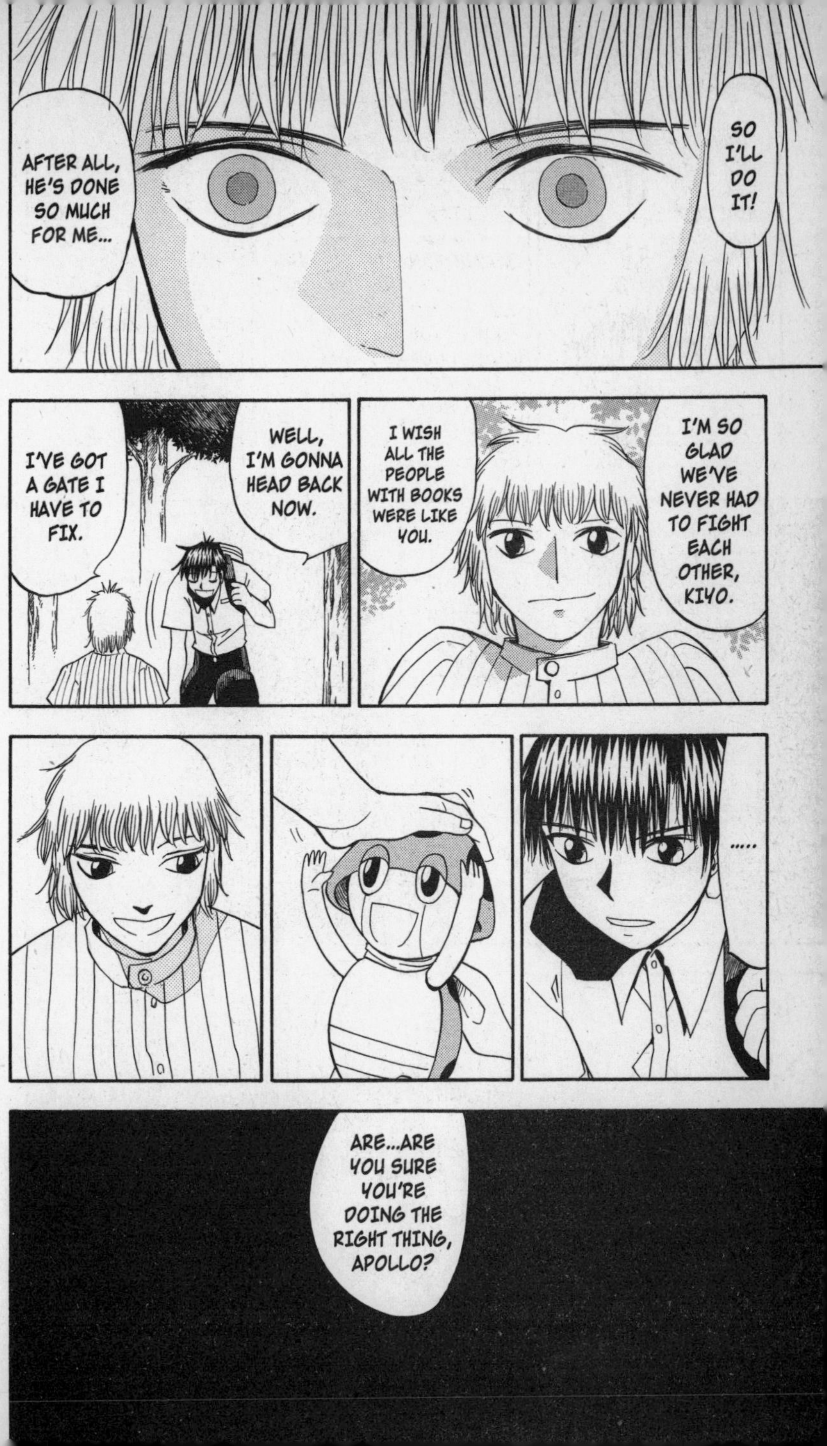
AFTER ALL, HE'S DONE SO MUCH FOR ME...
SO I'LL DO IT!
I'M SO GLAD WE'VE NEVER HAD TO FIGHT EACH OTHER, KIYO.
I WISH ALL THE PEOPLE WITH BOOKS WERE LIKE YOU.
WELL, I'M GONNA HEAD BACK NOW.
I'VE GOT A GATE I HAVE TO FIX.
.....
ARE...ARE YOU SURE YOU'RE DOING THE RIGHT THING, APOLLO?

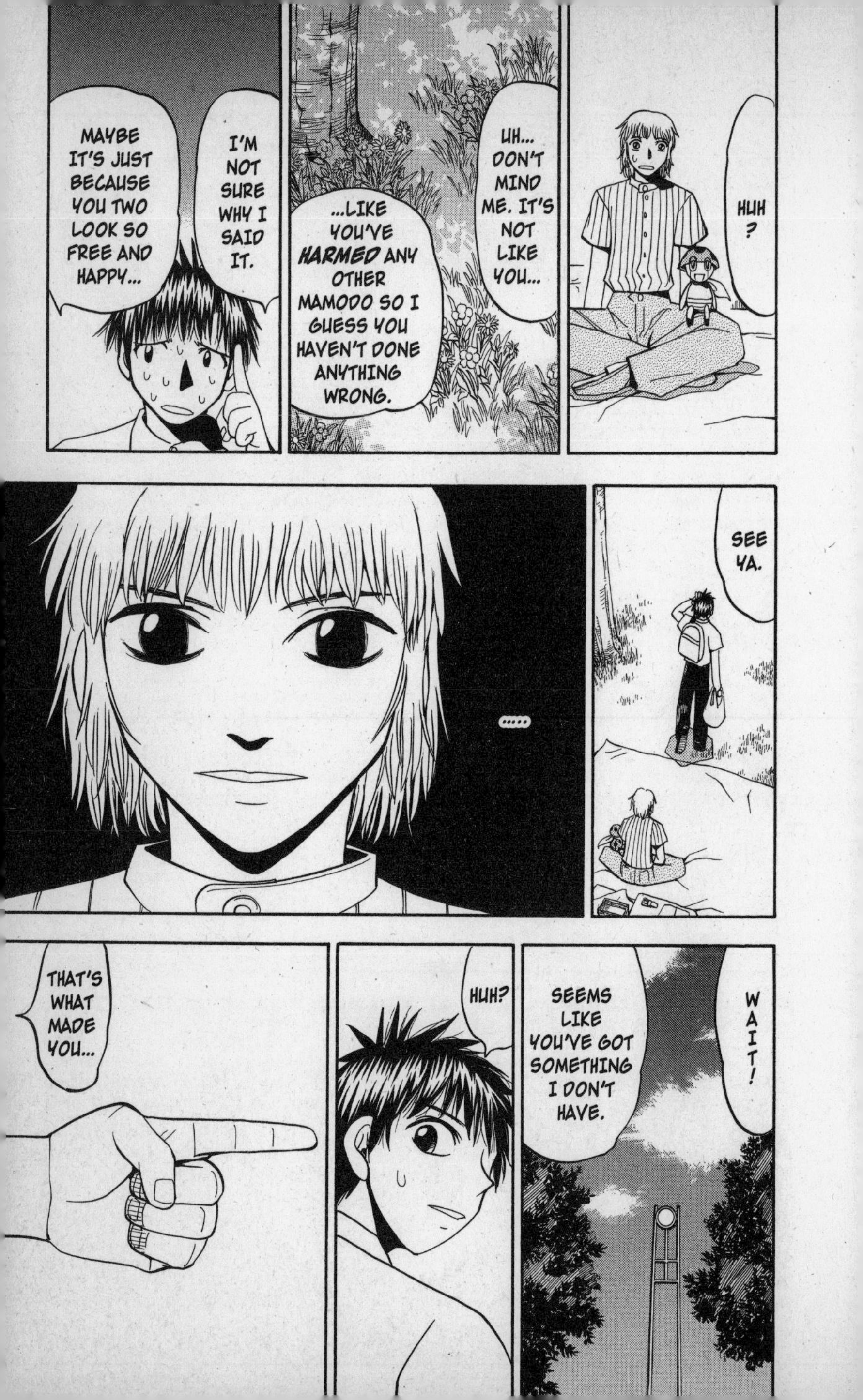
HUH?
UH... DON'T MIND ME. IT'S NOT LIKE YOU...
...LIKE YOU'VE *HARMED* ANY OTHER MAMODO SO I GUESS YOU HAVEN'T DONE ANYTHING WRONG.
I'M NOT SURE WHY I SAID IT.
MAYBE IT'S JUST BECAUSE YOU TWO LOOK SO FREE AND HAPPY...
SEE YA.
......
WAIT!
SEEMS LIKE YOU'VE GOT SOMETHING I DON'T HAVE.
HUH?
THAT'S WHAT MADE YOU...

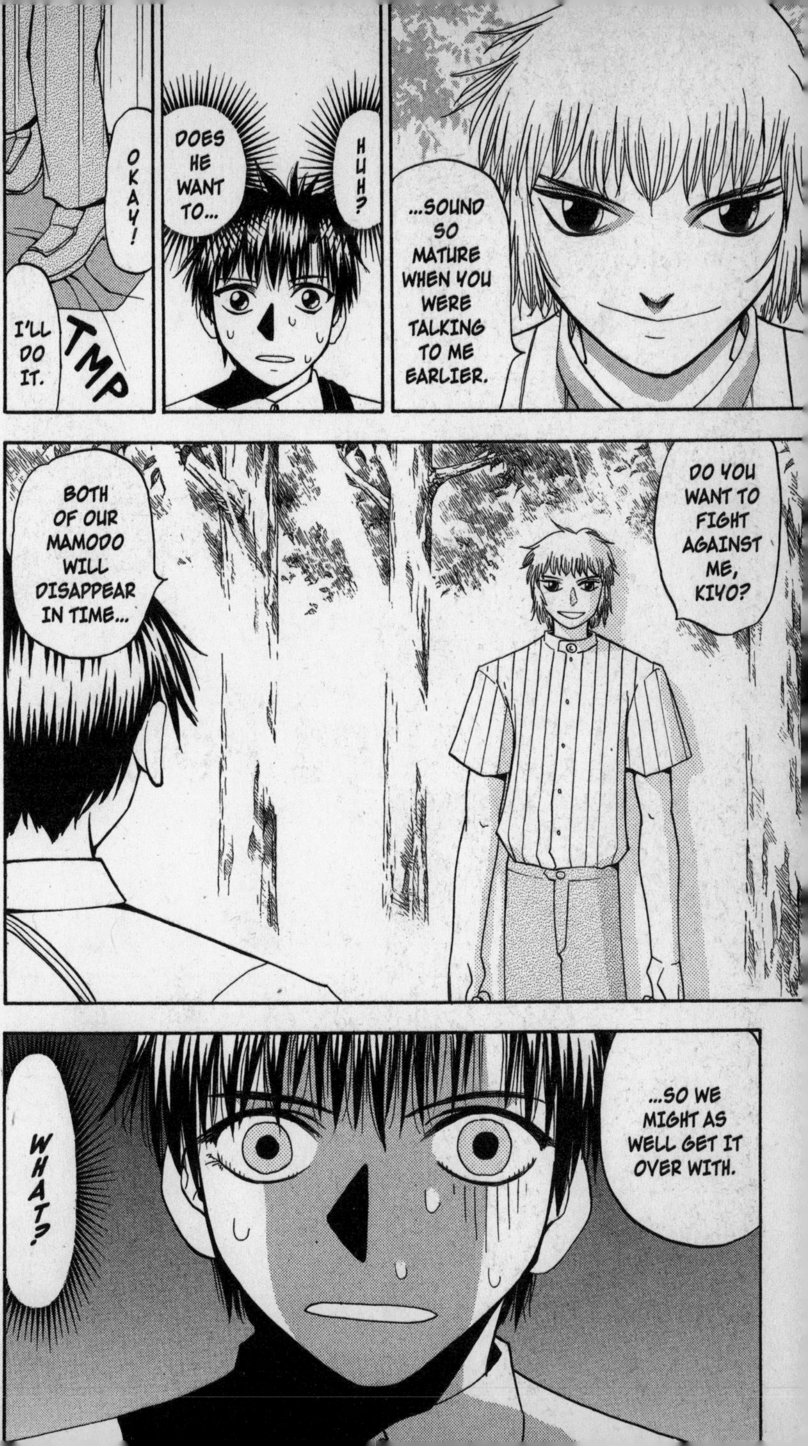
...SOUND SO MATURE WHEN YOU WERE TALKING TO ME EARLIER.
HUH?
DOES HE WANT TO...
OKAY!
TMP
I'LL DO IT.
DO YOU WANT TO FIGHT AGAINST ME, KIYO?
BOTH OF OUR MAMODO WILL DISAPPEAR IN TIME...
...SO WE MIGHT AS WELL GET IT OVER WITH.
WHAT?

LEVEL 60: Unlimited Power

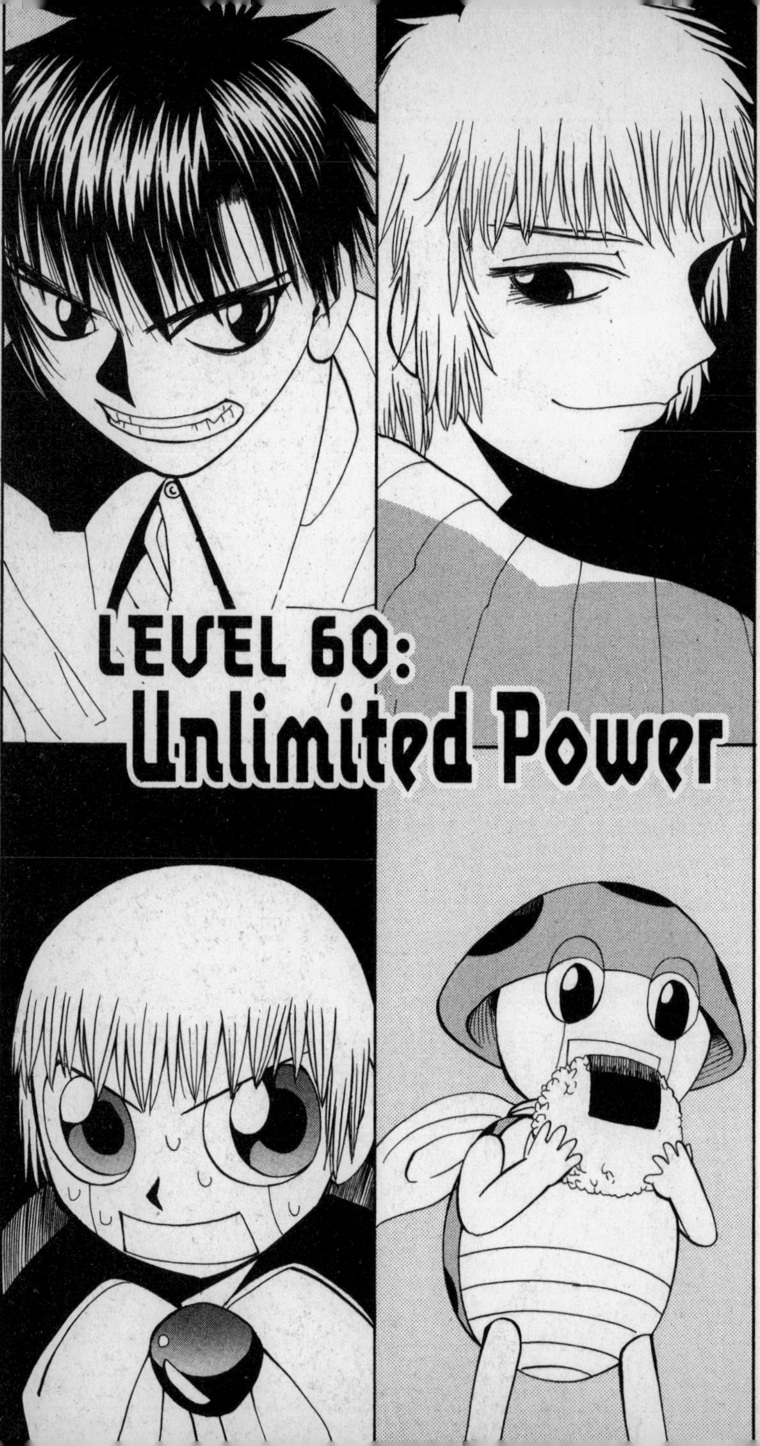

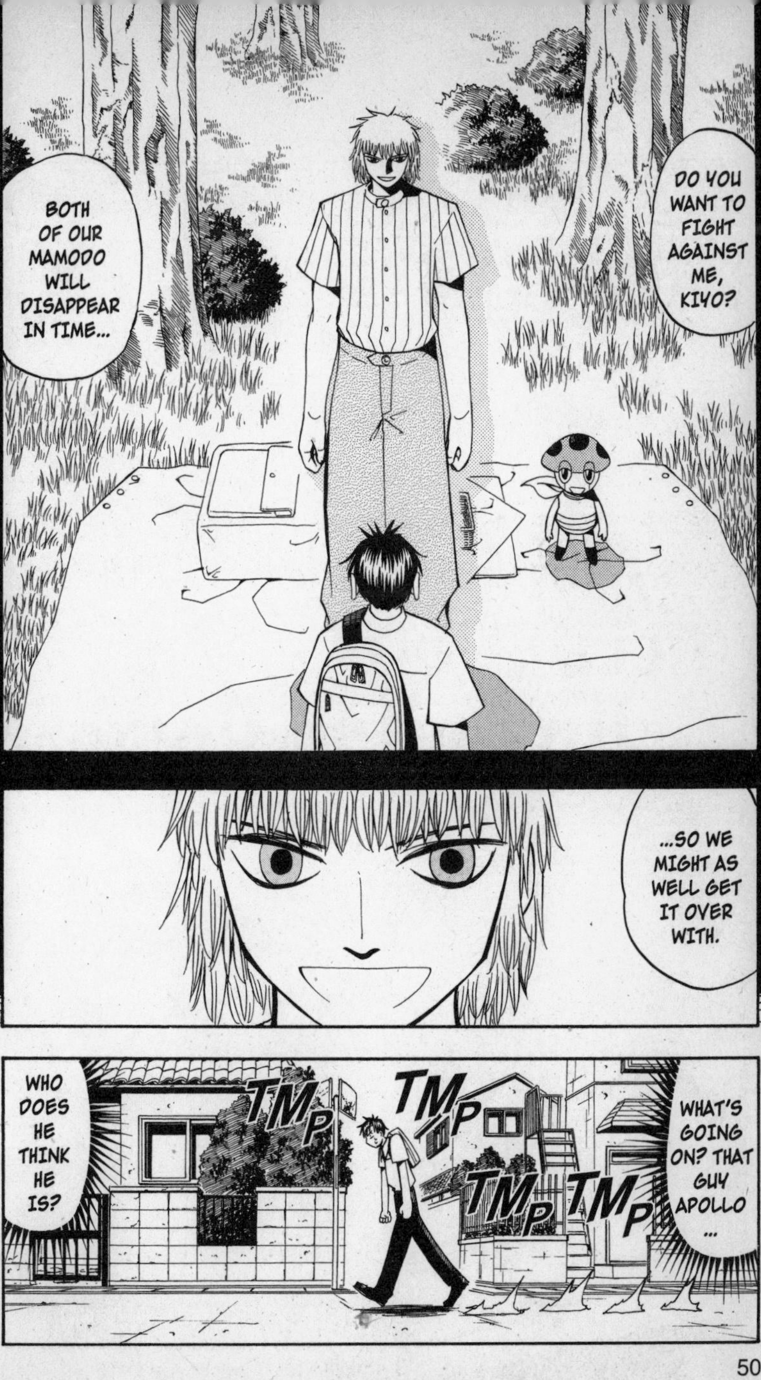
DO YOU WANT TO FIGHT AGAINST ME, KIYO?
BOTH OF OUR MAMODO WILL DISAPPEAR IN TIME...
...SO WE MIGHT AS WELL GET IT OVER WITH.
WHAT'S GOING ON? THAT GUY APOLLO ...
TMP TMP TMP TMP
WHO DOES HE THINK HE IS?

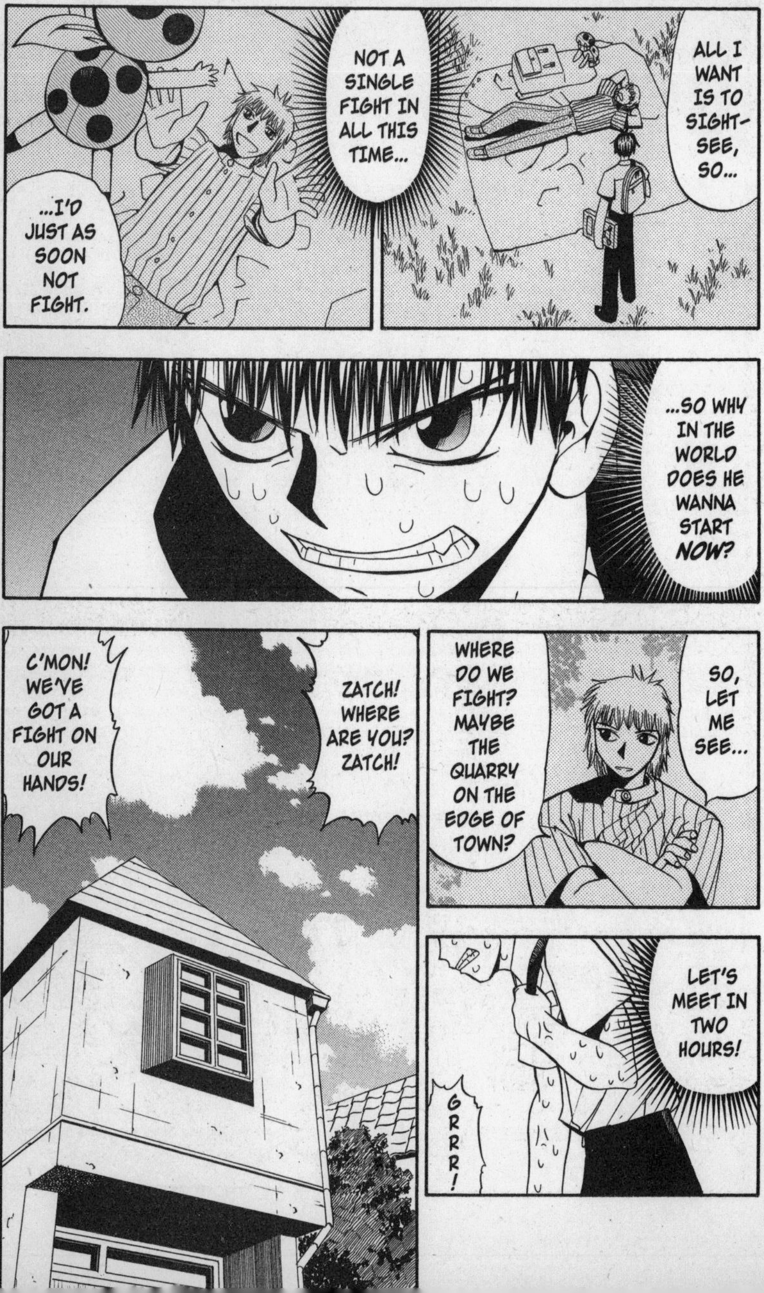
ALL I WANT IS TO SIGHT-SEE, SO...
NOT A SINGLE FIGHT IN ALL THIS TIME...
...I'D JUST AS SOON NOT FIGHT.
...SO WHY IN THE WORLD DOES HE WANNA START *NOW*?
SO, LET ME SEE...
WHERE DO WE FIGHT? MAYBE THE QUARRY ON THE EDGE OF TOWN?
LET'S MEET IN TWO HOURS!
GRRR!
ZATCH! WHERE ARE YOU? ZATCH!
C'MON! WE'VE GOT A FIGHT ON OUR HANDS!

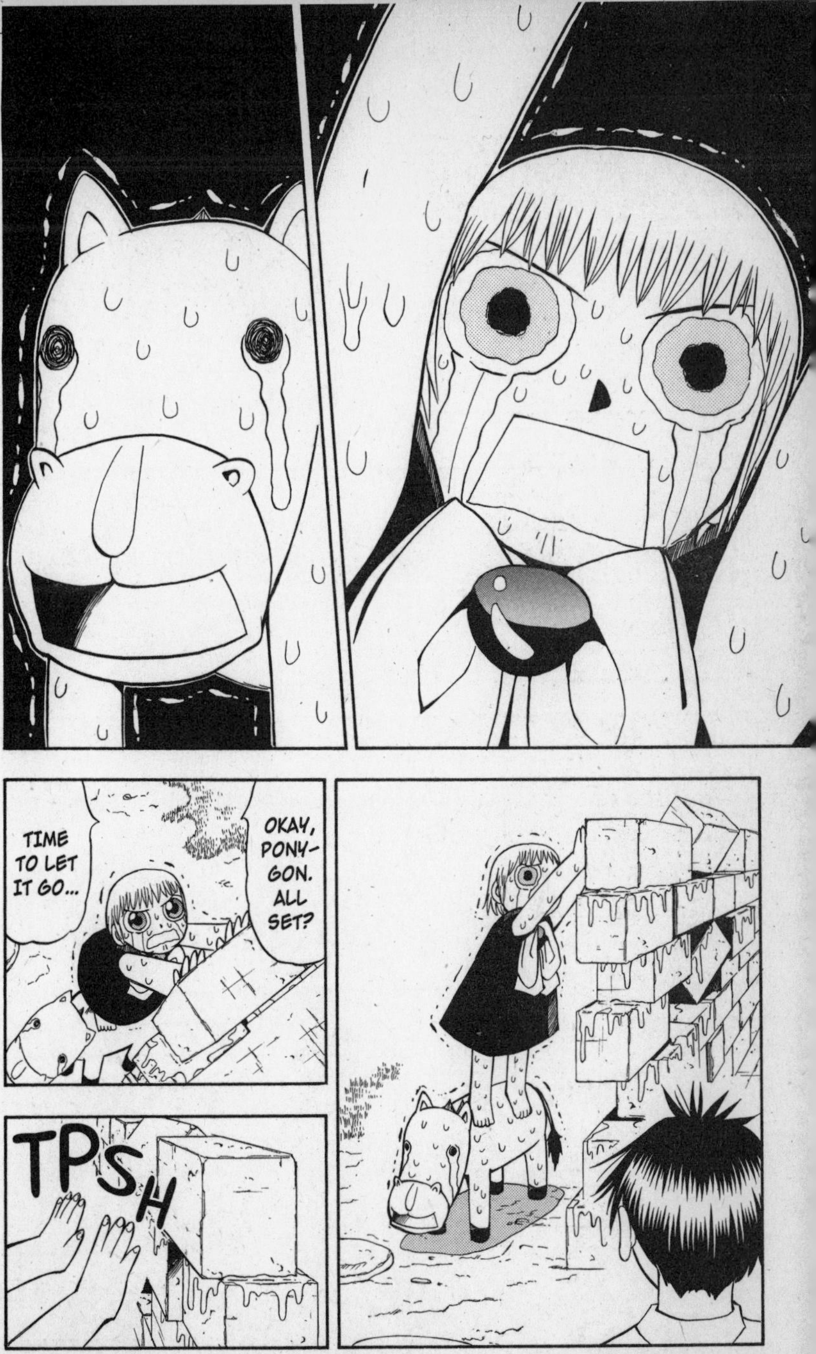
OKAY, PONY-GON. ALL SET?
TIME TO LET IT GO...
TPSH

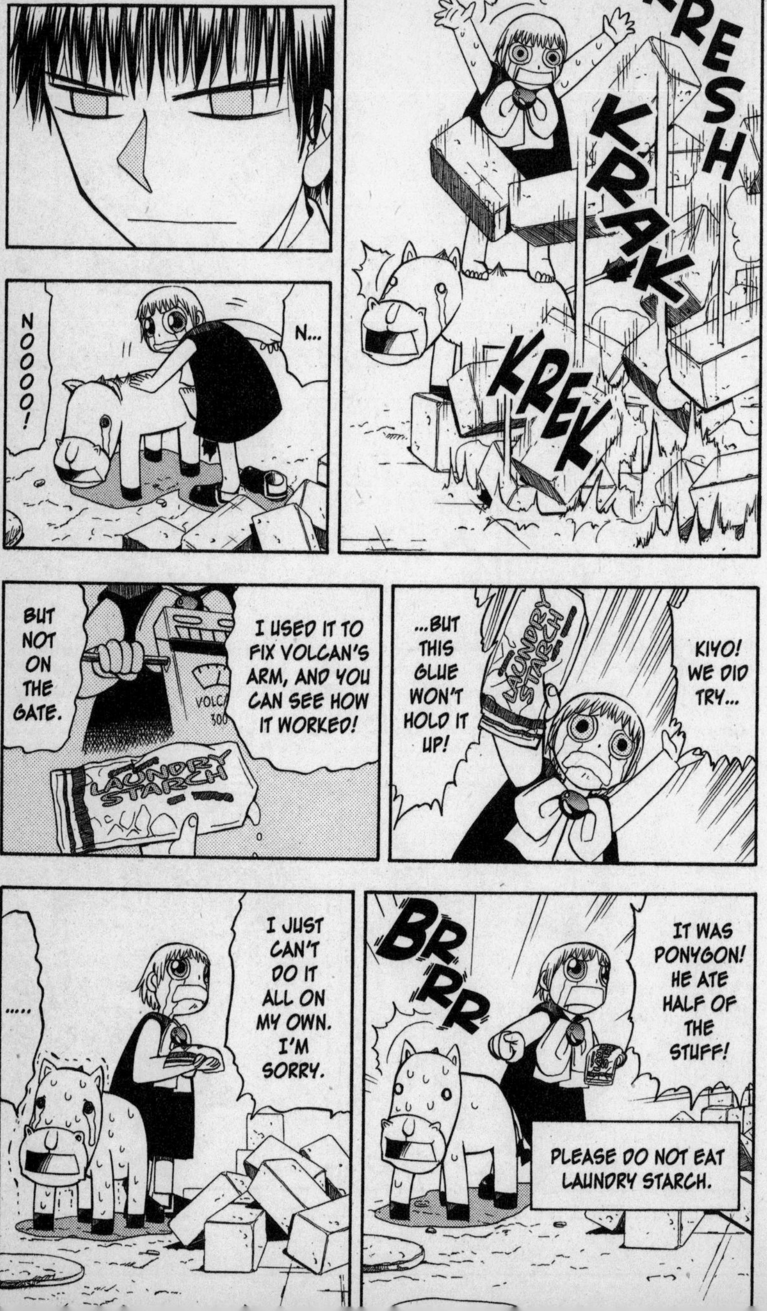
KRESH
KRAK
KREK
N...
NOOOOO!
KIYO! WE DID TRY...
...BUT THIS GLUE WON'T HOLD IT UP!
LAUNDRY STARCH
I USED IT TO FIX VOLCAN'S ARM, AND YOU CAN SEE HOW IT WORKED!
BUT NOT ON THE GATE.
LAUNDRY STARCH
IT WAS PONYGON! HE ATE HALF OF THE STUFF!
BRRR
PLEASE DO NOT EAT LAUNDRY STARCH.
I JUST CAN'T DO IT ALL ON MY OWN. I'M SORRY.
.....

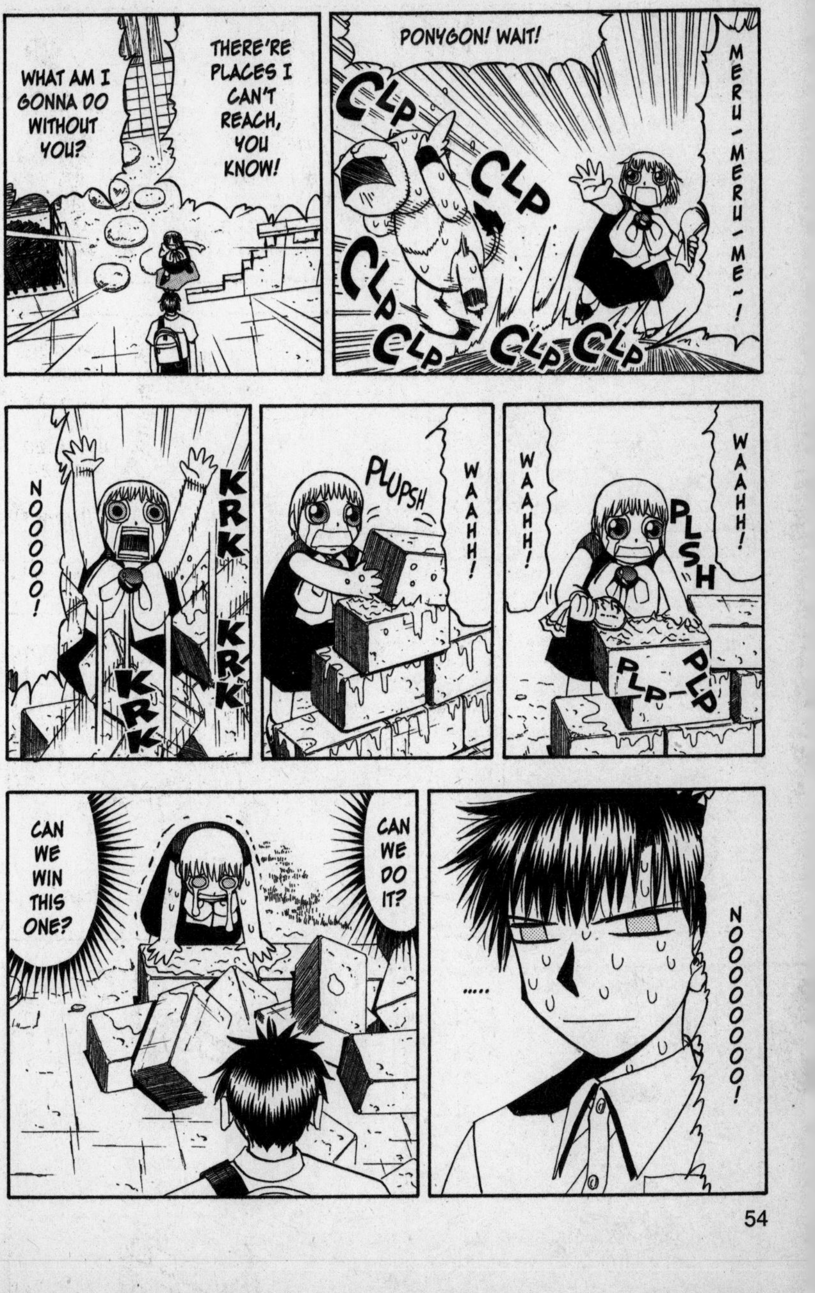
MERU-MERU-ME~!
PONYGON! WAIT!
CLP CLP CLP CLP CLP CLP
THERE'RE PLACES I CAN'T REACH, YOU KNOW!
WHAT AM I GONNA DO WITHOUT YOU?
WAAHH!
PLSH
WAAHH!
PLP PLP
WAAHH!
PLUPSH
KRK KRK KRK
NOOOOOO!
NOOOOOOOOO!
.....
CAN WE DO IT?
CAN WE WIN THIS ONE?

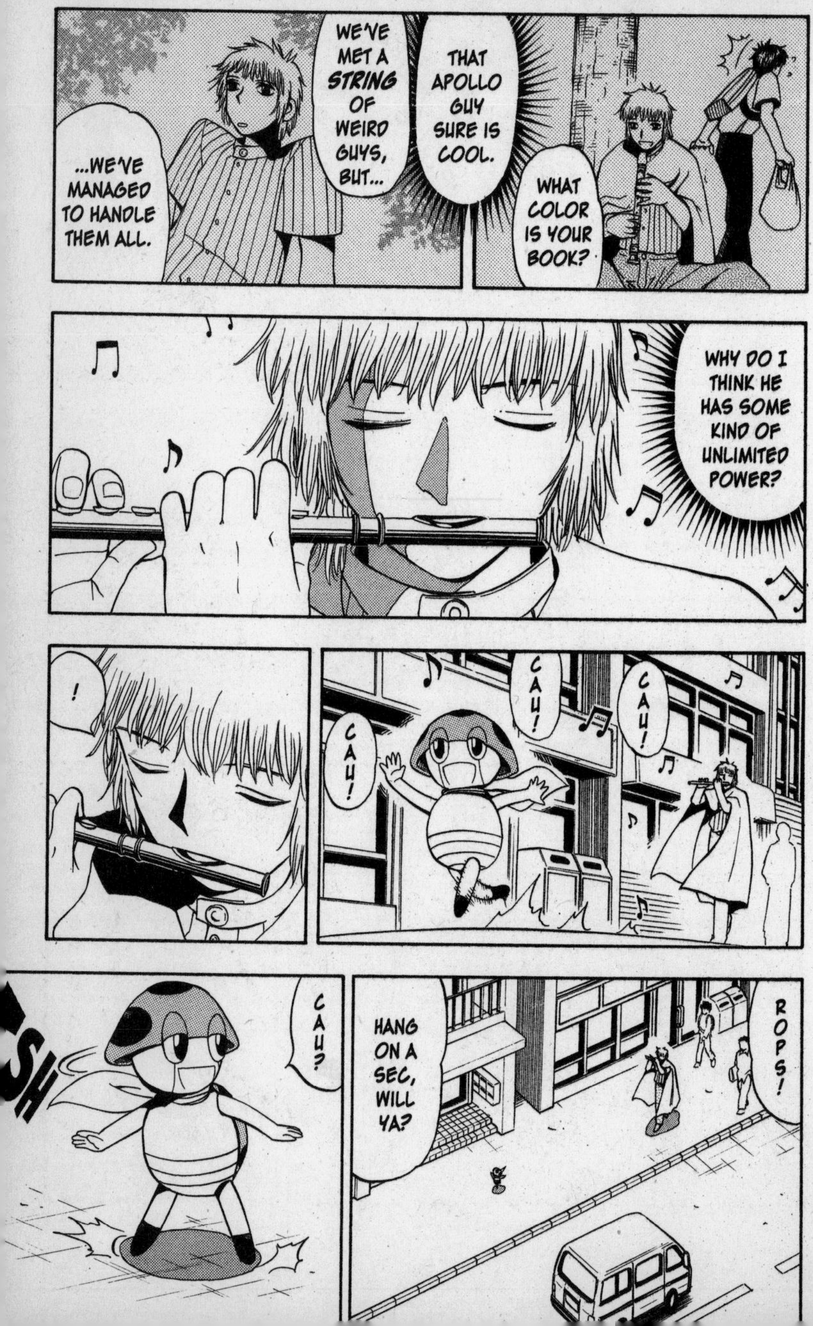
WHAT COLOR IS YOUR BOOK?
THAT APOLLO GUY SURE IS COOL.
WE'VE MET A STRING OF WEIRD GUYS, BUT...
...WE'VE MANAGED TO HANDLE THEM ALL.
WHY DO I THINK HE HAS SOME KIND OF UNLIMITED POWER?
CAU!
CAU!
CAU!
!
ROPS!
HANG ON A SEC, WILL YA?
CAU?
SH

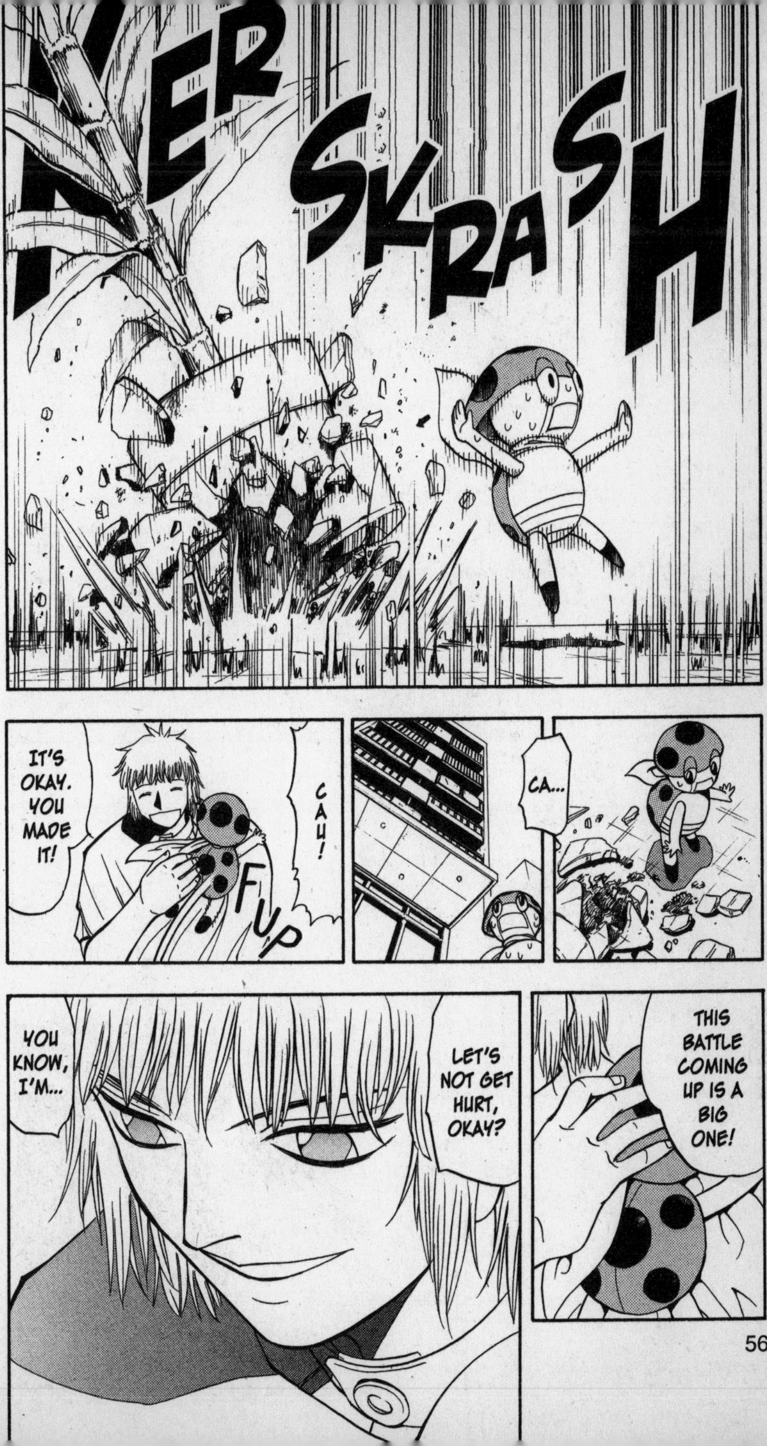
KER SKRASH
CA...
CAU!
IT'S OKAY. YOU MADE IT!
FUP
THIS BATTLE COMING UP IS A BIG ONE!
LET'S NOT GET HURT, OKAY?
YOU KNOW, I'M...

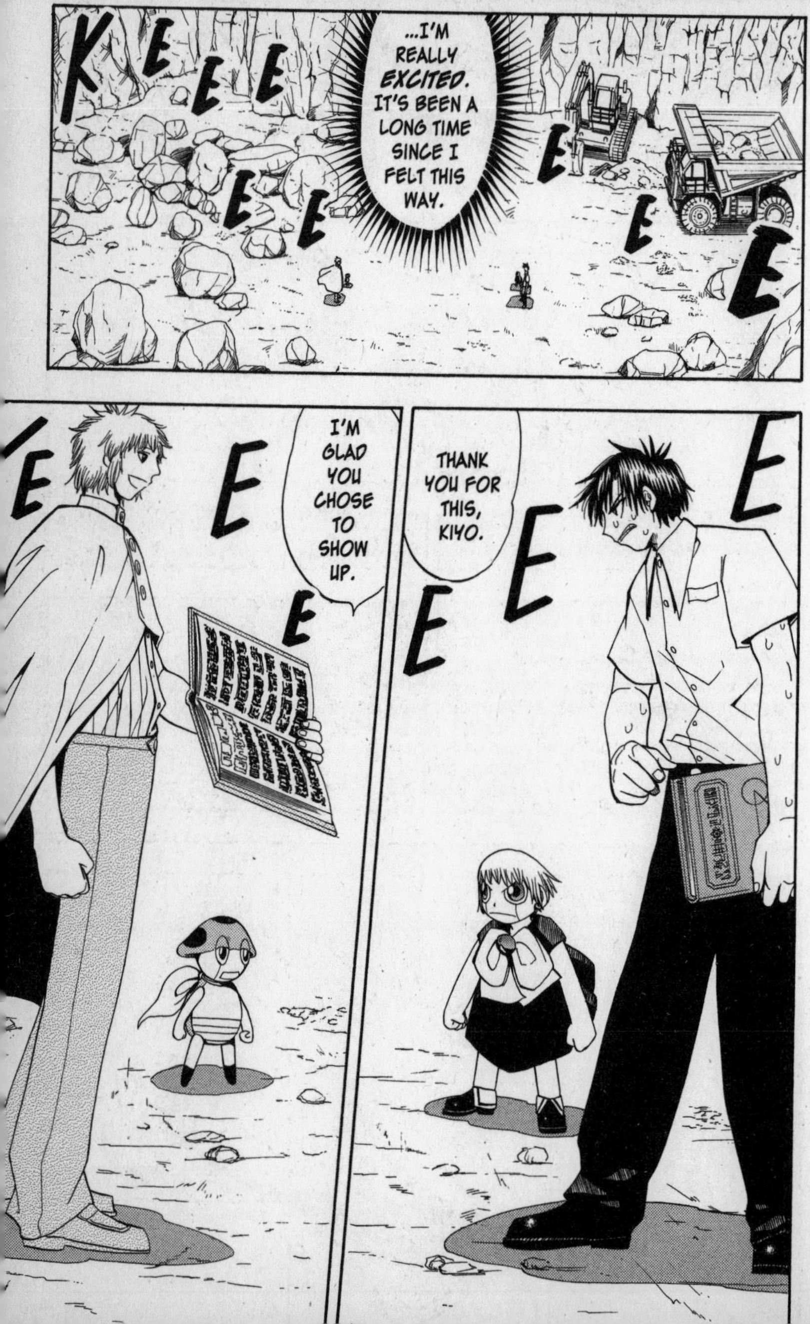
KEEEEEEEE
...I'M REALLY EXCITED. IT'S BEEN A LONG TIME SINCE I FELT THIS WAY.
EEEE
THANK YOU FOR THIS, KIYO.
EEEE
I'M GLAD YOU CHOSE TO SHOW UP.

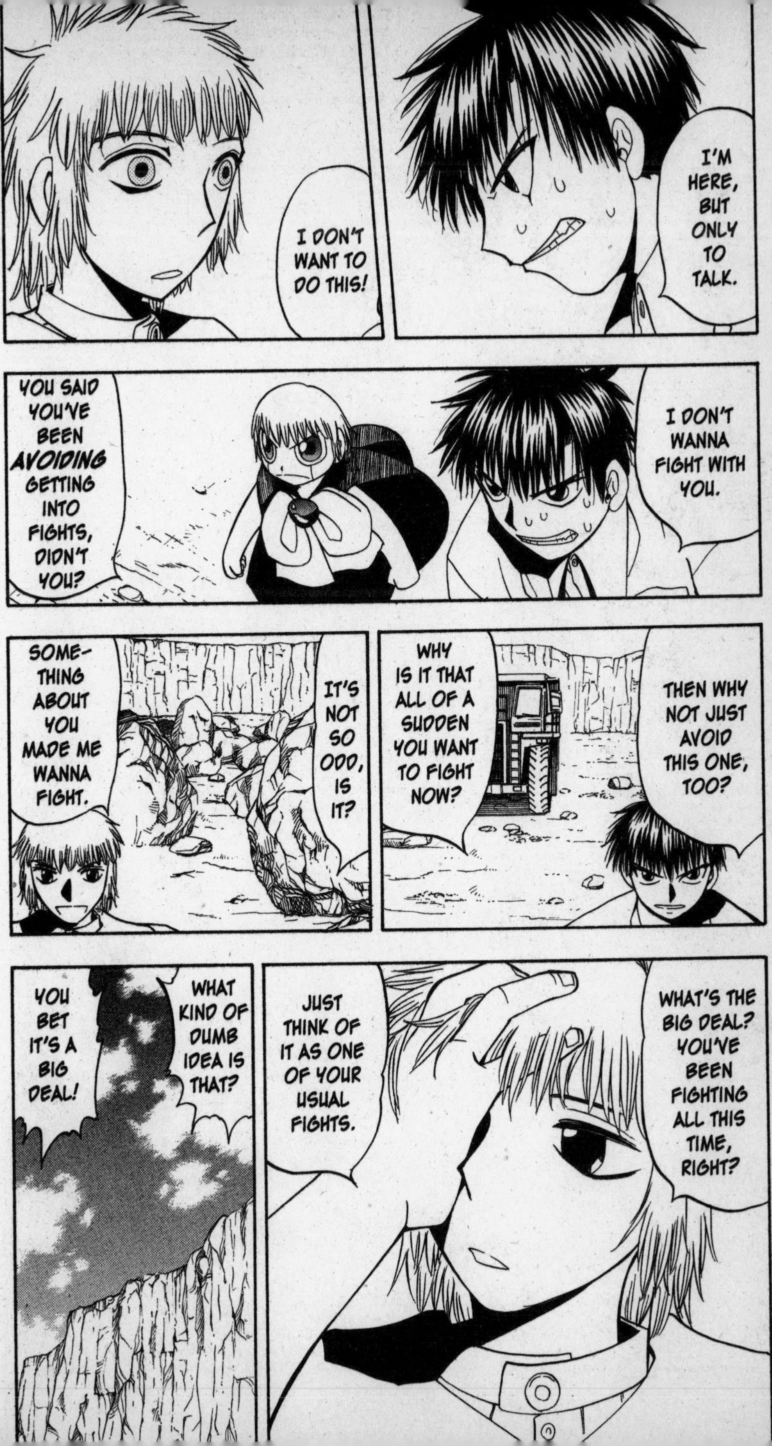
I'M HERE, BUT ONLY TO TALK.
I DON'T WANT TO DO THIS!
I DON'T WANNA FIGHT WITH YOU.
YOU SAID YOU'VE BEEN AVOIDING GETTING INTO FIGHTS, DIDN'T YOU?
THEN WHY NOT JUST AVOID THIS ONE, TOO?
WHY IS IT THAT ALL OF A SUDDEN YOU WANT TO FIGHT NOW?
IT'S NOT SO ODD, IS IT?
SOME-THING ABOUT YOU MADE ME WANNA FIGHT.
WHAT'S THE BIG DEAL? YOU'VE BEEN FIGHTING ALL THIS TIME, RIGHT?
JUST THINK OF IT AS ONE OF YOUR USUAL FIGHTS.
WHAT KIND OF DUMB IDEA IS THAT?
YOU BET IT'S A BIG DEAL!

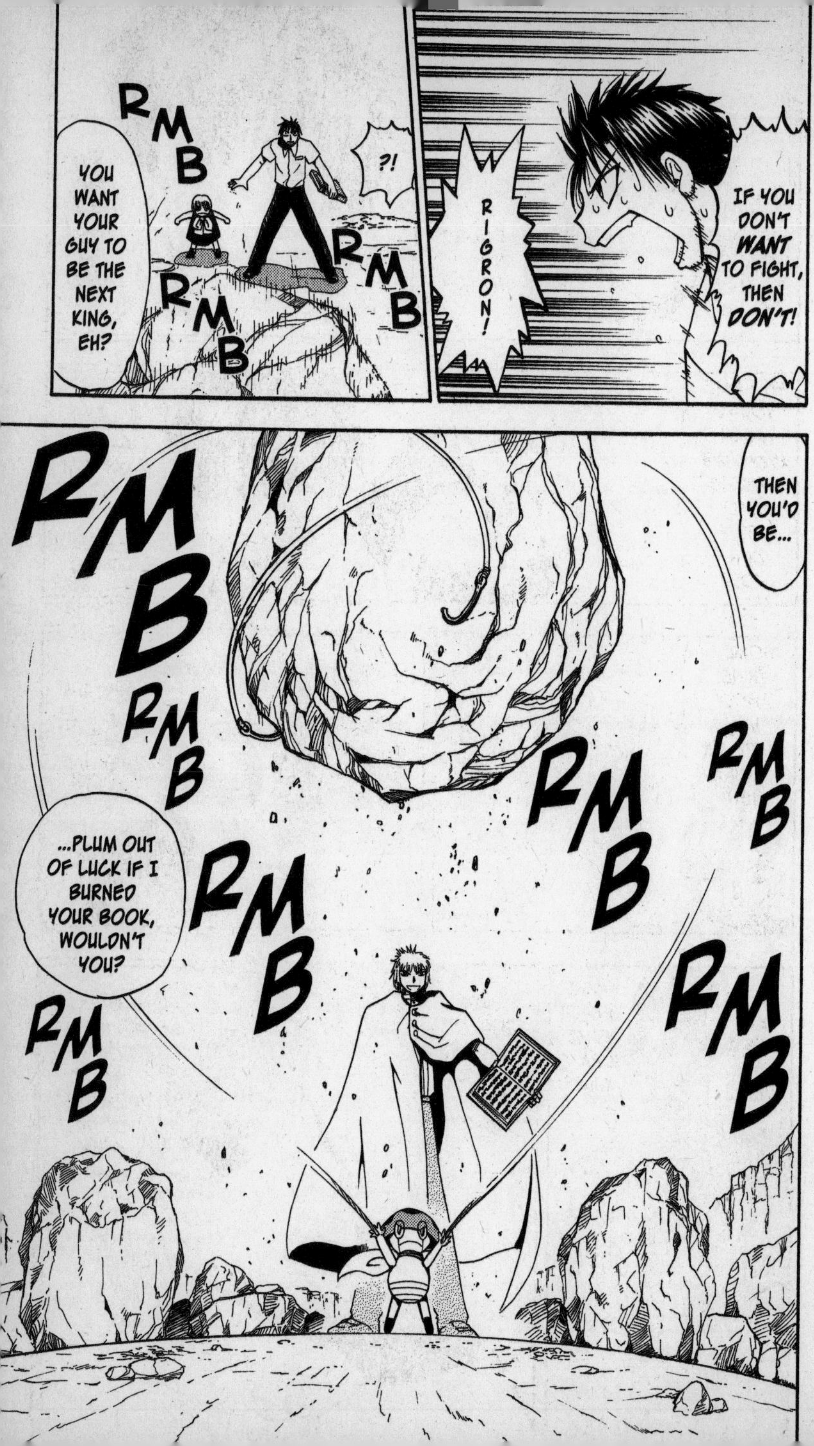
IF YOU DON'T WANT TO FIGHT, THEN DON'T!
RIGRON!
?!
YOU WANT YOUR GUY TO BE THE NEXT KING, EH?
RMB
RMB
RMB
THEN YOU'D BE...
RMB
RMB
RMB
RMB
...PLUM OUT OF LUCK IF I BURNED YOUR BOOK, WOULDN'T YOU?
RMB
RMB
RMB

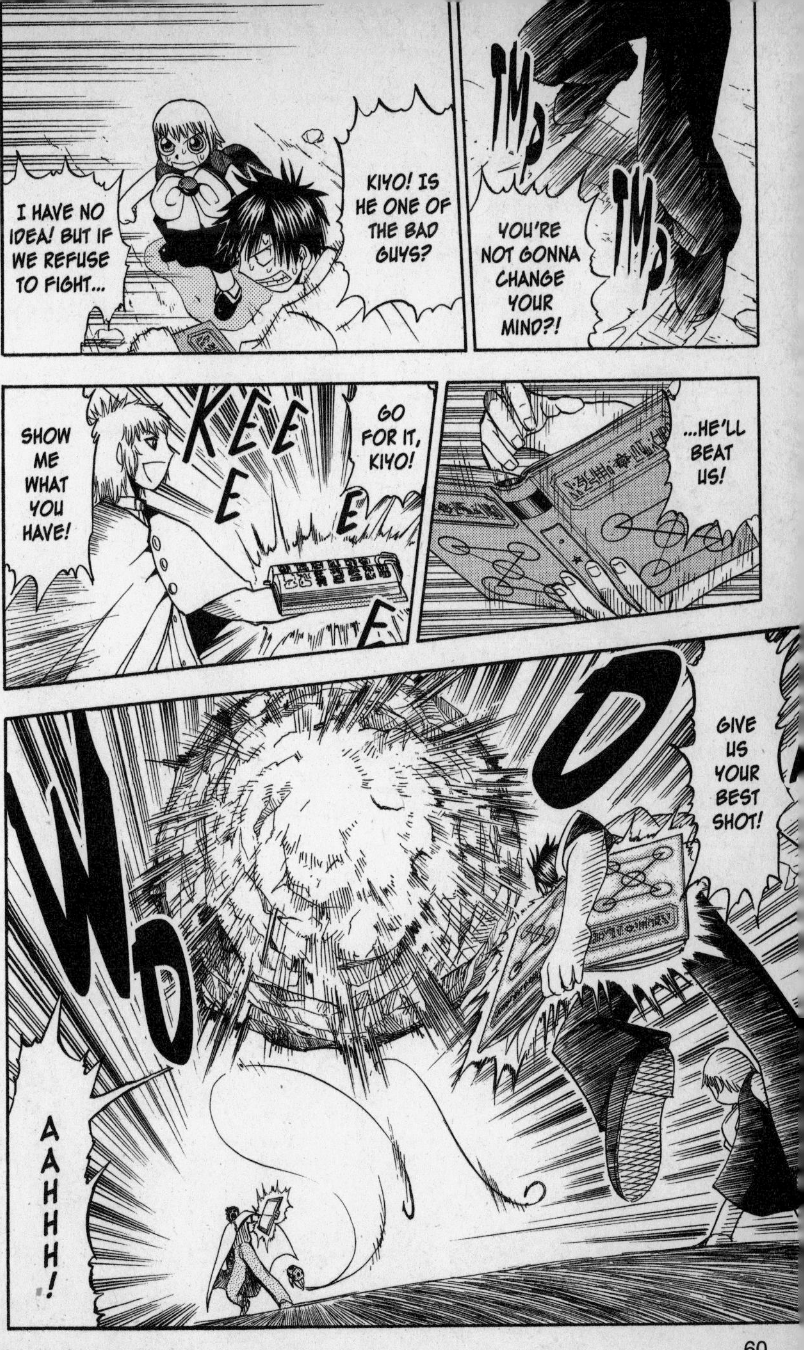
TMP
TMP
YOU'RE NOT GONNA CHANGE YOUR MIND?!
KIYO! IS HE ONE OF THE BAD GUYS?
I HAVE NO IDEA! BUT IF WE REFUSE TO FIGHT...
...HE'LL BEAT US!
GO FOR IT, KIYO!
KEEEEE
SHOW ME WHAT YOU HAVE!
GIVE US YOUR BEST SHOT!
AAHHH!

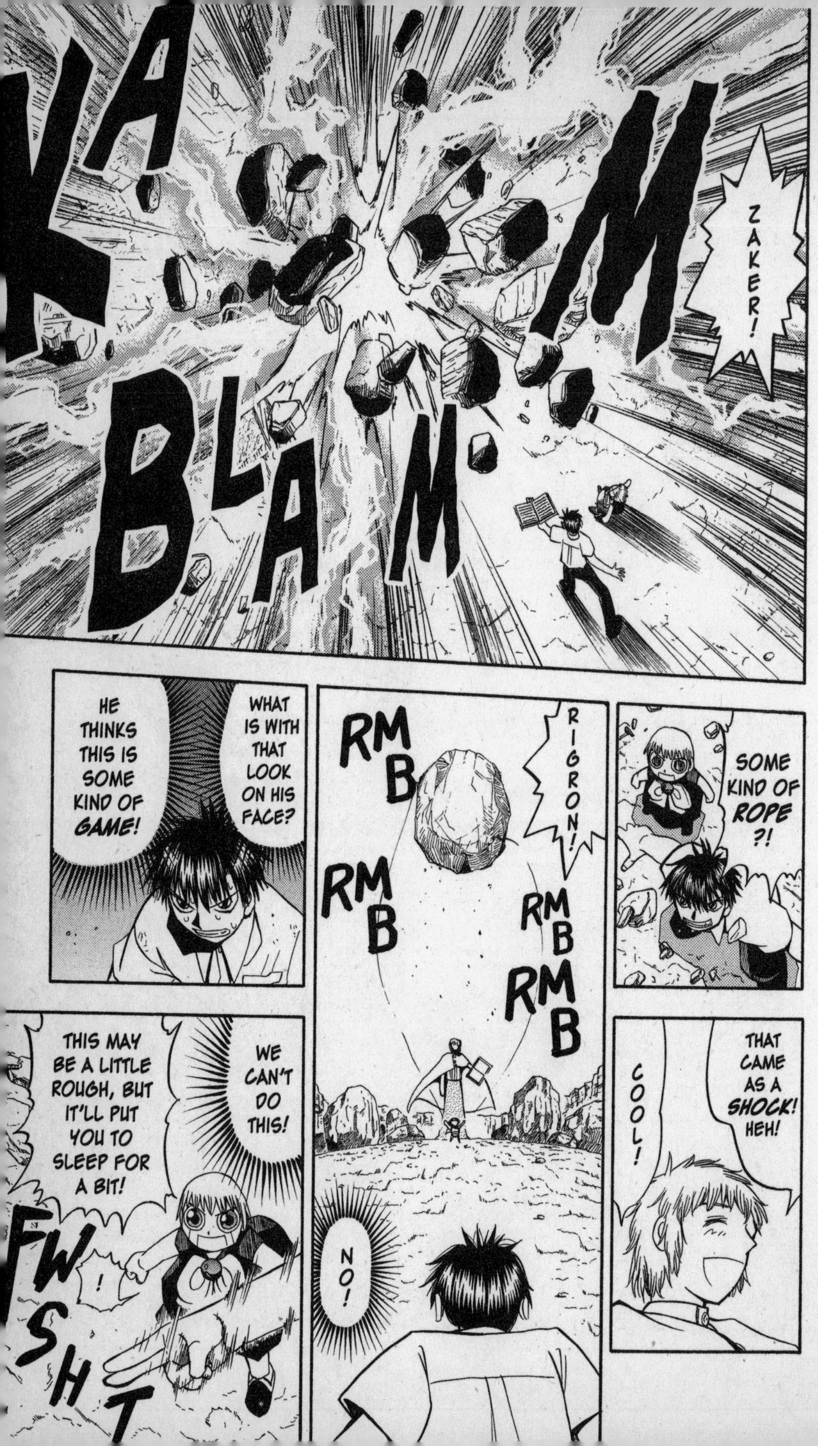
ZAKER!
KA-BLAM
SOME KIND OF ROPE?!
THAT CAME AS A SHOCK! HEH!
COOL!
RIGRON!
RMB
RMB
RMB
RMB
NO!
WHAT IS WITH THAT LOOK ON HIS FACE?
HE THINKS THIS IS SOME KIND OF GAME!
WE CAN'T DO THIS!
THIS MAY BE A LITTLE ROUGH, BUT IT'LL PUT YOU TO SLEEP FOR A BIT!
!
FWSHT

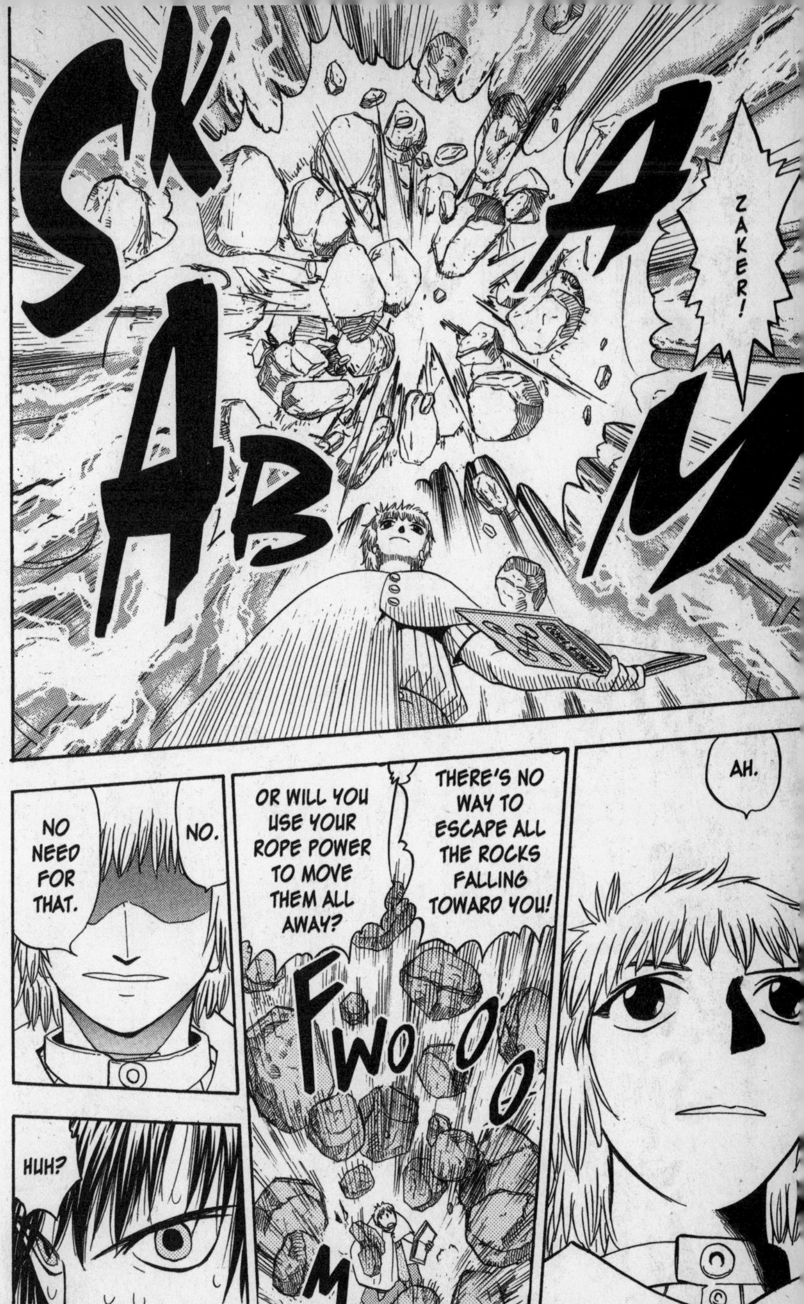
SKABAM
ZAKER!
AH.
THERE'S NO WAY TO ESCAPE ALL THE ROCKS FALLING TOWARD YOU!
OR WILL YOU USE YOUR ROPE POWER TO MOVE THEM ALL AWAY?
FWOOOMSH
NO.
NO NEED FOR THAT.
HUH?

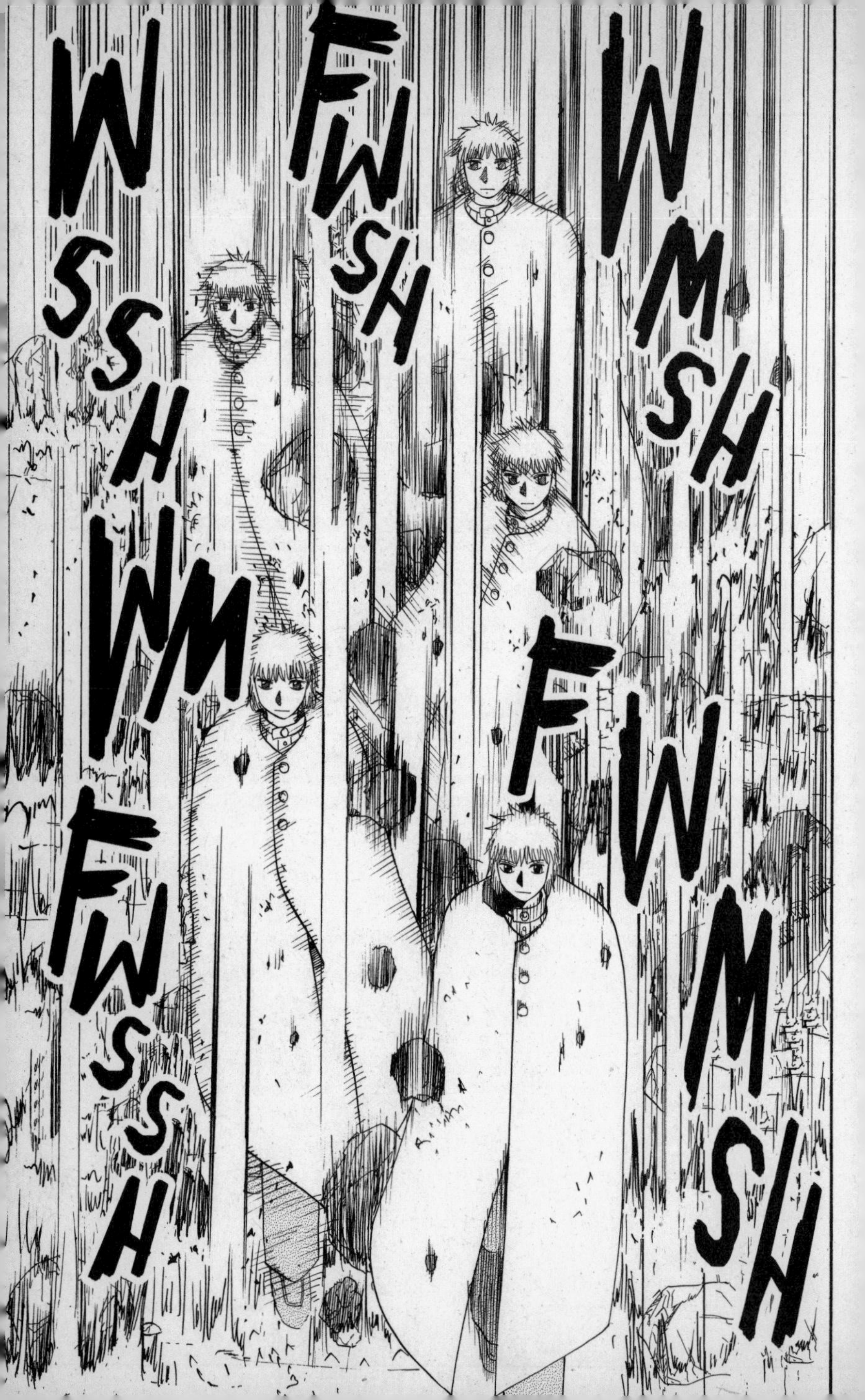
WMSH
FWMSH
FWSH
WSSH
WM
FWSSH

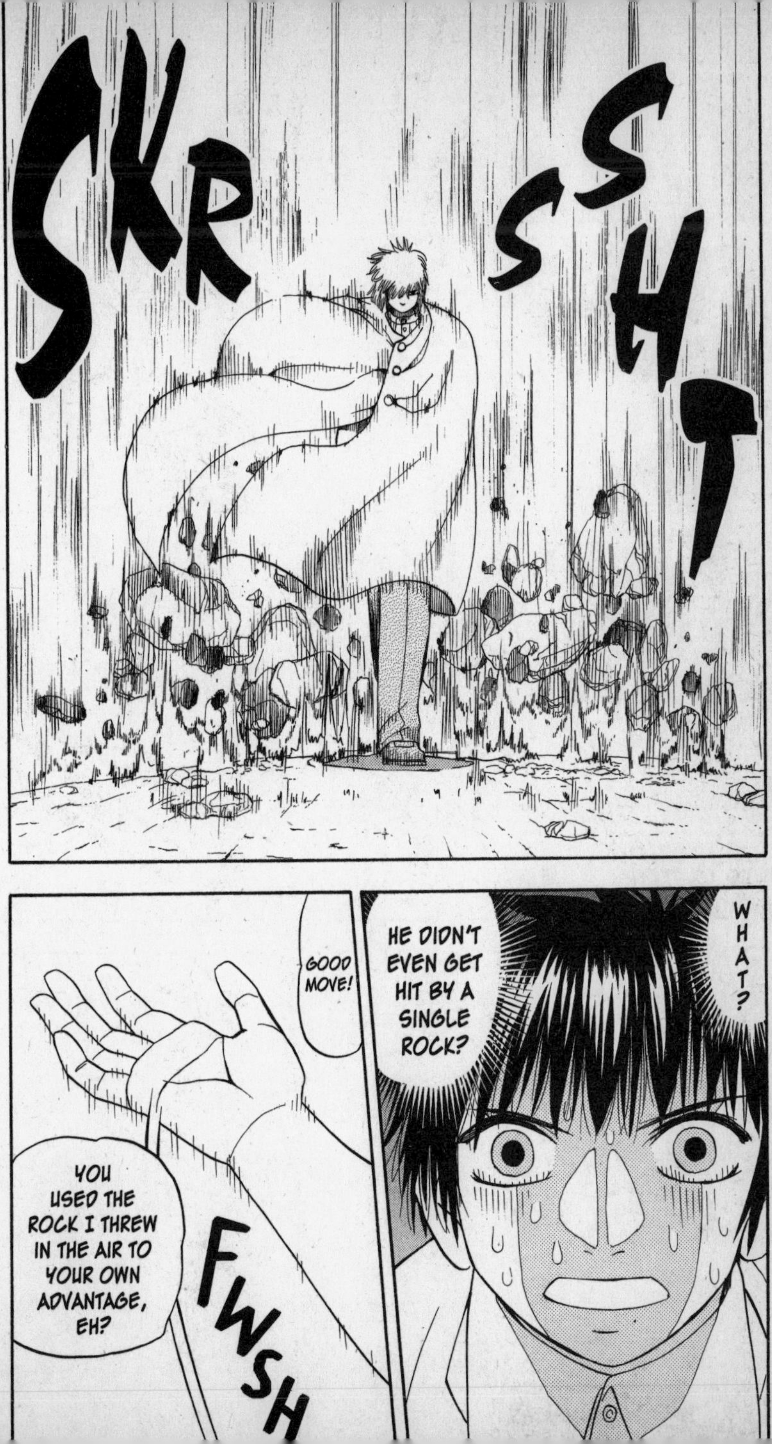
SKRSSHT
WHAT?
HE DIDN'T EVEN GET HIT BY A SINGLE ROCK?
GOOD MOVE!
YOU USED THE ROCK I THREW IN THE AIR TO YOUR OWN ADVANTAGE, EH?
FWSH

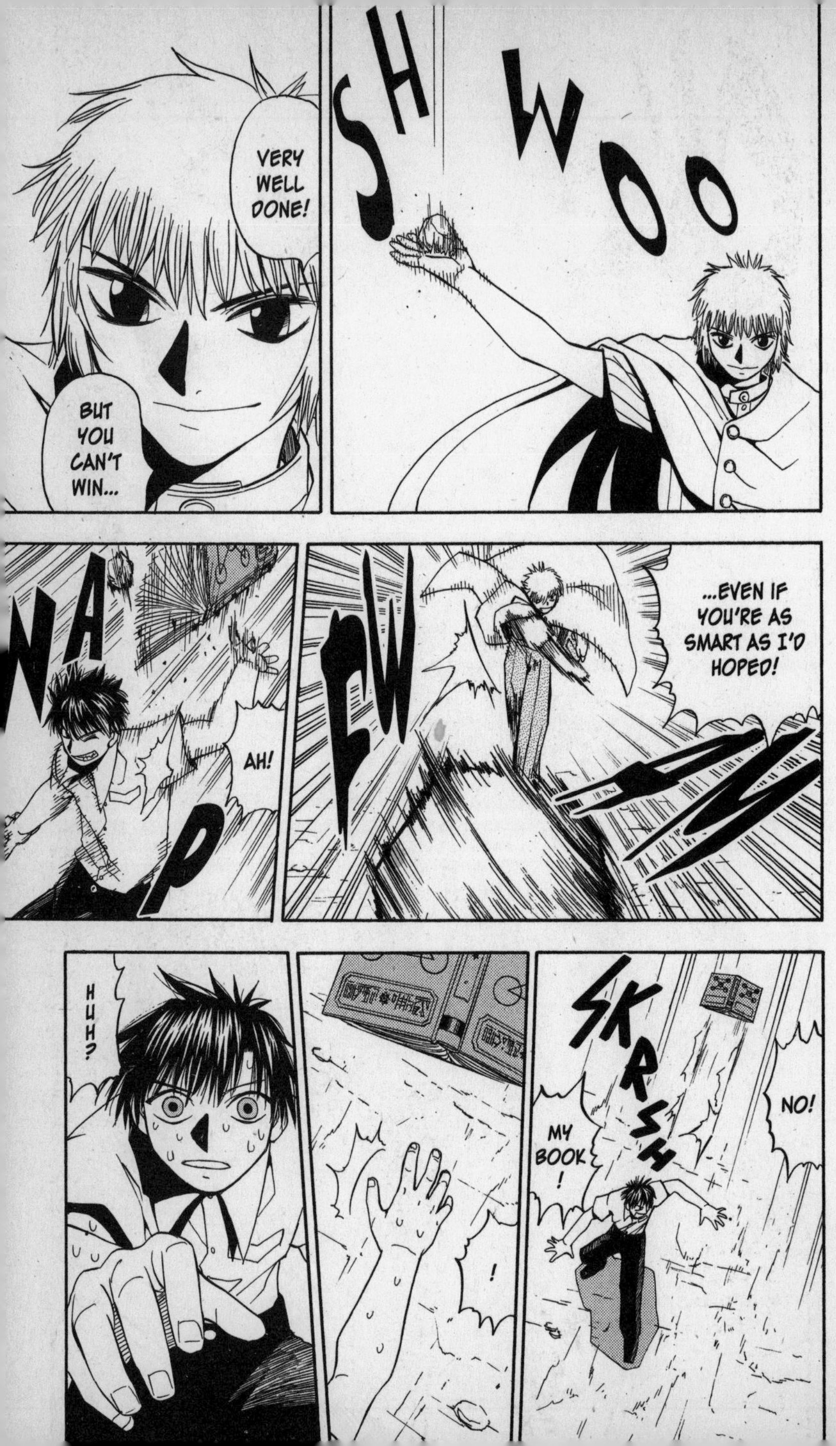
SHWOO
VERY WELL DONE!
BUT YOU CAN'T WIN...
...EVEN IF YOU'RE AS SMART AS I'D HOPED!
AH!
SKRSH
NO!
MY BOOK!
!
HUH?

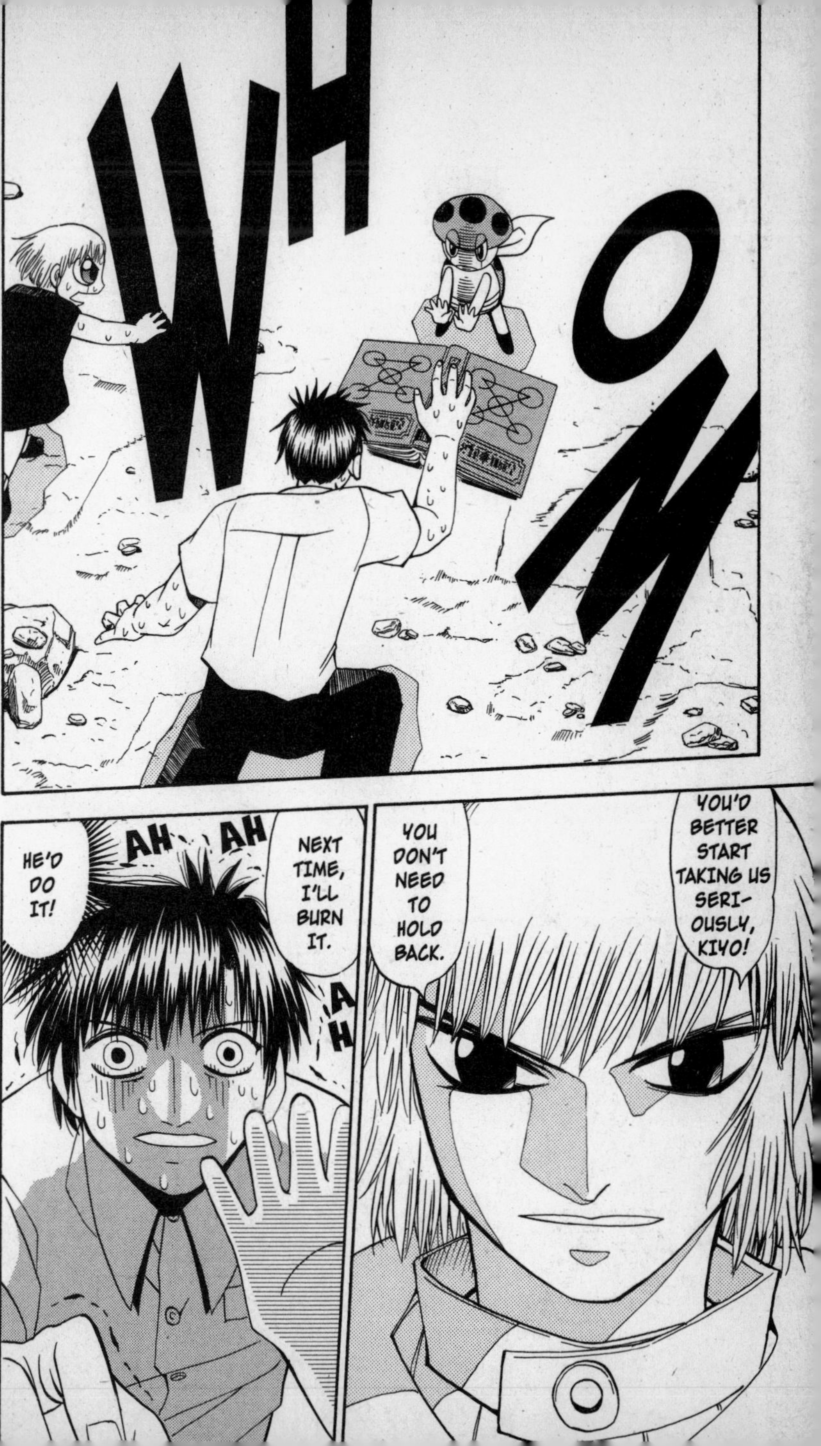
WHOM
YOU'D BETTER START TAKING US SERI-OUSLY, KIYO!
YOU DON'T NEED TO HOLD BACK.
NEXT TIME, I'LL BURN IT.
AH AH AH
HE'D DO IT!

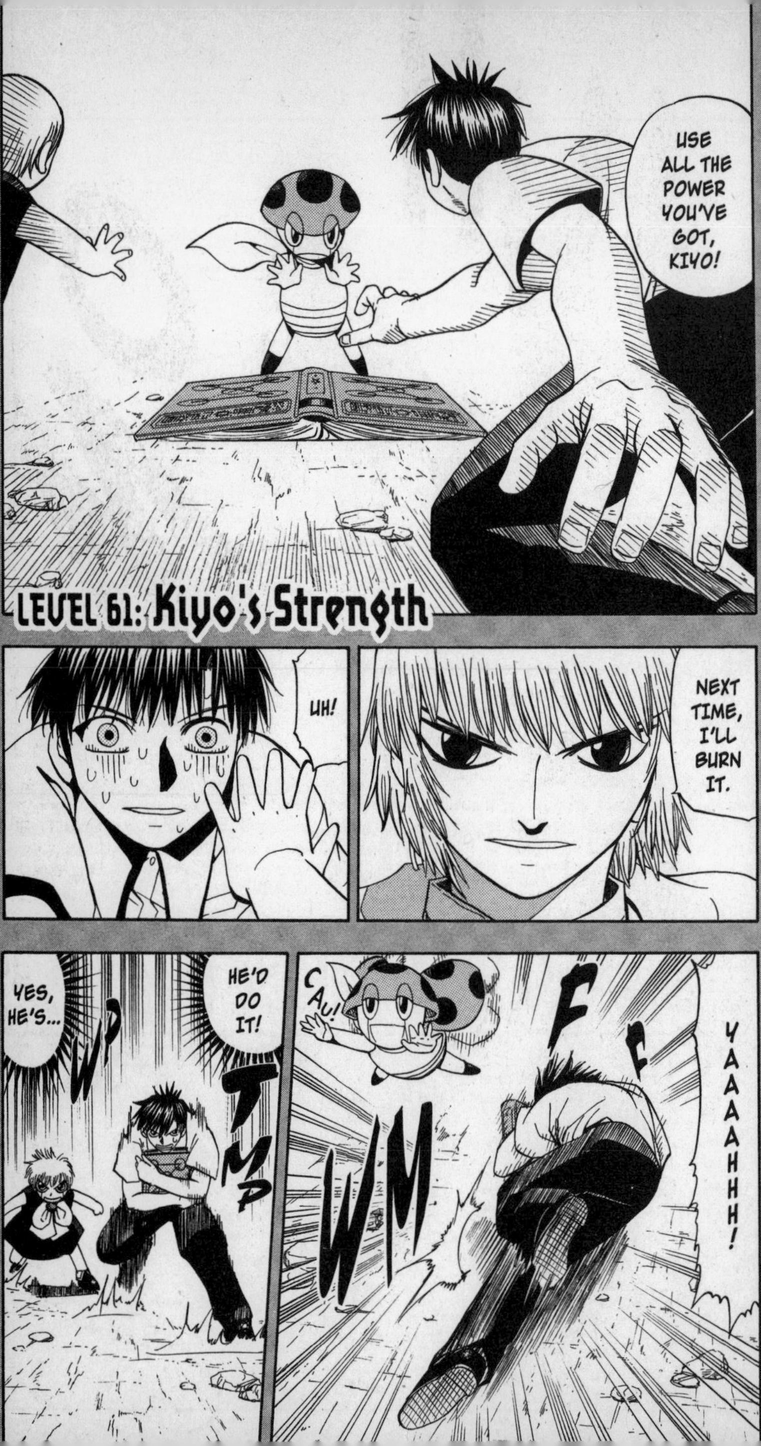
USE ALL THE POWER YOU'VE GOT, KIYO!
LEVEL 61: Kiyo's Strength
NEXT TIME, I'LL BURN IT.
UH!
YAAAAHHH!
CAU!
HE'D DO IT!
YES, HE'S...

LEVEL 61: Kiyo's Strength

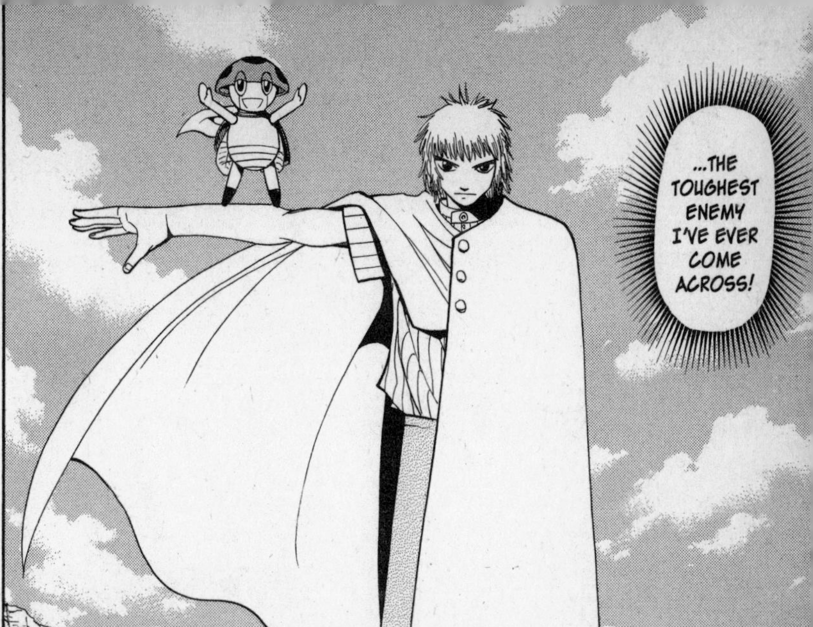
...THE TOUGHEST ENEMY I'VE EVER COME ACROSS!

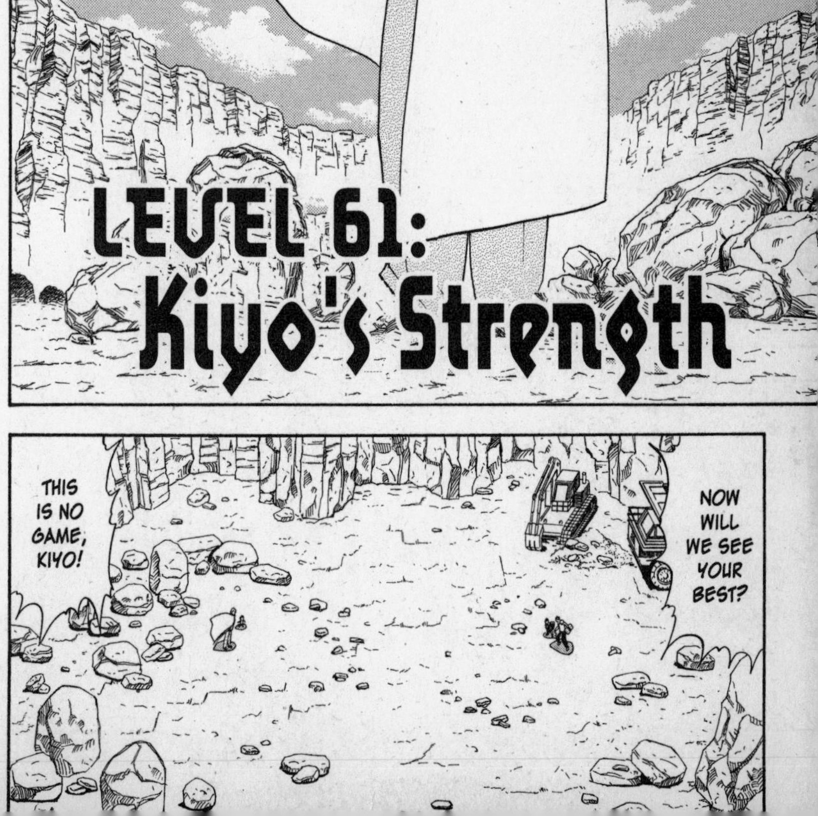
NOW WILL WE SEE YOUR BEST?
THIS IS NO GAME, KIYO!

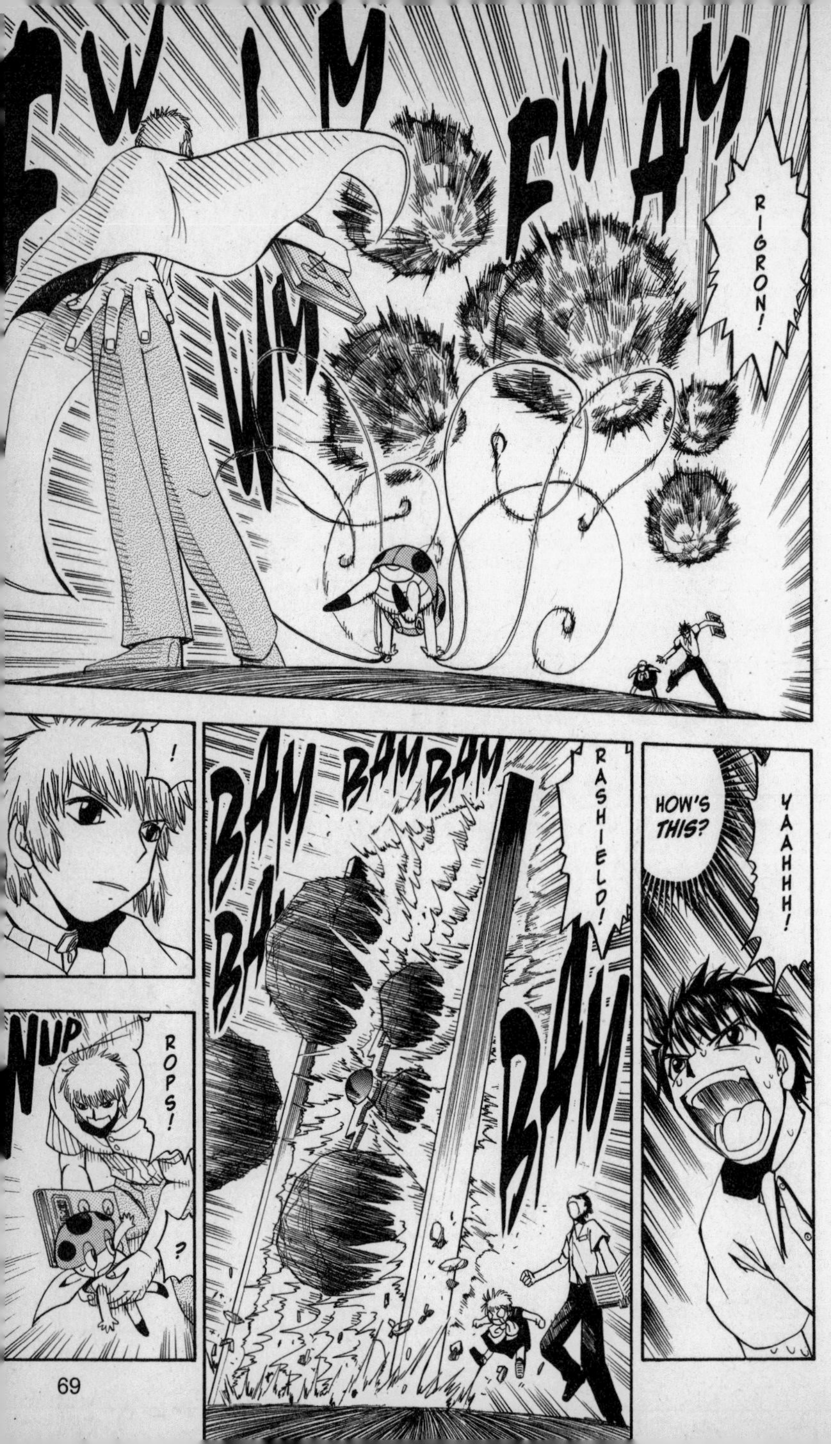
RIGRON!
FWAM
SWIM
WIM
YAAHHH!
HOW'S THIS?
RASHIELD!
BAM
BAMBAM
BAM
!
ROPS!
NUP
?

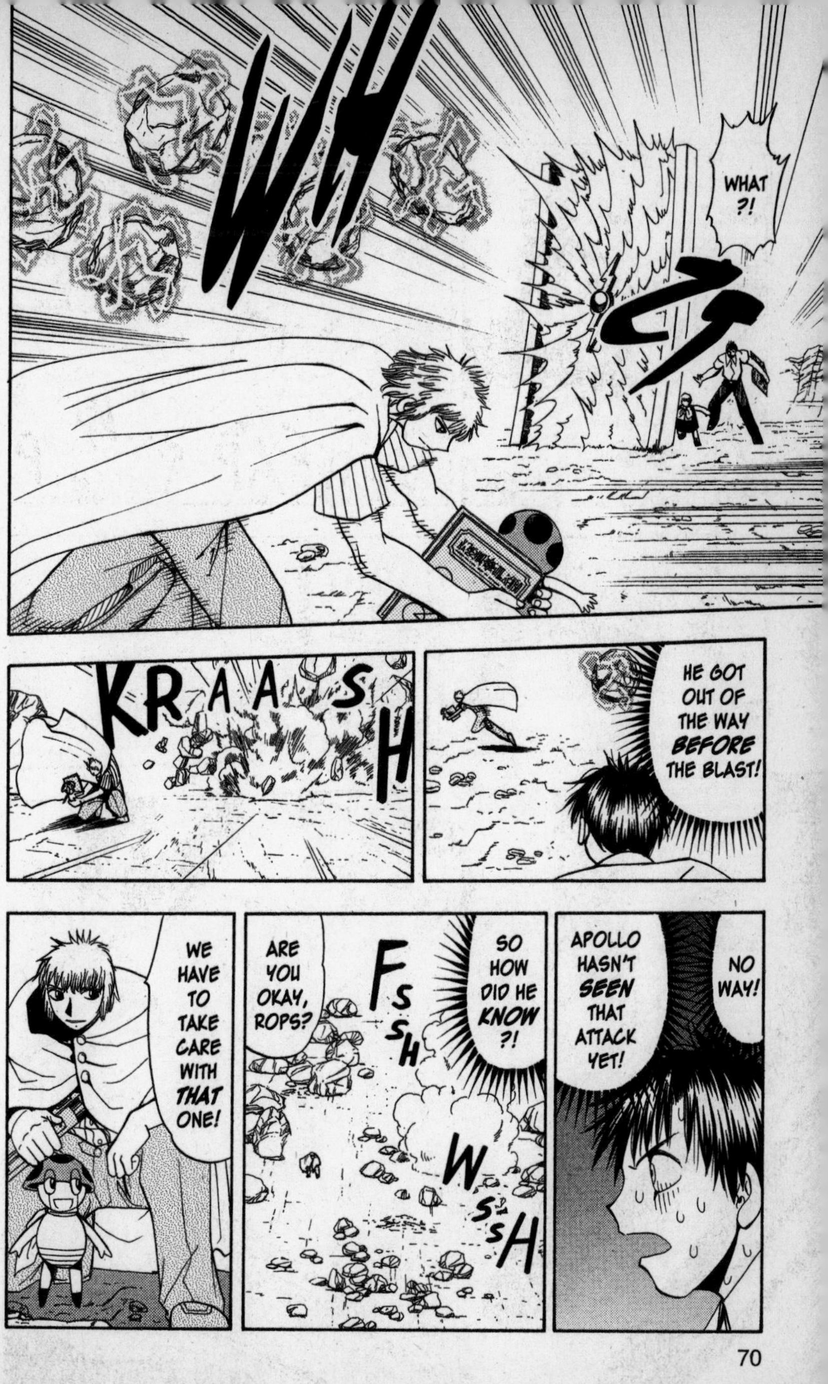
WHAT ?!
WH
HE GOT OUT OF THE WAY BEFORE THE BLAST!
KRAASH
NO WAY!
APOLLO HASN'T SEEN THAT ATTACK YET!
SO HOW DID HE KNOW ?!
FSSH
ARE YOU OKAY, ROPS?
WSSH
WE HAVE TO TAKE CARE WITH THAT ONE!

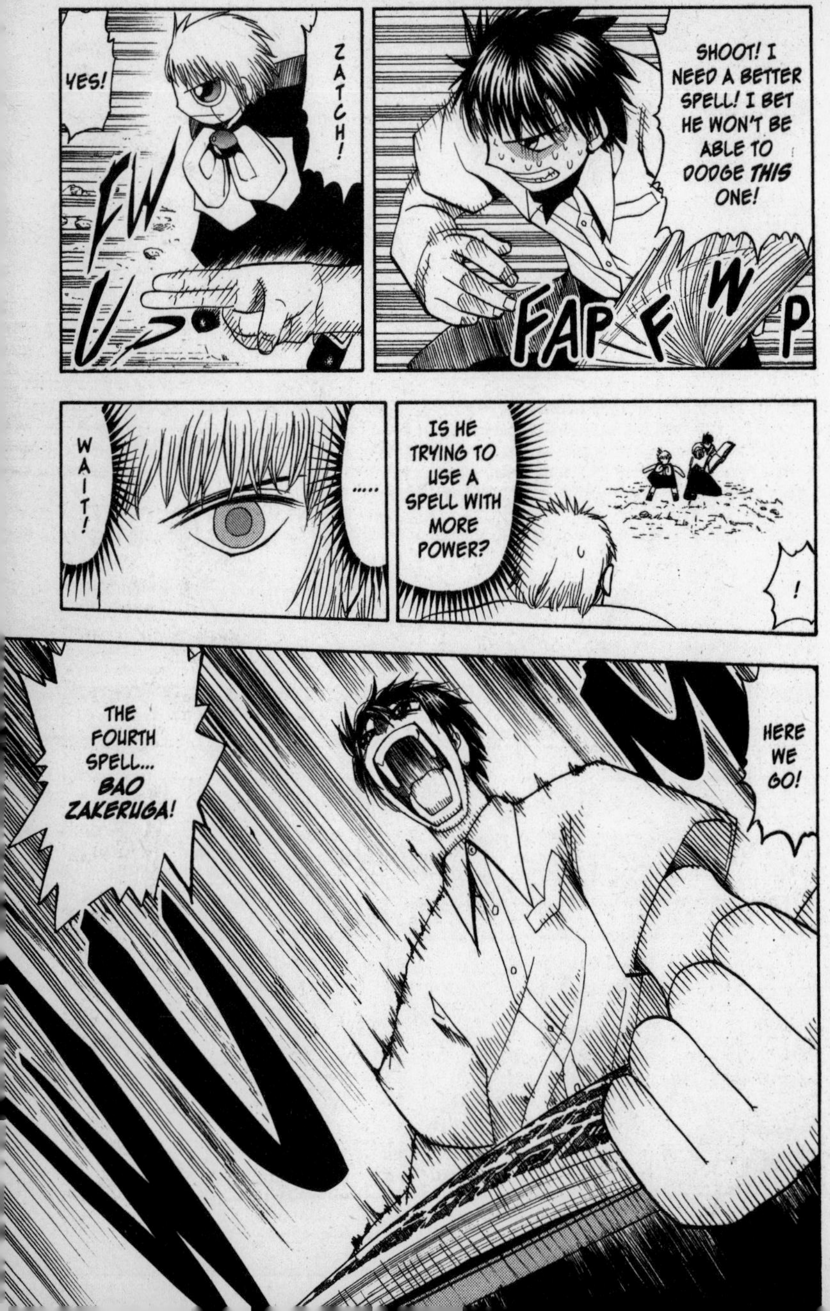
SHOOT! I NEED A BETTER SPELL! I BET HE WON'T BE ABLE TO DODGE THIS ONE!
FAP F W P
ZATCH!
YES!
FW
!
IS HE TRYING TO USE A SPELL WITH MORE POWER?
.....
WAIT!
HERE WE GO!
THE FOURTH SPELL... BAO ZAKERUGA!

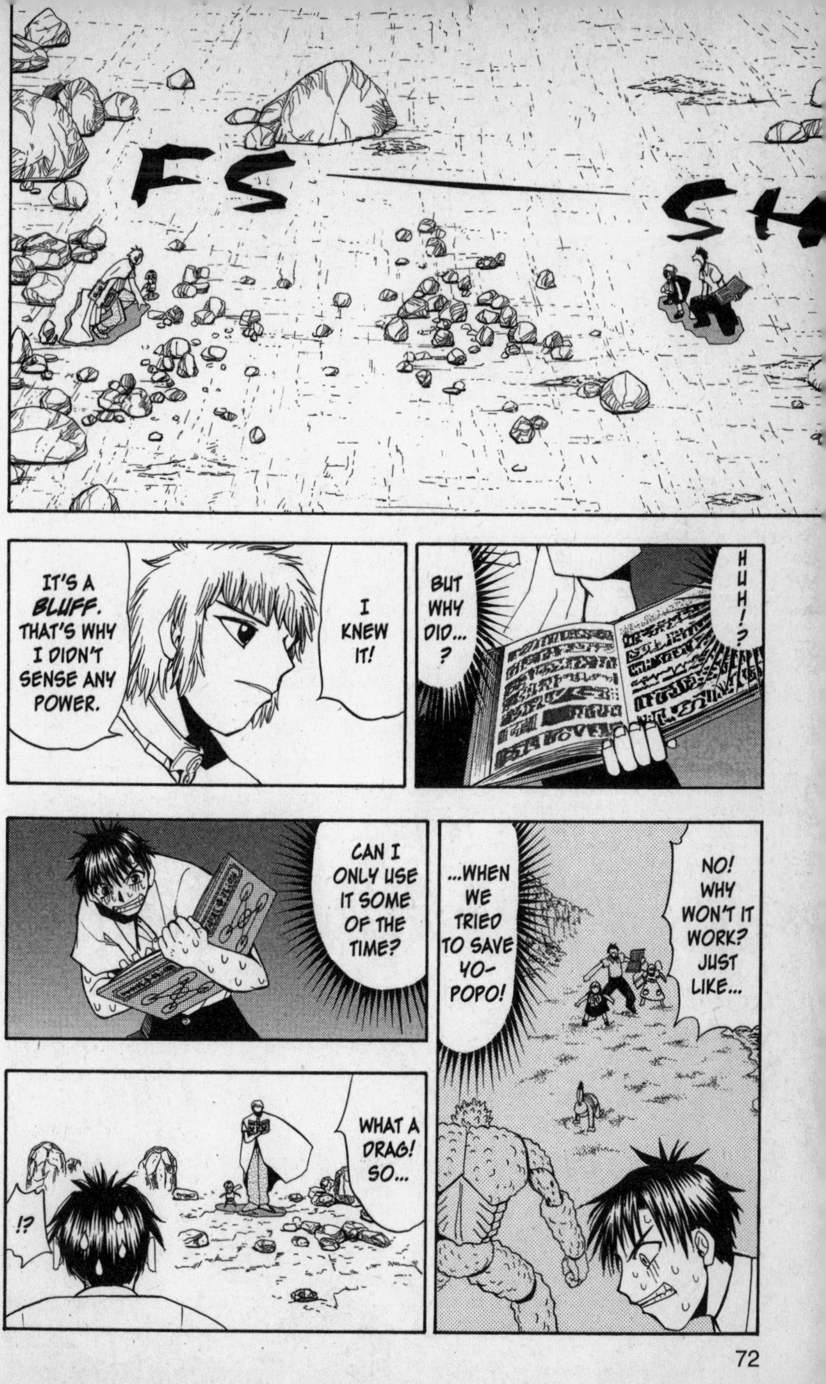
FS—SH
HUH!?
BUT WHY DID...?
I KNEW IT!
IT'S A BLUFF. THAT'S WHY I DIDN'T SENSE ANY POWER.
NO! WHY WON'T IT WORK? JUST LIKE...
...WHEN WE TRIED TO SAVE YO-POPO!
CAN I ONLY USE IT SOME OF THE TIME?
WHAT A DRAG! SO...
!?

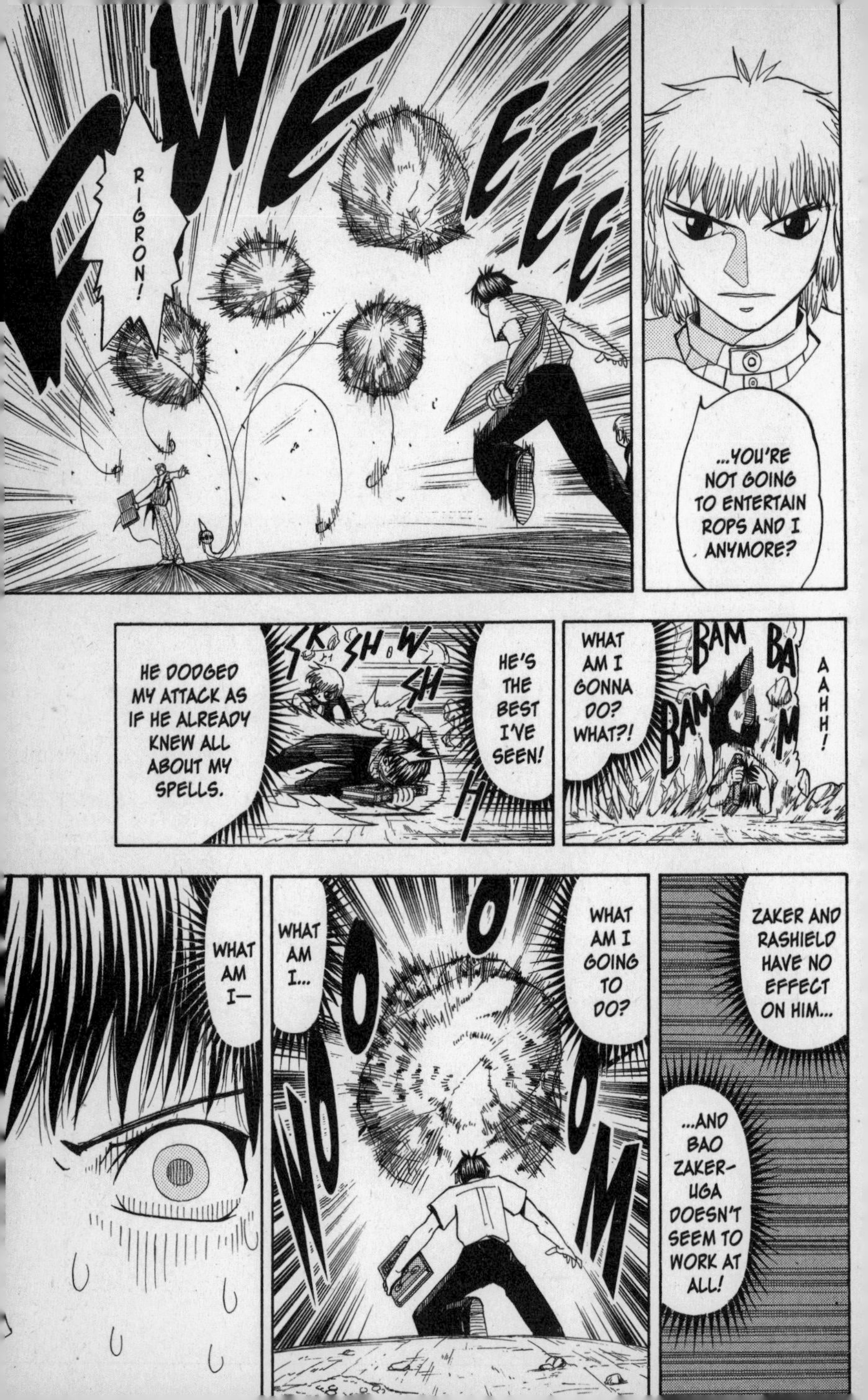
...YOU'RE NOT GOING TO ENTERTAIN ROPS AND I ANYMORE?
RIGRON!
CHWEEEE
BAM BAM BAM
AAHH!
WHAT AM I GONNA DO? WHAT?!
HE'S THE BEST I'VE SEEN!
SHOW SHH
SK
HE DODGED MY ATTACK AS IF HE ALREADY KNEW ALL ABOUT MY SPELLS.
ZAKER AND RASHIELD HAVE NO EFFECT ON HIM...
...AND BAO ZAKER-UGA DOESN'T SEEM TO WORK AT ALL!
WHAT AM I GOING TO DO?
WHAT AM I...
WHAT AM I—

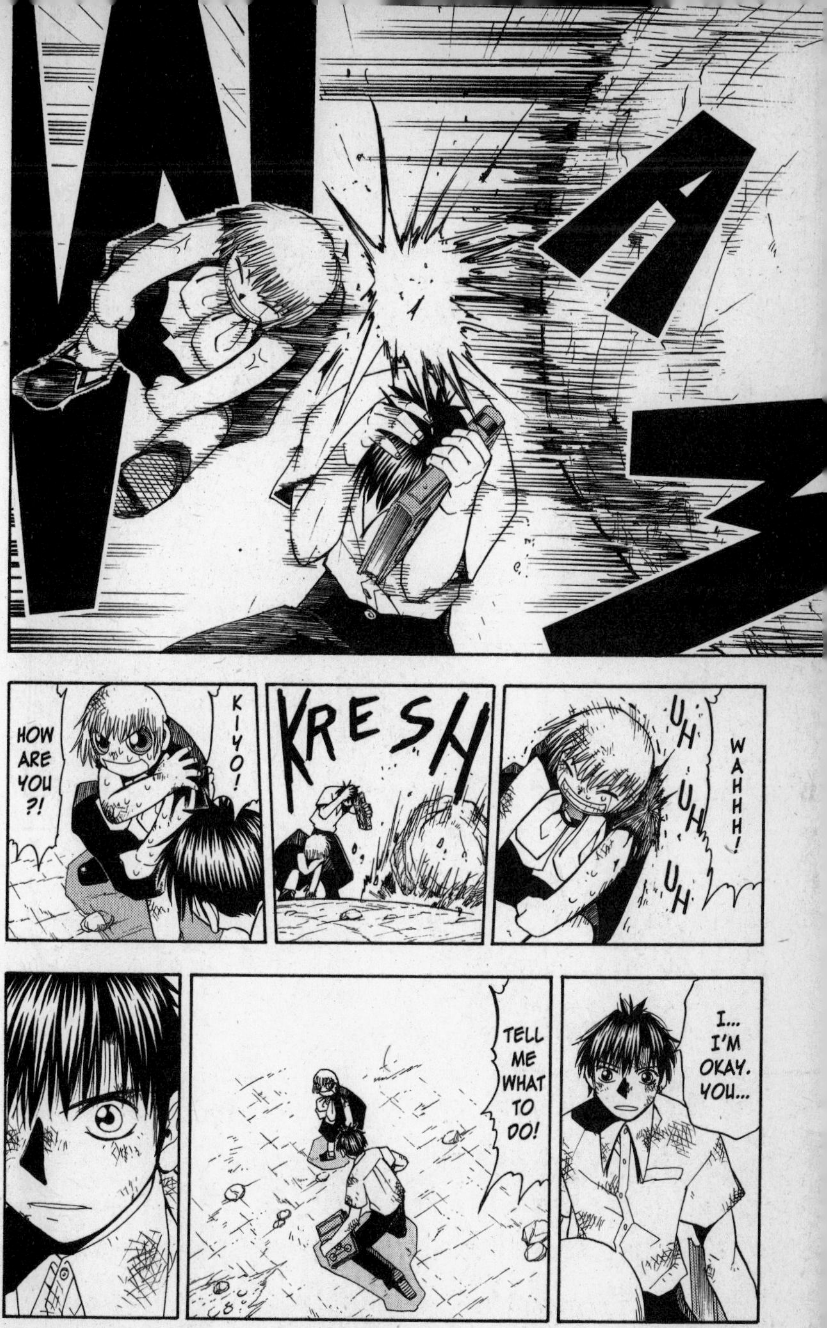
WAM
WAHHH!
UH UH UH
KRESH
KIYO!
HOW ARE YOU?!
I... I'M OKAY. YOU...
TELL ME WHAT TO DO!

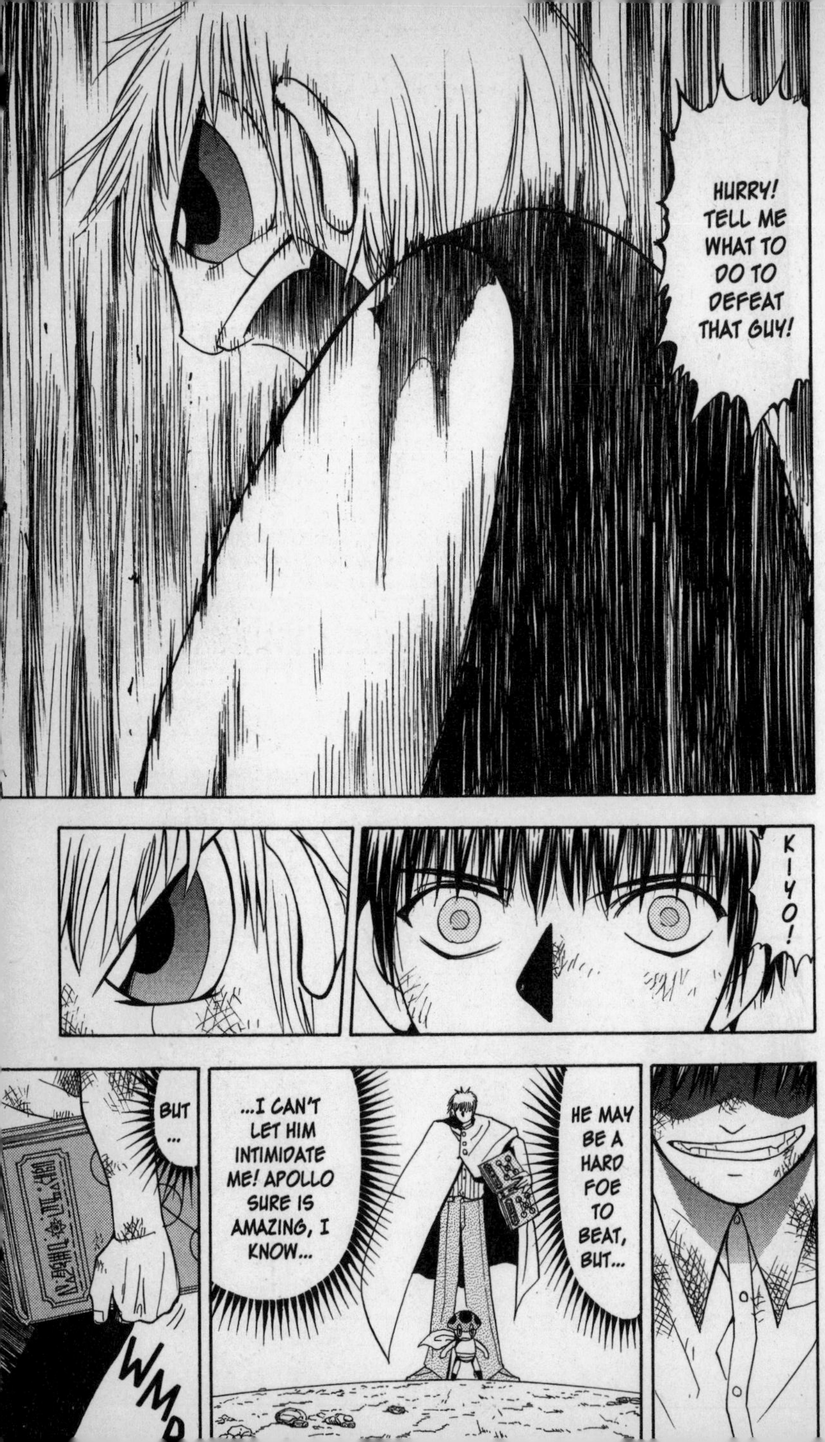
HURRY! TELL ME WHAT TO DO TO DEFEAT THAT GUY!
KIYO!
HE MAY BE A HARD FOE TO BEAT, BUT...
...I CAN'T LET HIM INTIMIDATE ME! APOLLO SURE IS AMAZING, I KNOW...
BUT ...
WM

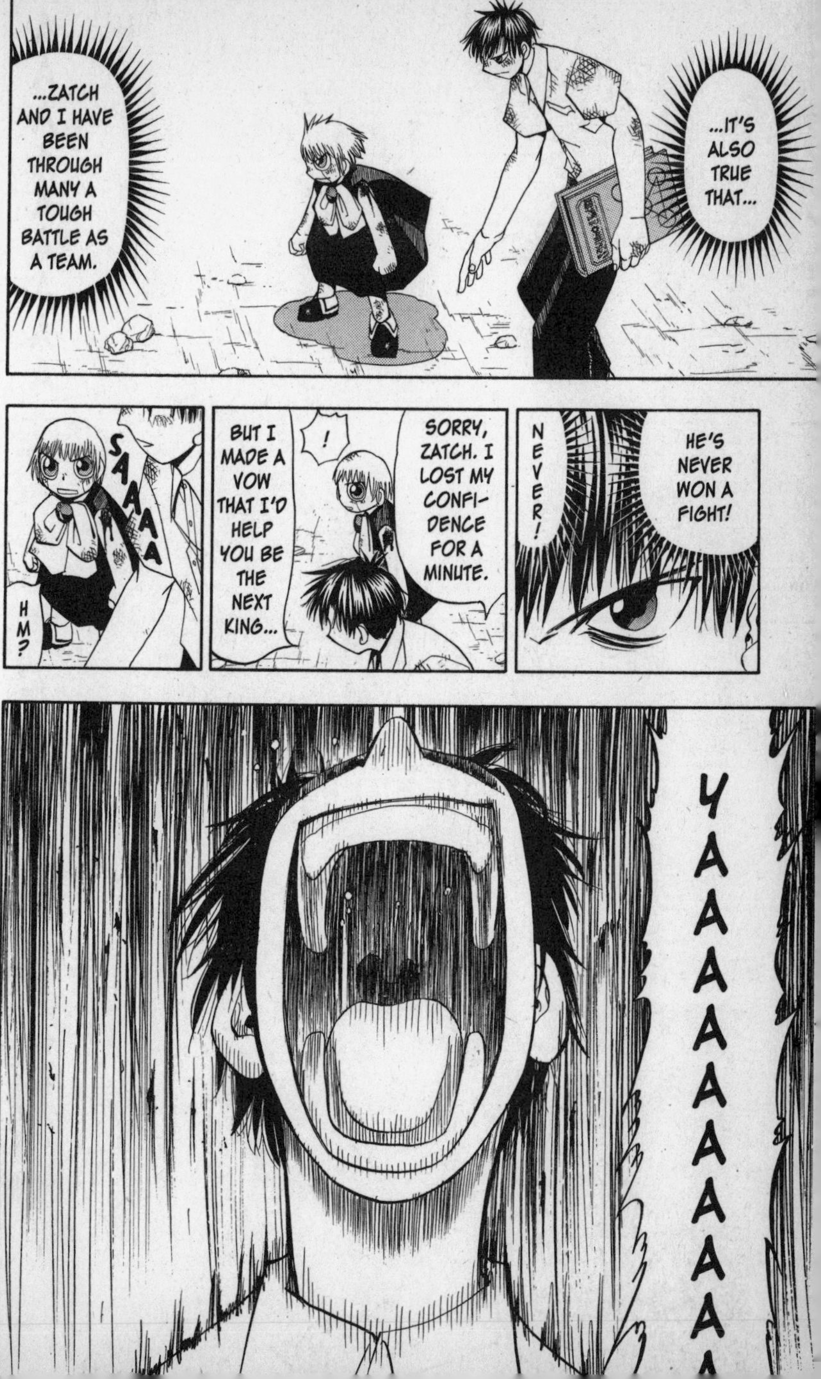
...IT'S ALSO TRUE THAT...
...ZATCH AND I HAVE BEEN THROUGH MANY A TOUGH BATTLE AS A TEAM.
HE'S NEVER WON A FIGHT!
NEVER!
SORRY, ZATCH. I LOST MY CONFIDENCE FOR A MINUTE.
!
BUT I MADE A VOW THAT I'D HELP YOU BE THE NEXT KING...
SAAAAA
HM?
YAAAAAAAAAAA

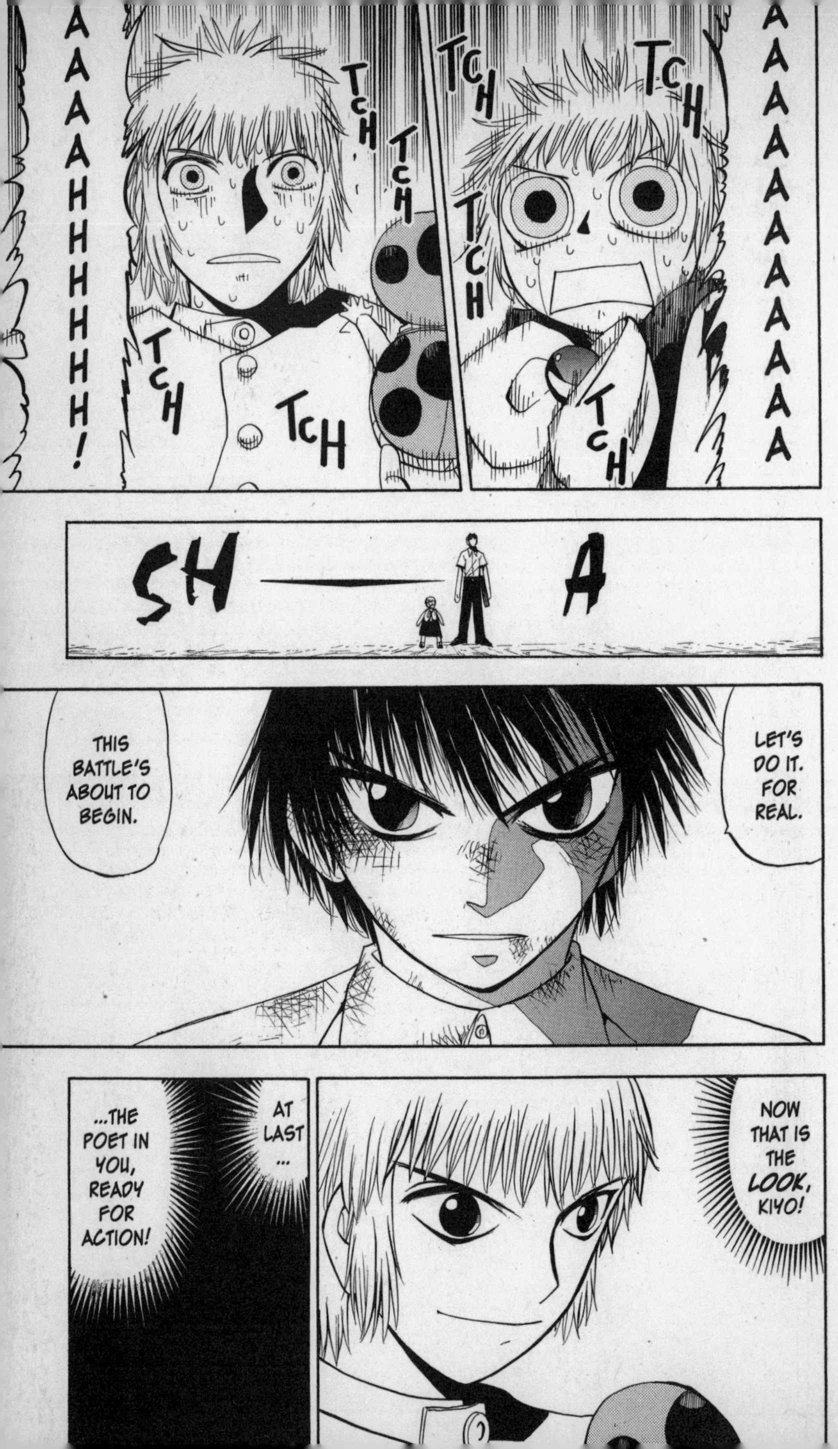

TCH TCH
TCH
TCH
AAAAAAAAAAAAAA
TCH TCH
TCH TCH
AAAAHHHHHHHHH!
SH—A
LET'S DO IT. FOR REAL.
THIS BATTLE'S ABOUT TO BEGIN.
NOW THAT IS THE *LOOK*, KIYO!
AT LAST...
...THE POET IN YOU, READY FOR ACTION!

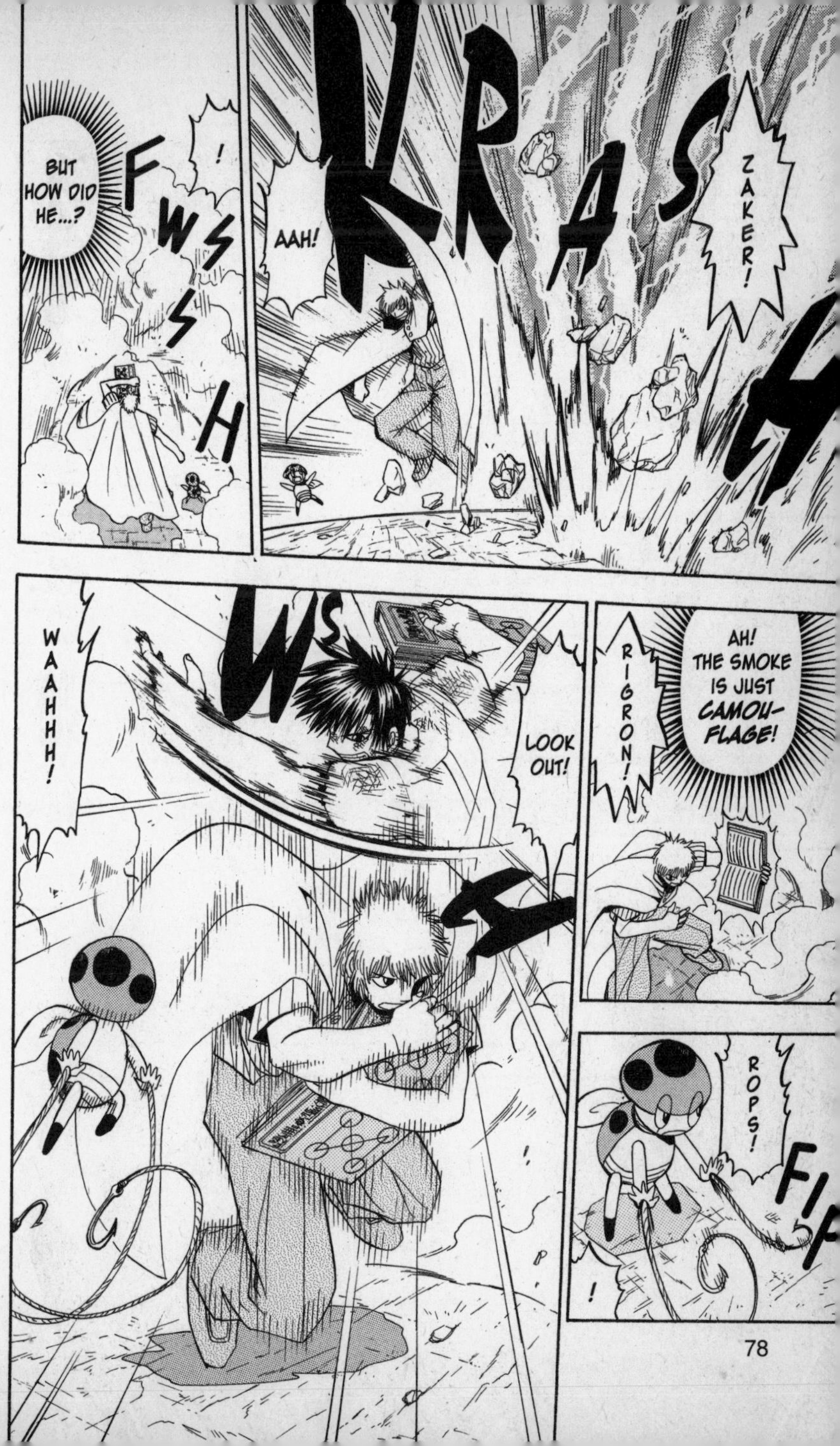
ZAKER!
KRASH
AAH!
!
FWSH
BUT HOW DID HE...?
AH! THE SMOKE IS JUST **CAMOUFLAGE!**
RIGRON!
ROPS!
FIP
!
LOOK OUT!
WS
WAAHHH!
!

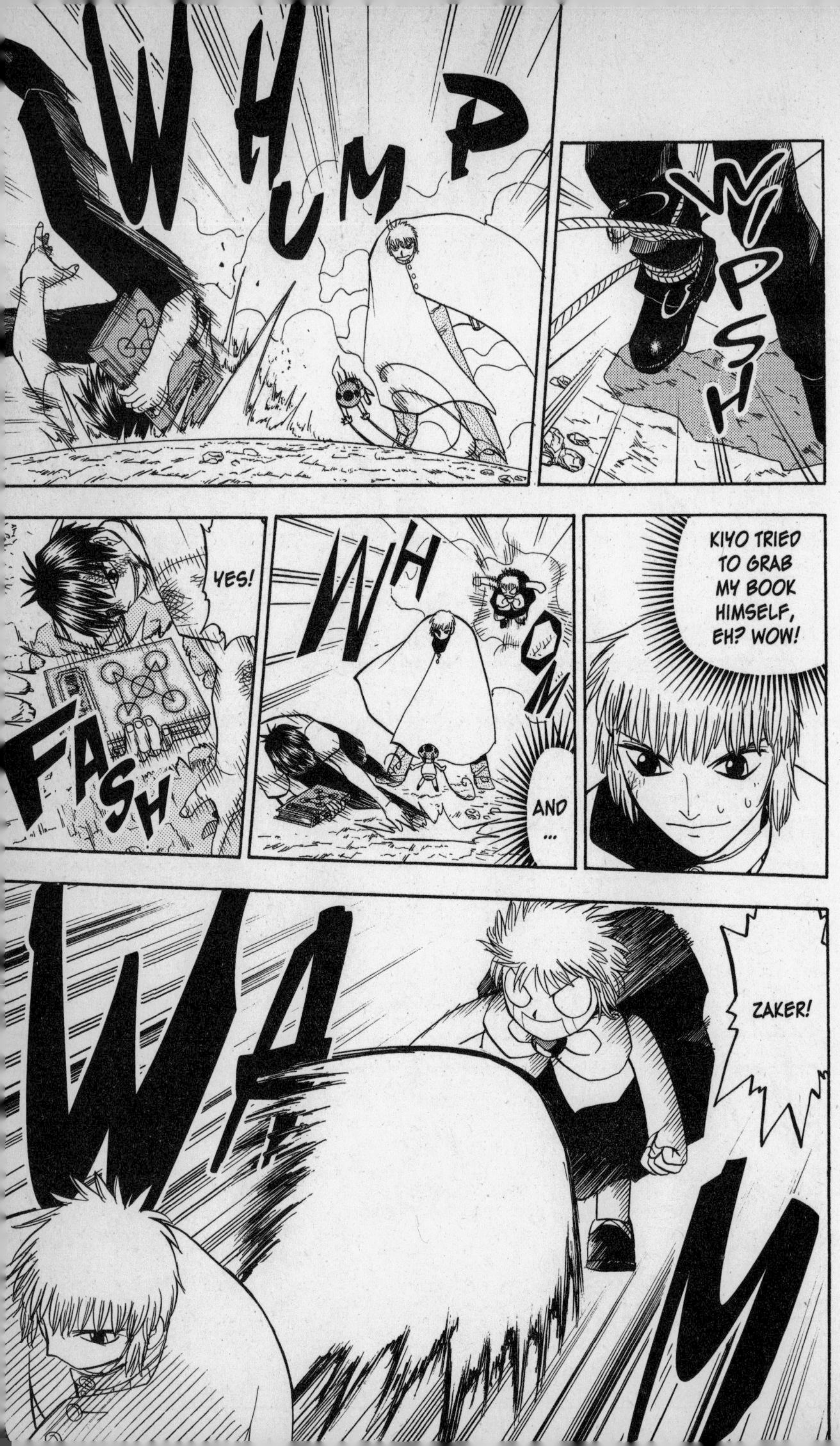
WIPSH
WHUMP
KIYO TRIED TO GRAB MY BOOK HIMSELF, EH? WOW!
AND ...
WHOM
YES!
FASH
ZAKER!
WAM

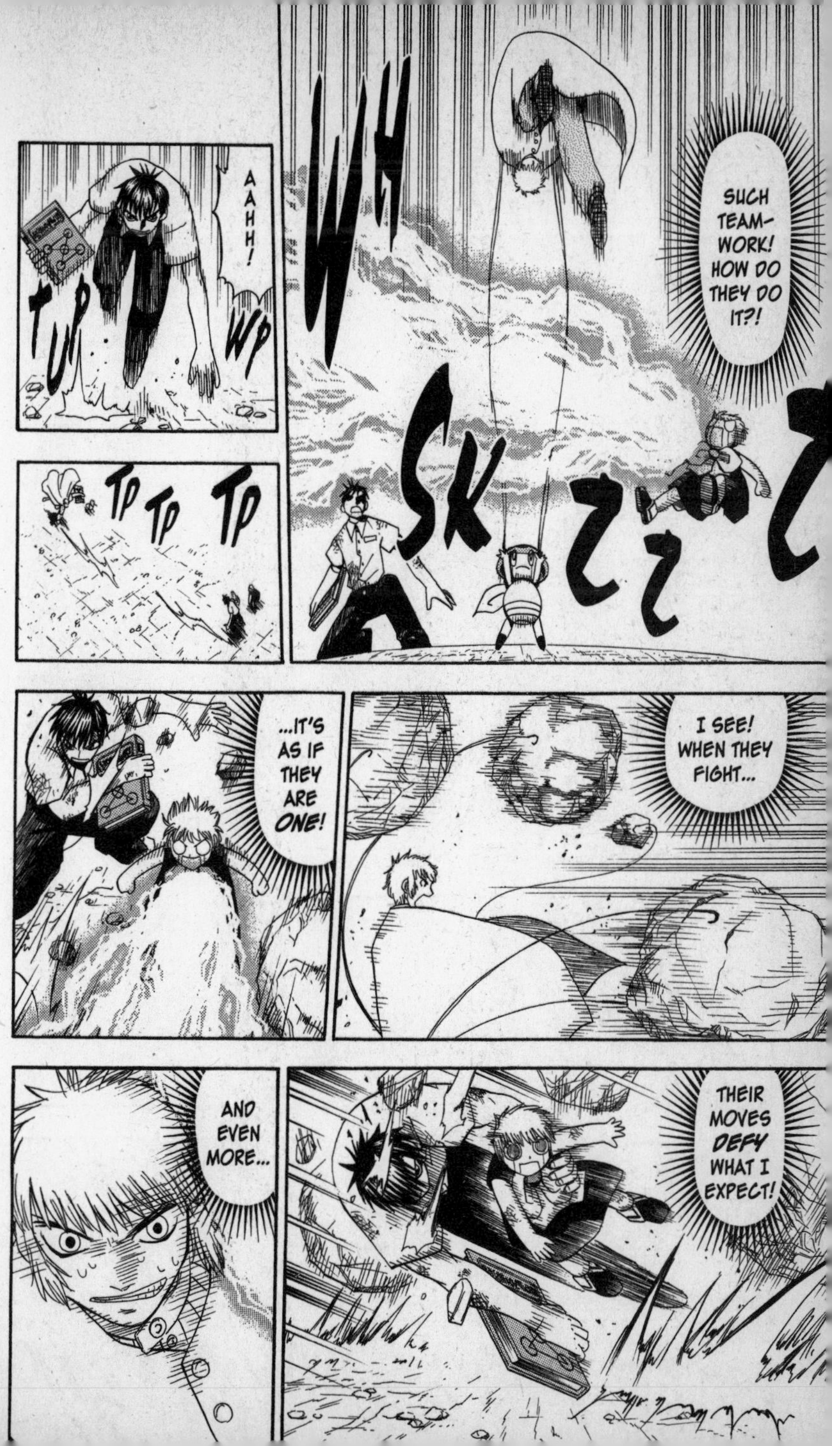
SUCH TEAM-WORK! HOW DO THEY DO IT?!
WH
SK
AAHH!
TUP
WP
TP TP TP
I SEE! WHEN THEY FIGHT...
...IT'S AS IF THEY ARE ONE!
THEIR MOVES DEFY WHAT I EXPECT!
AND EVEN MORE...

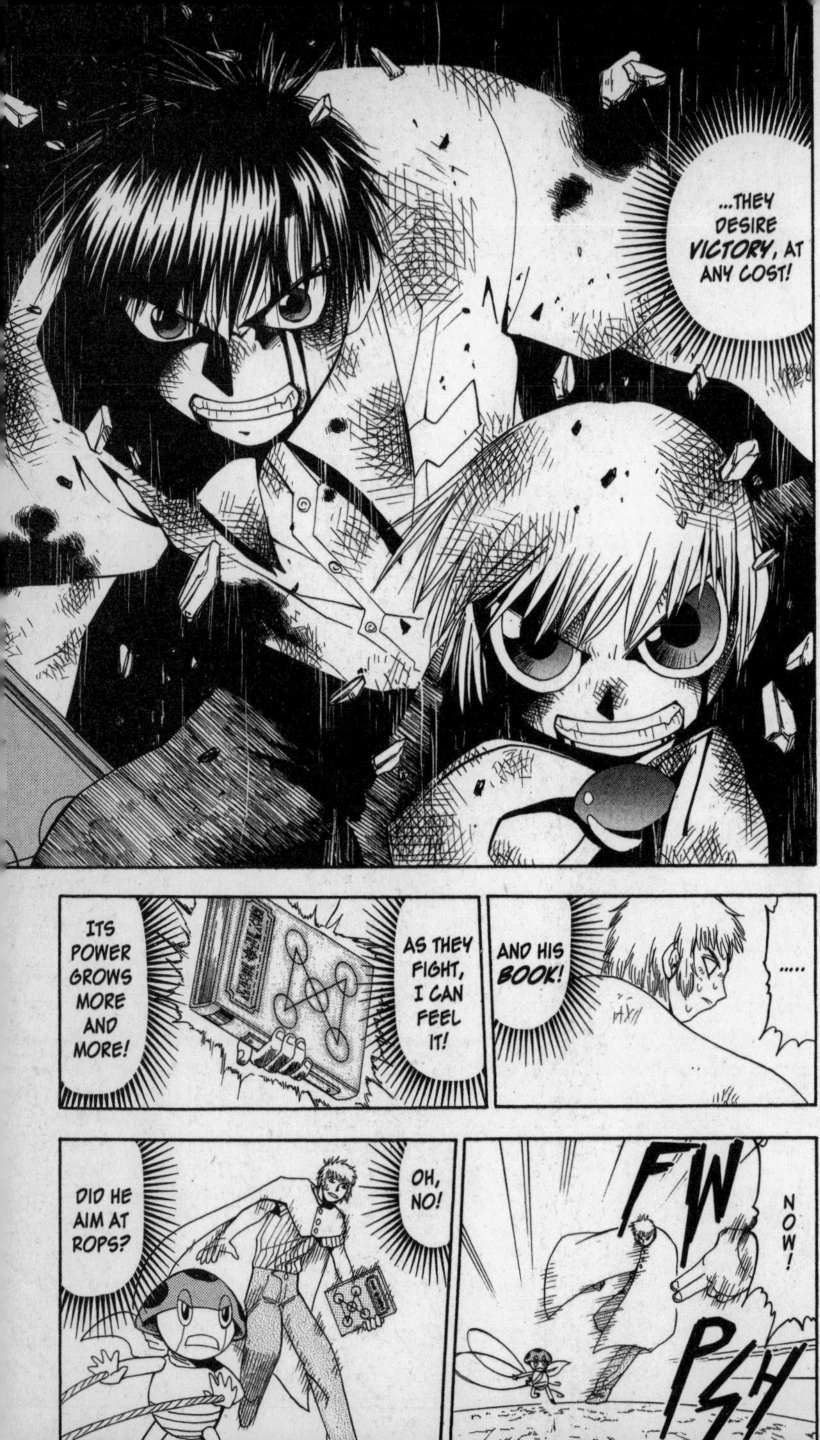
...THEY DESIRE VICTORY, AT ANY COST!
.....
AND HIS BOOK!
AS THEY FIGHT, I CAN FEEL IT!
ITS POWER GROWS MORE AND MORE!
NOW!
FW
PSH
OH, NO!
DID HE AIM AT ROPS?

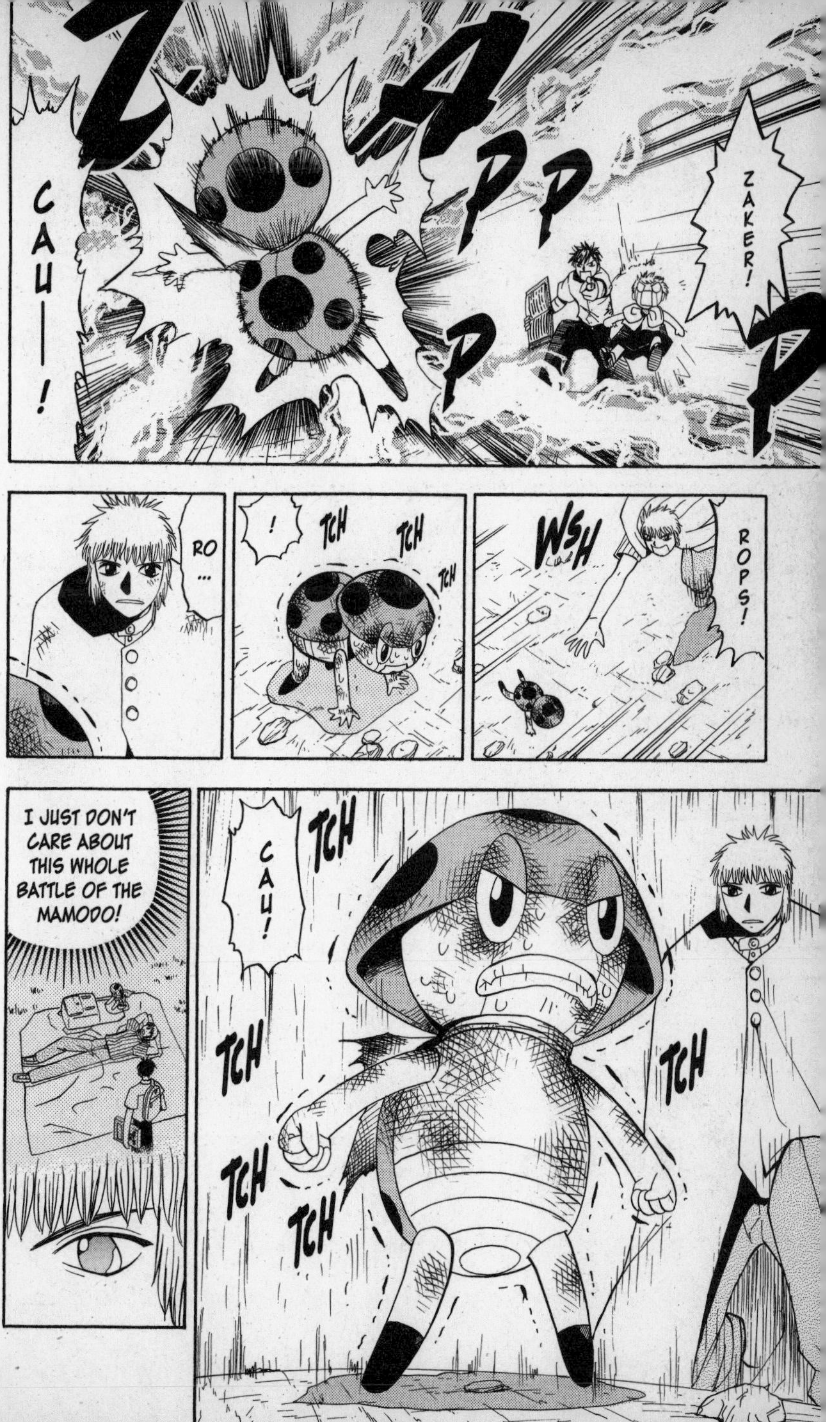
ZAKER!
ZAPPP
CAU—!
ROPS!
WSH
!
TCH
TCH
TCH
RO...
CAU!
TCH
TCH
TCH
TCH
TCH
I JUST DON'T CARE ABOUT THIS WHOLE BATTLE OF THE MAMODO!

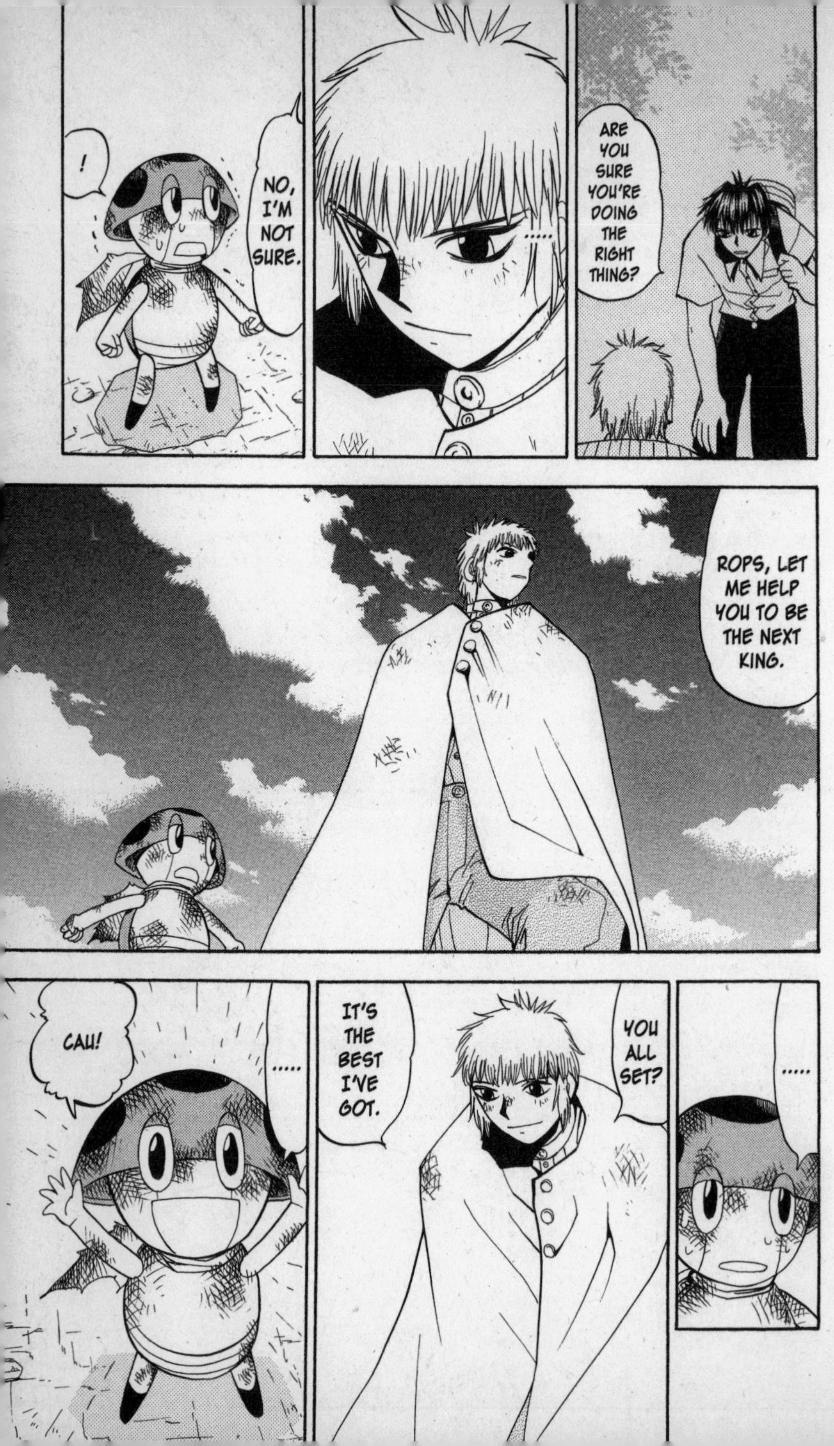
ARE YOU SURE YOU'RE DOING THE RIGHT THING?
.....
NO, I'M NOT SURE.
!
ROPS, LET ME HELP YOU TO BE THE NEXT KING.
.....
YOU ALL SET?
IT'S THE BEST I'VE GOT.
.....
CAU!

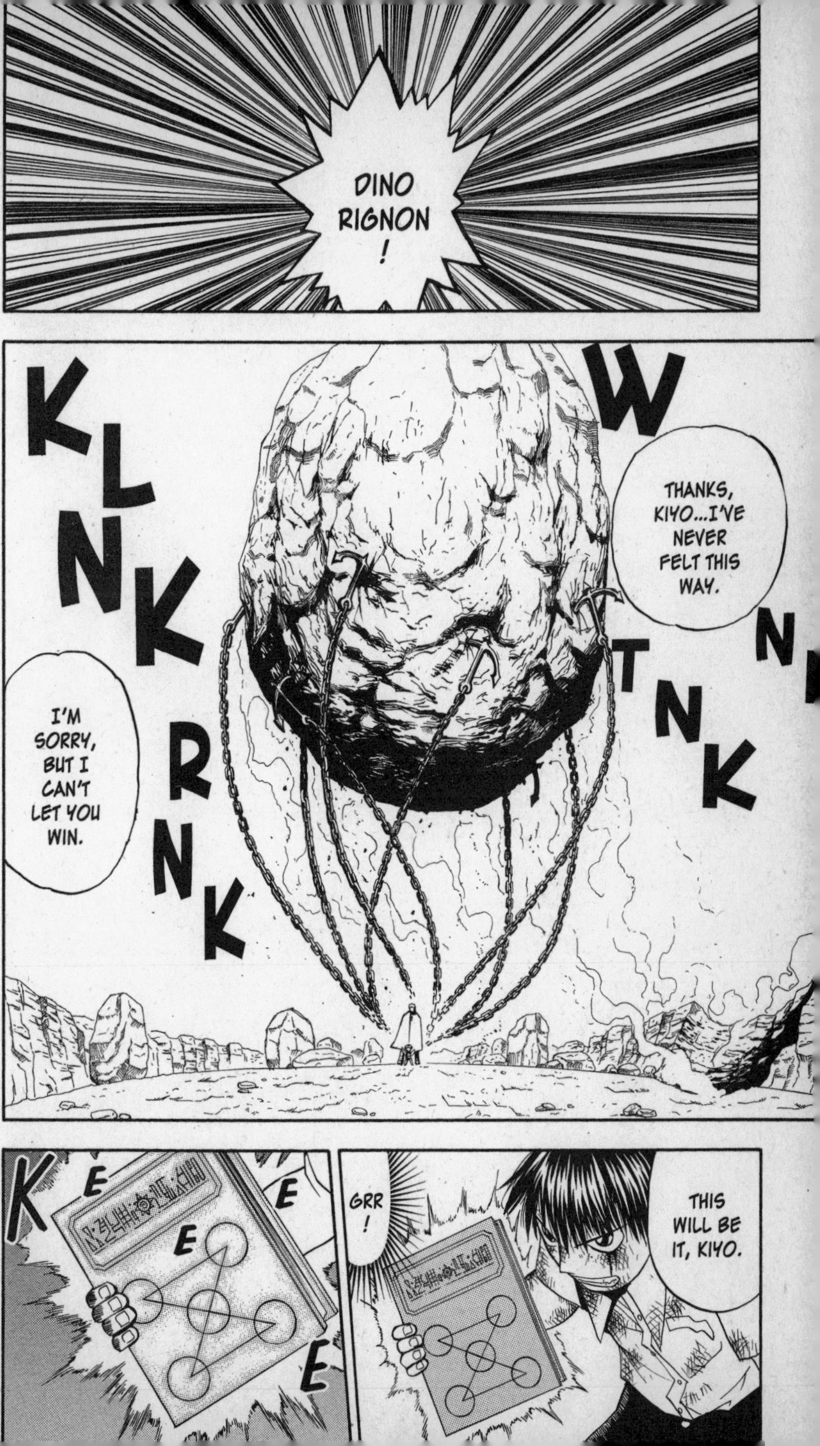
DINO RIGNON !
THANKS, KIYO...I'VE NEVER FELT THIS WAY.
TNK
KLNK
I'M SORRY, BUT I CAN'T LET YOU WIN.
RNK
THIS WILL BE IT, KIYO.
GRR !
KEEEE

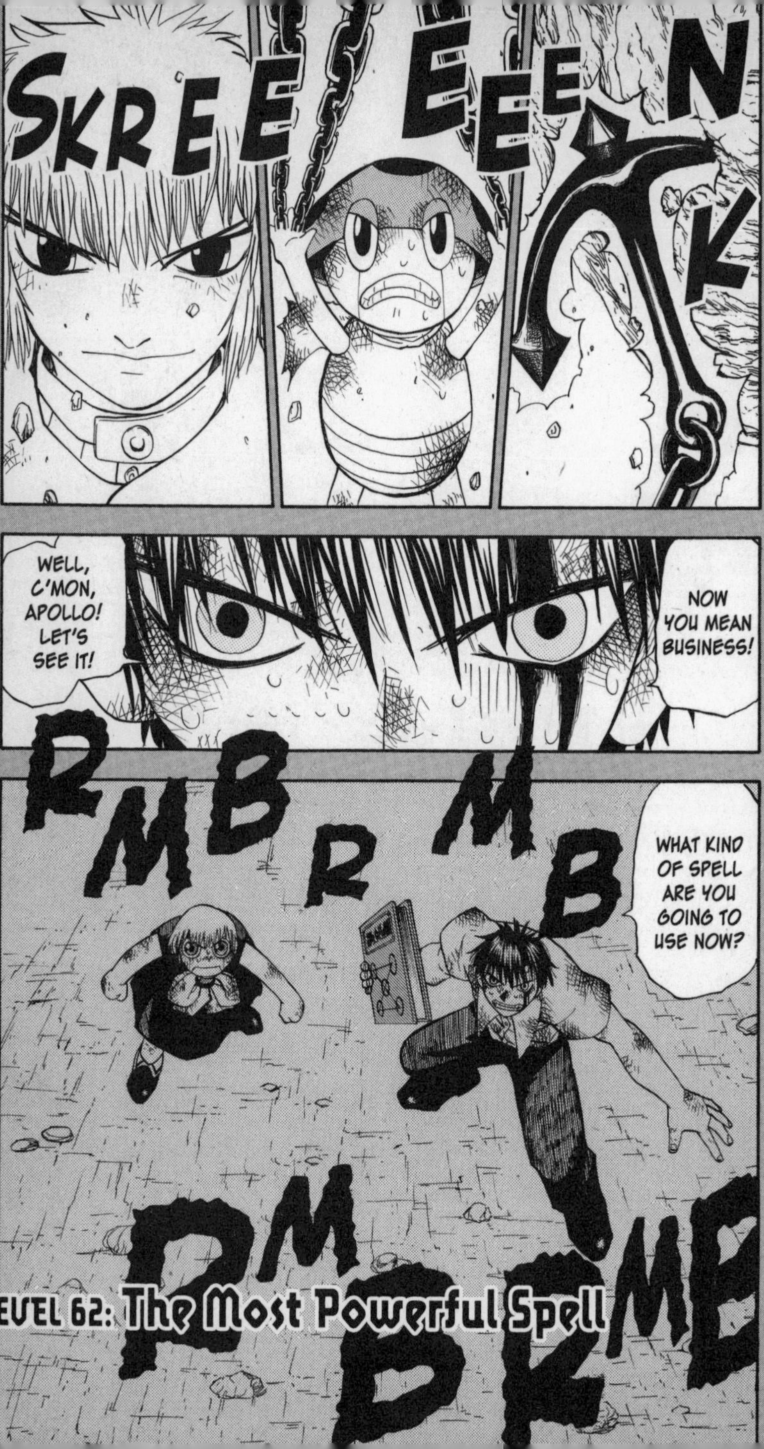
SKREEEEENK
NOW YOU MEAN BUSINESS!
WELL, C'MON, APOLLO! LET'S SEE IT!
RMB RMB
WHAT KIND OF SPELL ARE YOU GOING TO USE NOW?
LEVEL 62: The Most Powerful Spell

LEVEL 62: The Most Powerful Spell

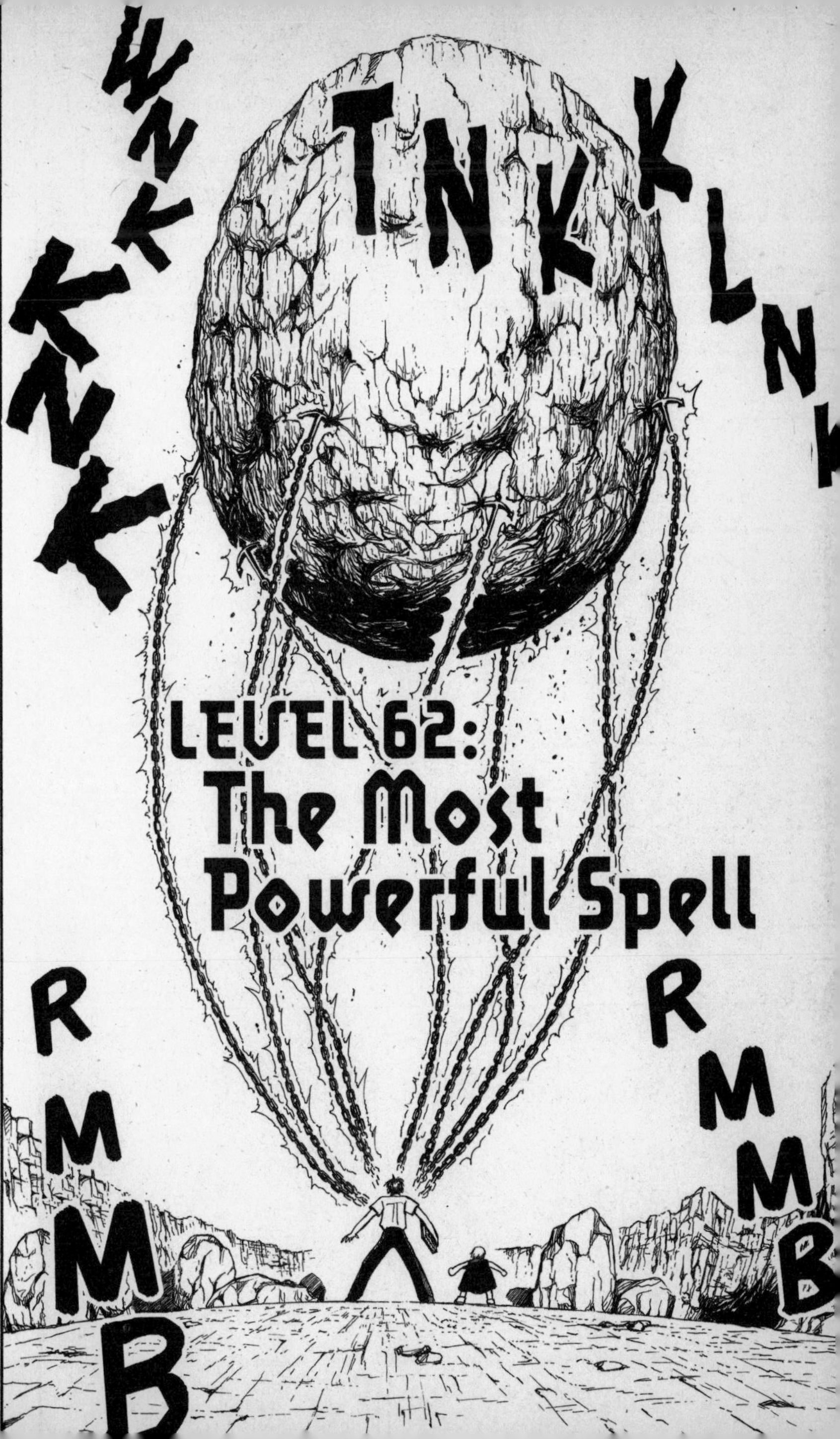
KLNK
TNK
WNK
KNK
RMMB
RMMB

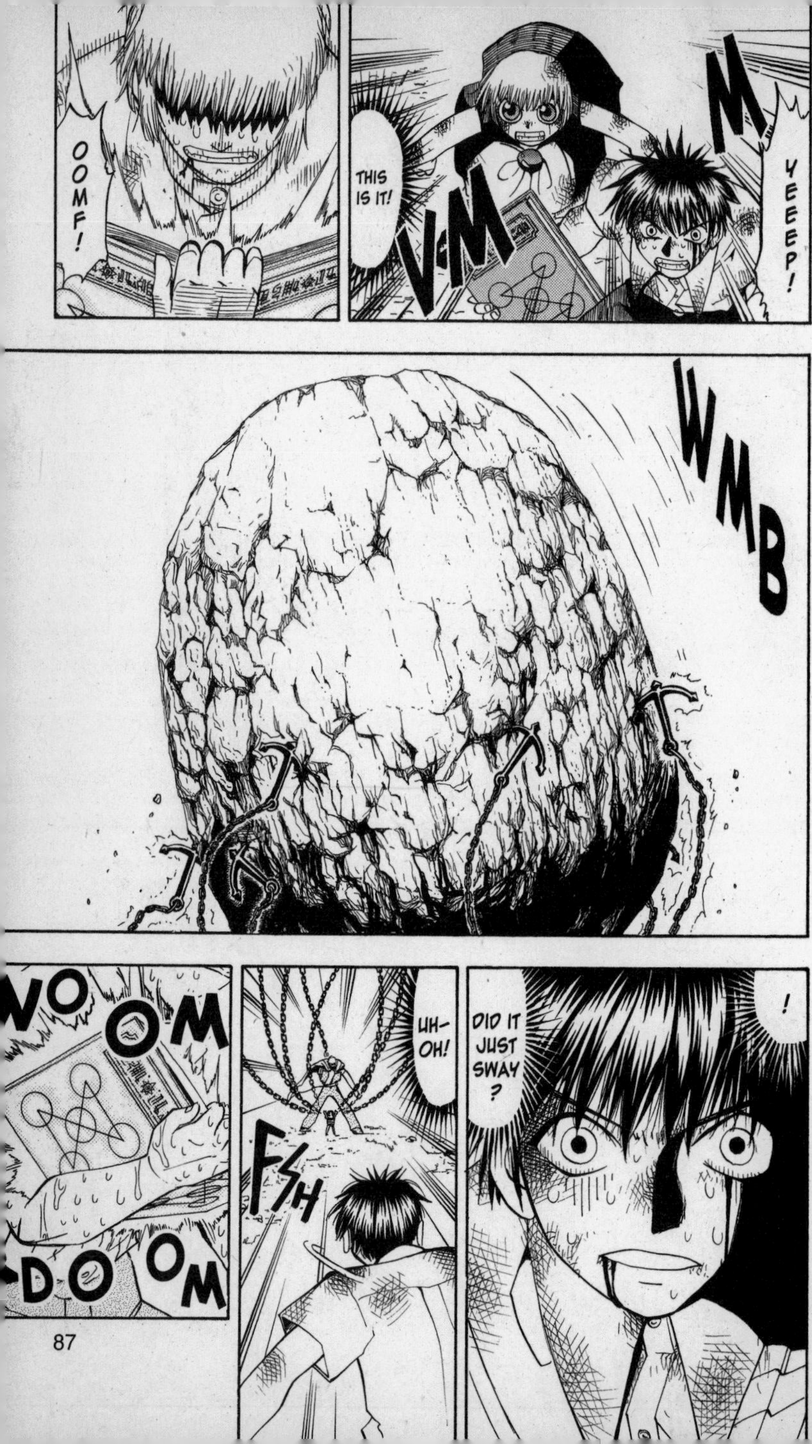
YEEEP!
THIS IS IT!
VMM
OOMF!
WMB
!
DID IT JUST SWAY?
UH-OH!
FSH
WOOM
-DOOM

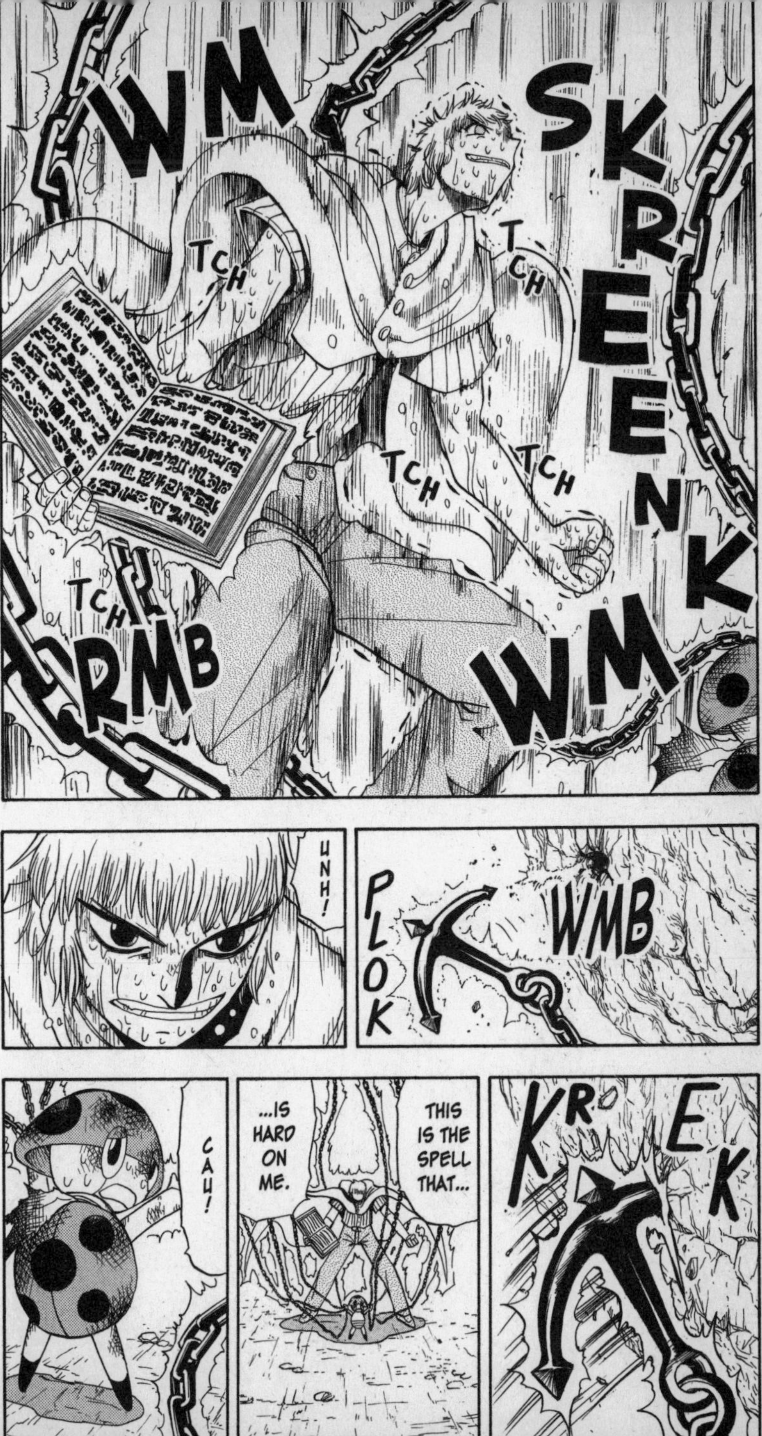
SKREENK
WM
TCH
TCH
TCH
TCH
WM
RMB
TCH
PLOK
WMB
UNH!
KREK
THIS IS THE SPELL THAT...
...IS HARD ON ME.
CAU!

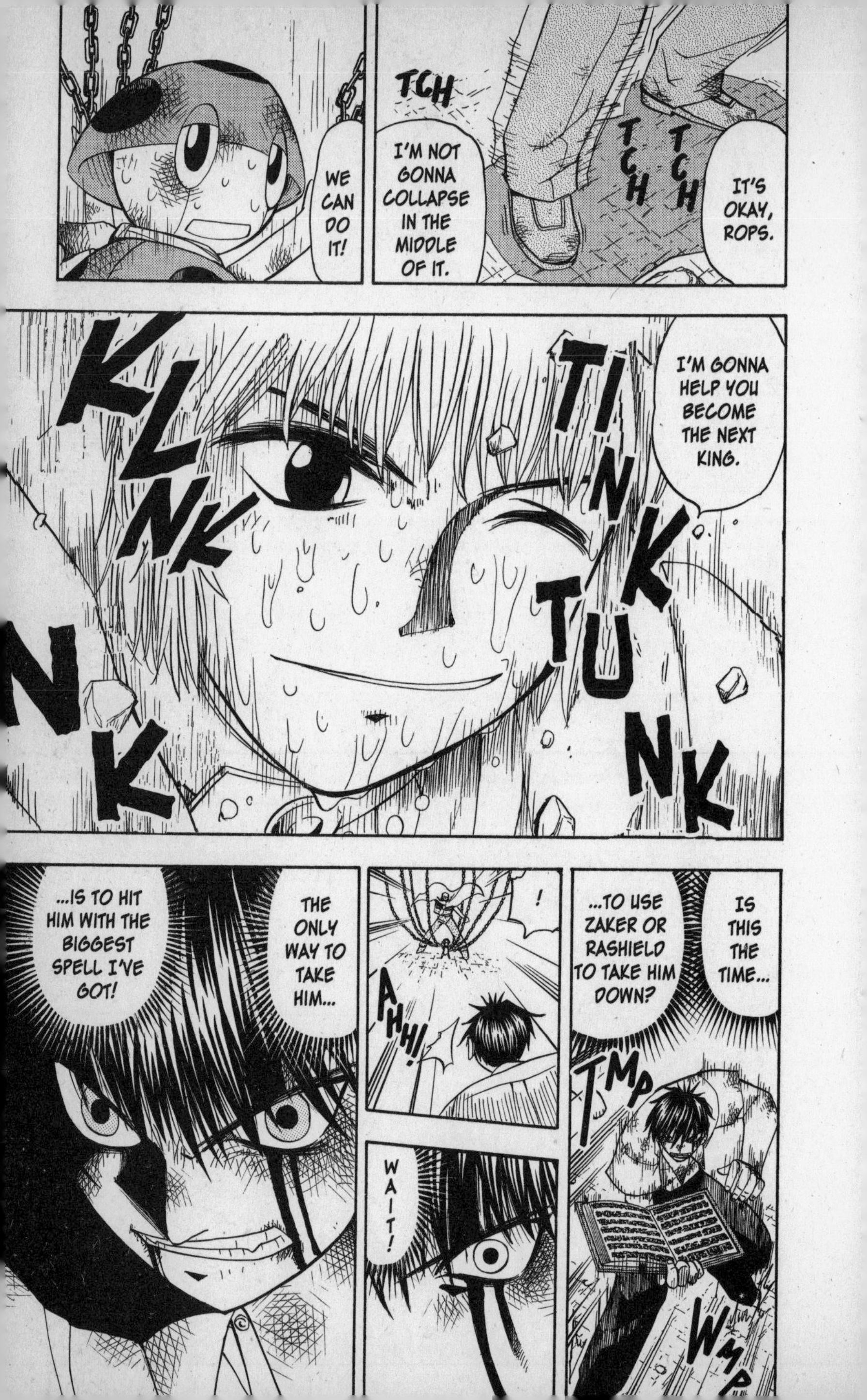
TCH
TCH
IT'S OKAY, ROPS.
TCH
I'M NOT GONNA COLLAPSE IN THE MIDDLE OF IT.
WE CAN DO IT!
I'M GONNA HELP YOU BECOME THE NEXT KING.
TINK
TUNK
KLNK
NK
NK
IS THIS THE TIME...
...TO USE ZAKER OR RASHIELD TO TAKE HIM DOWN?
TMP
WMP
!
AHH!
WAIT!
THE ONLY WAY TO TAKE HIM...
...IS TO HIT HIM WITH THE BIGGEST SPELL I'VE GOT!

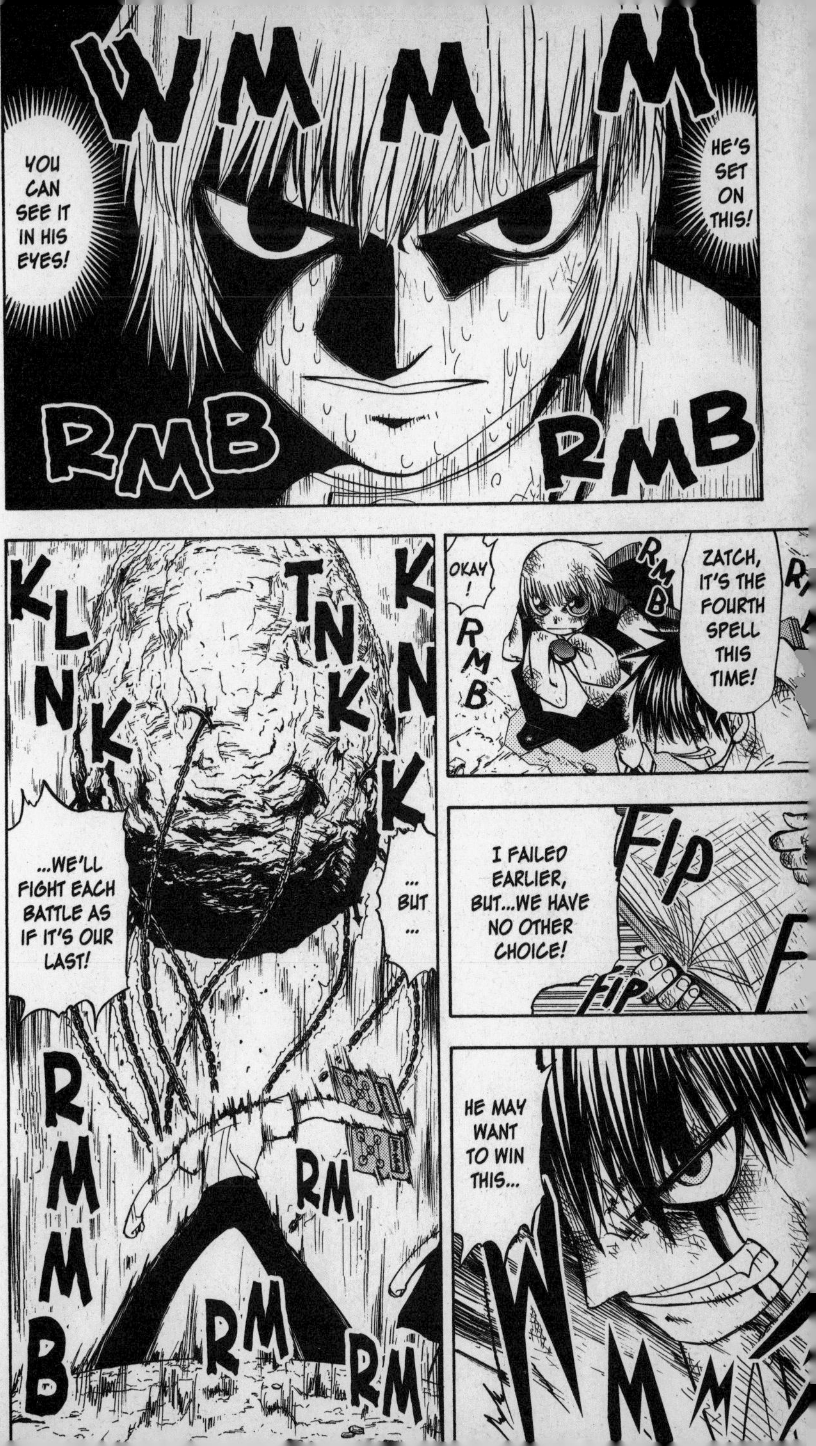
WMMM
HE'S SET ON THIS!
YOU CAN SEE IT IN HIS EYES!
RMB RMB
ZATCH, IT'S THE FOURTH SPELL THIS TIME!
RMB
OKAY!
RMB
I FAILED EARLIER, BUT...WE HAVE NO OTHER CHOICE!
HE MAY WANT TO WIN THIS...
KNK TNK KLNK
...BUT...
...WE'LL FIGHT EACH BATTLE AS IF IT'S OUR LAST!
RMM RM RM RMMMB

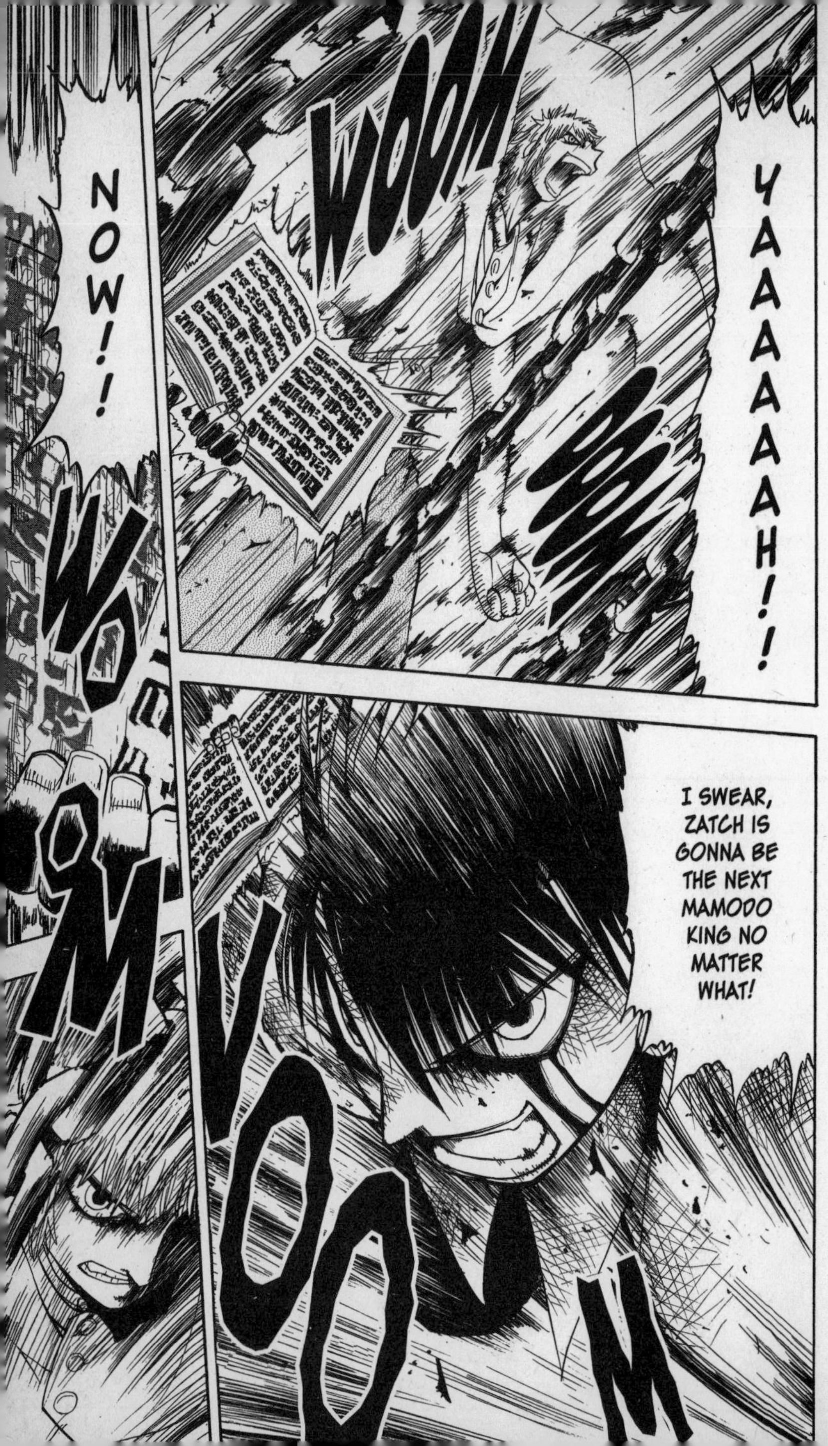
YAAAAAAH!!!
I SWEAR, ZATCH IS GONNA BE THE NEXT MAMODO KING NO MATTER WHAT!
NOW!!

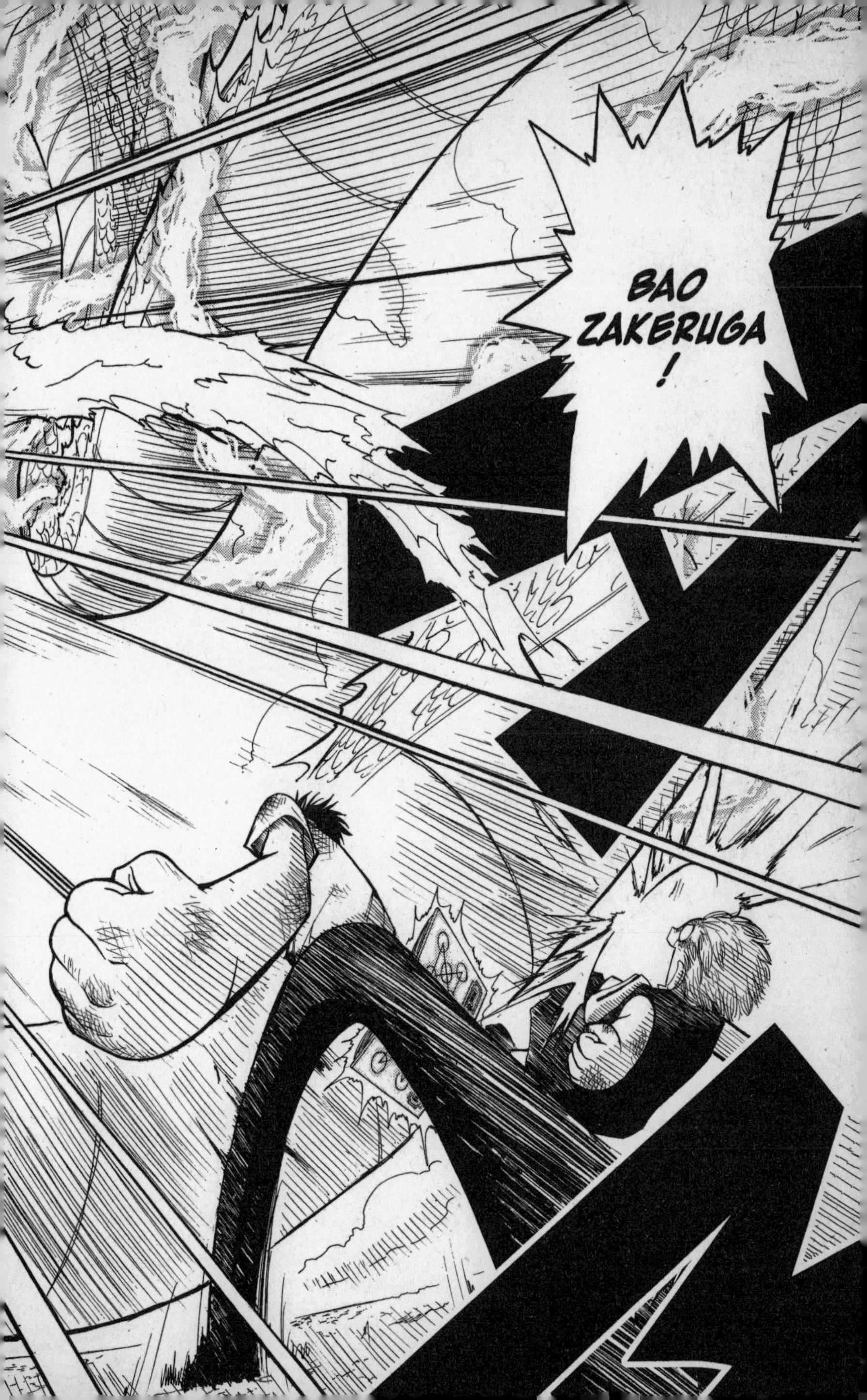
BAO ZAKERUGA!

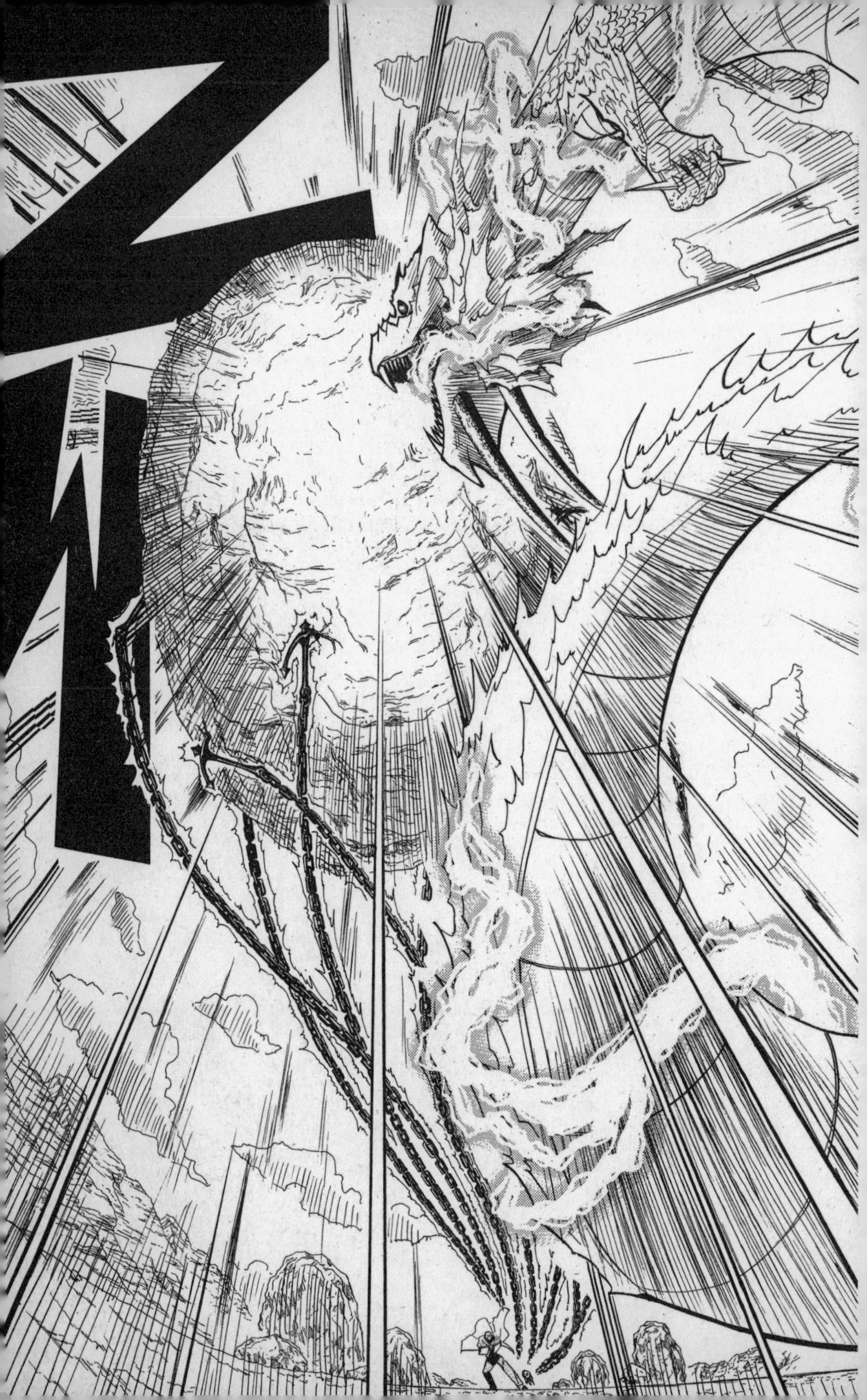

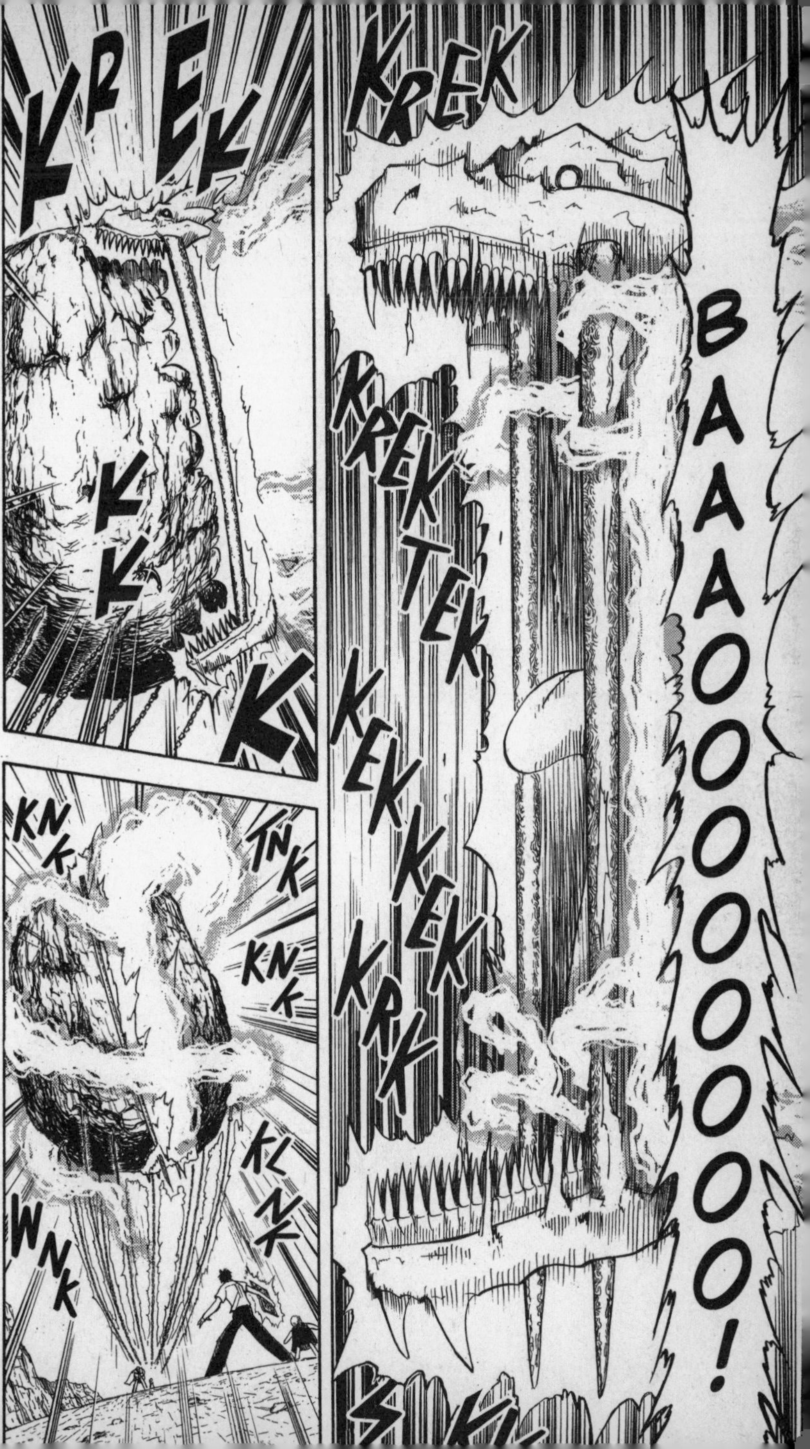
KREK
KREKTEK
KEKKEKKRK
BAAAOOOOOOOO!
KREK
KK
K
TNK
KNK
KNK
KLNK
WNK

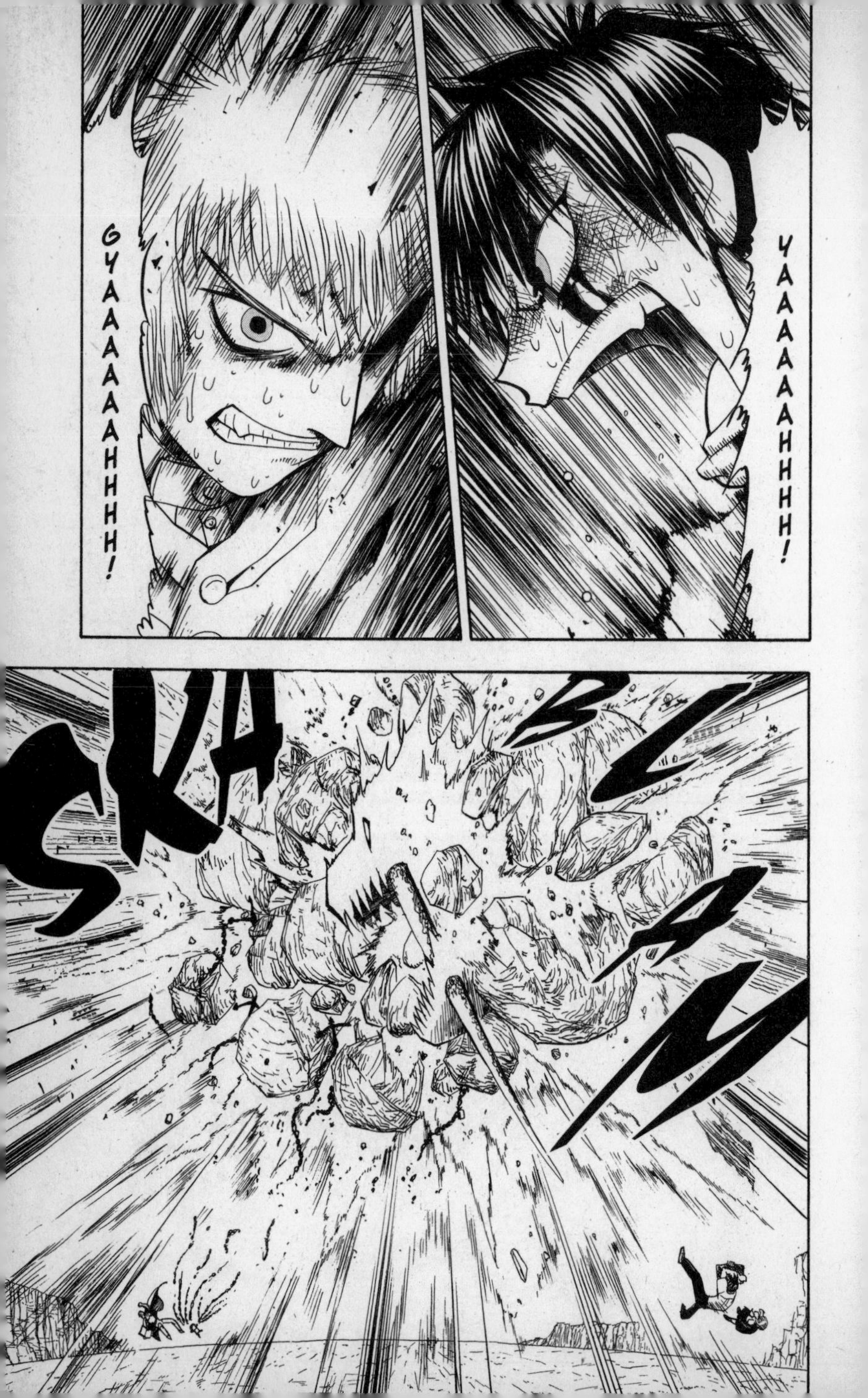
YAAAAAAHHHH!
GYAAAAAAHHHH!
SKA
BLAM

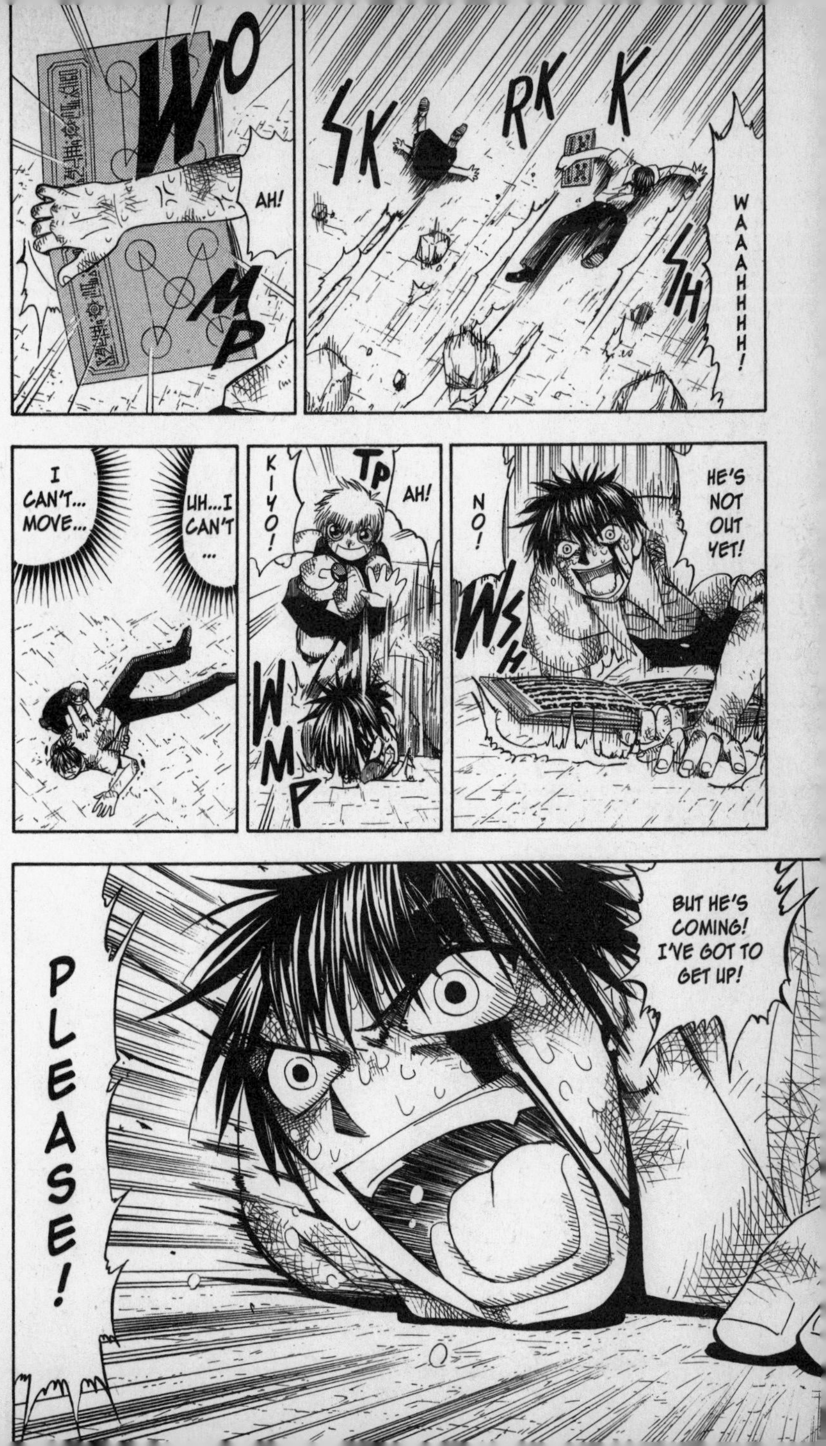
SK RK K
WAAAHHHH!
SH
WO MP
AH!
HE'S NOT OUT YET!
NO!
WSH
AH!
KIYO!
TP
WMP
UH...I CAN'T ...
I CAN'T... MOVE...
BUT HE'S COMING! I'VE GOT TO GET UP!
PLEASE!

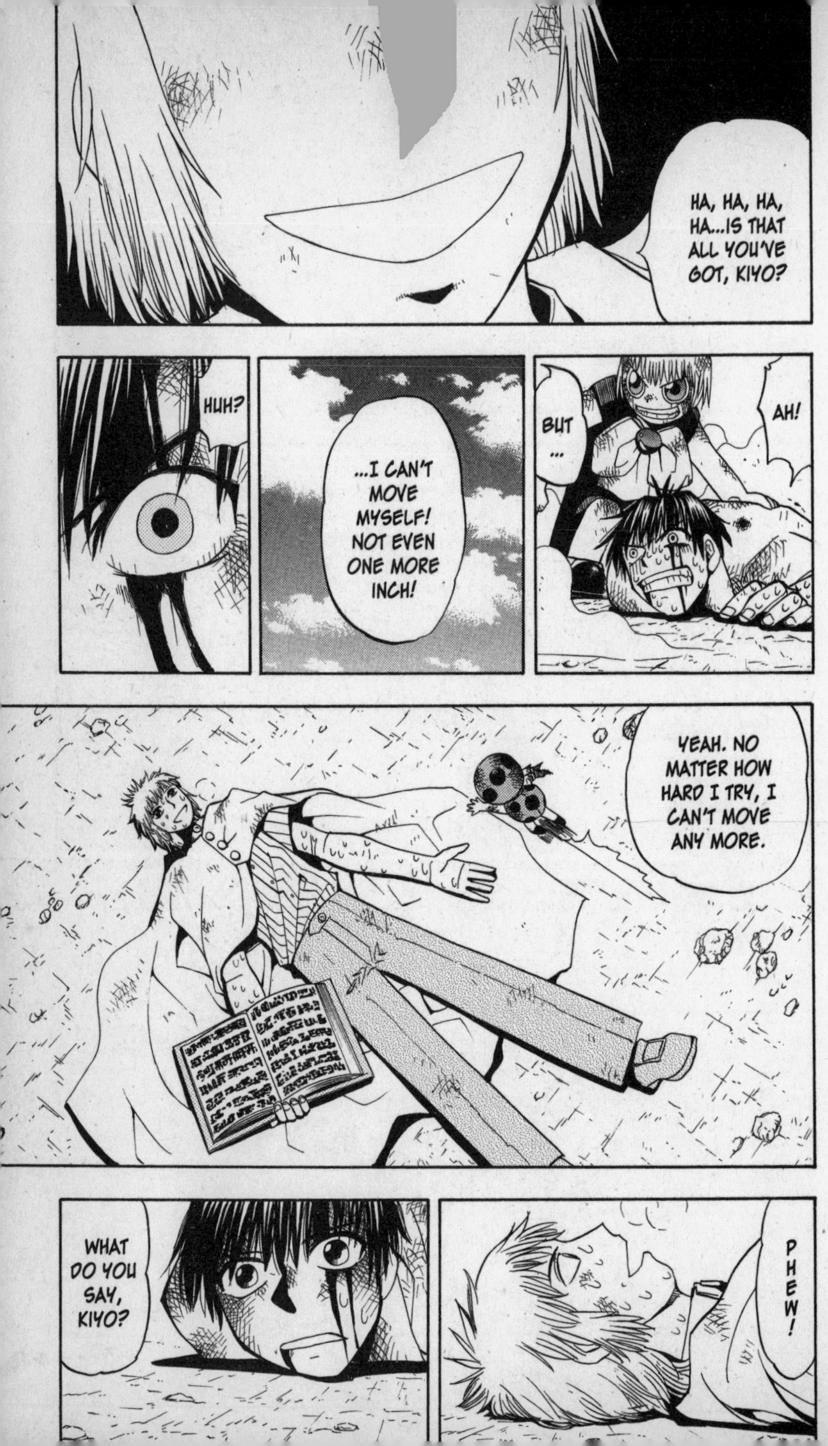
HA, HA, HA, HA...IS THAT ALL YOU'VE GOT, KIYO?
AH!
BUT ...
...I CAN'T MOVE MYSELF! NOT EVEN ONE MORE INCH!
HUH?
YEAH. NO MATTER HOW HARD I TRY, I CAN'T MOVE ANY MORE.
PHEW!
WHAT DO YOU SAY, KIYO?

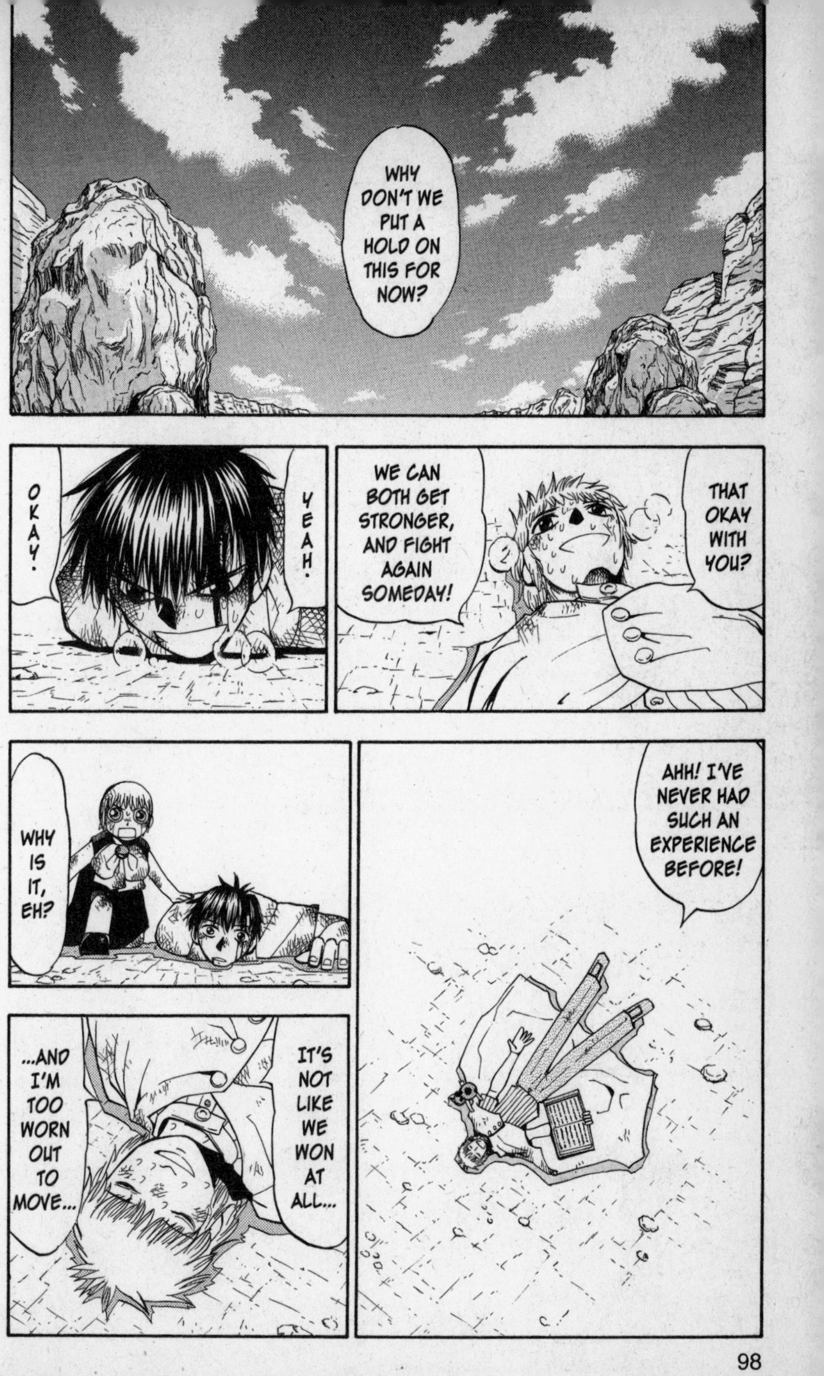
WHY DON'T WE PUT A HOLD ON THIS FOR NOW?
THAT OKAY WITH YOU?
WE CAN BOTH GET STRONGER, AND FIGHT AGAIN SOMEDAY!
YEAH.
OKAY.
AHH! I'VE NEVER HAD SUCH AN EXPERIENCE BEFORE!
WHY IS IT, EH?
IT'S NOT LIKE WE WON AT ALL...
...AND I'M TOO WORN OUT TO MOVE...

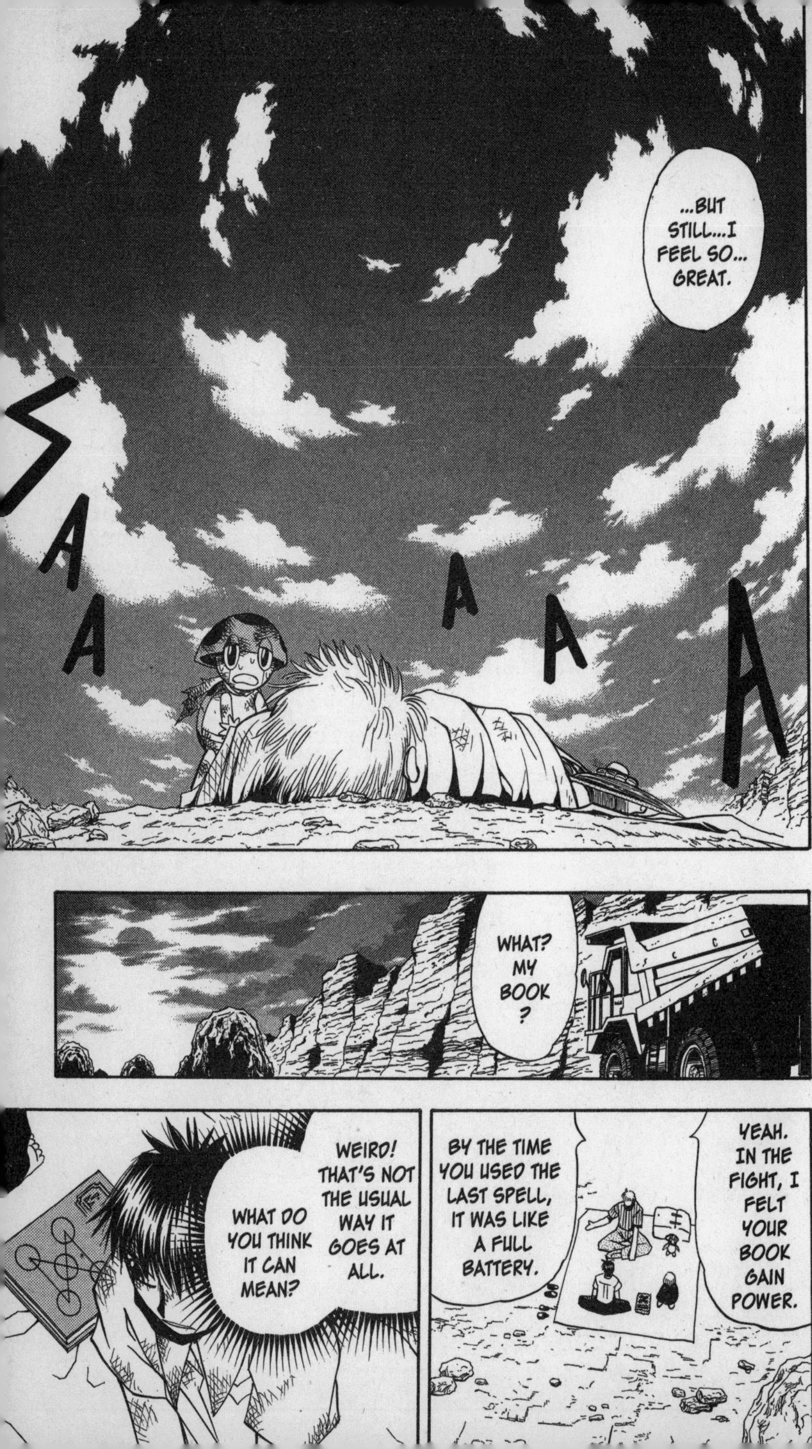
...BUT STILL...I FEEL SO... GREAT.
SAAAAA
WHAT? MY BOOK ?
YEAH. IN THE FIGHT, I FELT YOUR BOOK GAIN POWER.
BY THE TIME YOU USED THE LAST SPELL, IT WAS LIKE A FULL BATTERY.
WEIRD! THAT'S NOT THE USUAL WAY IT GOES AT ALL.
WHAT DO YOU THINK IT CAN MEAN?

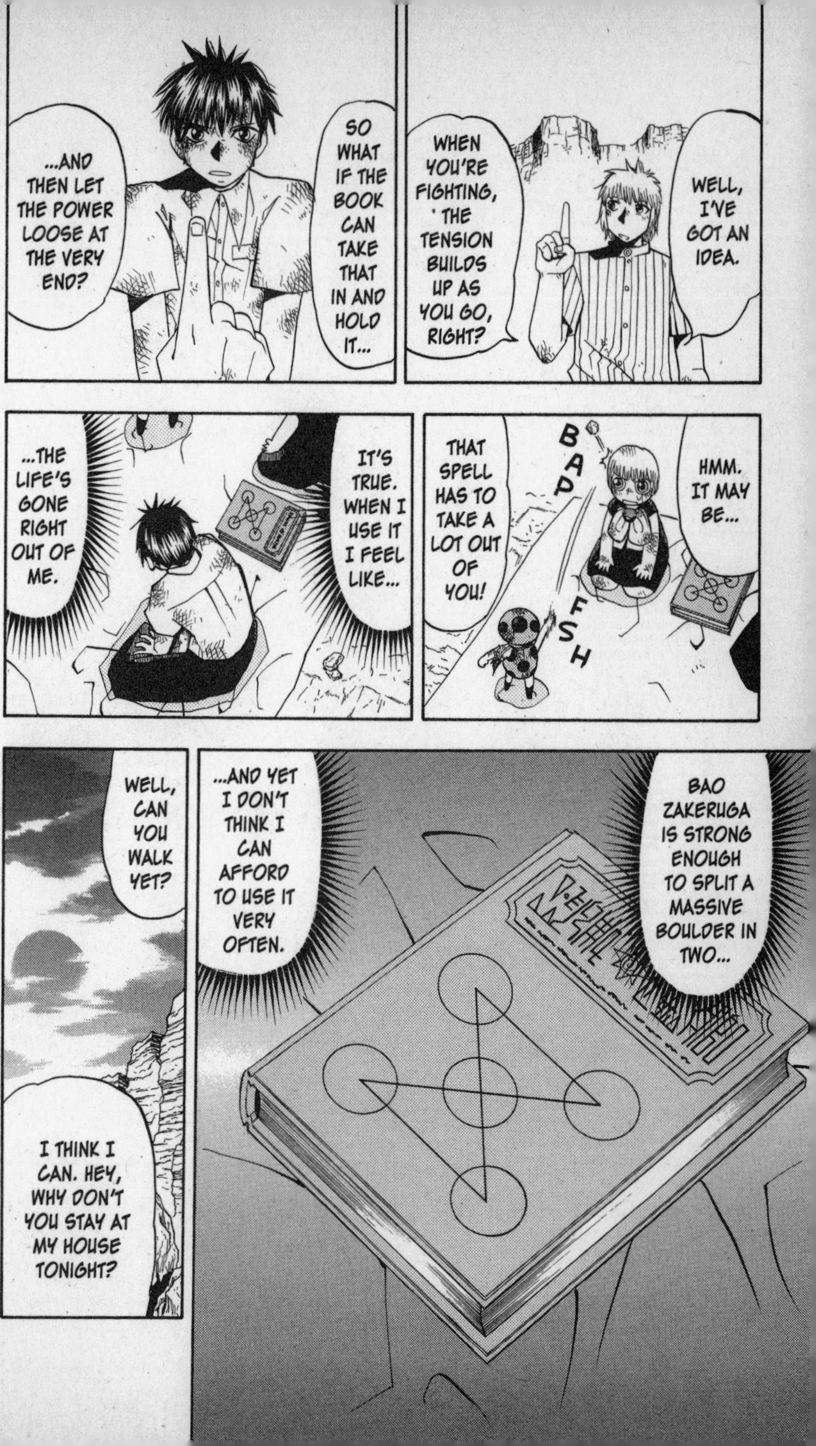
WELL, I'VE GOT AN IDEA.
WHEN YOU'RE FIGHTING, THE TENSION BUILDS UP AS YOU GO, RIGHT?
SO WHAT IF THE BOOK CAN TAKE THAT IN AND HOLD IT...
...AND THEN LET THE POWER LOOSE AT THE VERY END?
HMM. IT MAY BE...
BAP
THAT SPELL HAS TO TAKE A LOT OUT OF YOU!
FSH
IT'S TRUE. WHEN I USE IT I FEEL LIKE...
...THE LIFE'S GONE RIGHT OUT OF ME.
BAO ZAKERUGA IS STRONG ENOUGH TO SPLIT A MASSIVE BOULDER IN TWO...
...AND YET I DON'T THINK I CAN AFFORD TO USE IT VERY OFTEN.
WELL, CAN YOU WALK YET?
I THINK I CAN. HEY, WHY DON'T YOU STAY AT MY HOUSE TONIGHT?

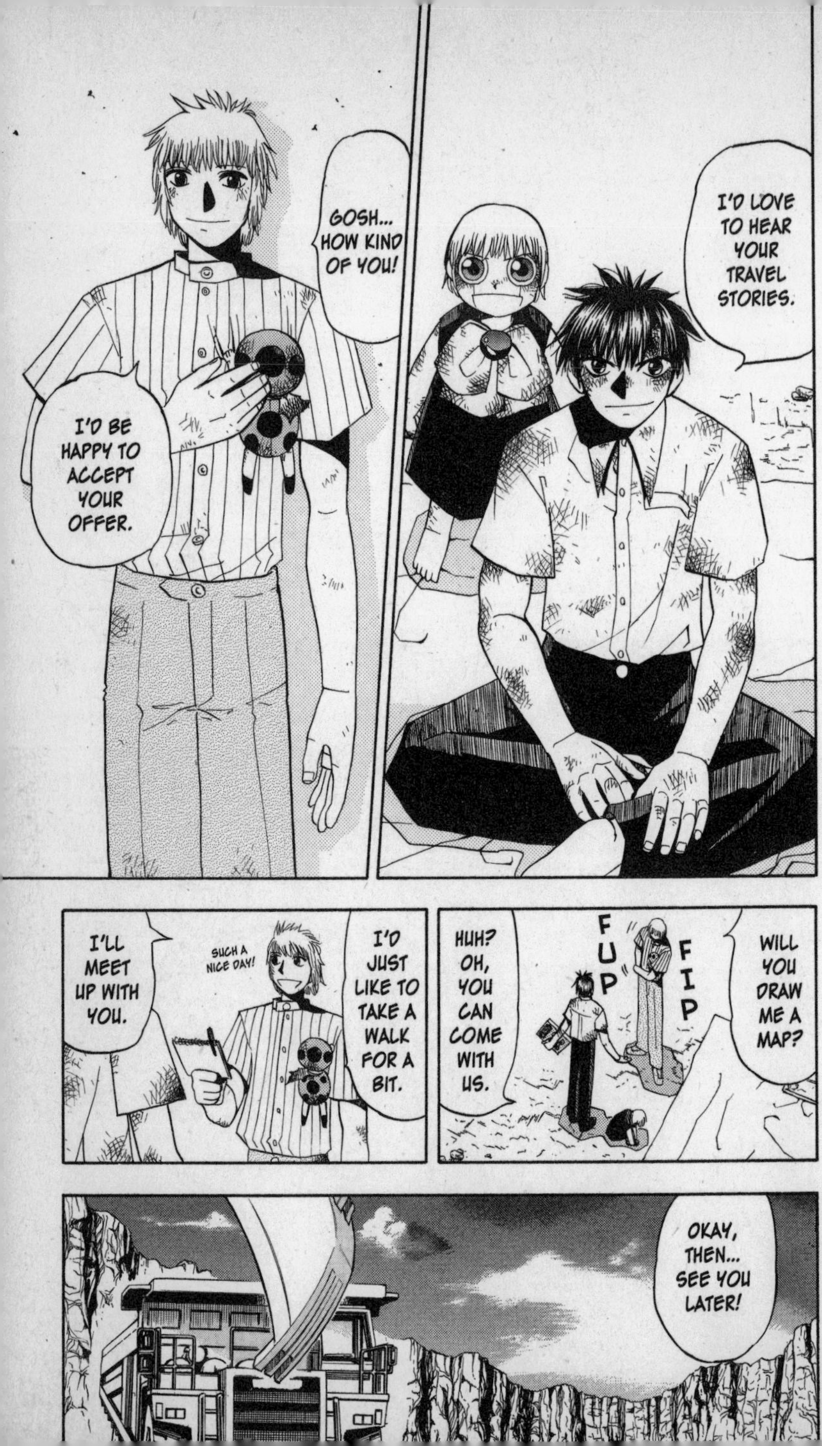
I'D LOVE TO HEAR YOUR TRAVEL STORIES.
GOSH... HOW KIND OF YOU!
I'D BE HAPPY TO ACCEPT YOUR OFFER.
WILL YOU DRAW ME A MAP?
FIP
FUP
HUH? OH, YOU CAN COME WITH US.
I'D JUST LIKE TO TAKE A WALK FOR A BIT.
SUCH A NICE DAY!
I'LL MEET UP WITH YOU.
OKAY, THEN... SEE YOU LATER!

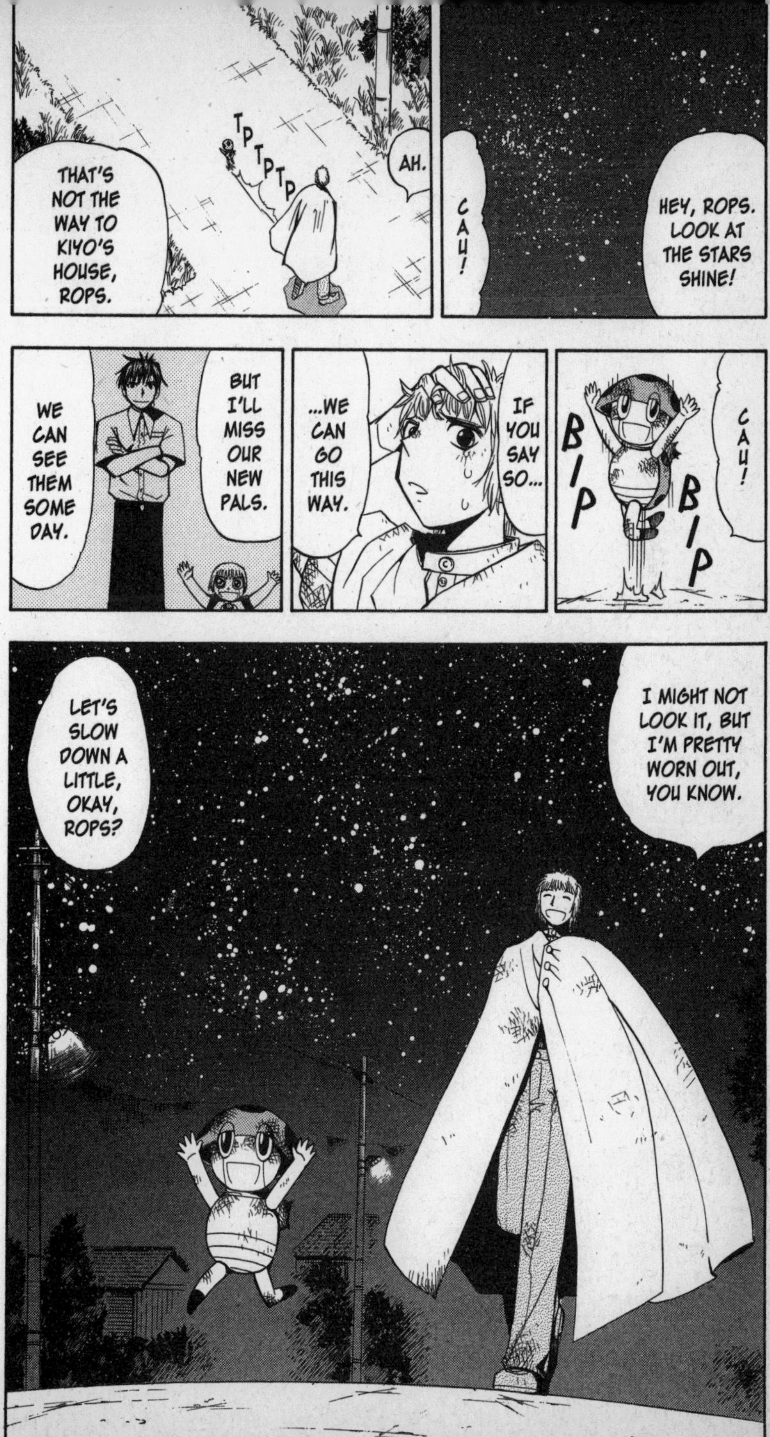
HEY, ROPS. LOOK AT THE STARS SHINE!
CAU!
AH.
TPTPTPTP
THAT'S NOT THE WAY TO KIYO'S HOUSE, ROPS.
CAU!
BIP
BIP
IF YOU SAY SO...
...WE CAN GO THIS WAY.
BUT I'LL MISS OUR NEW PALS.
WE CAN SEE THEM SOME DAY.
I MIGHT NOT LOOK IT, BUT I'M PRETTY WORN OUT, YOU KNOW.
LET'S SLOW DOWN A LITTLE, OKAY, ROPS?

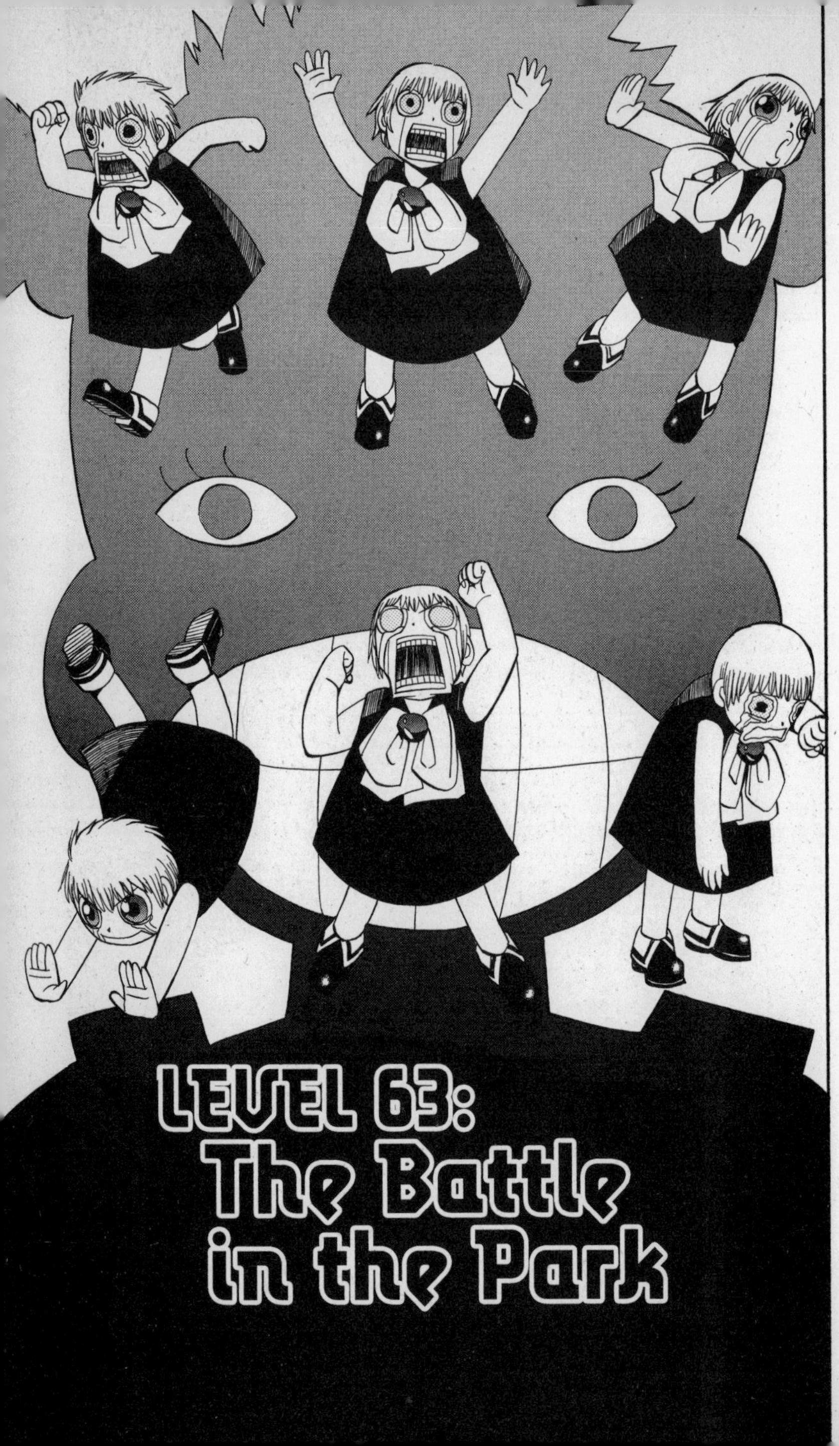
LEVEL 63:
The Battle in the Park

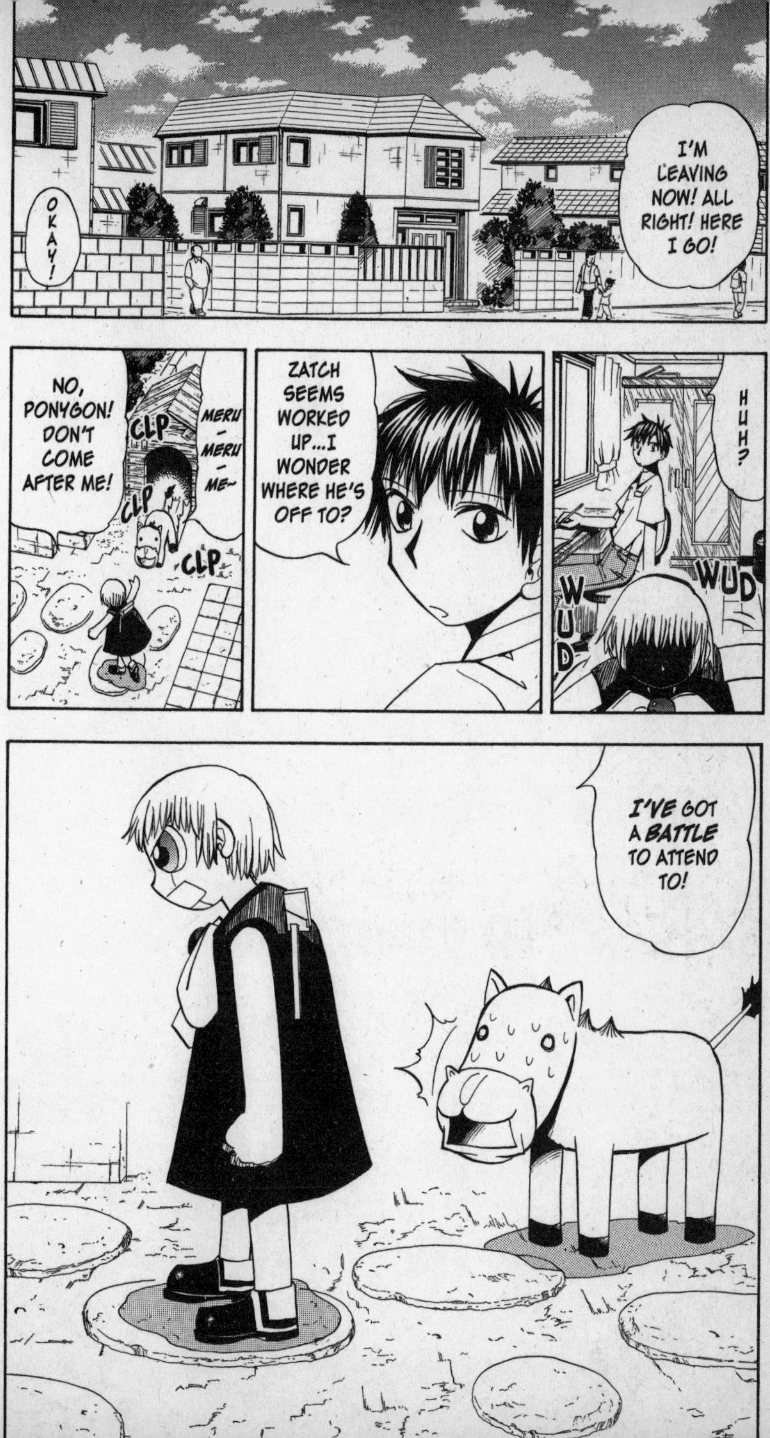
I'M LEAVING NOW! ALL RIGHT! HERE I GO!
OKAY!
HUH?
WUD
WUD
WUD
ZATCH SEEMS WORKED UP...I WONDER WHERE HE'S OFF TO?
NO, PONYGON! DON'T COME AFTER ME!
MERU-MERU-ME~
CLP
CLP
CLP
I'VE GOT A BATTLE TO ATTEND TO!

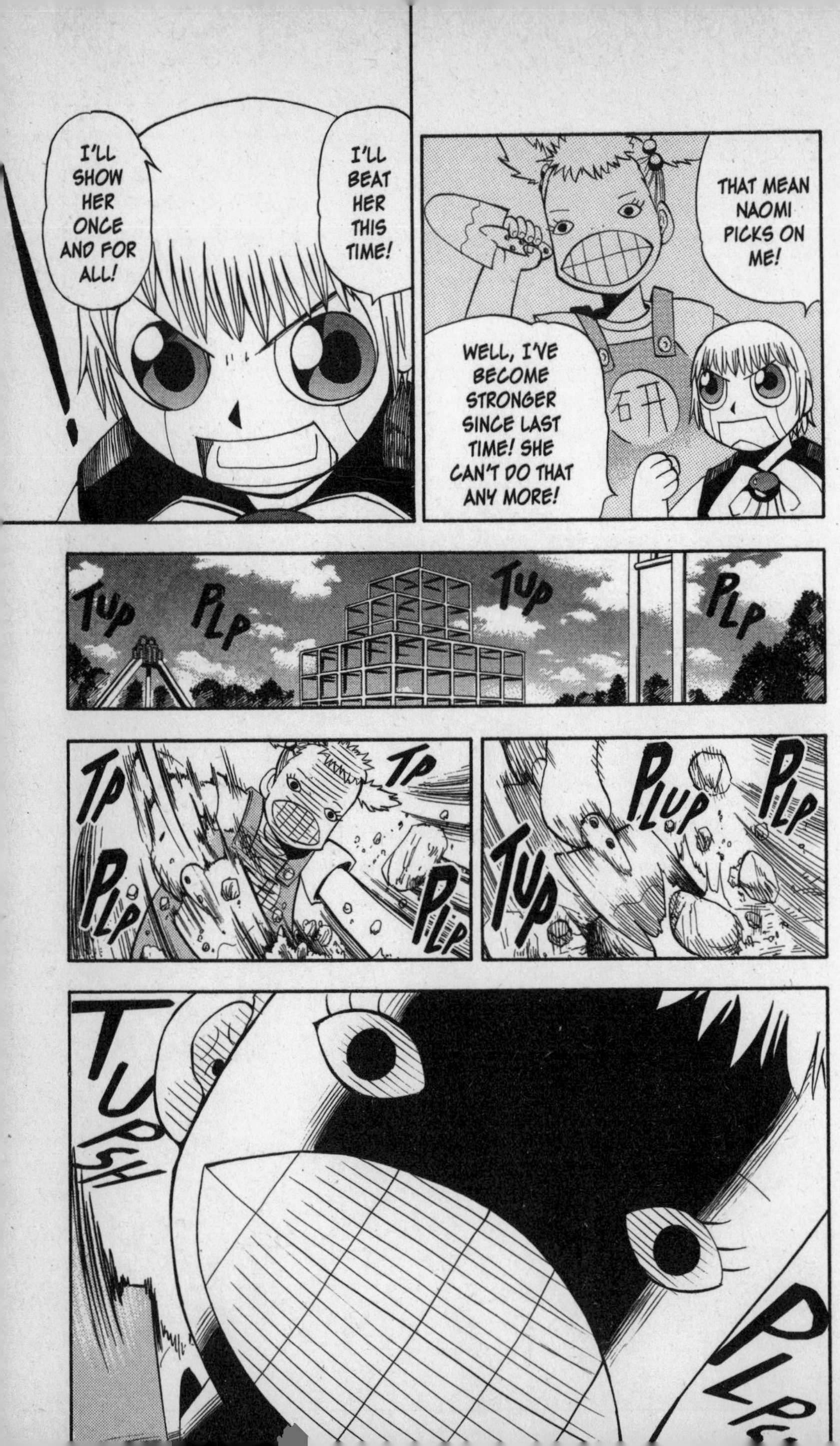

THAT MEAN NAOMI PICKS ON ME!
WELL, I'VE BECOME STRONGER SINCE LAST TIME! SHE CAN'T DO THAT ANY MORE!
I'LL BEAT HER THIS TIME!
I'LL SHOW HER ONCE AND FOR ALL!
!
PLP
TUP
PLP
TUP
PLP
PLUP
TUP
TP
PLP
TP
PLP
PLPL
TUPISH

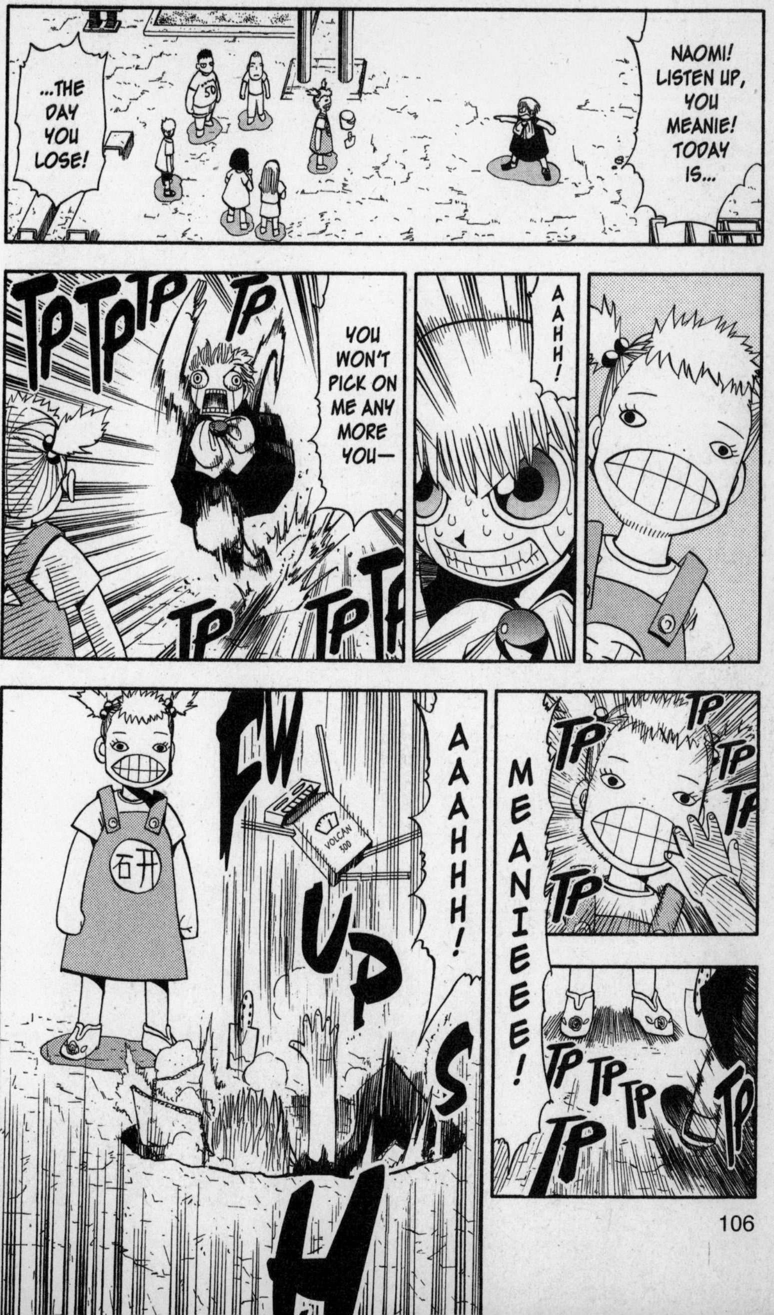
NAOMI! LISTEN UP, YOU MEANIE! TODAY IS...
...THE DAY YOU LOSE!
AAHH!
YOU WON'T PICK ON ME ANY MORE YOU—
TP TP TP TP
TP TP TP
TP TP TP TP TP
MEANIEEEE!
TP TP TP TP TP
AAAHHH!
VOLCAN 300
FW UP S H

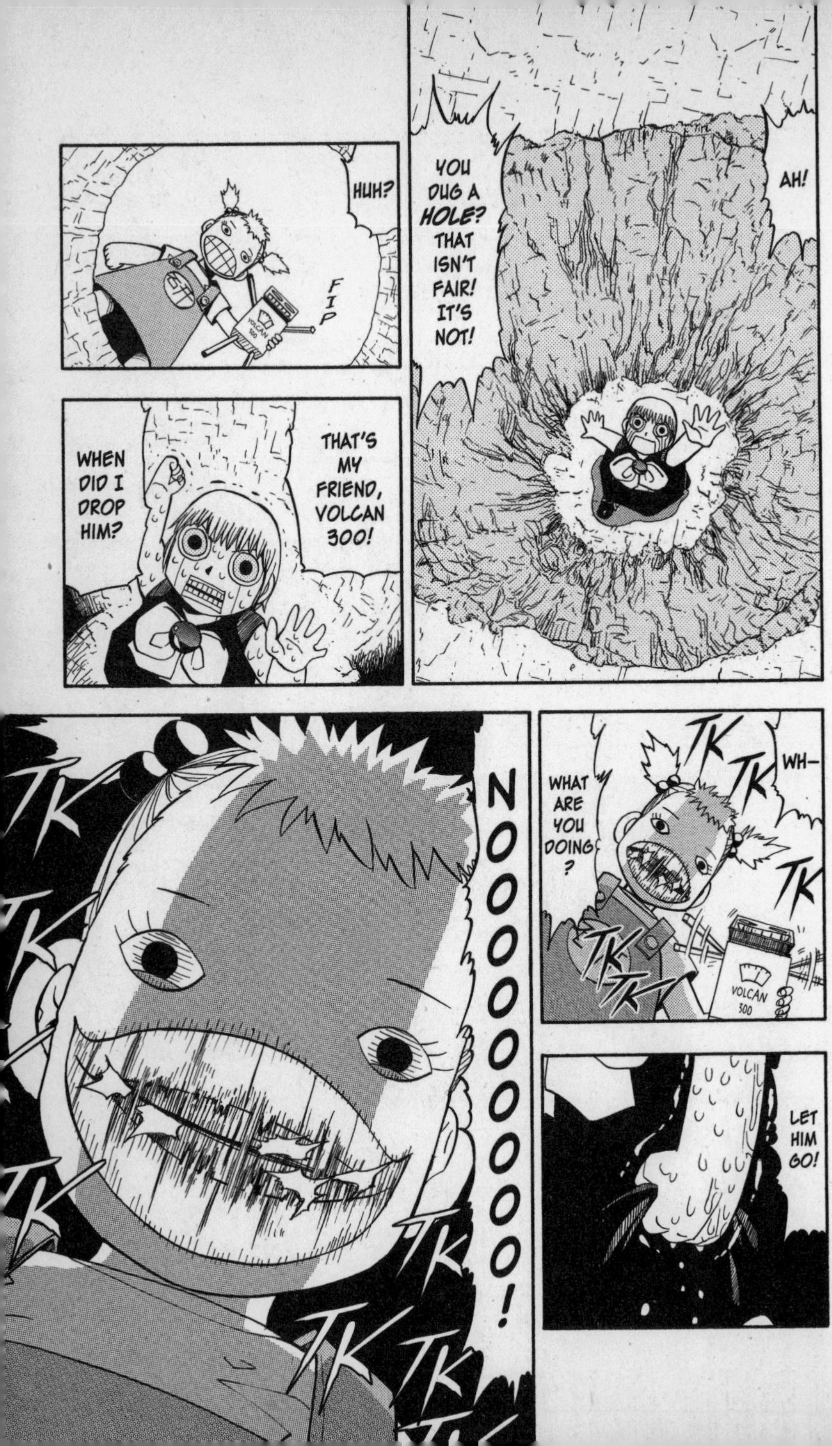
AH!
YOU DUG A HOLE? THAT ISN'T FAIR! IT'S NOT!
HUH?
FIP
VOLCAN 300
THAT'S MY FRIEND, VOLCAN 300!
WHEN DID I DROP HIM?
WH-
TK TK
WHAT ARE YOU DOING?
TK
TK TK TK
VOLCAN 300
LET HIM GO!
NOOOOOOOOOO!
TK TK TK
TK TK TK

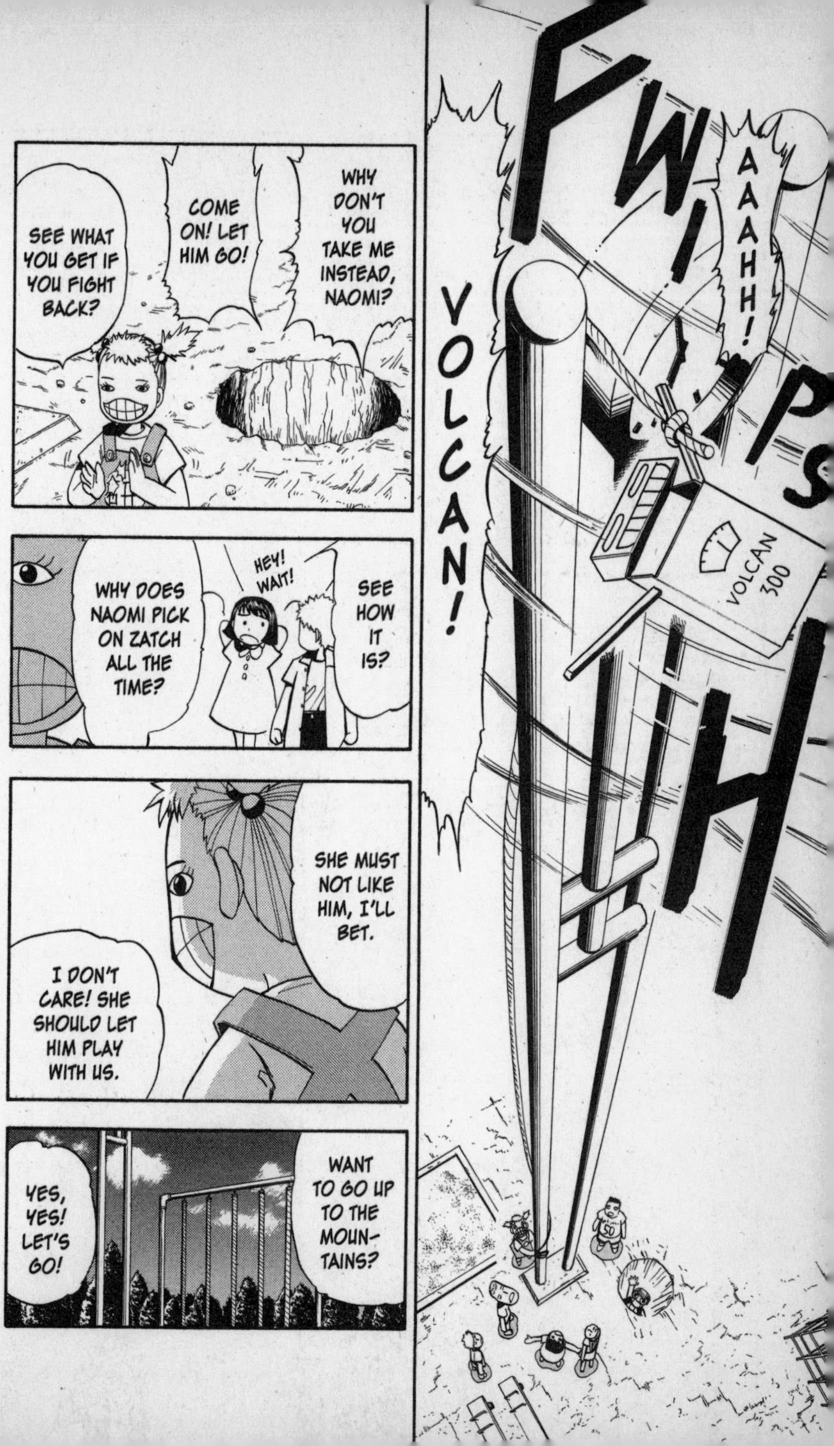
FWIPSH
AAAHH!
VOLCAN!
VOLCAN 300
WHY DON'T YOU TAKE ME INSTEAD, NAOMI?
COME ON! LET HIM GO!
SEE WHAT YOU GET IF YOU FIGHT BACK?
SEE HOW IT IS?
HEY! WAIT!
WHY DOES NAOMI PICK ON ZATCH ALL THE TIME?
SHE MUST NOT LIKE HIM, I'LL BET.
I DON'T CARE! SHE SHOULD LET HIM PLAY WITH US.
WANT TO GO UP TO THE MOUN-TAINS?
YES, YES! LET'S GO!

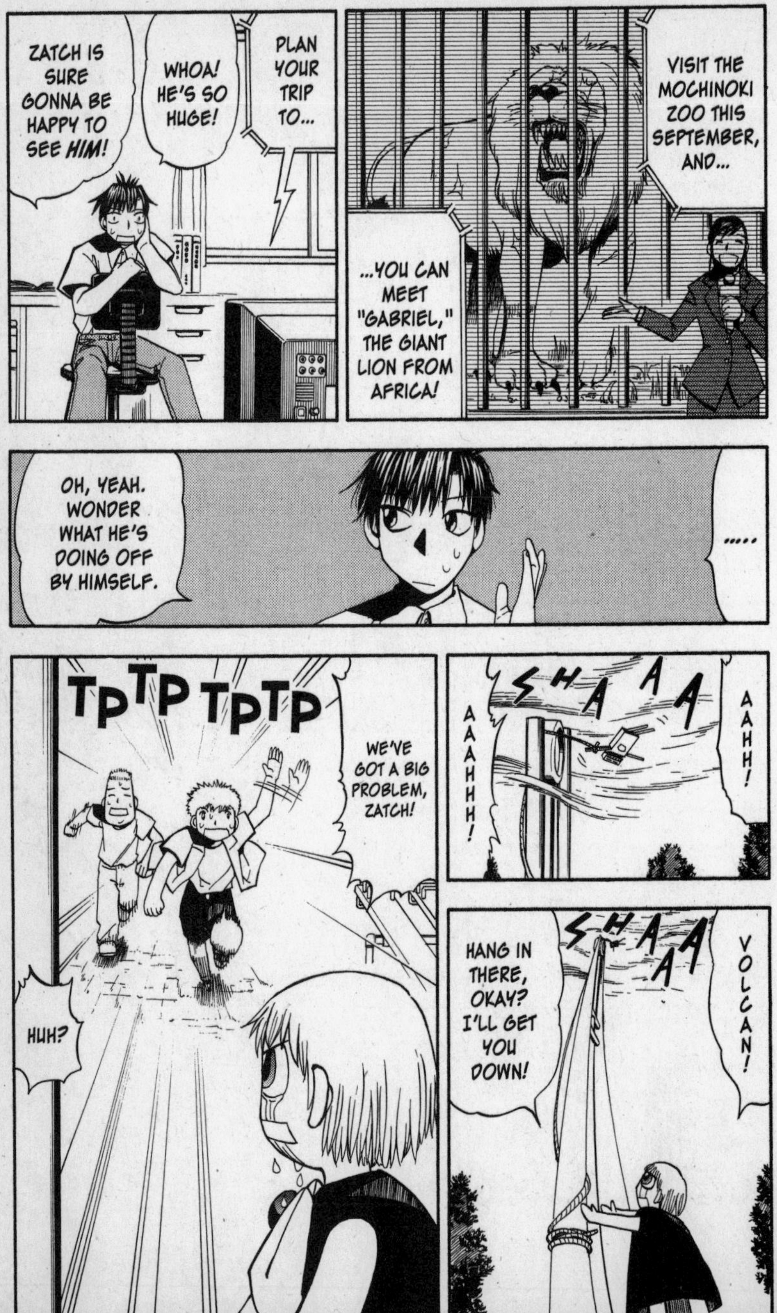
VISIT THE MOCHINOKI ZOO THIS SEPTEMBER, AND...
...YOU CAN MEET "GABRIEL," THE GIANT LION FROM AFRICA!
PLAN YOUR TRIP TO...
WHOA! HE'S SO HUGE!
ZATCH IS SURE GONNA BE HAPPY TO SEE HIM!
.....
OH, YEAH. WONDER WHAT HE'S DOING OFF BY HIMSELF.
AAHH!
SHAAAA
AAAAHHHH!
VOLCAN!
SHAAAA
HANG IN THERE, OKAY? I'LL GET YOU DOWN!
TPTP TPTP
WE'VE GOT A BIG PROBLEM, ZATCH!
HUH?

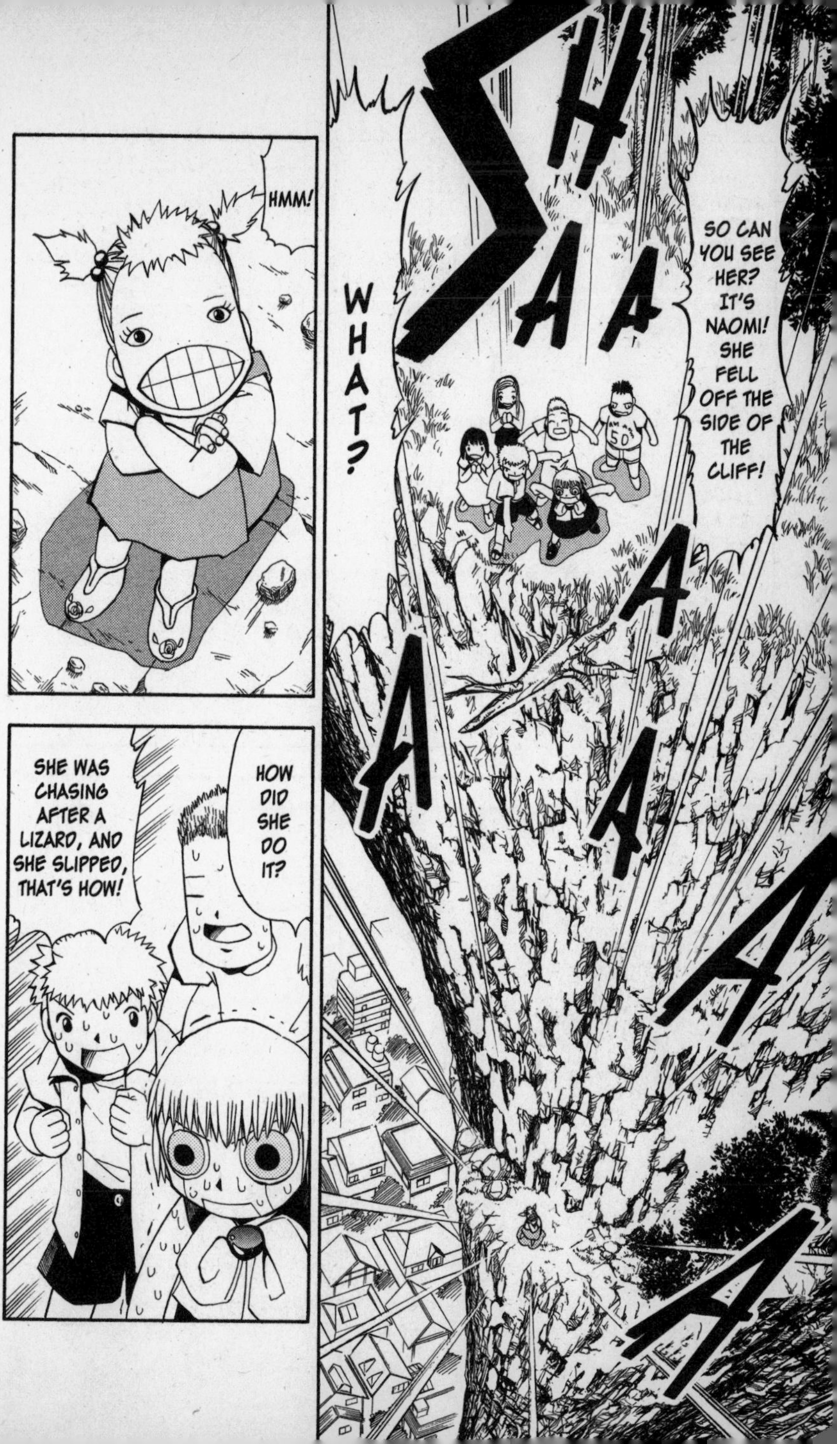
SO CAN YOU SEE HER? IT'S NAOMI! SHE FELL OFF THE SIDE OF THE CLIFF!
SHAAAAAAAAAA
WHAT?
HMM!
HOW DID SHE DO IT?
SHE WAS CHASING AFTER A LIZARD, AND SHE SLIPPED, THAT'S HOW!

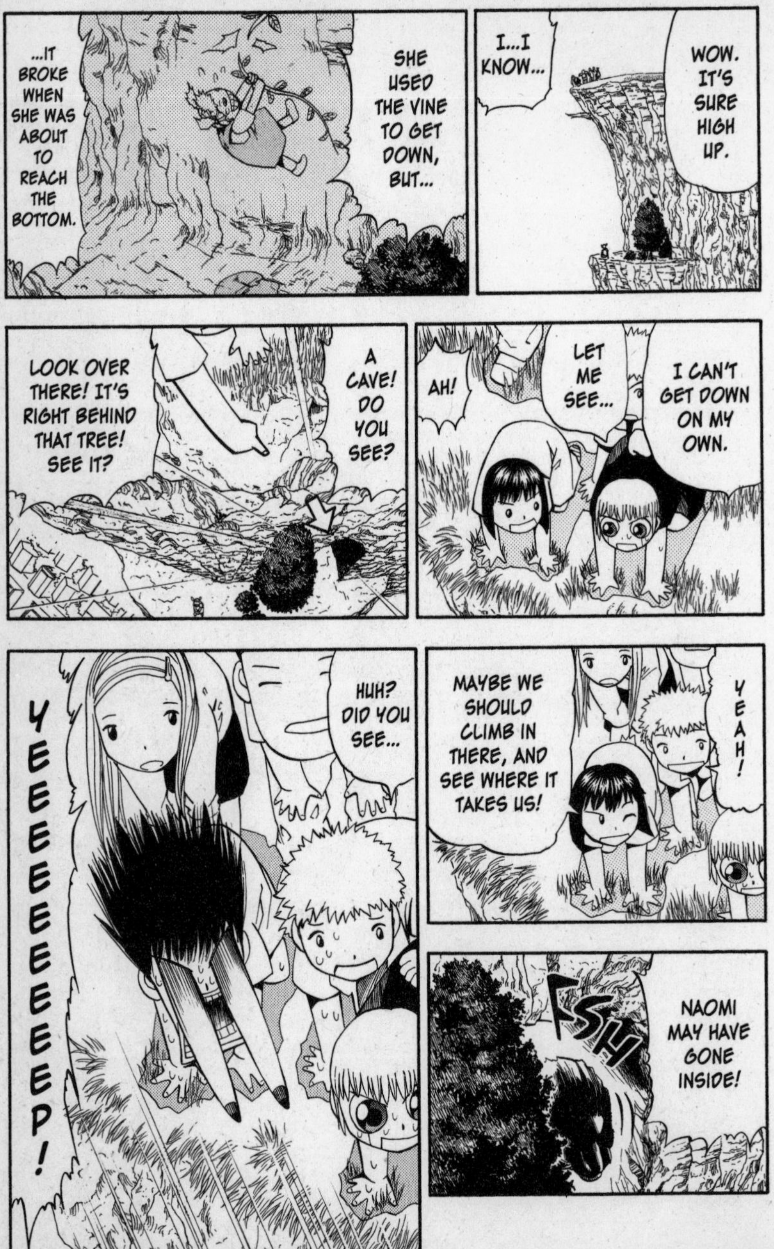
WOW. IT'S SURE HIGH UP.
I...I KNOW...
SHE USED THE VINE TO GET DOWN, BUT...
...IT BROKE WHEN SHE WAS ABOUT TO REACH THE BOTTOM.
I CAN'T GET DOWN ON MY OWN.
LET ME SEE...
AH!
A CAVE! DO YOU SEE?
LOOK OVER THERE! IT'S RIGHT BEHIND THAT TREE! SEE IT?
YEAH!
MAYBE WE SHOULD CLIMB IN THERE, AND SEE WHERE IT TAKES US!
NAOMI MAY HAVE GONE INSIDE!
FSH
HUH? DID YOU SEE...
YEEEEEEEEEEEP!

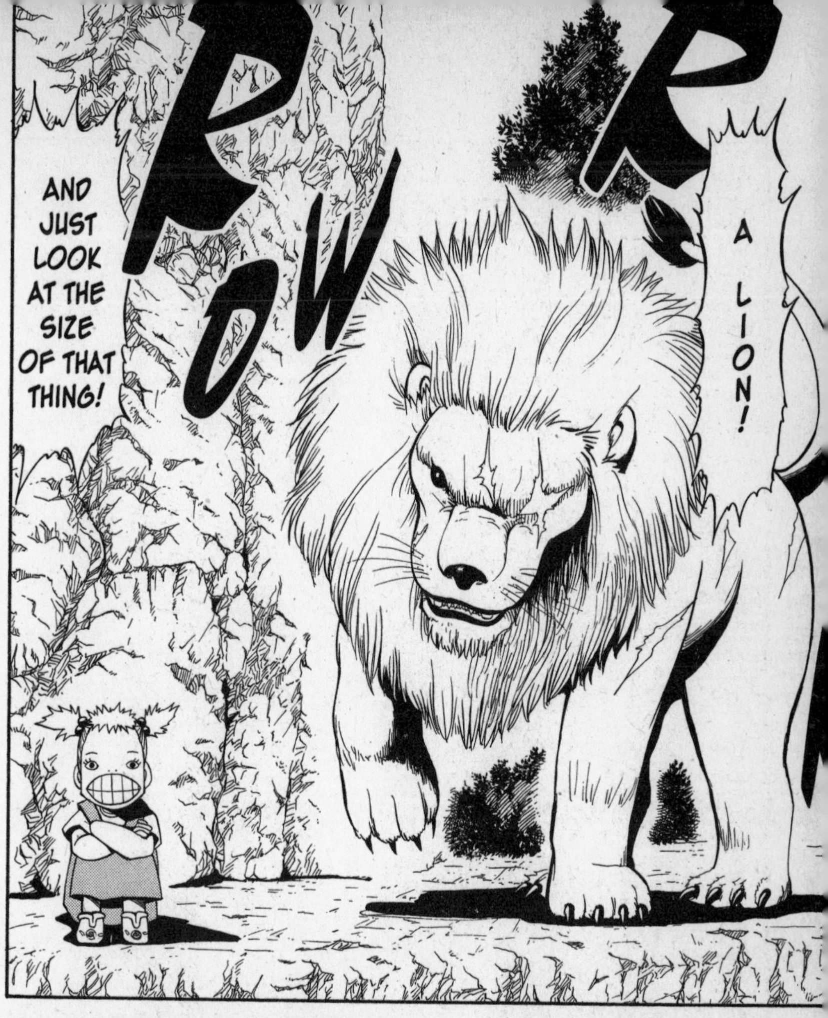
ROWR
A LION!
AND JUST LOOK AT THE SIZE OF THAT THING!

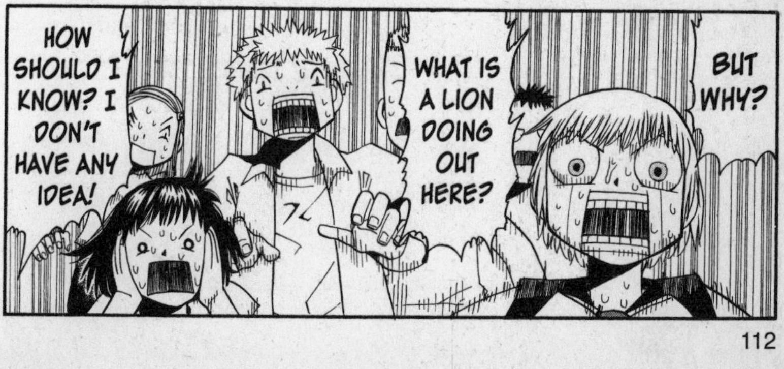
BUT WHY?
WHAT IS A LION DOING OUT HERE?
HOW SHOULD I KNOW? I DON'T HAVE ANY IDEA!

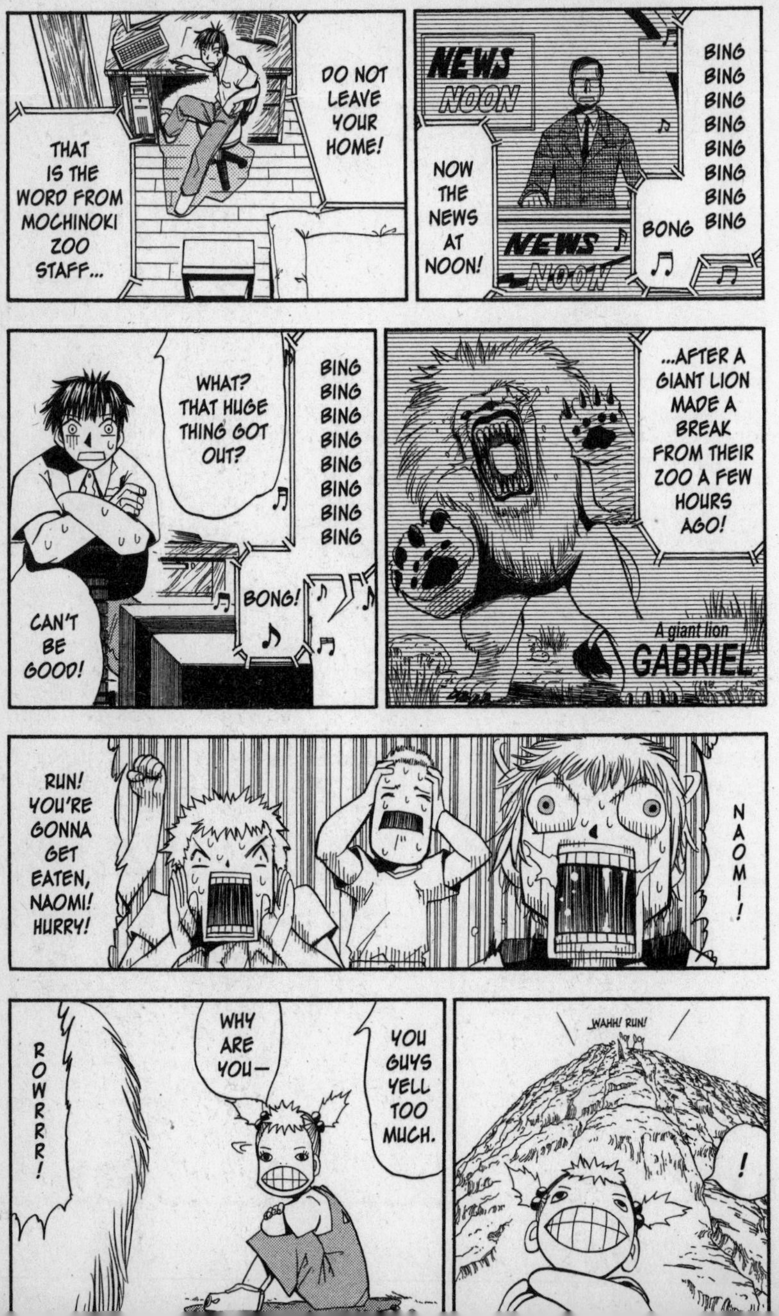
BING BING BING BING BING BING BING BING
BONG
NOW THE NEWS AT NOON!
NEWS NOON
DO NOT LEAVE YOUR HOME!
THAT IS THE WORD FROM MOCHINOKI ZOO STAFF...
...AFTER A GIANT LION MADE A BREAK FROM THEIR ZOO A FEW HOURS AGO!
A giant lion
GABRIEL
BING BING BING BING BING BING BING BING
BONG!
WHAT? THAT HUGE THING GOT OUT?
CAN'T BE GOOD!
NAOMI!
RUN! YOU'RE GONNA GET EATEN, NAOMI! HURRY!
WAHH! RUN!
!
YOU GUYS YELL TOO MUCH.
WHY ARE YOU—
ROWRRRR!

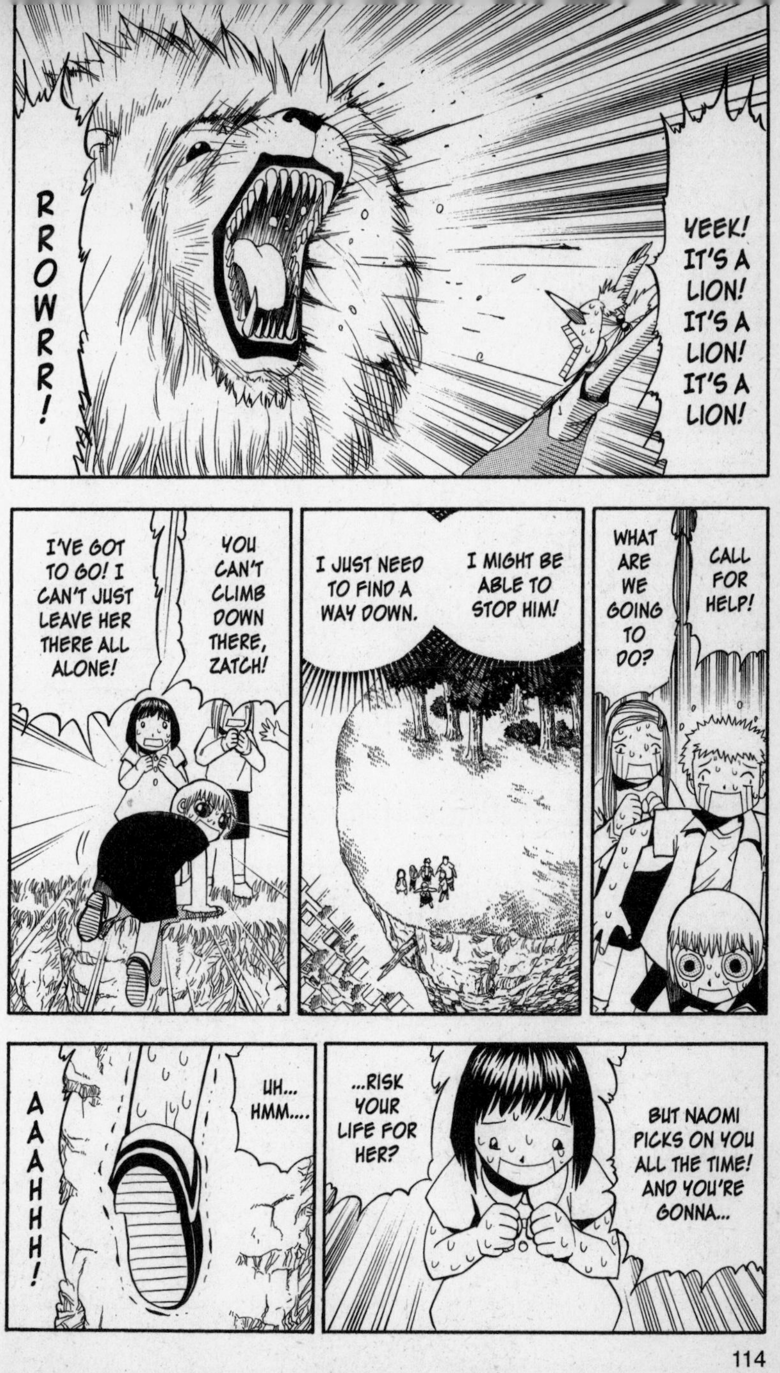
YEEK! IT'S A LION! IT'S A LION! IT'S A LION!
RROWRRR!
CALL FOR HELP!
WHAT ARE WE GOING TO DO?
I MIGHT BE ABLE TO STOP HIM!
I JUST NEED TO FIND A WAY DOWN.
YOU CAN'T CLIMB DOWN THERE, ZATCH!
I'VE GOT TO GO! I CAN'T JUST LEAVE HER THERE ALL ALONE!
BUT NAOMI PICKS ON YOU ALL THE TIME! AND YOU'RE GONNA...
...RISK YOUR LIFE FOR HER?
UH... HMM....
AAAHHH!

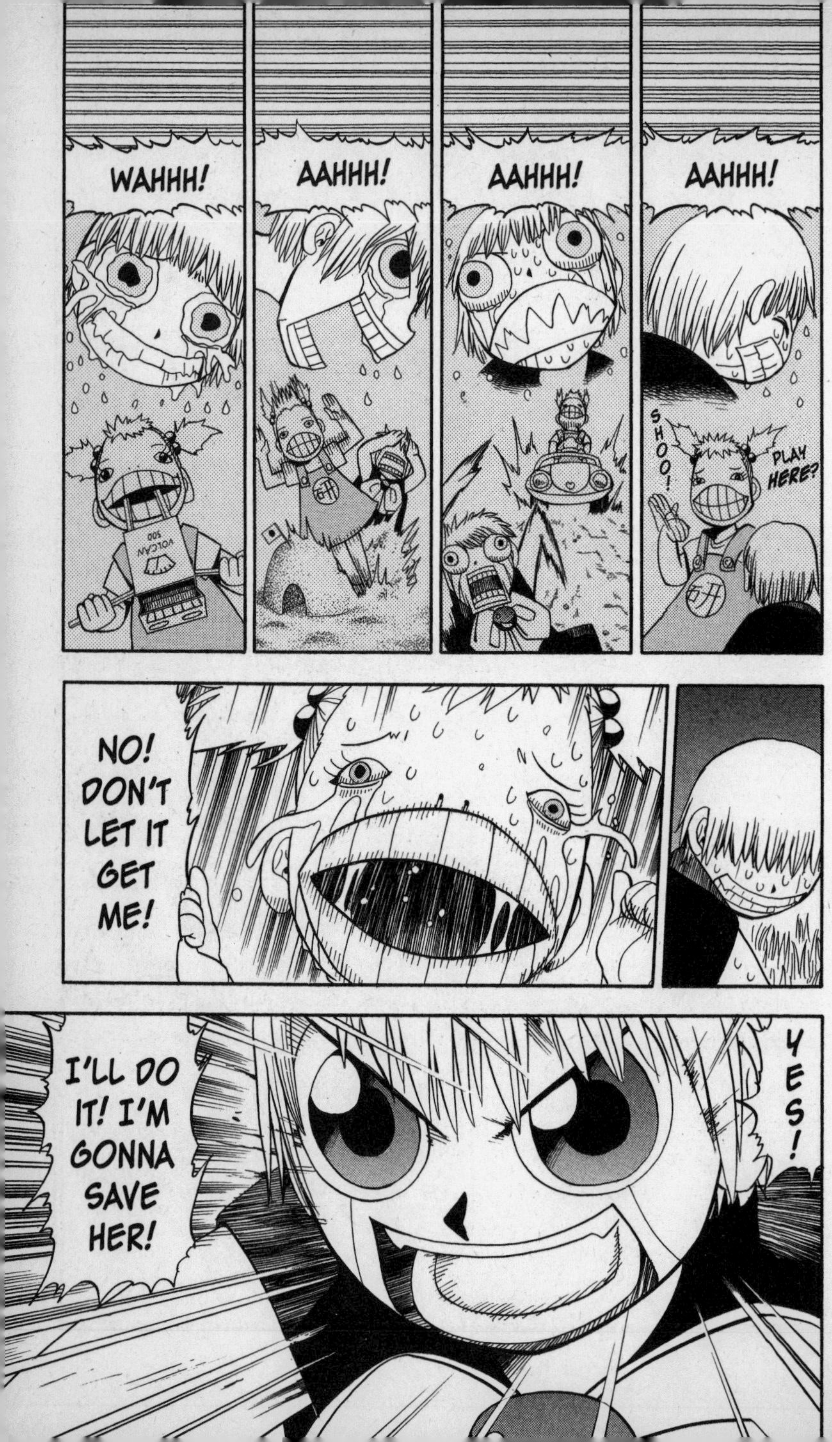
AAHHH!
PLAY HERE?
SHOO!
AAHHH!
AAHHH!
WAHHH!
NO! DON'T LET IT GET ME!
YES!
I'LL DO IT! I'M GONNA SAVE HER!

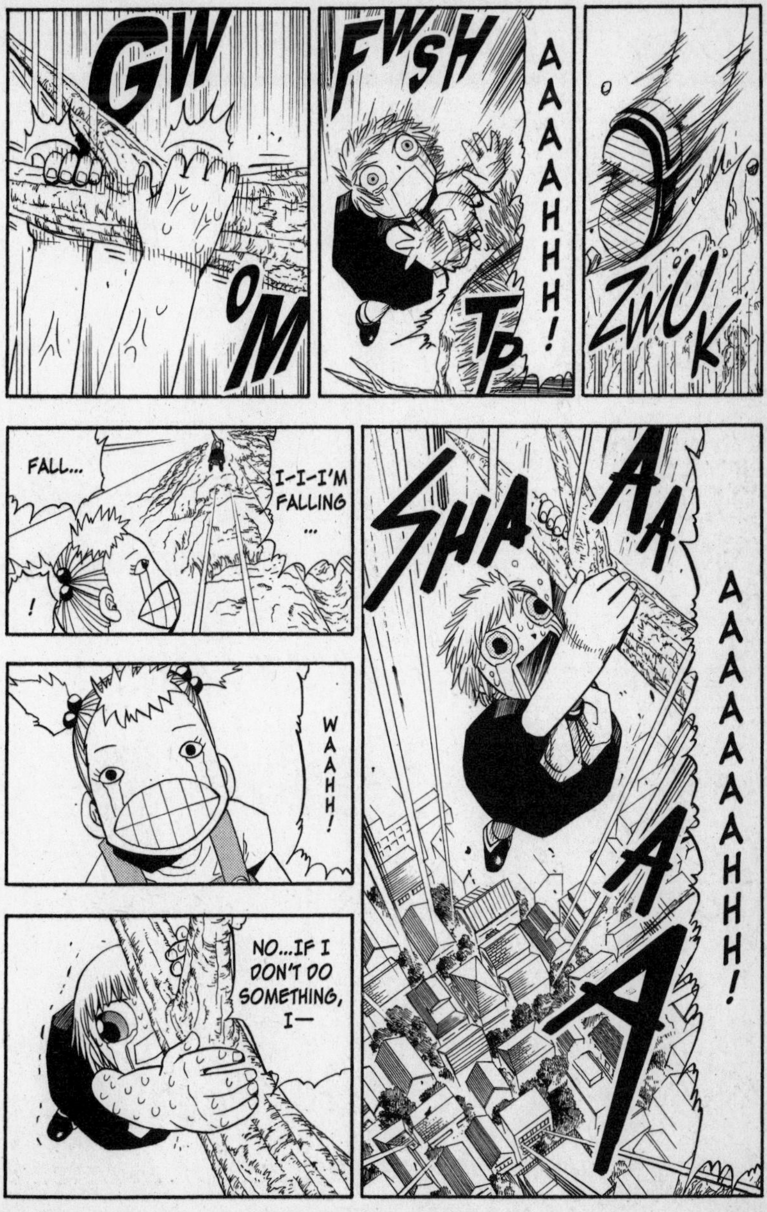
ZWUCK
FWSH
AAAAHHH!
TP
GW
OM
SHAAAAA
AAAAAAAHHH!
FALL...
I-I-I'M FALLING...
!
WAAAHH!
NO...IF I DON'T DO SOMETHING, I—

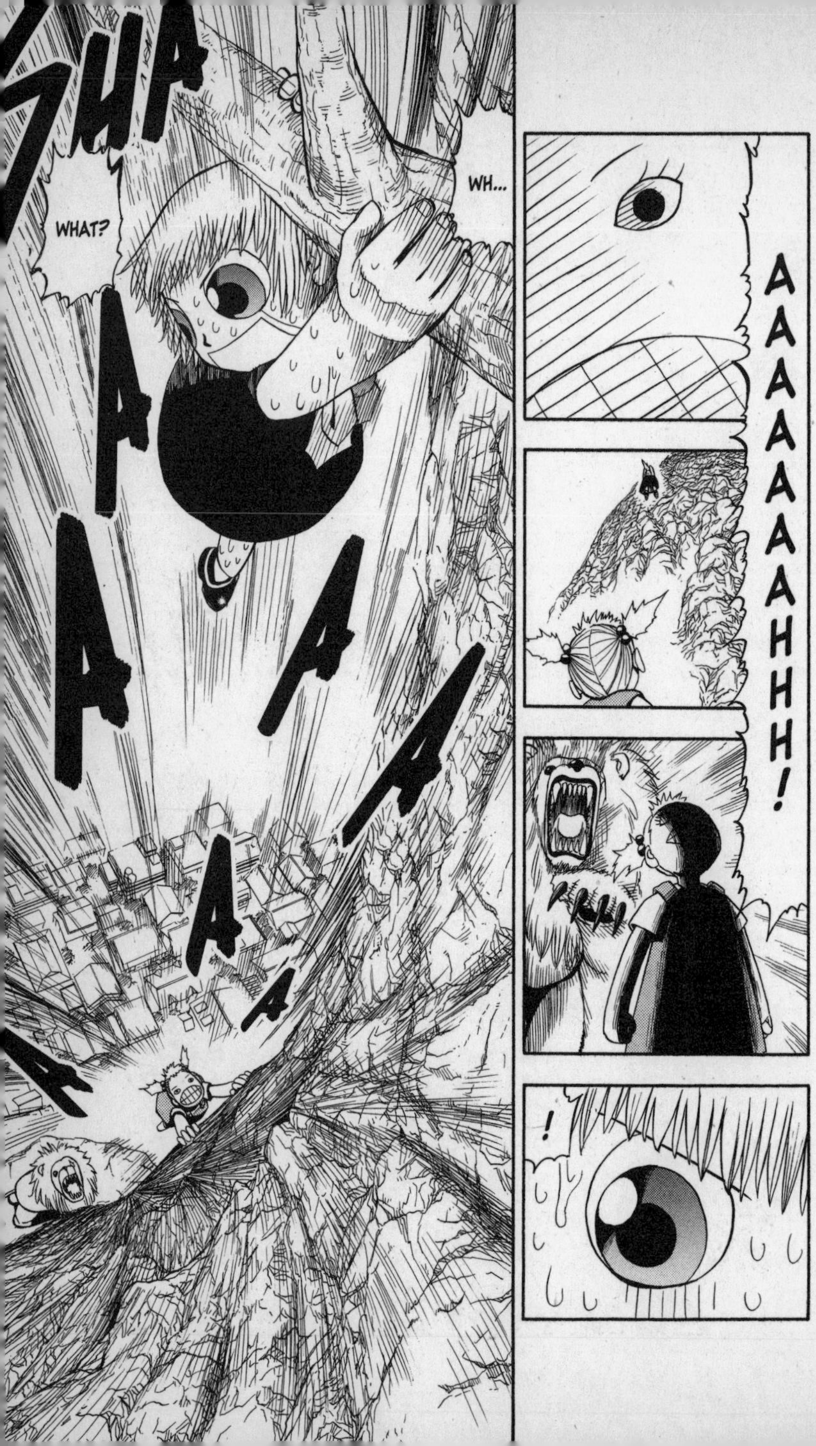
AAAAAAAHHH!
!
WH...
WHAT?
SHA

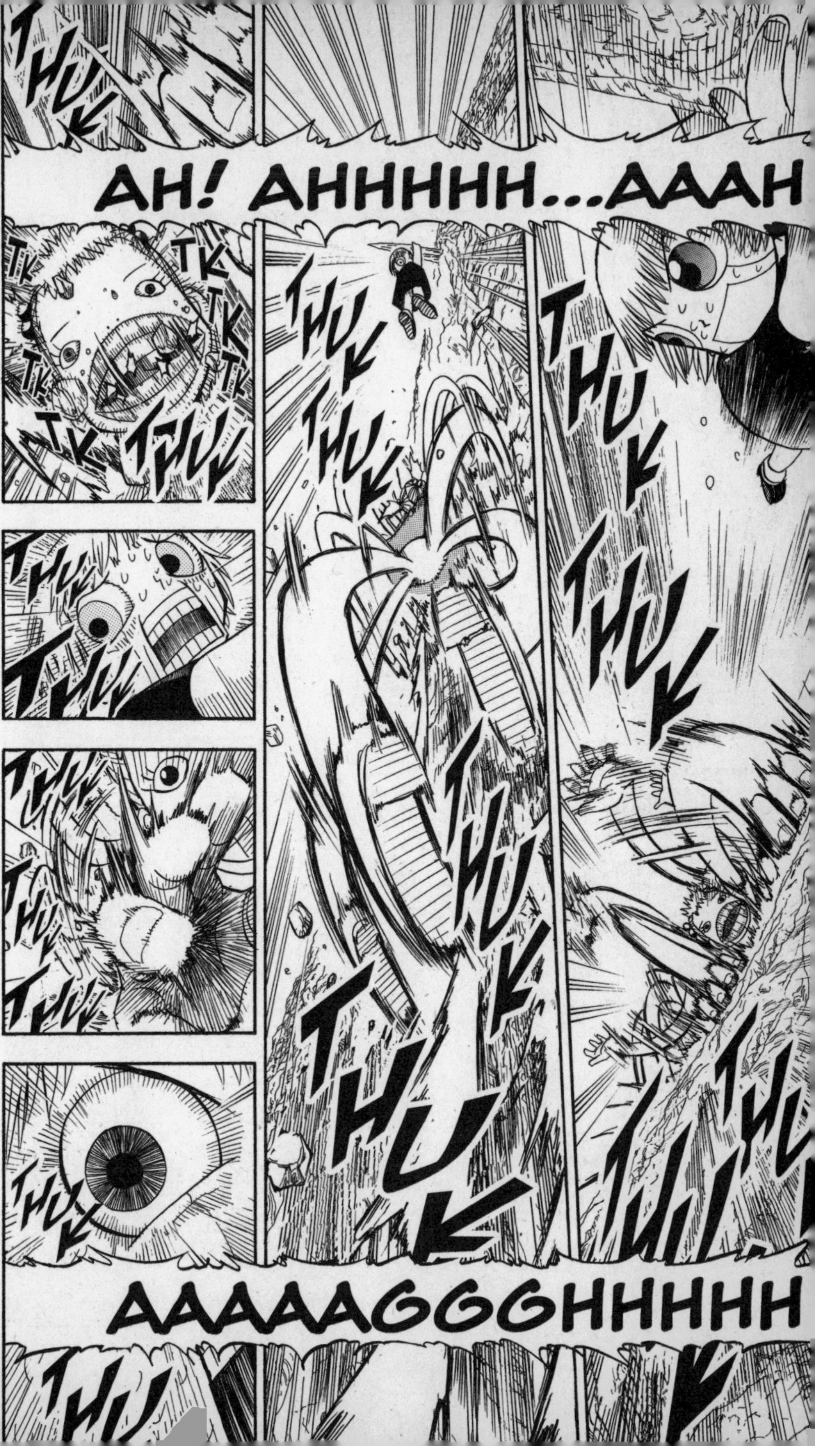

THUK
AH! AHHHHH...AAAH
THUK
THUK
THUK
THUK
THUK
THUK
THUK
TK TK TK TK TK TK
THUK
THUK
THUK
THUK
THUK
THUK
THUK
THUK
AAAAAGGGHHHHH

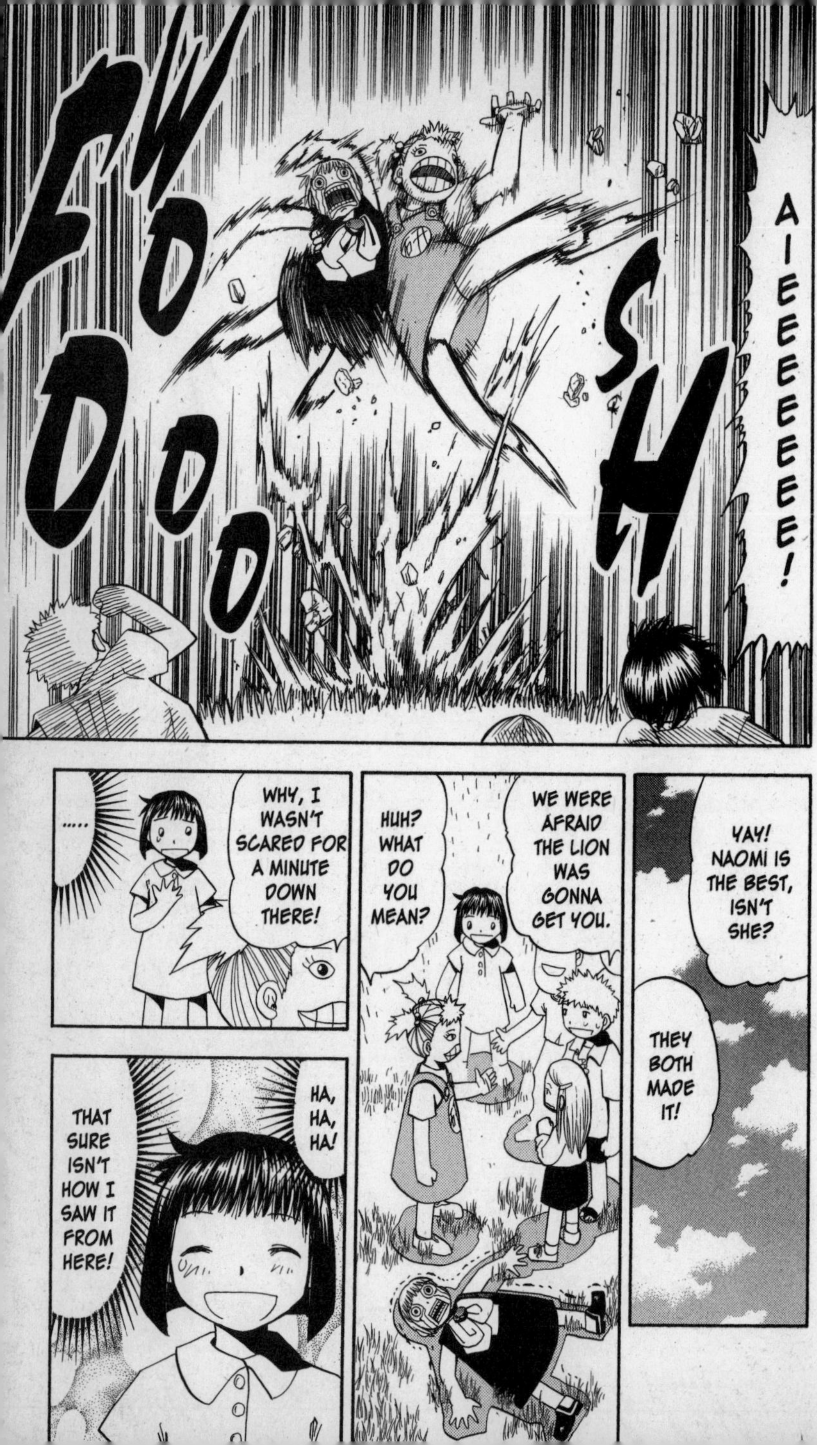
SH
AIEEEEEEE!
YAY! NAOMI IS THE BEST, ISN'T SHE?
THEY BOTH MADE IT!
WE WERE AFRAID THE LION WAS GONNA GET YOU.
HUH? WHAT DO YOU MEAN?
WHY, I WASN'T SCARED FOR A MINUTE DOWN THERE!
.....
HA, HA, HA!
THAT SURE ISN'T HOW I SAW IT FROM HERE!

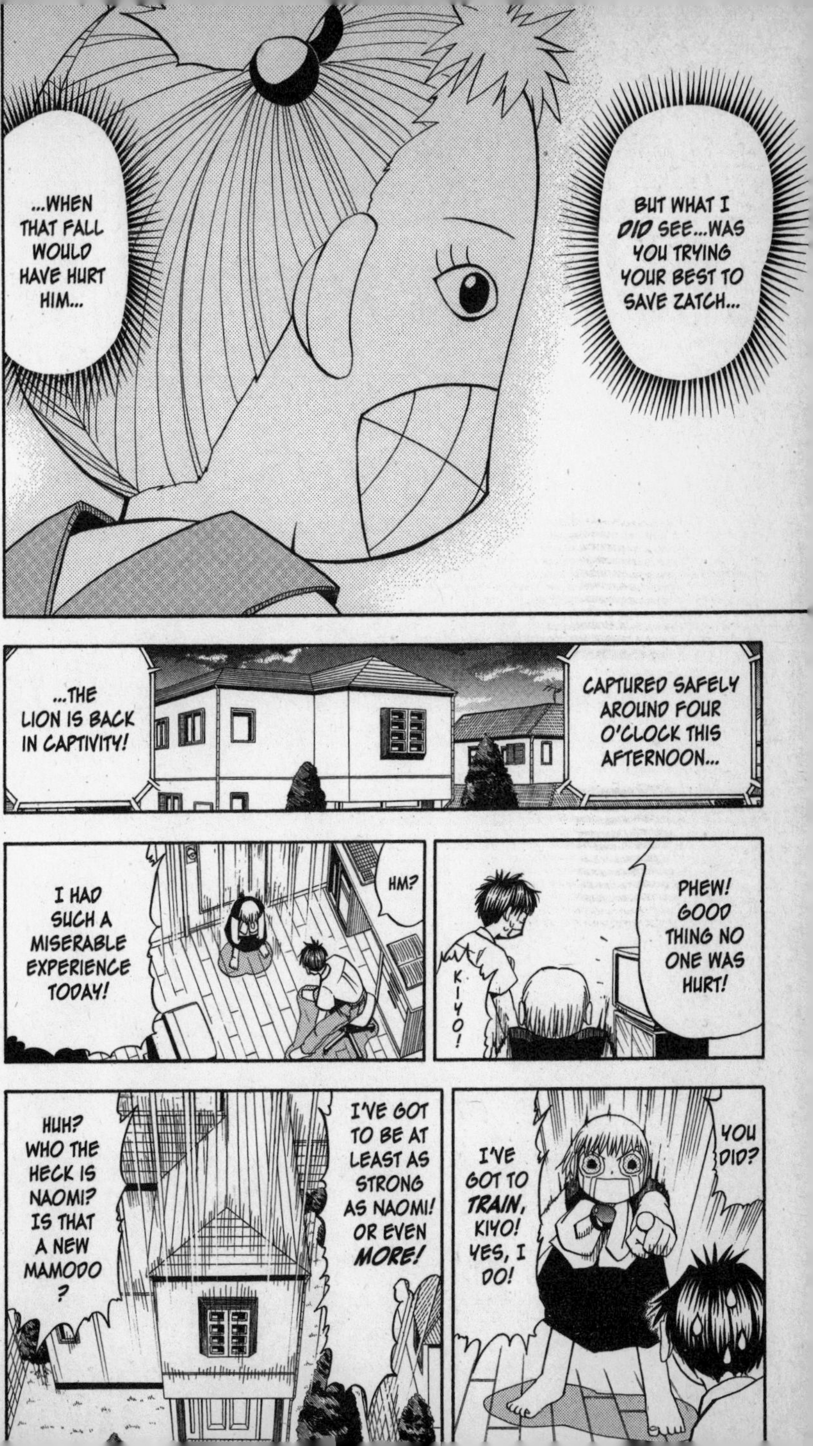
BUT WHAT I DID SEE...WAS YOU TRYING YOUR BEST TO SAVE ZATCH...
...WHEN THAT FALL WOULD HAVE HURT HIM...
CAPTURED SAFELY AROUND FOUR O'CLOCK THIS AFTERNOON...
...THE LION IS BACK IN CAPTIVITY!
PHEW! GOOD THING NO ONE WAS HURT!
KIYO!
HM?
I HAD SUCH A MISERABLE EXPERIENCE TODAY!
YOU DID?
I'VE GOT TO TRAIN, KIYO! YES, I DO!
I'VE GOT TO BE AT LEAST AS STRONG AS NAOMI! OR EVEN MORE!
HUH? WHO THE HECK IS NAOMI? IS THAT A NEW MAMODO?

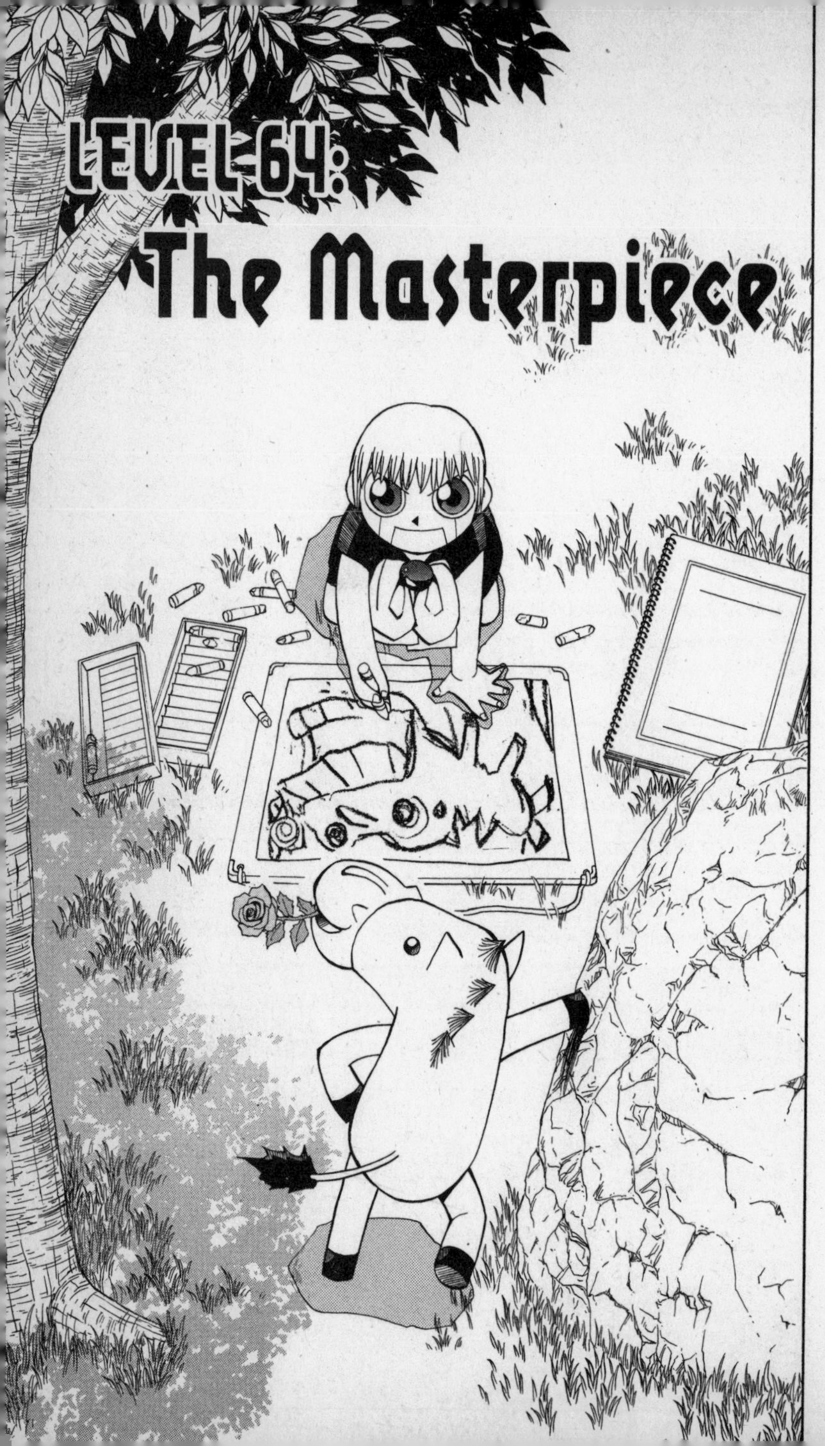
LEVEL 64:
The Masterpiece

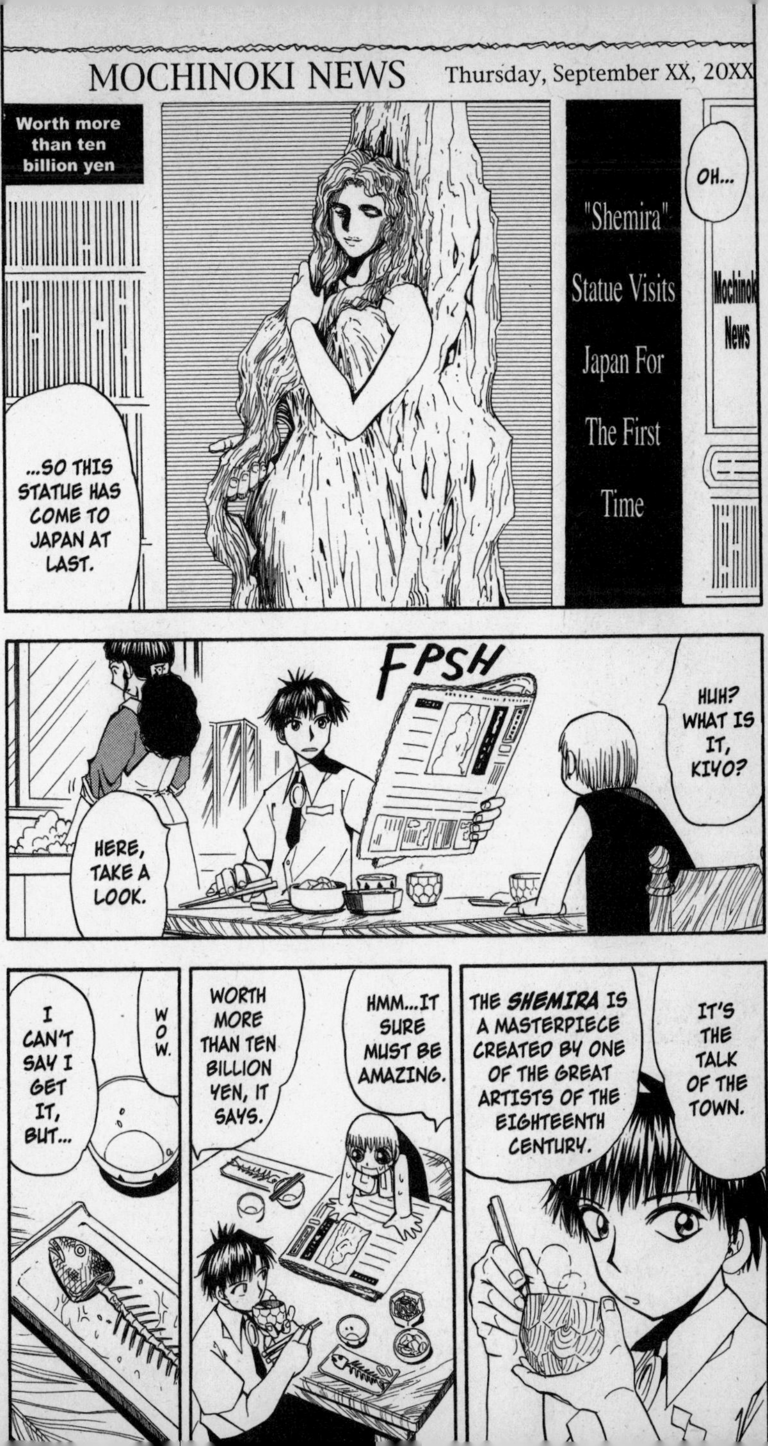
MOCHINOKI NEWS
Thursday, September XX, 20XX
OH...
Mochinoki News
"Shemira" Statue Visits Japan For The First Time
Worth more than ten billion yen
...SO THIS STATUE HAS COME TO JAPAN AT LAST.
HUH? WHAT IS IT, KIYO?
FPSH
HERE, TAKE A LOOK.
IT'S THE TALK OF THE TOWN.
THE SHEMIRA IS A MASTERPIECE CREATED BY ONE OF THE GREAT ARTISTS OF THE EIGHTEENTH CENTURY.
HMM...IT SURE MUST BE AMAZING.
WORTH MORE THAN TEN BILLION YEN, IT SAYS.
WOW.
I CAN'T SAY I GET IT, BUT...

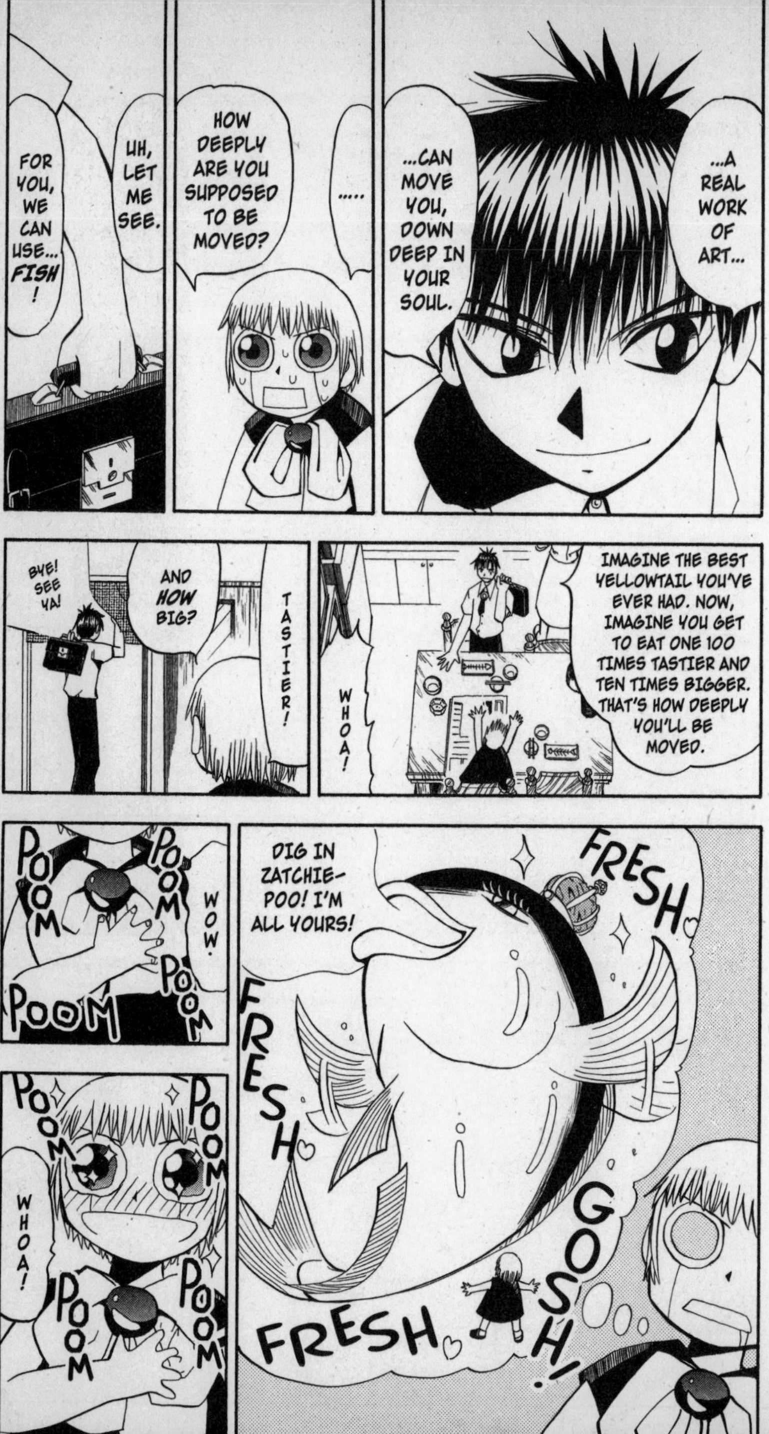
...A REAL WORK OF ART...
...CAN MOVE YOU, DOWN DEEP IN YOUR SOUL.
.....
HOW DEEPLY ARE YOU SUPPOSED TO BE MOVED?
UH, LET ME SEE.
FOR YOU, WE CAN USE... FISH!
IMAGINE THE BEST YELLOWTAIL YOU'VE EVER HAD. NOW, IMAGINE YOU GET TO EAT ONE 100 TIMES TASTIER AND TEN TIMES BIGGER. THAT'S HOW DEEPLY YOU'LL BE MOVED.
WHOA!
TASTIER!
AND HOW BIG?
BYE! SEE YA!
FRESH
DIG IN ZATCHIE-POO! I'M ALL YOURS!
FRESH
FRESH
GOSH!
POOM
POOM
WOW.
POOM
POOM
POOM
POOM
POOM
WHOA!
POOM
POOM

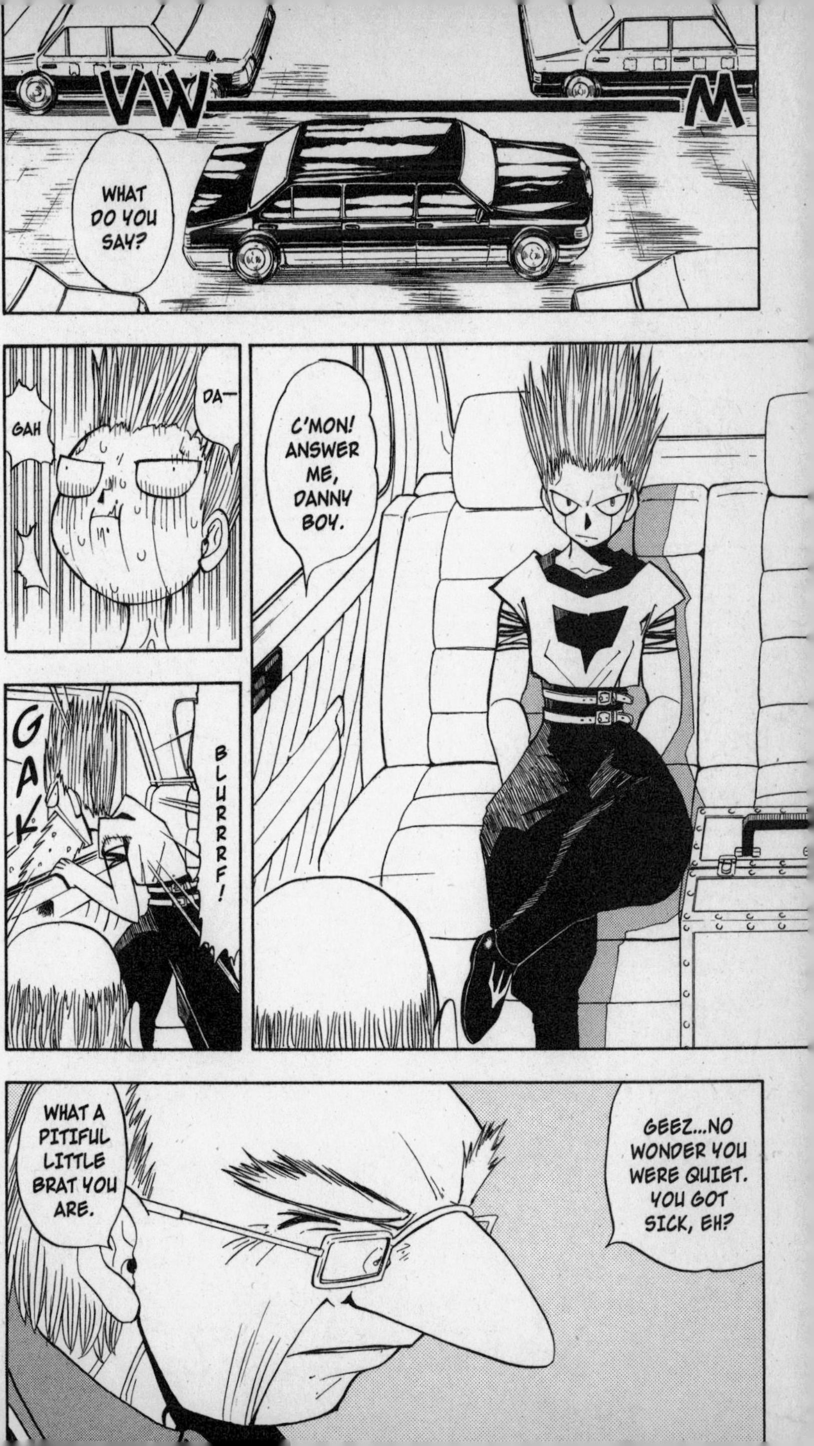
VWM
WHAT DO YOU SAY?
C'MON! ANSWER ME, DANNY BOY.
DA—
GAH
GAK
BLURRRF!
GEEZ...NO WONDER YOU WERE QUIET. YOU GOT SICK, EH?
WHAT A PITIFUL LITTLE BRAT YOU ARE.

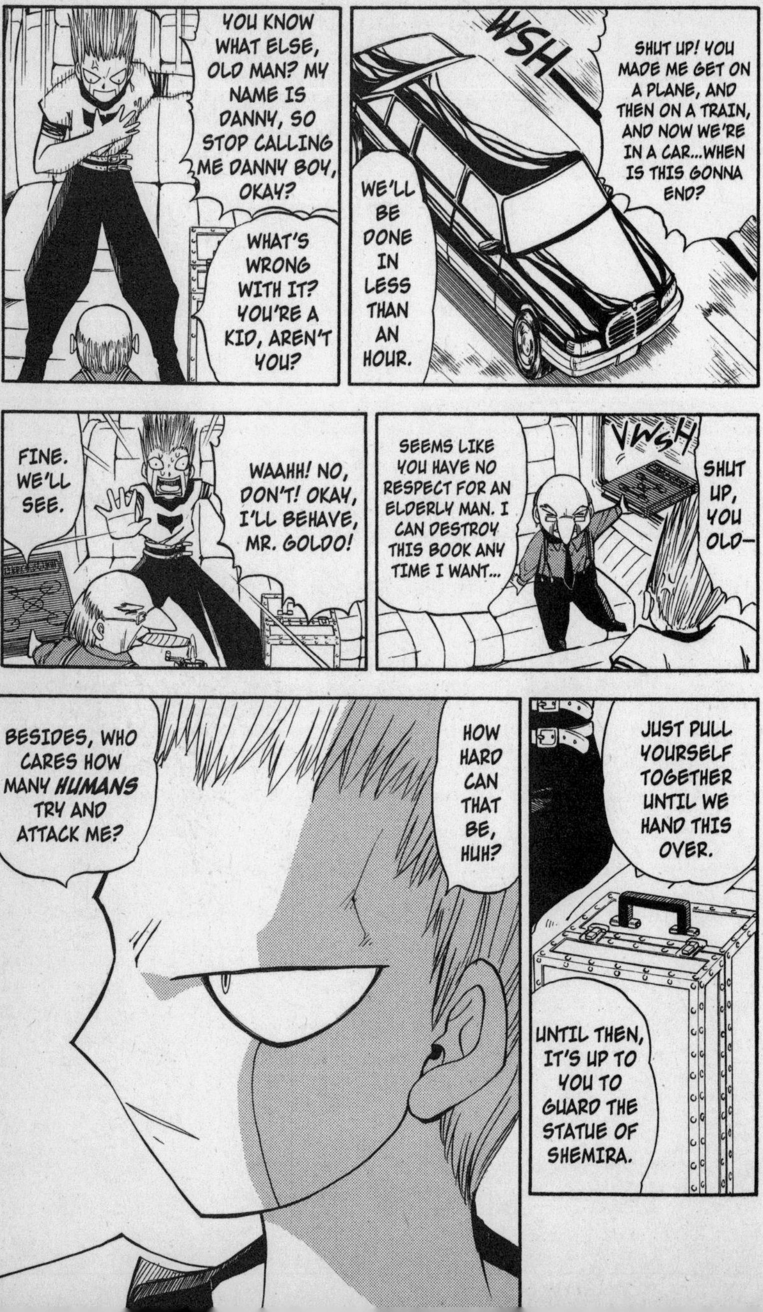
WSH
SHUT UP! YOU MADE ME GET ON A PLANE, AND THEN ON A TRAIN, AND NOW WE'RE IN A CAR...WHEN IS THIS GONNA END?
WE'LL BE DONE IN LESS THAN AN HOUR.
YOU KNOW WHAT ELSE, OLD MAN? MY NAME IS DANNY, SO STOP CALLING ME DANNY BOY, OKAY?
WHAT'S WRONG WITH IT? YOU'RE A KID, AREN'T YOU?
VWSH
SHUT UP, YOU OLD—
SEEMS LIKE YOU HAVE NO RESPECT FOR AN ELDERLY MAN. I CAN DESTROY THIS BOOK ANY TIME I WANT...
WAAHH! NO, DON'T! OKAY, I'LL BEHAVE, MR. GOLDO!
FINE. WE'LL SEE.
JUST PULL YOURSELF TOGETHER UNTIL WE HAND THIS OVER.
UNTIL THEN, IT'S UP TO YOU TO GUARD THE STATUE OF SHEMIRA.
HOW HARD CAN THAT BE, HUH?
BESIDES, WHO CARES HOW MANY ***HUMANS*** TRY AND ATTACK ME?

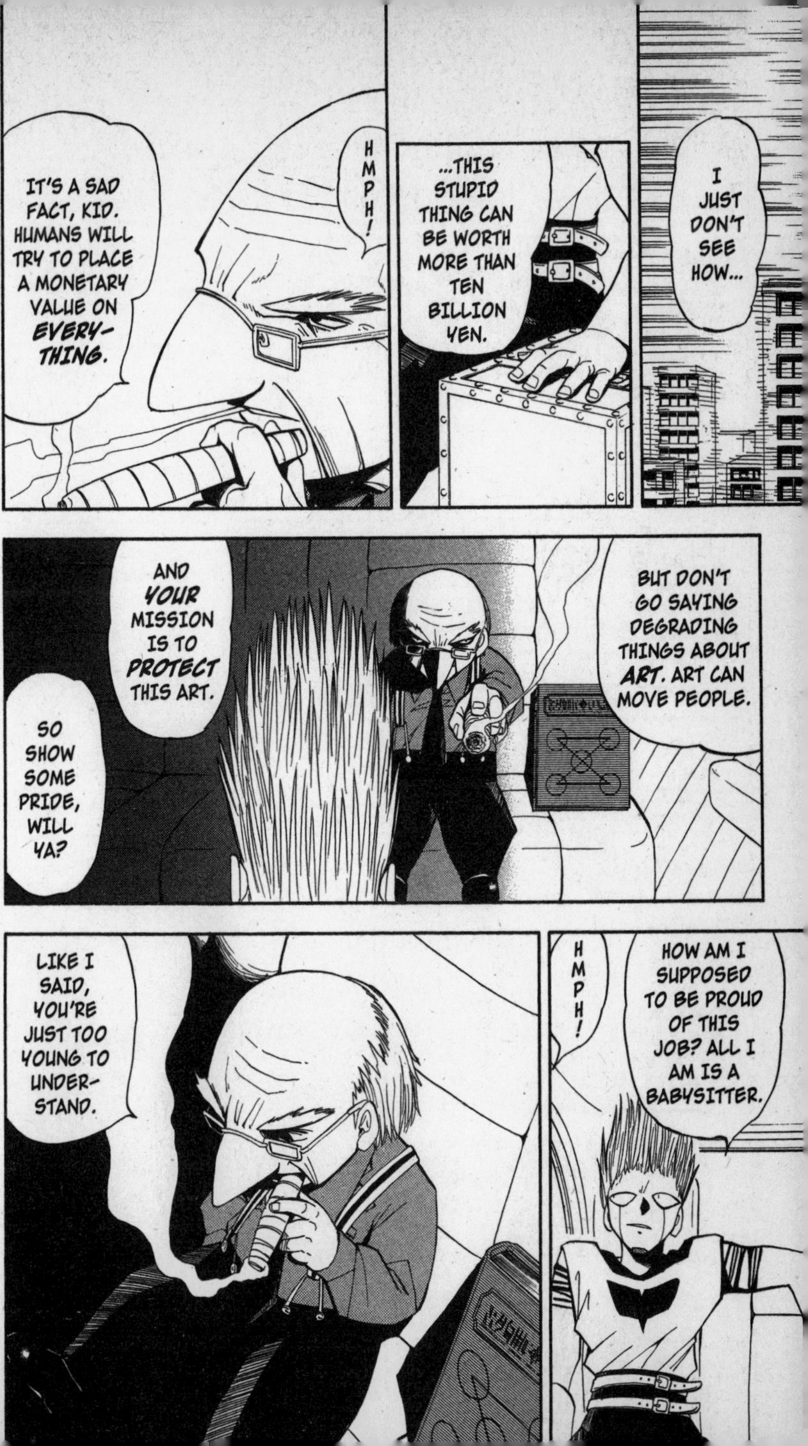
I JUST DON'T SEE HOW...
...THIS STUPID THING CAN BE WORTH MORE THAN TEN BILLION YEN.
HMPH!
IT'S A SAD FACT, KID. HUMANS WILL TRY TO PLACE A MONETARY VALUE ON *EVERY-THING*.
BUT DON'T GO SAYING DEGRADING THINGS ABOUT *ART*. ART CAN MOVE PEOPLE.
AND *YOUR* MISSION IS TO *PROTECT* THIS ART.
SO SHOW SOME PRIDE, WILL YA?
HOW AM I SUPPOSED TO BE PROUD OF THIS JOB? ALL I AM IS A BABYSITTER.
HMPH!
LIKE I SAID, YOU'RE JUST TOO YOUNG TO UNDER-STAND.

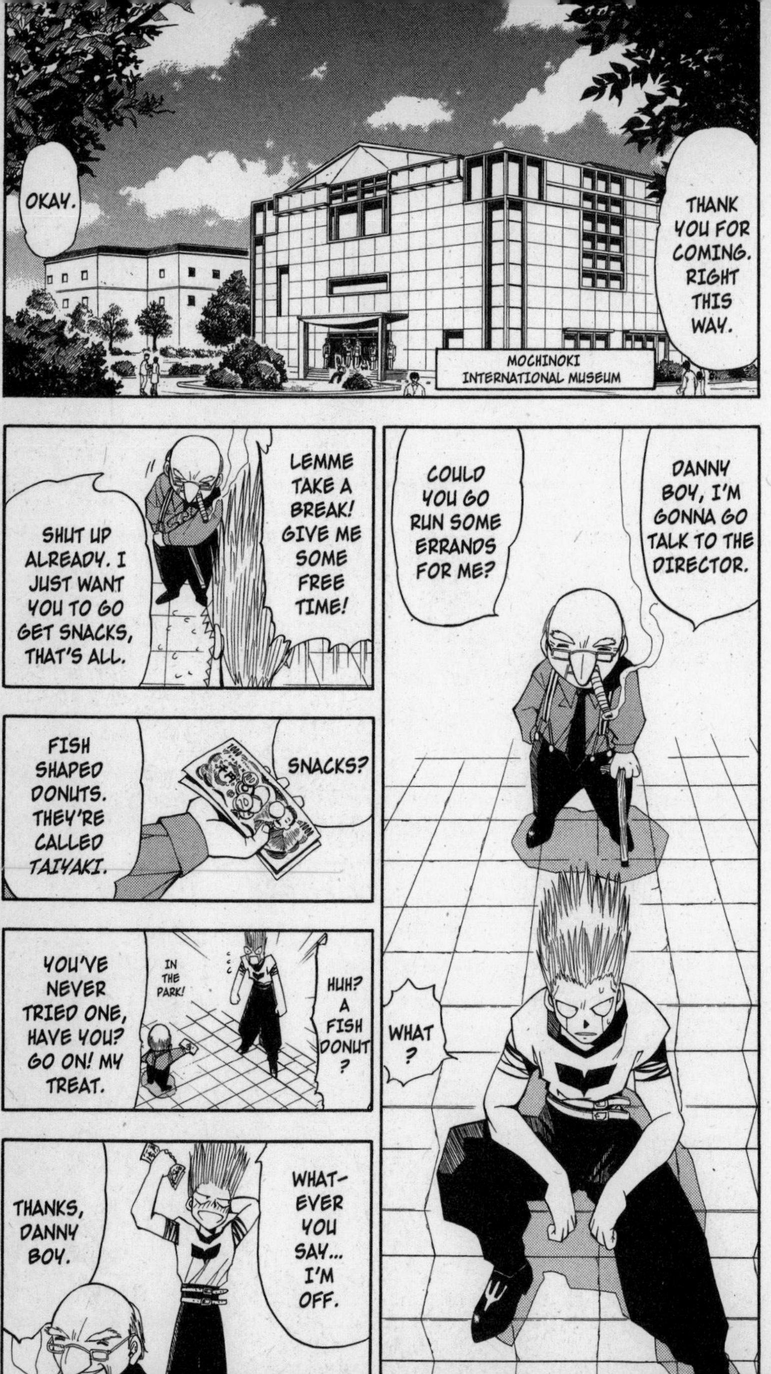
THANK YOU FOR COMING. RIGHT THIS WAY.
OKAY.
MOCHINOKI INTERNATIONAL MUSEUM
DANNY BOY, I'M GONNA GO TALK TO THE DIRECTOR.
COULD YOU GO RUN SOME ERRANDS FOR ME?
WHAT?
LEMME TAKE A BREAK! GIVE ME SOME FREE TIME!
SHUT UP ALREADY. I JUST WANT YOU TO GO GET SNACKS, THAT'S ALL.
SNACKS?
FISH SHAPED DONUTS. THEY'RE CALLED *TAIYAKI*.
HUH? A FISH DONUT?
IN THE PARK!
YOU'VE NEVER TRIED ONE, HAVE YOU? GO ON! MY TREAT.
WHAT-EVER YOU SAY... I'M OFF.
THANKS, DANNY BOY.

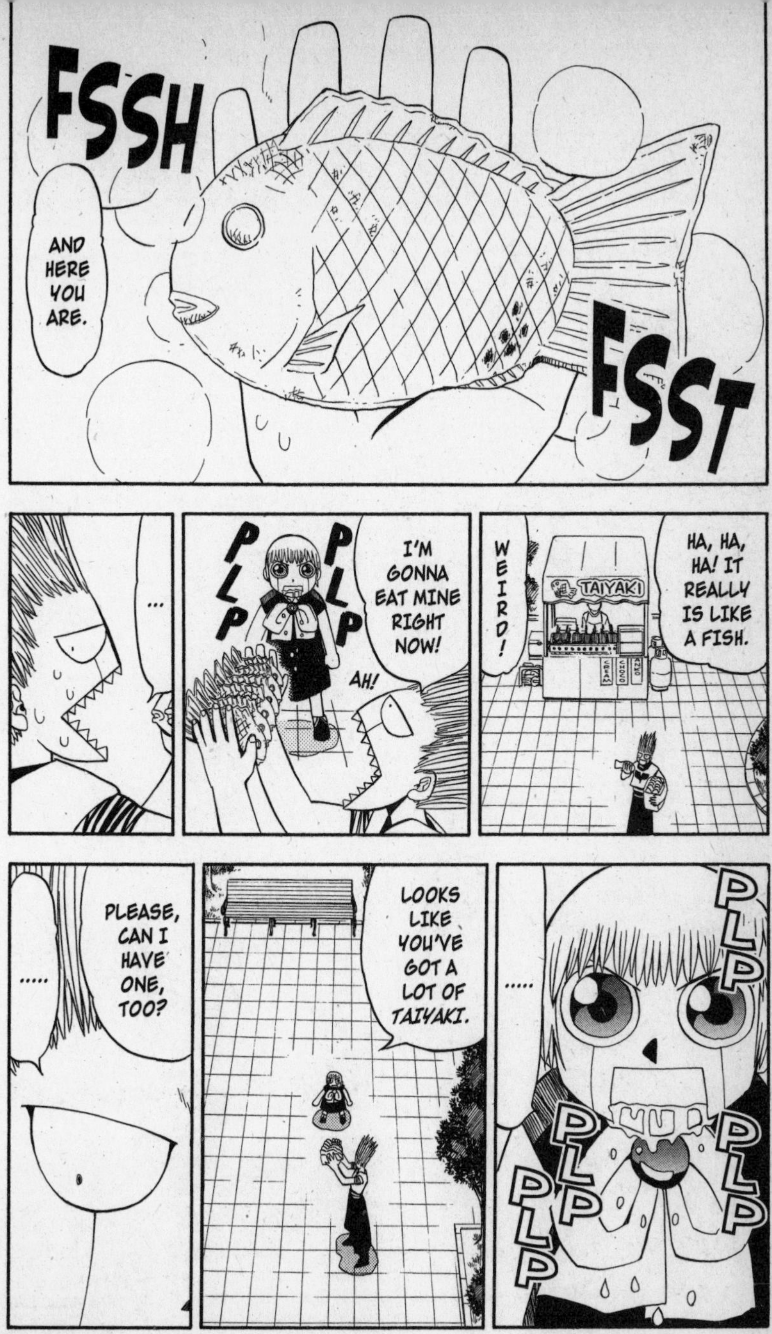
FSST
AND HERE YOU ARE.
FSSH
HA, HA, HA! IT REALLY IS LIKE A FISH.
TAIYAKI
CREAM
CHOCO
ANKO
WEIRD!
I'M GONNA EAT MINE RIGHT NOW!
PLP PLP
AH!
...
.....
PLP PLP PLP PLP PLP
LOOKS LIKE YOU'VE GOT A LOT OF TAIYAKI.
PLEASE, CAN I HAVE ONE, TOO?
.....

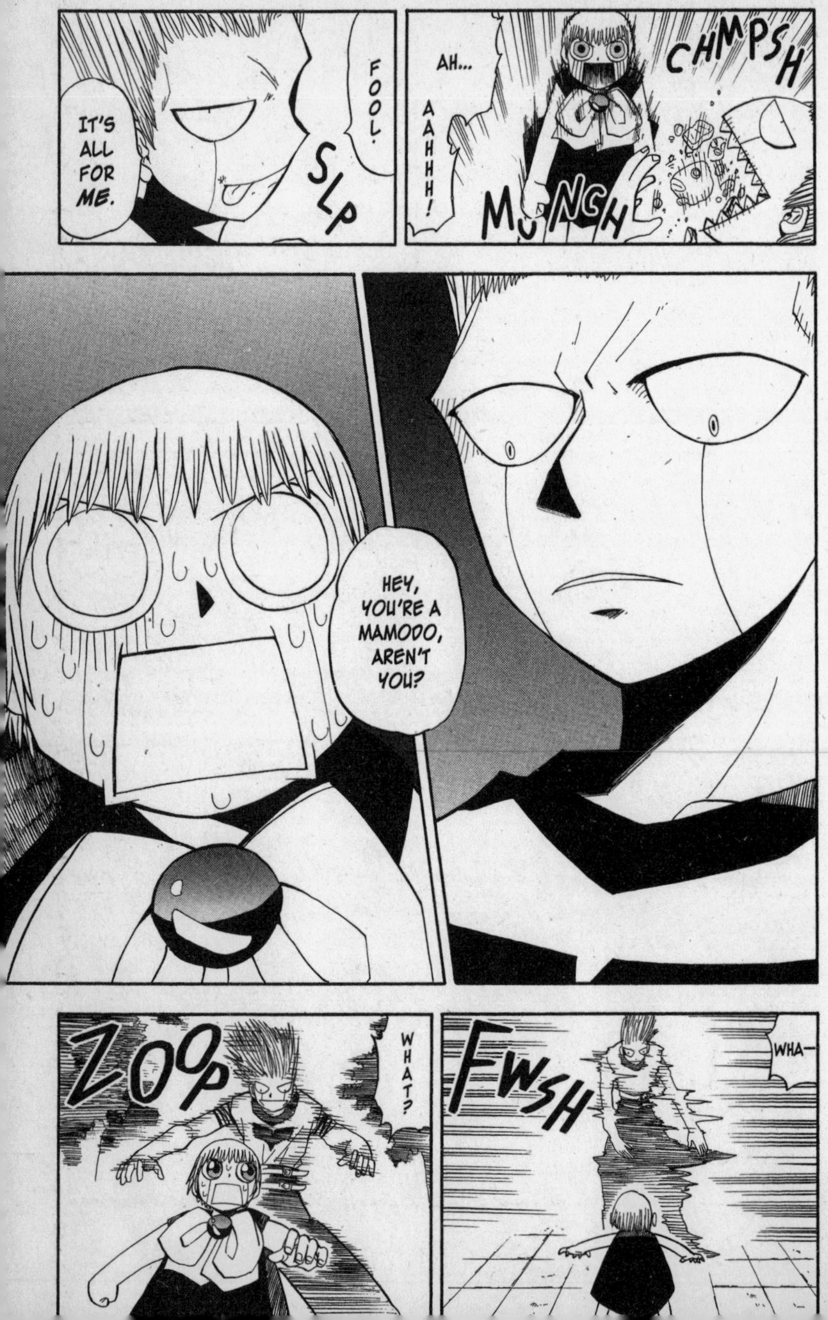
CHMPSH
AH...
AAHHHH!
MUNCH
FOOL.
SLP
IT'S ALL FOR ME.
HEY, YOU'RE A MAMODO, AREN'T YOU?
WHA—
FWSH
WHAT?
ZOOP

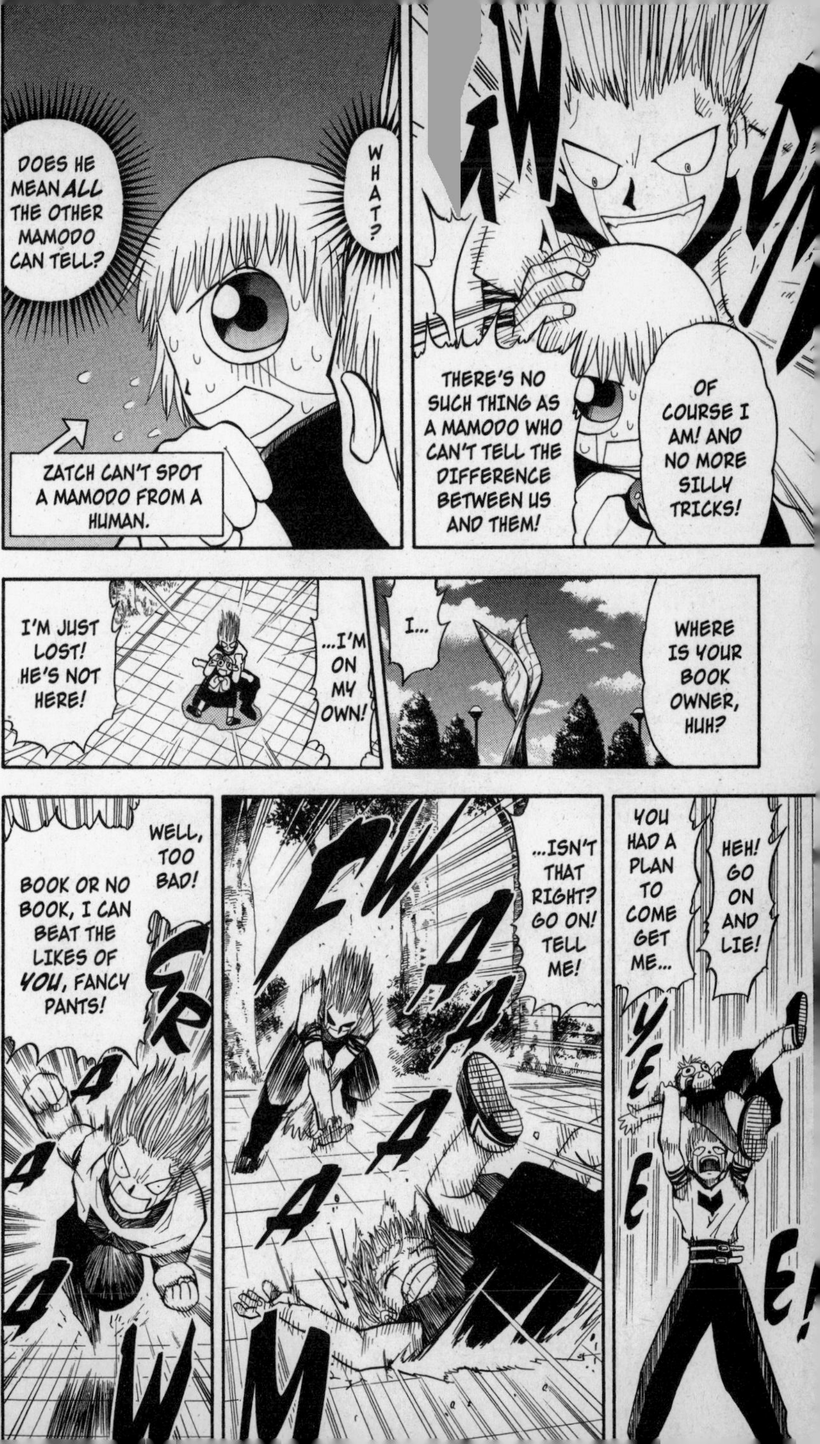
OF COURSE I AM! AND NO MORE SILLY TRICKS!
THERE'S NO SUCH THING AS A MAMODO WHO CAN'T TELL THE DIFFERENCE BETWEEN US AND THEM!
WHAT?
DOES HE MEAN ALL THE OTHER MAMODO CAN TELL?
ZATCH CAN'T SPOT A MAMODO FROM A HUMAN.
WHERE IS YOUR BOOK OWNER, HUH?
I...
...I'M ON MY OWN!
I'M JUST LOST! HE'S NOT HERE!
HEH! GO ON AND LIE!
YOU HAD A PLAN TO COME GET ME...
YEEE!
...ISN'T THAT RIGHT? GO ON! TELL ME!
WELL, TOO BAD!
BOOK OR NO BOOK, I CAN BEAT THE LIKES OF YOU, FANCY PANTS!

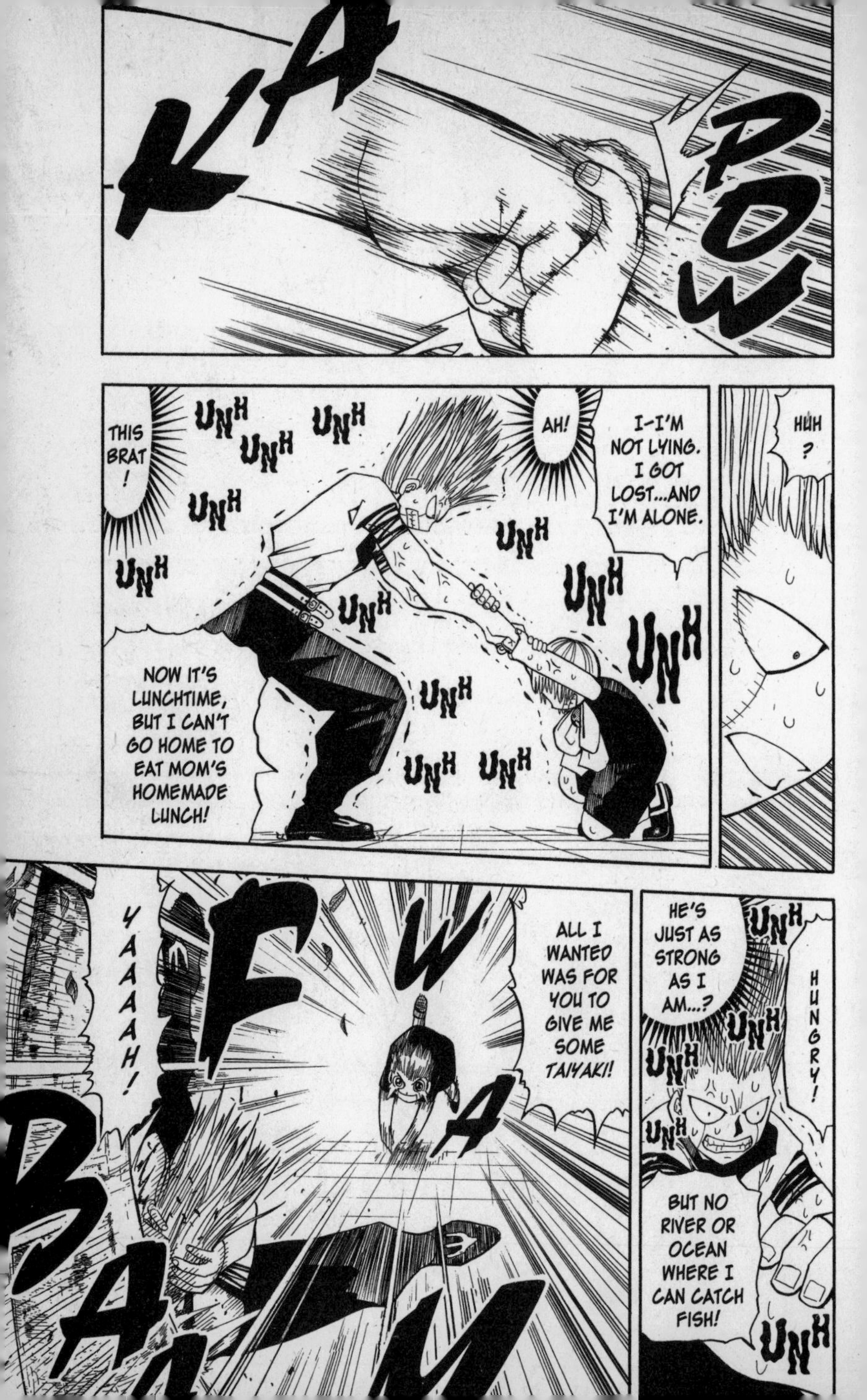
KA
POW
HUH?
AH!
I-I'M NOT LYING. I GOT LOST...AND I'M ALONE.
UNH UNH UNH UNH
THIS BRAT!
UNH UNH UNH UNH UNH
NOW IT'S LUNCHTIME, BUT I CAN'T GO HOME TO EAT MOM'S HOMEMADE LUNCH!
UNH UNH UNH
HE'S JUST AS STRONG AS I AM...?
HUNGRY!
UNH UNH UNH UNH
BUT NO RIVER OR OCEAN WHERE I CAN CATCH FISH!
UNH
ALL I WANTED WAS FOR YOU TO GIVE ME SOME *TAIYAKI*!
FWA
YAAAAAH!
BAM

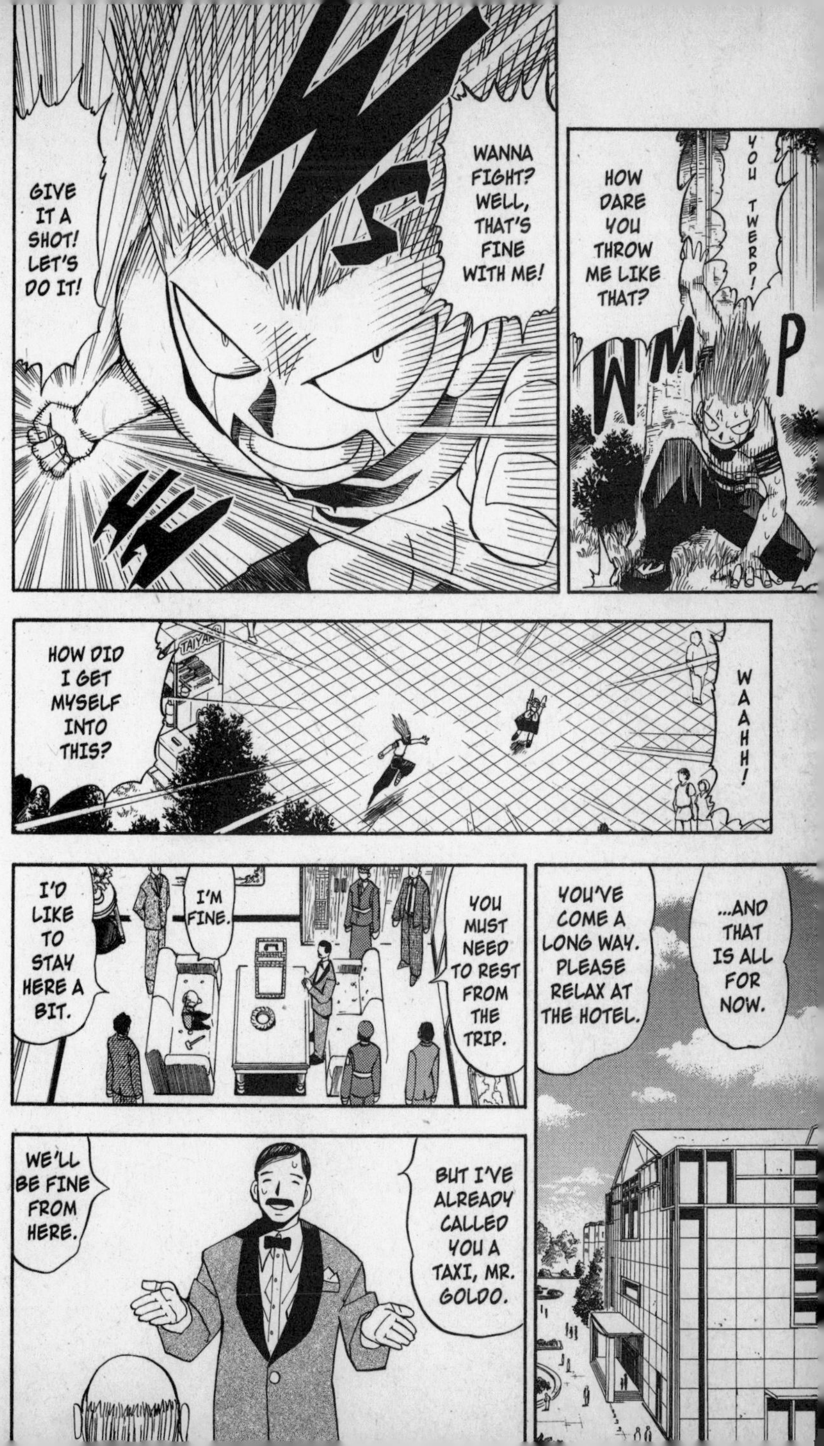
YOU TWERP!
HOW DARE YOU THROW ME LIKE THAT?
WMP
WANNA FIGHT? WELL, THAT'S FINE WITH ME!
GIVE IT A SHOT! LET'S DO IT!
WAAHH!
HOW DID I GET MYSELF INTO THIS?
...AND THAT IS ALL FOR NOW.
YOU'VE COME A LONG WAY. PLEASE RELAX AT THE HOTEL.
YOU MUST NEED TO REST FROM THE TRIP.
I'M FINE.
I'D LIKE TO STAY HERE A BIT.
BUT I'VE ALREADY CALLED YOU A TAXI, MR. GOLDO.
WE'LL BE FINE FROM HERE.

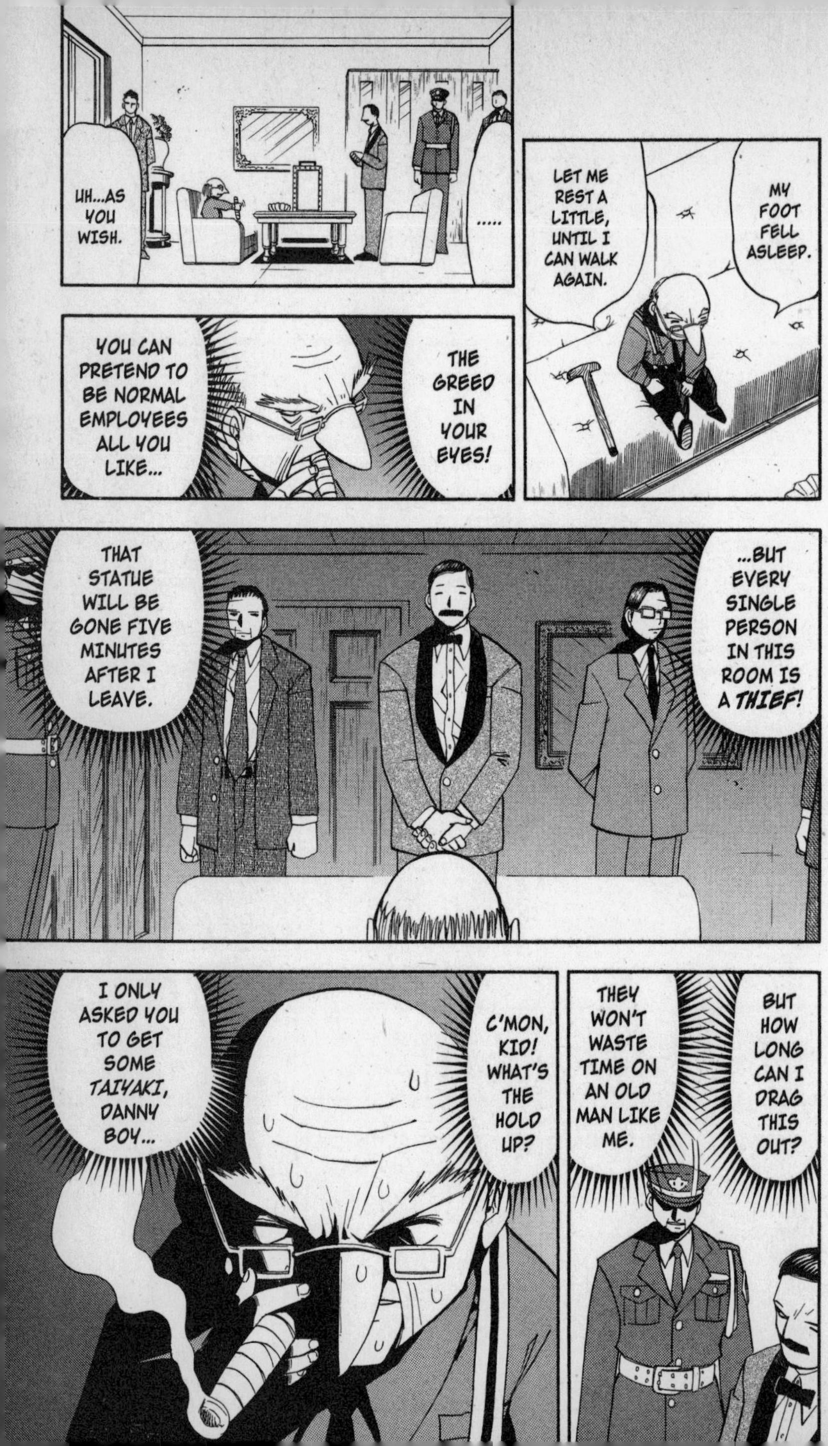
MY FOOT FELL ASLEEP.
LET ME REST A LITTLE, UNTIL I CAN WALK AGAIN.
.....
UH...AS YOU WISH.
THE GREED IN YOUR EYES!
YOU CAN PRETEND TO BE NORMAL EMPLOYEES ALL YOU LIKE...
...BUT EVERY SINGLE PERSON IN THIS ROOM IS A *THIEF*!
THAT STATUE WILL BE GONE FIVE MINUTES AFTER I LEAVE.
BUT HOW LONG CAN I DRAG THIS OUT?
THEY WON'T WASTE TIME ON AN OLD MAN LIKE ME.
C'MON, KID! WHAT'S THE HOLD UP?
I ONLY ASKED YOU TO GET SOME *TAIYAKI*, DANNY BOY...

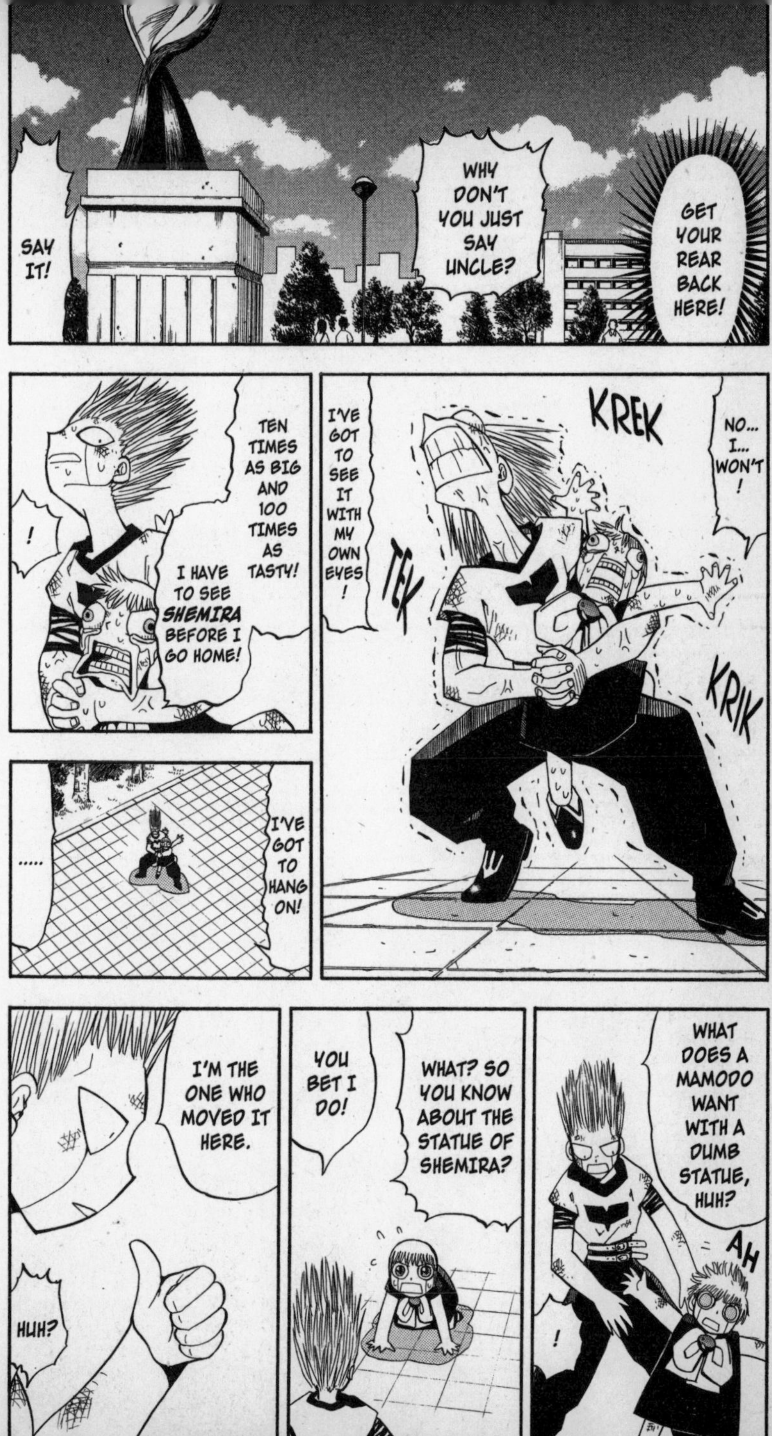
GET YOUR REAR BACK HERE!
WHY DON'T YOU JUST SAY UNCLE?
SAY IT!
NO... I... WON'T!
KREK
I'VE GOT TO SEE IT WITH MY OWN EYES!
TEK
KRIK
TEN TIMES AS BIG AND 100 TIMES AS TASTY!
I HAVE TO SEE **SHEMIRA** BEFORE I GO HOME!
!
I'VE GOT TO HANG ON!
.....
WHAT DOES A MAMODO WANT WITH A DUMB STATUE, HUH?
AH
!
WHAT? SO YOU KNOW ABOUT THE STATUE OF SHEMIRA?
YOU BET I DO!
I'M THE ONE WHO MOVED IT HERE.
HUH?

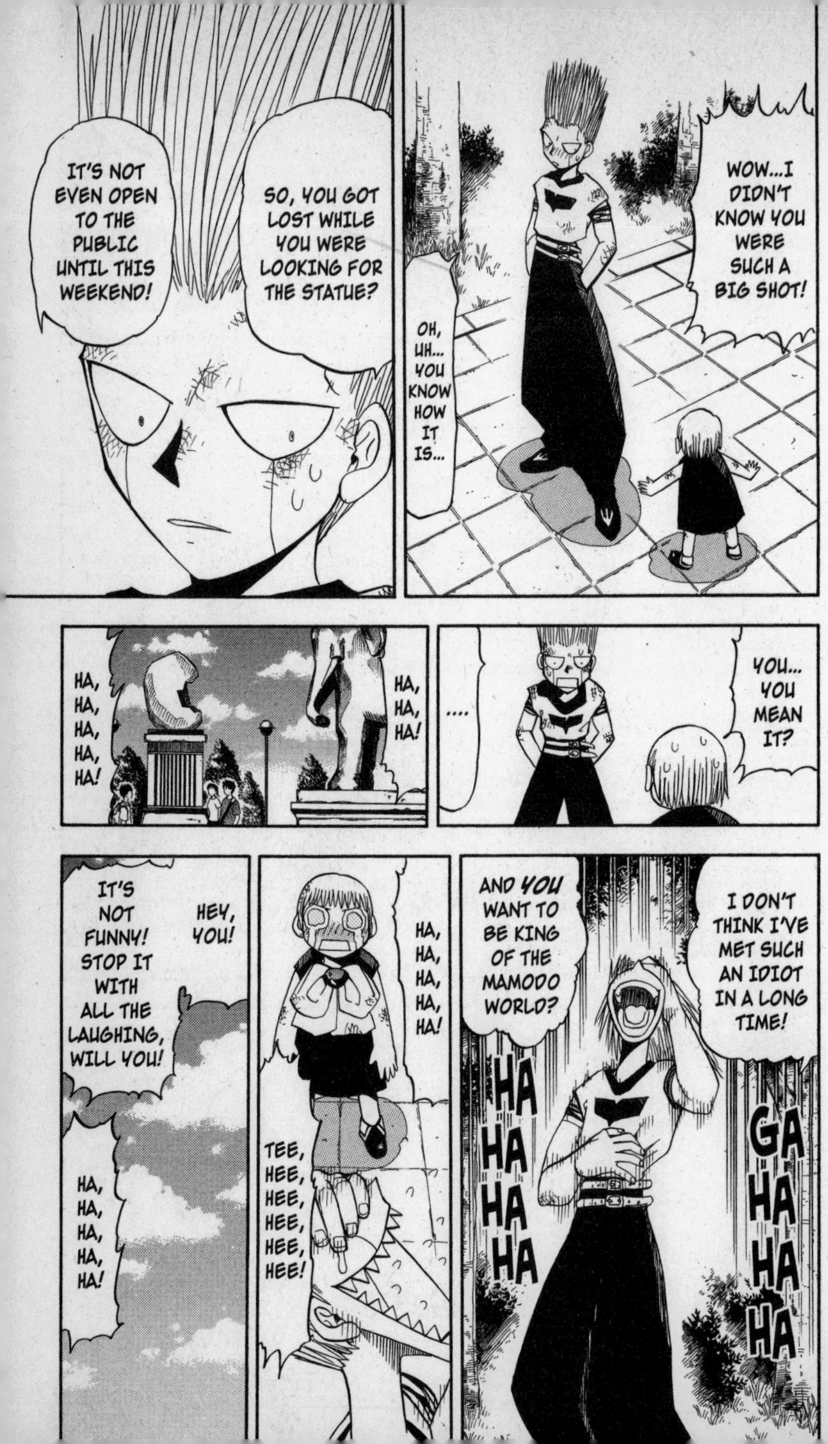
WOW...I DIDN'T KNOW YOU WERE SUCH A BIG SHOT!
OH, UH... YOU KNOW HOW IT IS...
SO, YOU GOT LOST WHILE YOU WERE LOOKING FOR THE STATUE?
IT'S NOT EVEN OPEN TO THE PUBLIC UNTIL THIS WEEKEND!
YOU... YOU MEAN IT?
....
HA, HA, HA!
HA, HA, HA, HA, HA!
I DON'T THINK I'VE MET SUCH AN IDIOT IN A LONG TIME!
AND YOU WANT TO BE KING OF THE MAMODO WORLD?
GA HA HA HA HA
HA HA HA HA HA
HA, HA, HA, HA, HA!
TEE, HEE, HEE, HEE, HEE, HEE!
HEY, YOU!
IT'S NOT FUNNY! STOP IT WITH ALL THE LAUGHING, WILL YOU!
HA, HA, HA, HA, HA!

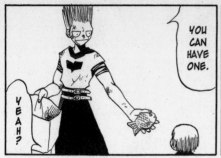

TCH TCH TCH
OKAY, OKAY. I'M SORRY ABOUT THAT.
TCH
TCH TCH TCH
YOU CAN HAVE ONE.
YEAH?
ARE YOU SURE?
YEAH, THEY'RE NOT MINE ANYWAY.
SINCE YOU'RE REALLY NOT WITH YOUR BOOK OWNER, AND...
...MINE IS AT THE MUSEUM NOW, I GUESS IT'S NOT A GOOD TIME TO FIGHT ANYHOW.
WHO ARE YOU, EH?
MY NAME IS ZATCH BELL! AND YOU?
ZATCH, EH? I'M DANNY BOY. ER, WELL...
...JUST DANNY. FORGET THE BOY PART.
MNCH
MNCH
OKAY, YOU'RE DANNY. THANK YOU!
OKAY, ZATCH. COME WITH ME, AND I'LL SHOW YOU THE STATUE OF SHEMIRA.

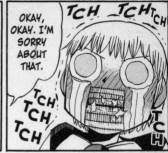

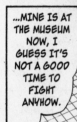

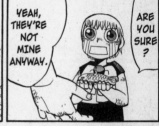

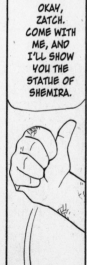

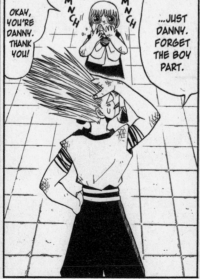

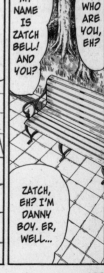

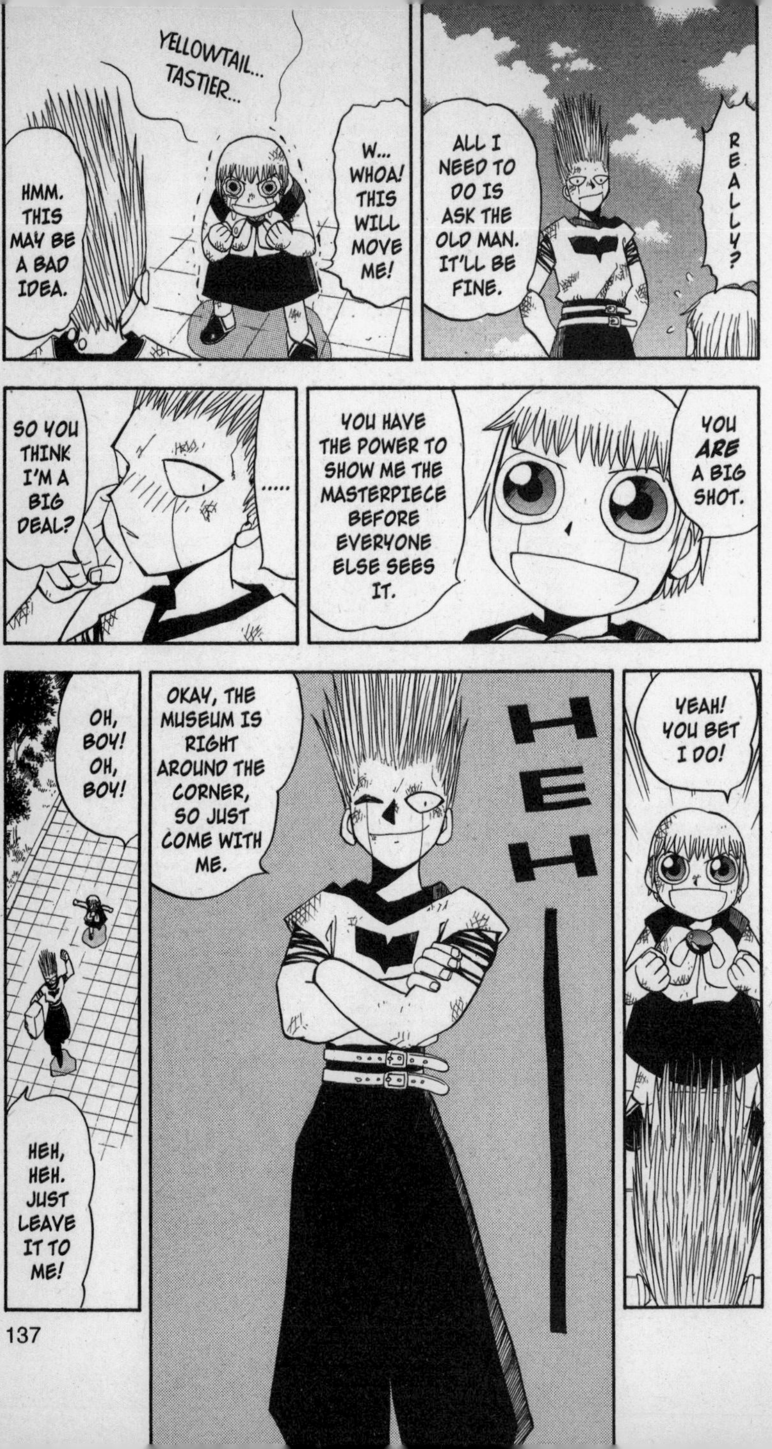
REALLY?
ALL I NEED TO DO IS ASK THE OLD MAN. IT'LL BE FINE.
W... WHOA! THIS WILL MOVE ME!
YELLOWTAIL... TASTIER...
HMM. THIS MAY BE A BAD IDEA.
YOU *ARE* A BIG SHOT.
YOU HAVE THE POWER TO SHOW ME THE MASTERPIECE BEFORE EVERYONE ELSE SEES IT.
.....
SO YOU THINK I'M A BIG DEAL?
YEAH! YOU BET I DO!
HEH HEH—
OKAY, THE MUSEUM IS RIGHT AROUND THE CORNER, SO JUST COME WITH ME.
OH, BOY! OH, BOY!
HEH, HEH. JUST LEAVE IT TO ME!

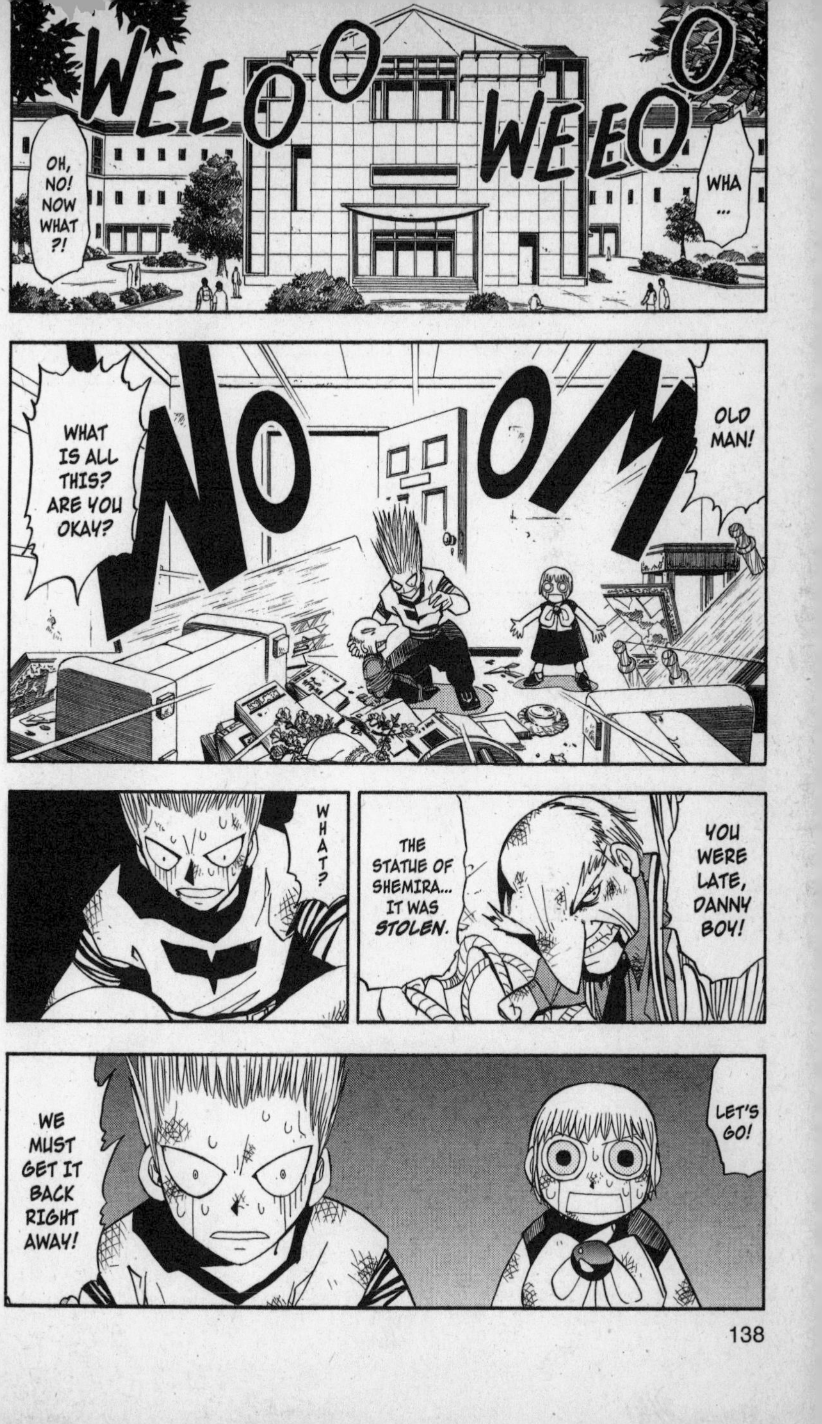
WEEOO
WEEOO
WHA...
OH, NO! NOW WHAT?!
OLD MAN!
NOOM
WHAT IS ALL THIS? ARE YOU OKAY?
YOU WERE LATE, DANNY BOY!
THE STATUE OF SHEMIRA... IT WAS STOLEN.
WHAT?
LET'S GO!
WE MUST GET IT BACK RIGHT AWAY!

LEVEL 65: Danny's Power

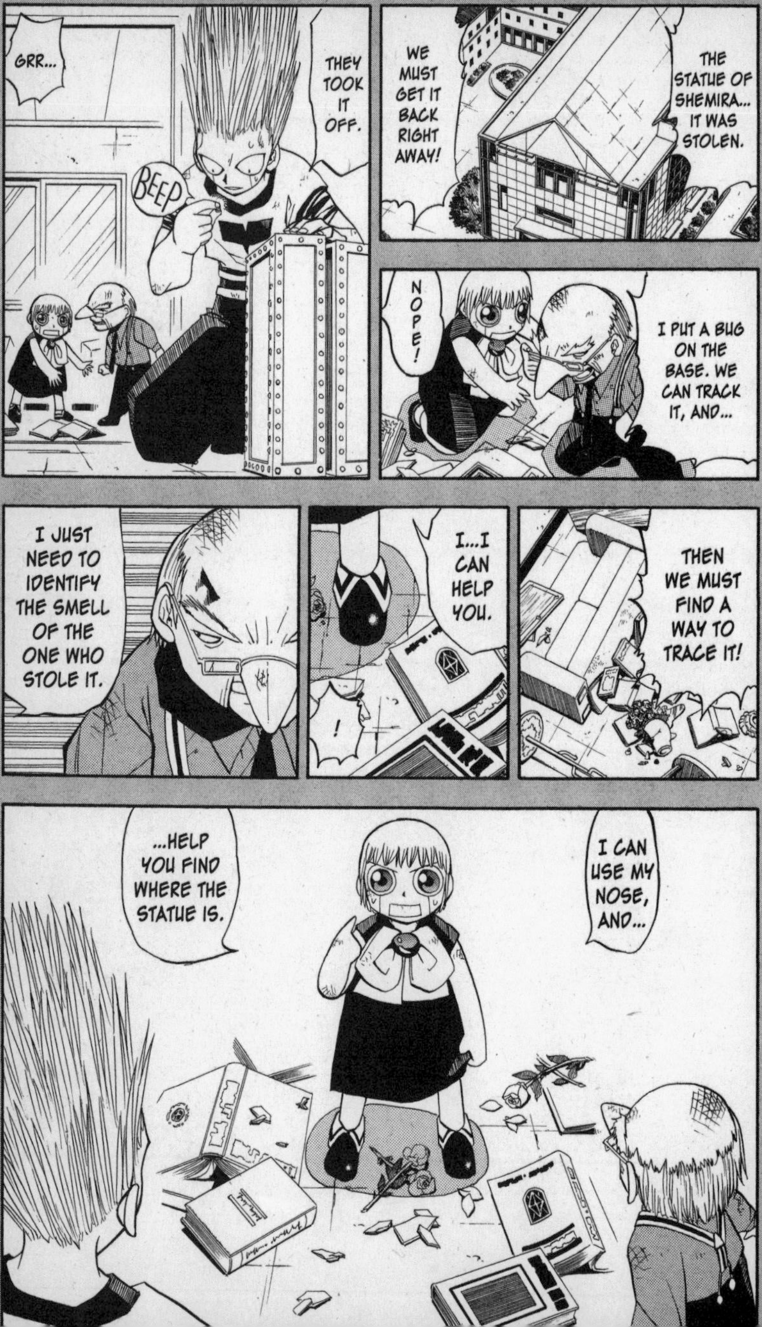
THE STATUE OF SHEMIRA... IT WAS STOLEN.
WE MUST GET IT BACK RIGHT AWAY!
I PUT A BUG ON THE BASE. WE CAN TRACK IT, AND...
NOPE!
THEY TOOK IT OFF.
BEEP
GRR...
THEN WE MUST FIND A WAY TO TRACE IT!
I...I CAN HELP YOU.
!
I JUST NEED TO IDENTIFY THE SMELL OF THE ONE WHO STOLE IT.
I CAN USE MY NOSE, AND...
...HELP YOU FIND WHERE THE STATUE IS.

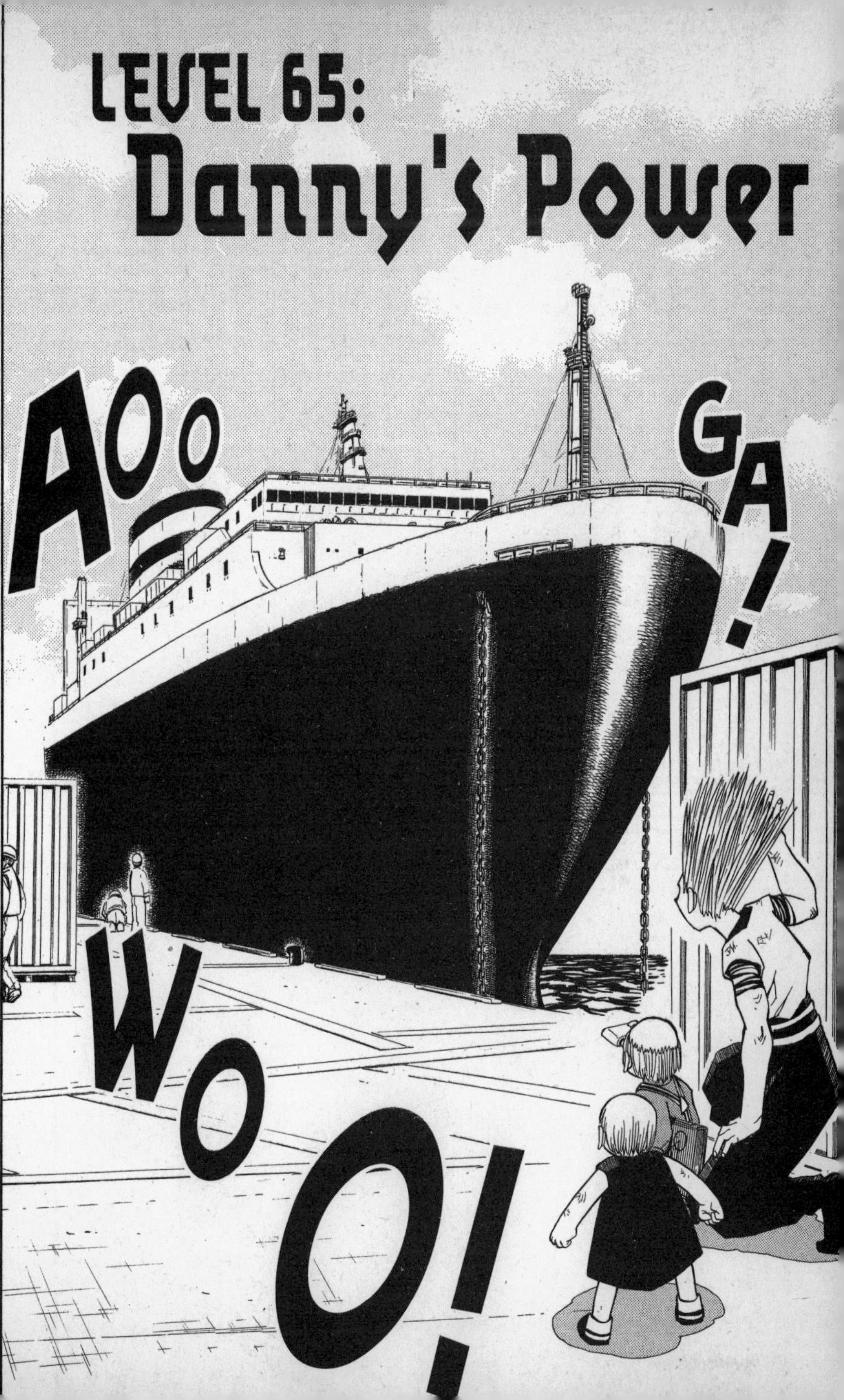
LEVEL 65:
Danny's Power
AOOGA!
WOO!

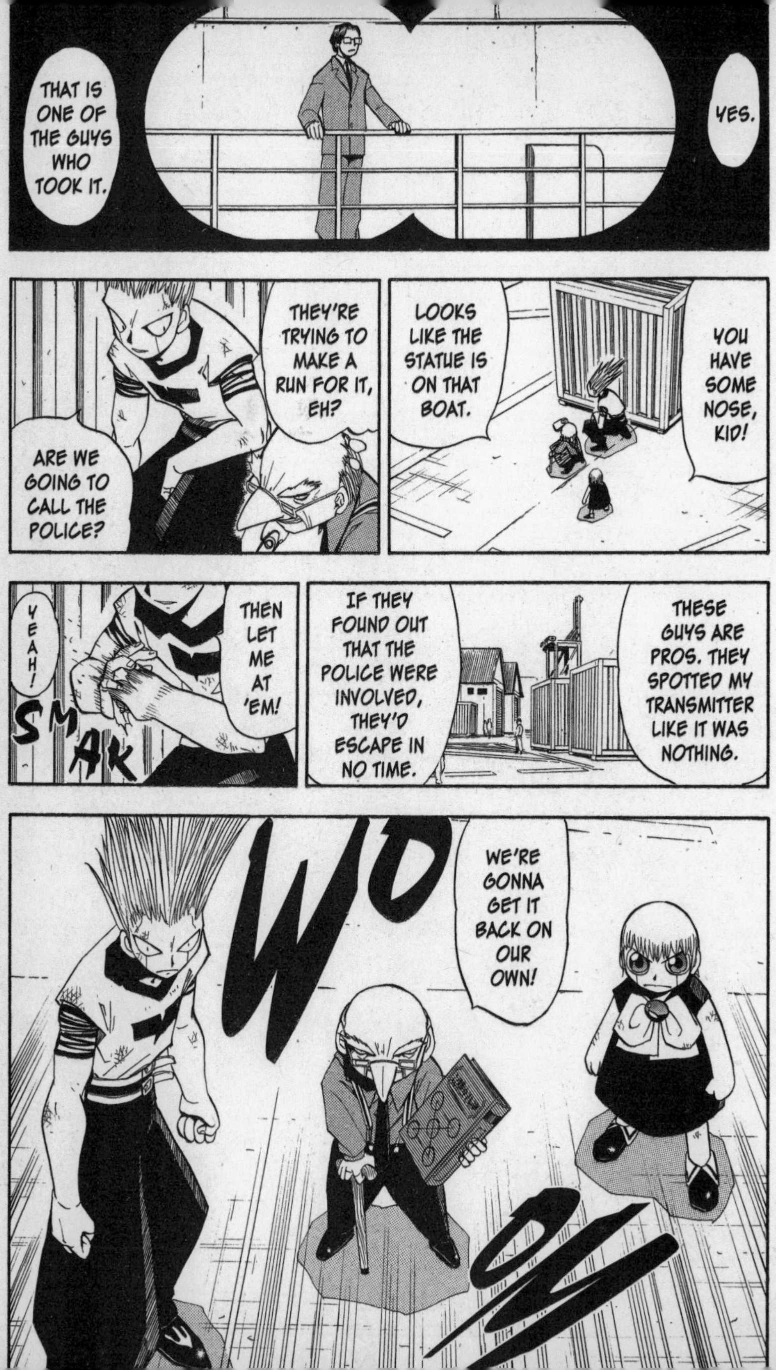
THAT IS ONE OF THE GUYS WHO TOOK IT.
YES.
YOU HAVE SOME NOSE, KID!
LOOKS LIKE THE STATUE IS ON THAT BOAT.
THEY'RE TRYING TO MAKE A RUN FOR IT, EH?
ARE WE GOING TO CALL THE POLICE?
THESE GUYS ARE PROS. THEY SPOTTED MY TRANSMITTER LIKE IT WAS NOTHING.
IF THEY FOUND OUT THAT THE POLICE WERE INVOLVED, THEY'D ESCAPE IN NO TIME.
THEN LET ME AT 'EM!
YEAH!
SMAK
WE'RE GONNA GET IT BACK ON OUR OWN!
WO

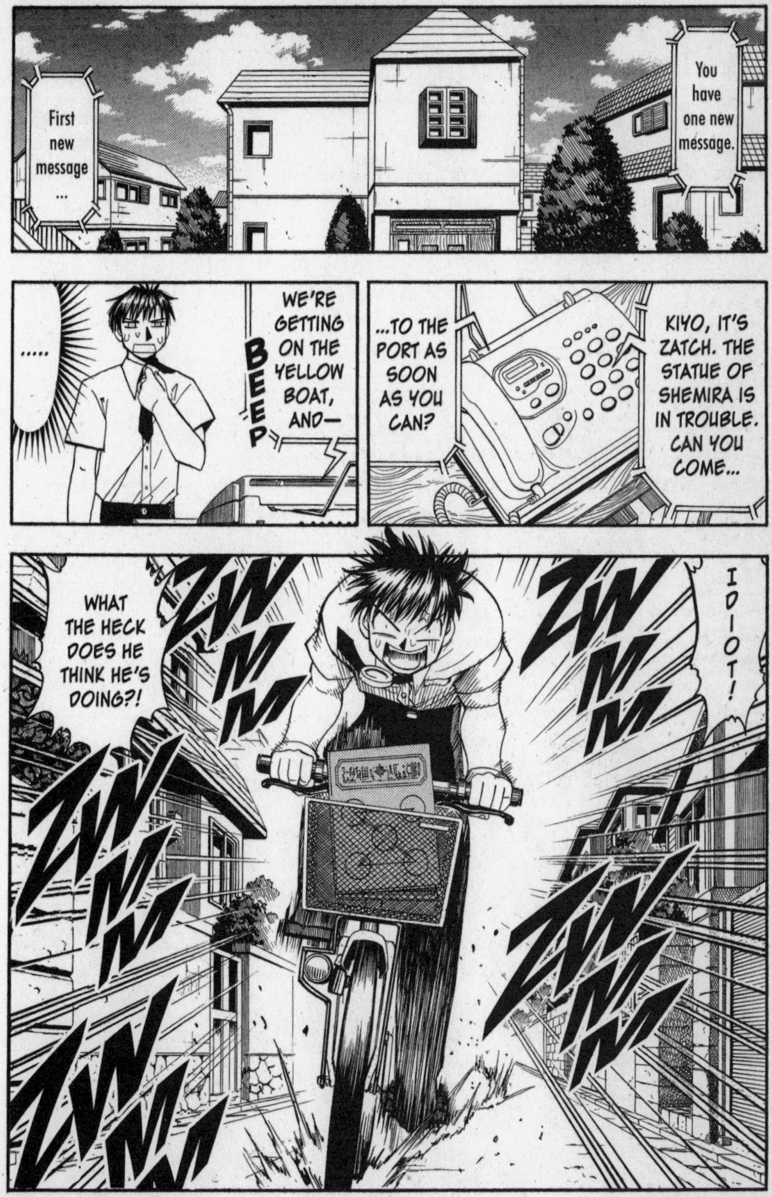
You have one new message.
First new message ...
KIYO, IT'S ZATCH. THE STATUE OF SHEMIRA IS IN TROUBLE. CAN YOU COME...
...TO THE PORT AS SOON AS YOU CAN?
WE'RE GETTING ON THE YELLOW BOAT, AND—
BEEP
.....
IDIOT!
WHAT THE HECK DOES HE THINK HE'S DOING?!

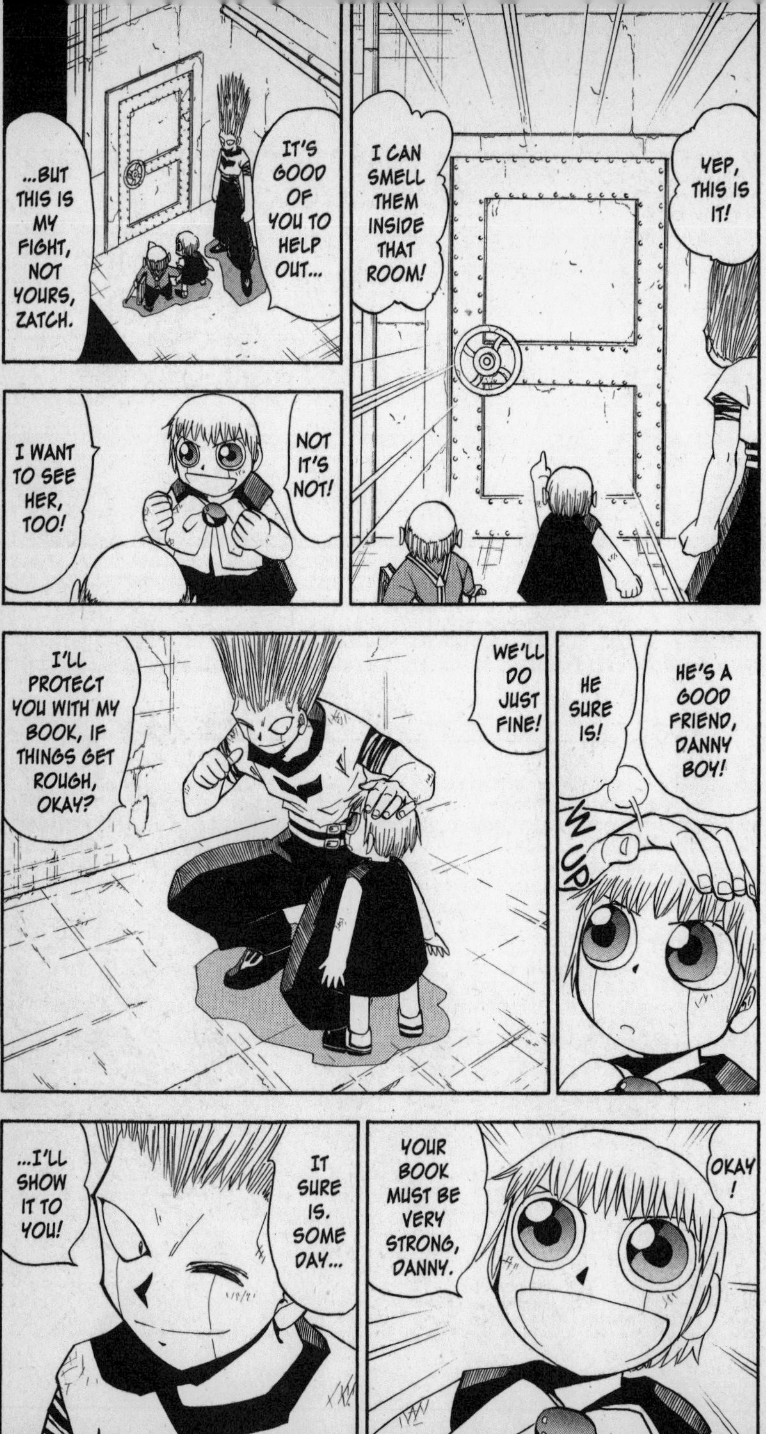
YEP, THIS IS IT!
I CAN SMELL THEM INSIDE THAT ROOM!
IT'S GOOD OF YOU TO HELP OUT...
...BUT THIS IS MY FIGHT, NOT YOURS, ZATCH.
NOT IT'S NOT!
I WANT TO SEE HER, TOO!
HE'S A GOOD FRIEND, DANNY BOY!
HE SURE IS!
WUP
WE'LL DO JUST FINE!
I'LL PROTECT YOU WITH MY BOOK, IF THINGS GET ROUGH, OKAY?
OKAY!
YOUR BOOK MUST BE VERY STRONG, DANNY.
IT SURE IS. SOME DAY...
...I'LL SHOW IT TO YOU!

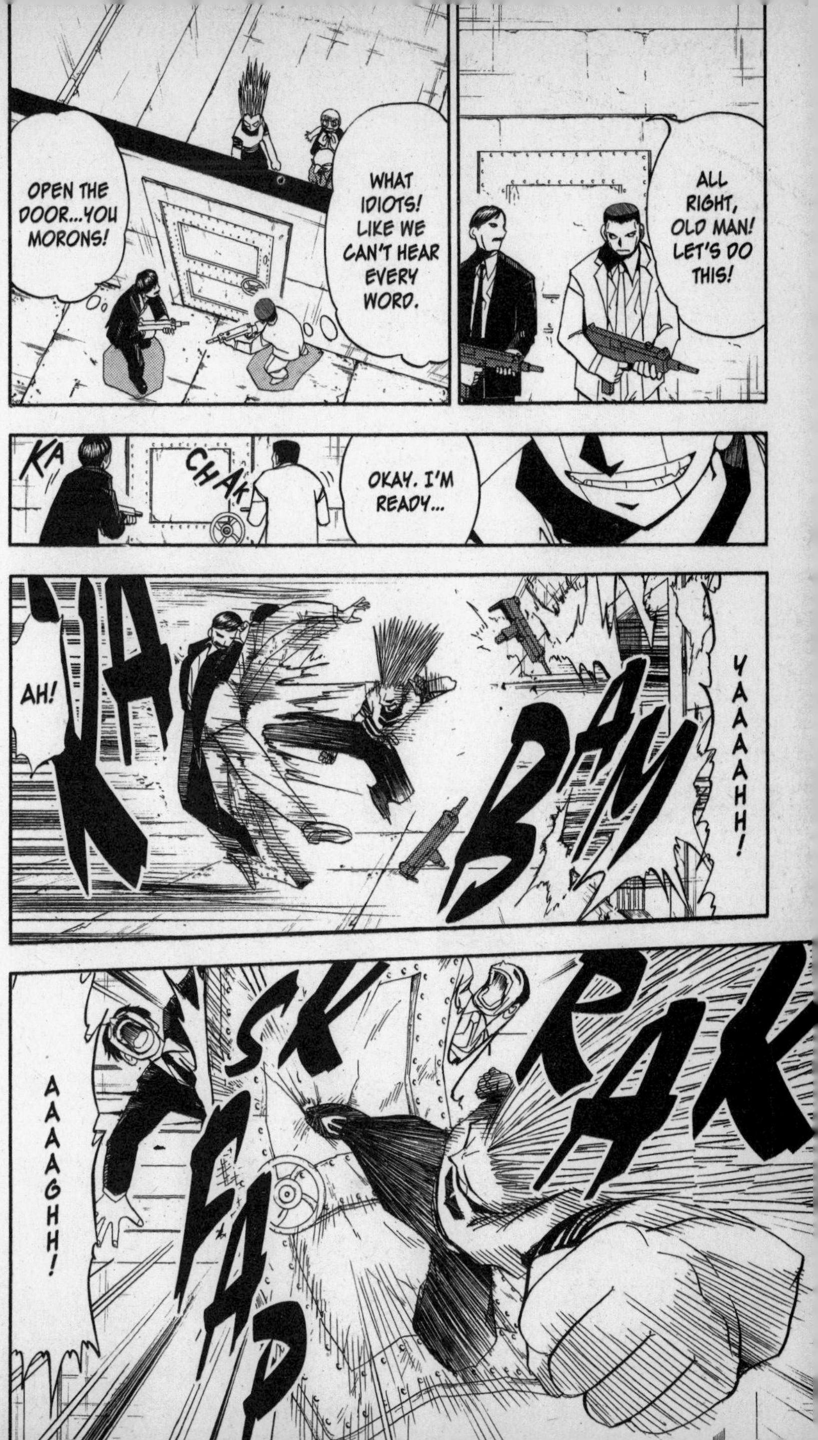
ALL RIGHT, OLD MAN! LET'S DO THIS!
WHAT IDIOTS! LIKE WE CAN'T HEAR EVERY WORD.
OPEN THE DOOR...YOU MORONS!
OKAY. I'M READY...
KA CHAK
YAAAAAHH!
BAM
AH!
RAK
SK
AAAAGHH!

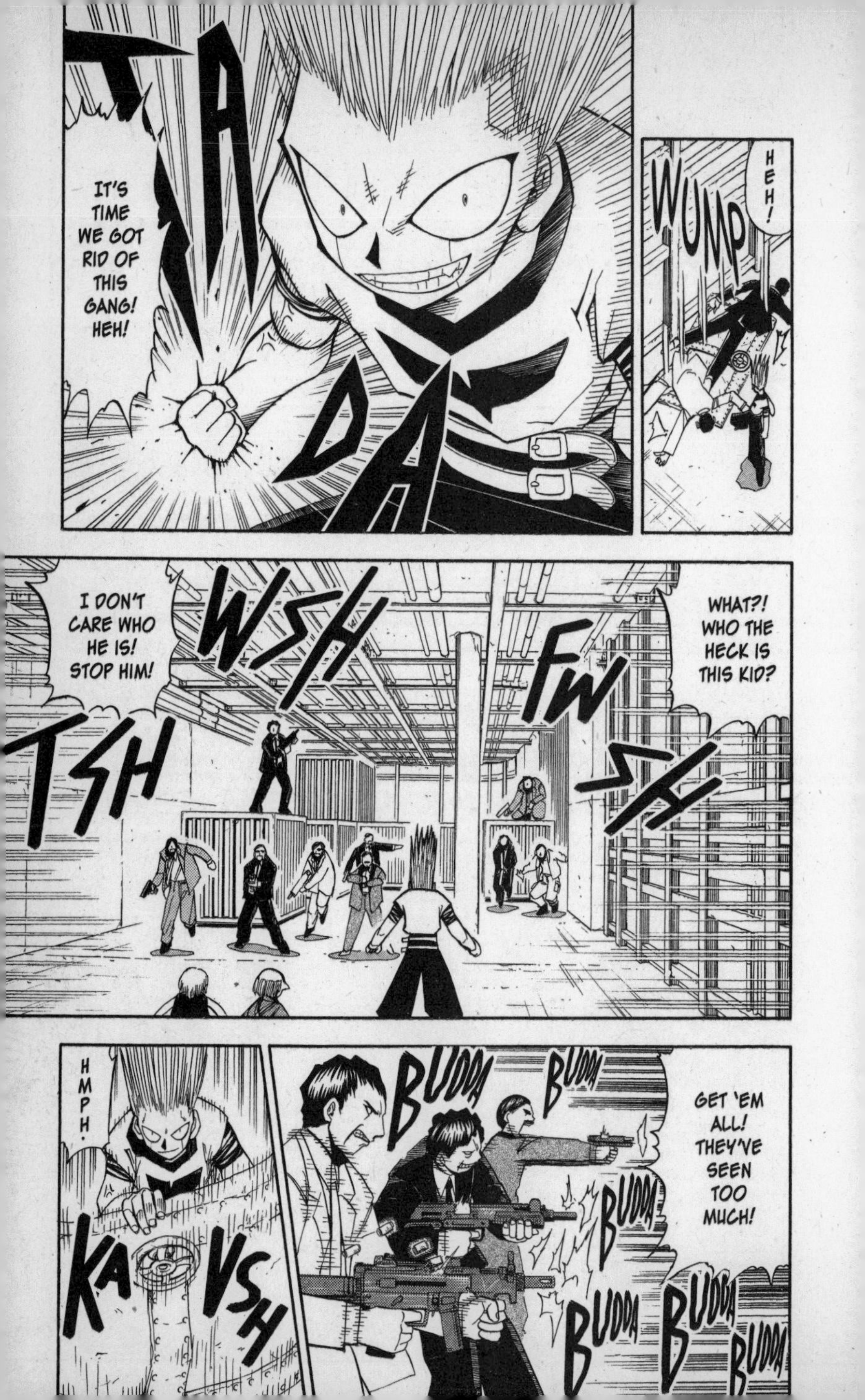

HEH!
WUMP
TA
IT'S TIME WE GOT RID OF THIS GANG! HEH!
DA
WHAT?! WHO THE HECK IS THIS KID?
FWSH
WSH
I DON'T CARE WHO HE IS! STOP HIM!
TSH
BUDDA
BUDDA
GET 'EM ALL! THEY'VE SEEN TOO MUCH!
BUDDA
BUDDA
BUDDA
BUDDA
HMPH.
KA
VSH

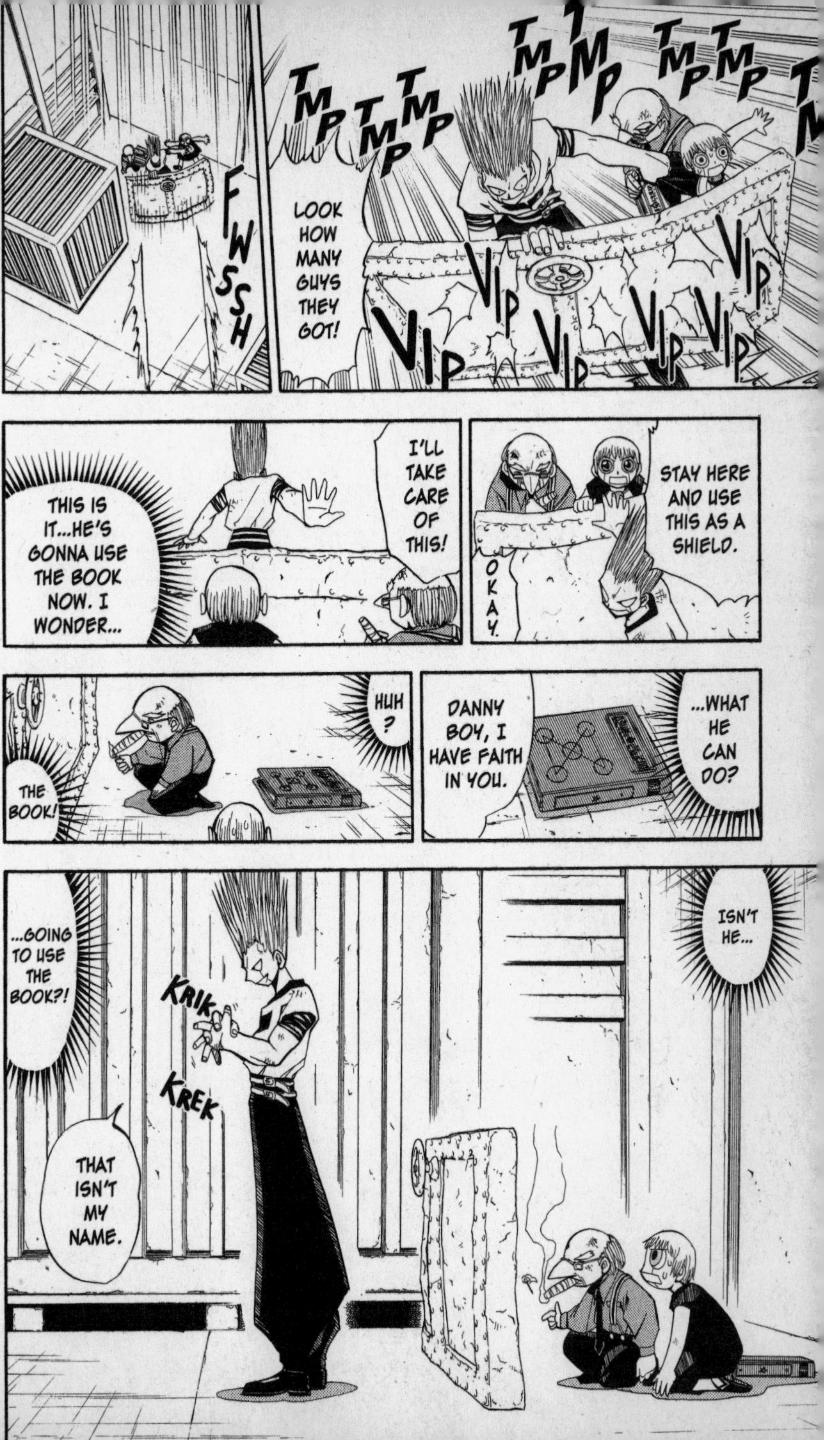
TMP TMP TMP TMP TMP TMP TMP
LOOK HOW MANY GUYS THEY GOT!
VIP VIP VIP VIP VIP VIP
FWSSH
STAY HERE AND USE THIS AS A SHIELD.
OKAY.
I'LL TAKE CARE OF THIS!
THIS IS IT...HE'S GONNA USE THE BOOK NOW. I WONDER...
...WHAT HE CAN DO?
DANNY BOY, I HAVE FAITH IN YOU.
HUH?
THE BOOK!
ISN'T HE...
...GOING TO USE THE BOOK?!
KRIK
KREK
THAT ISN'T MY NAME.

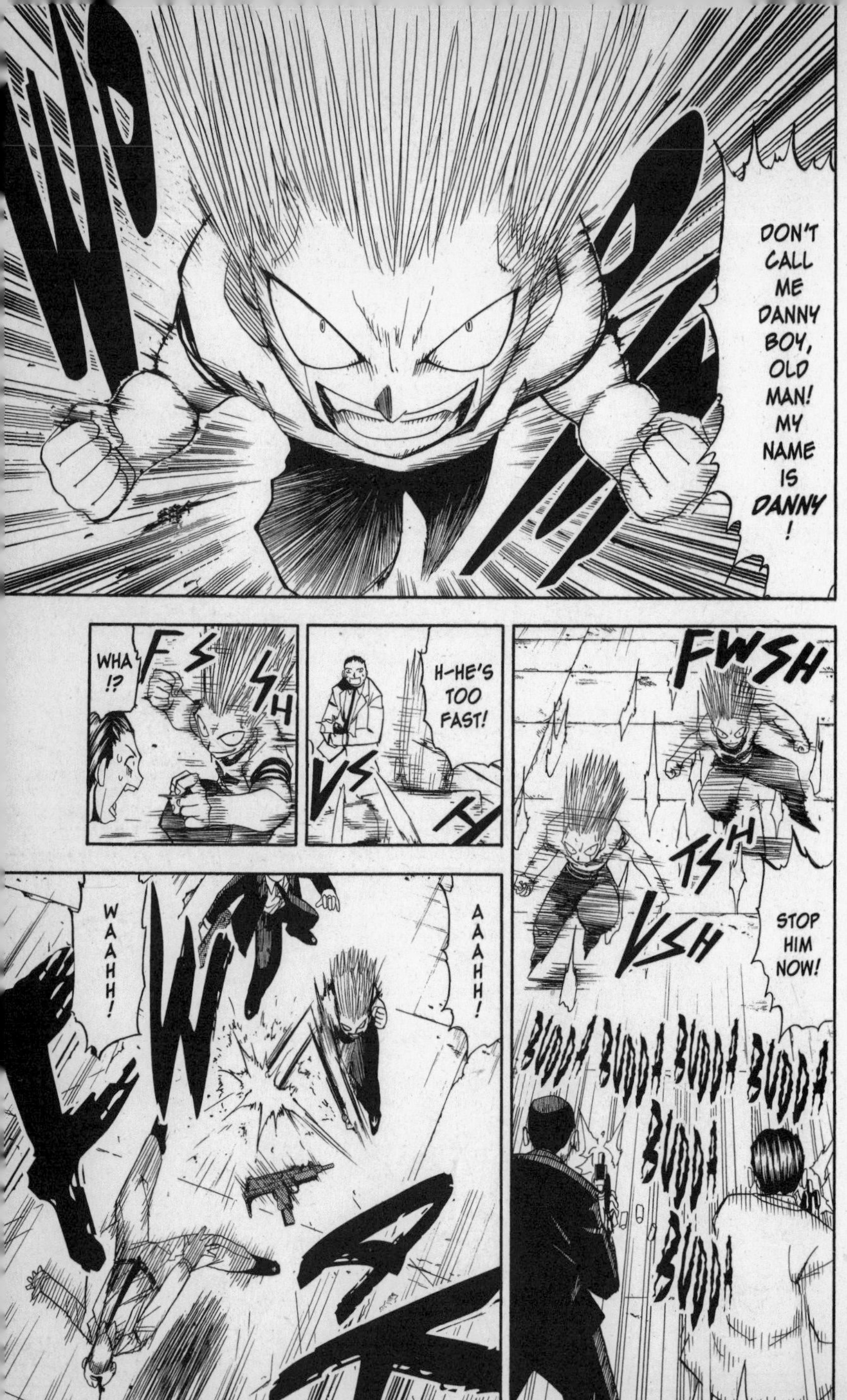
DON'T CALL ME DANNY BOY, OLD MAN! MY NAME IS DANNY!
FWSH
TSH
VSH
STOP HIM NOW!
BUDDA BUDDA BUDDA BUDDA BUDDA BUDDA BUDDA
H-HE'S TOO FAST!
VSH
WHA!?
FSSH
AAAAHH!
WAAAHH!

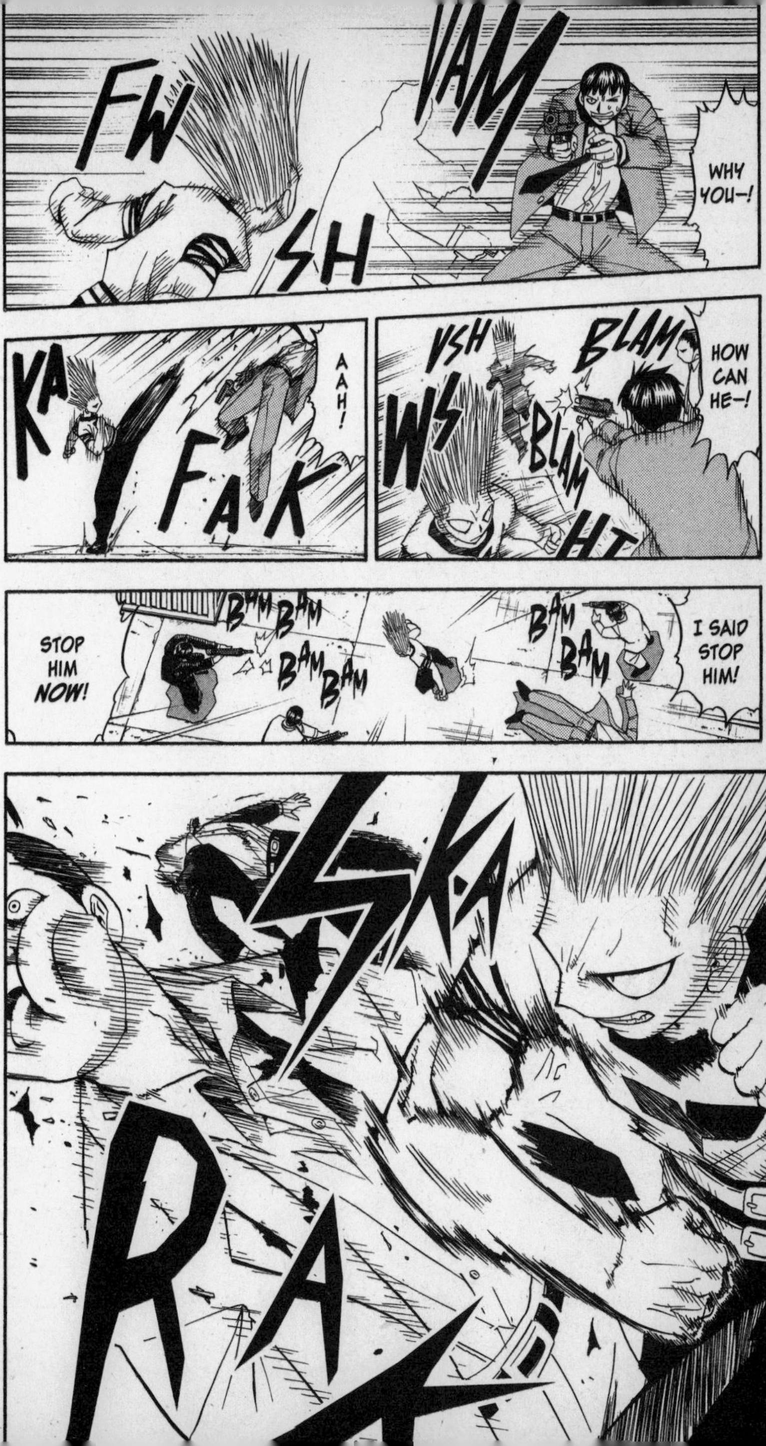
WHY YOU—!
VAM
SH
FW
HOW CAN HE—!
BLAM
VSH
BLAM
WS
AAH!
FAK
KA
I SAID STOP HIM!
BAM BAM
BAM BAM BAM BAM
STOP HIM **NOW!**

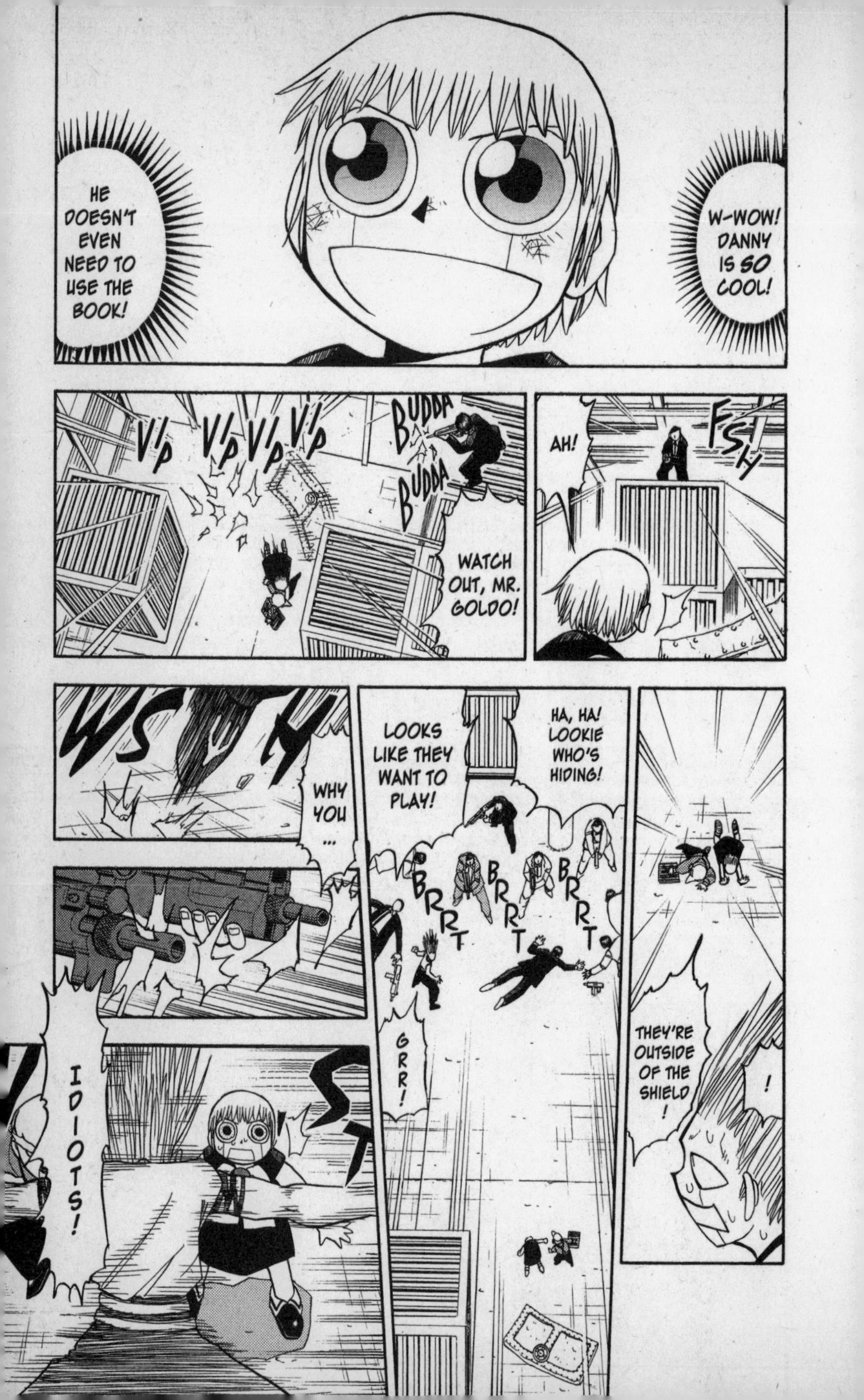
W-WOW! DANNY IS SO COOL!
HE DOESN'T EVEN NEED TO USE THE BOOK!
FSH
AH!
BUDDA
BUDDA
VIP VIP VIP VIP
WATCH OUT, MR. GOLDO!
!
THEY'RE OUTSIDE OF THE SHIELD!
HA, HA! LOOKIE WHO'S HIDING!
LOOKS LIKE THEY WANT TO PLAY!
BRRRT
BRRRT
BRRRT
GRR!
WSH
WHY YOU...
IDIOTS!

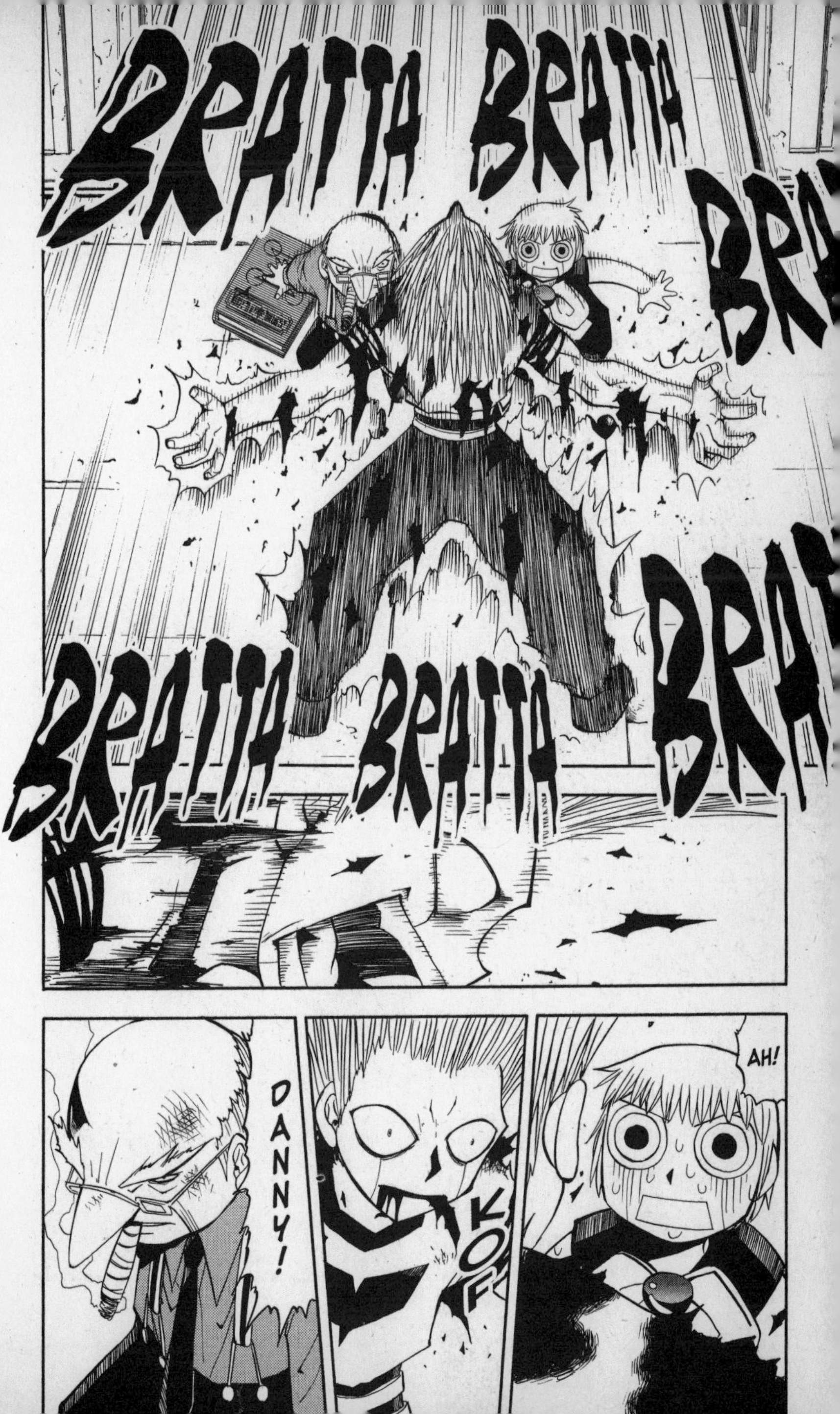
BRATTA BRATTA
BRA
BRA
BRATTA BRATTA
BRA
AH!
KOF
DANNY!

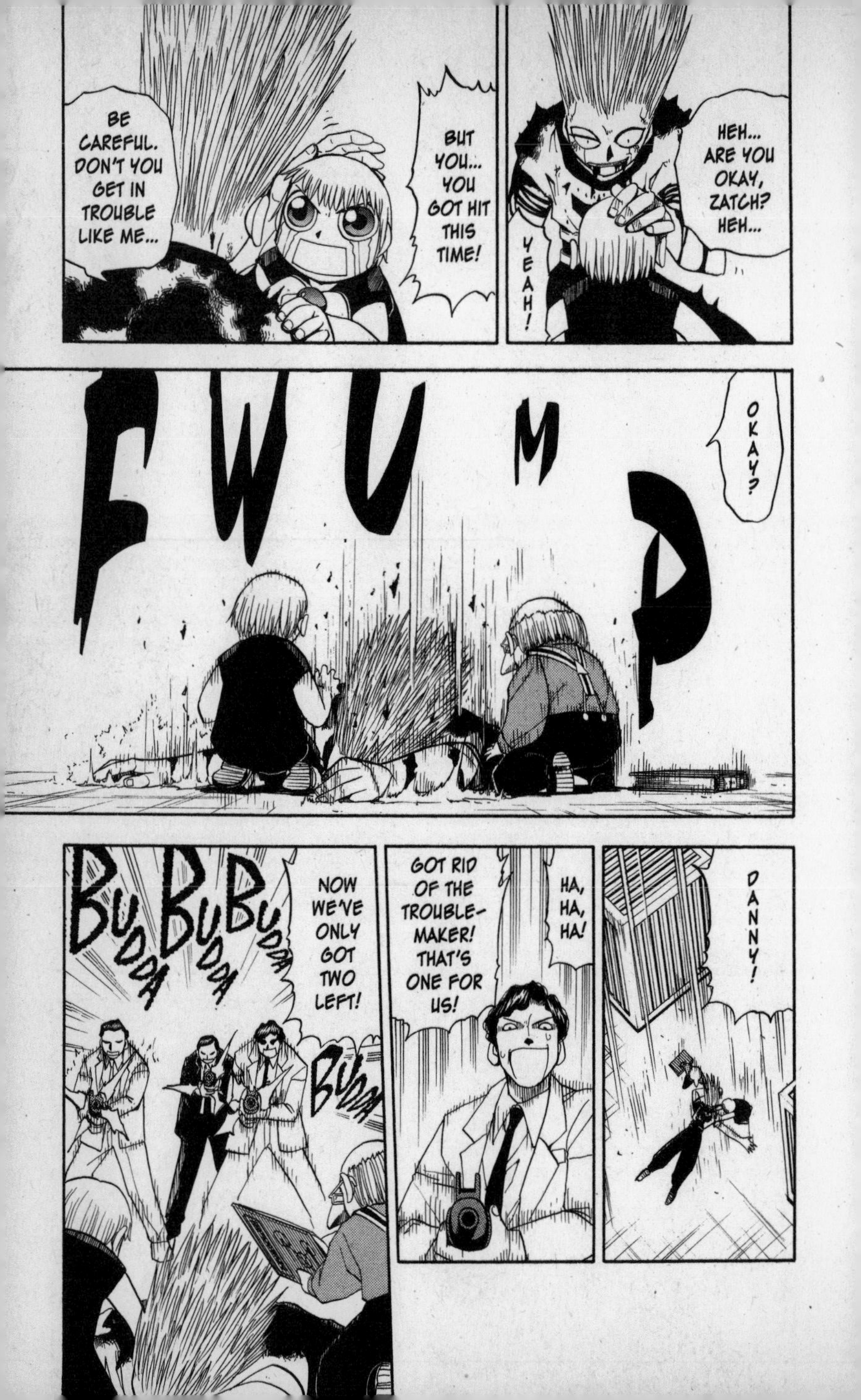
HEH... ARE YOU OKAY, ZATCH? HEH...
YEAH!
BUT YOU... YOU GOT HIT THIS TIME!
BE CAREFUL. DON'T YOU GET IN TROUBLE LIKE ME...
OKAY?
FWUMP
DANNY!
HA, HA, HA!
GOT RID OF THE TROUBLE-MAKER! THAT'S ONE FOR US!
NOW WE'VE ONLY GOT TWO LEFT!
BUDDA BUDDA BUDDA
BUDDA

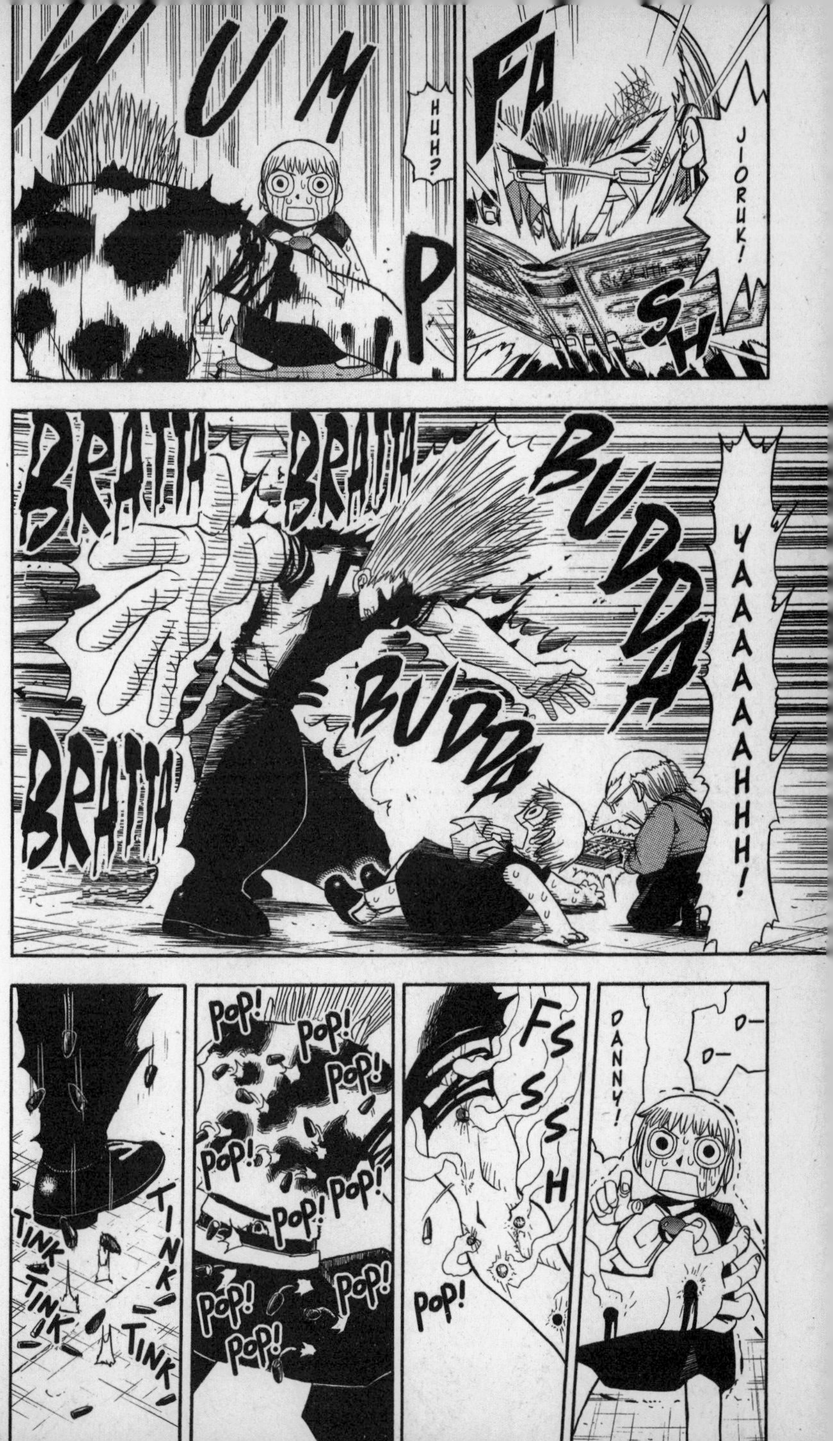
JIORUK!
FA
SH
WUMP
HUH?
YAAAAAAHHH!
BUDDA
BUDDA
BRATTA
BRATTA
BRATTA
D—
D—
DANNY!
FSSSH
POP!
POP!
POP!
POP!
POP!
POP!
POP!
POP!
POP!
POP!
TINK
TINK
TINK
TINK

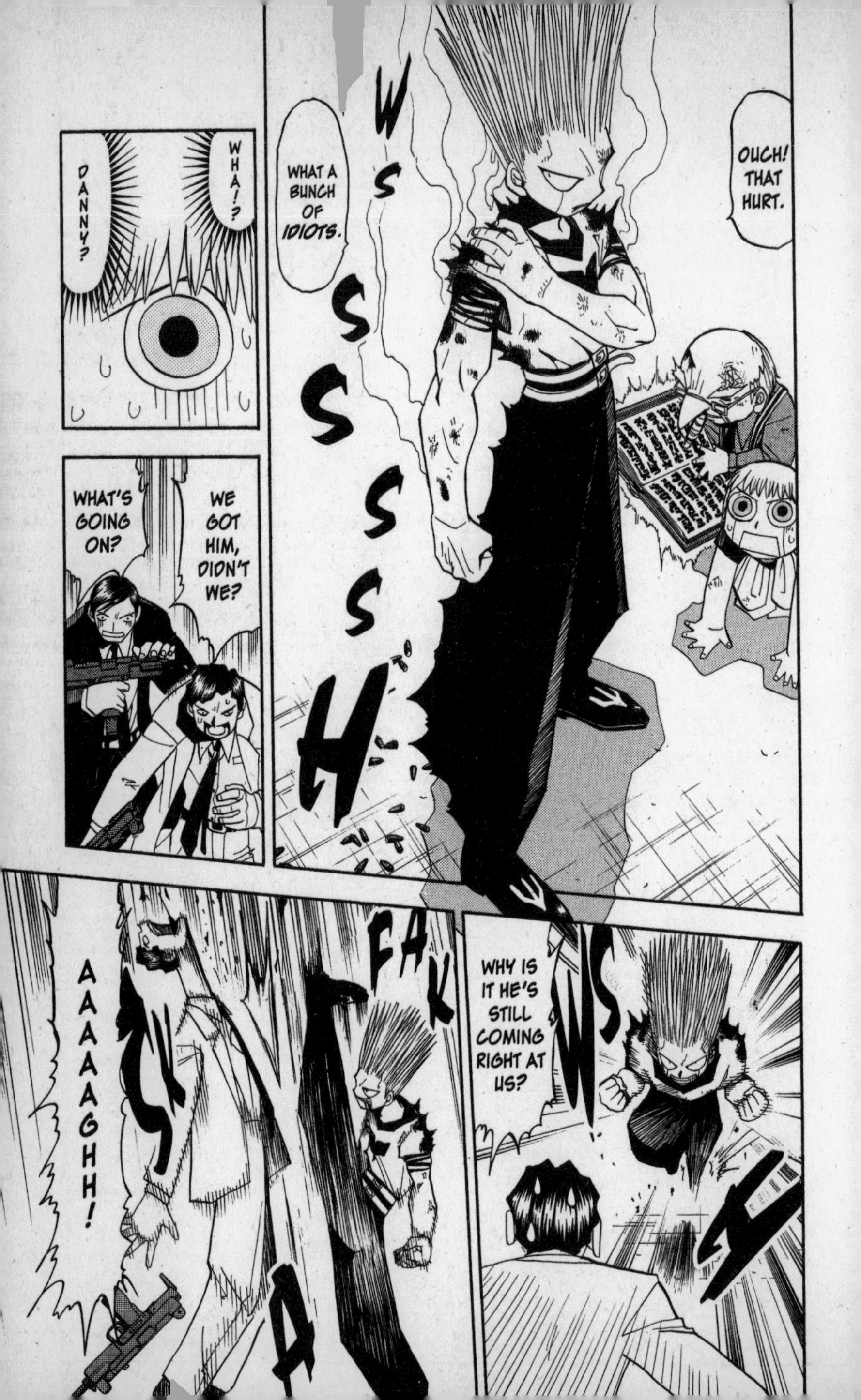
OUCH! THAT HURT.
WHAT A BUNCH OF IDIOTS.
WSSSSSH
WHA!?
DANNY?
WE GOT HIM, DIDN'T WE?
WHAT'S GOING ON?
WHY IS IT HE'S STILL COMING RIGHT AT US?
WS
FAK
AAAAAAGH!

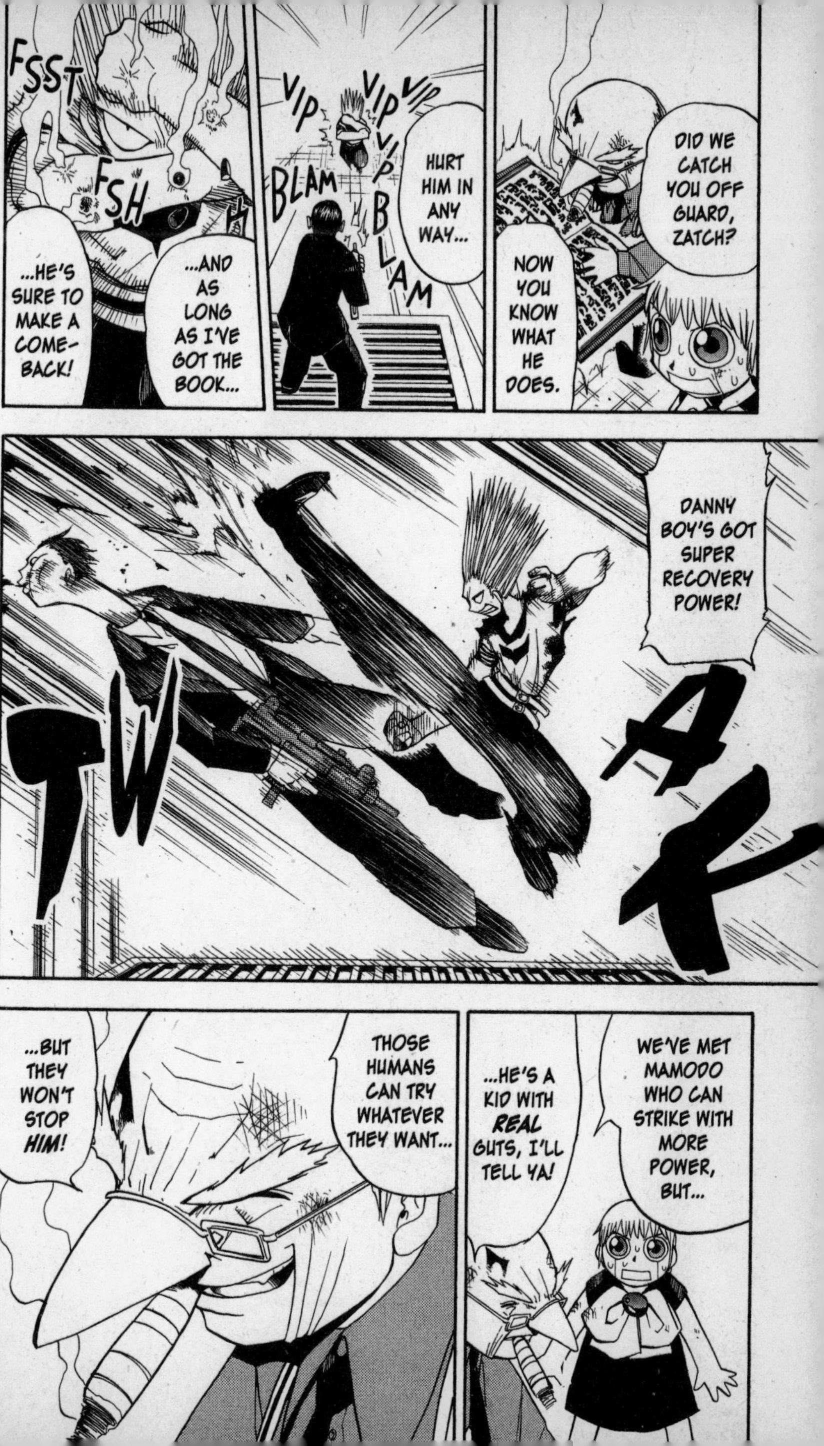
DID WE CATCH YOU OFF GUARD, ZATCH?
NOW YOU KNOW WHAT HE DOES.
VIP VIP VIP VIP
HURT HIM IN ANY WAY...
BLAM BLAM BLAM
FSST
FSH
...AND AS LONG AS I'VE GOT THE BOOK...
...HE'S SURE TO MAKE A COME-BACK!
DANNY BOY'S GOT SUPER RECOVERY POWER!
THWAK
WE'VE MET MAMODO WHO CAN STRIKE WITH MORE POWER, BUT...
...HE'S A KID WITH REAL GUTS, I'LL TELL YA!
THOSE HUMANS CAN TRY WHATEVER THEY WANT...
...BUT THEY WON'T STOP HIM!

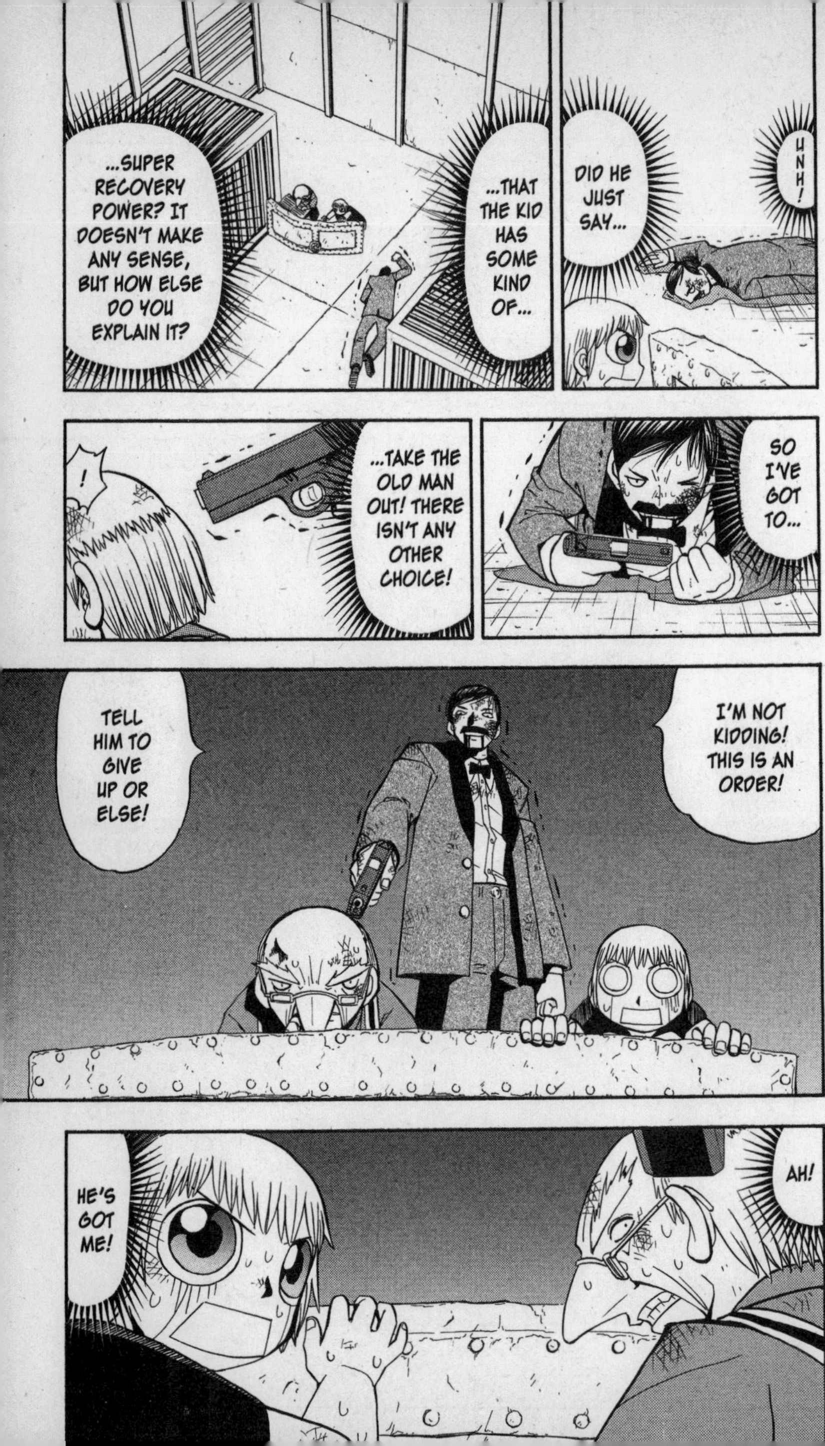
UNH!
DID HE JUST SAY...
...THAT THE KID HAS SOME KIND OF...
...SUPER RECOVERY POWER? IT DOESN'T MAKE ANY SENSE, BUT HOW ELSE DO YOU EXPLAIN IT?
SO I'VE GOT TO...
...TAKE THE OLD MAN OUT! THERE ISN'T ANY OTHER CHOICE!
!
I'M NOT KIDDING! THIS IS AN ORDER!
TELL HIM TO GIVE UP OR ELSE!
AH!
HE'S GOT ME!

EEE!

SORRY! MUST BE THE WRONG ROOM...

UH...

156

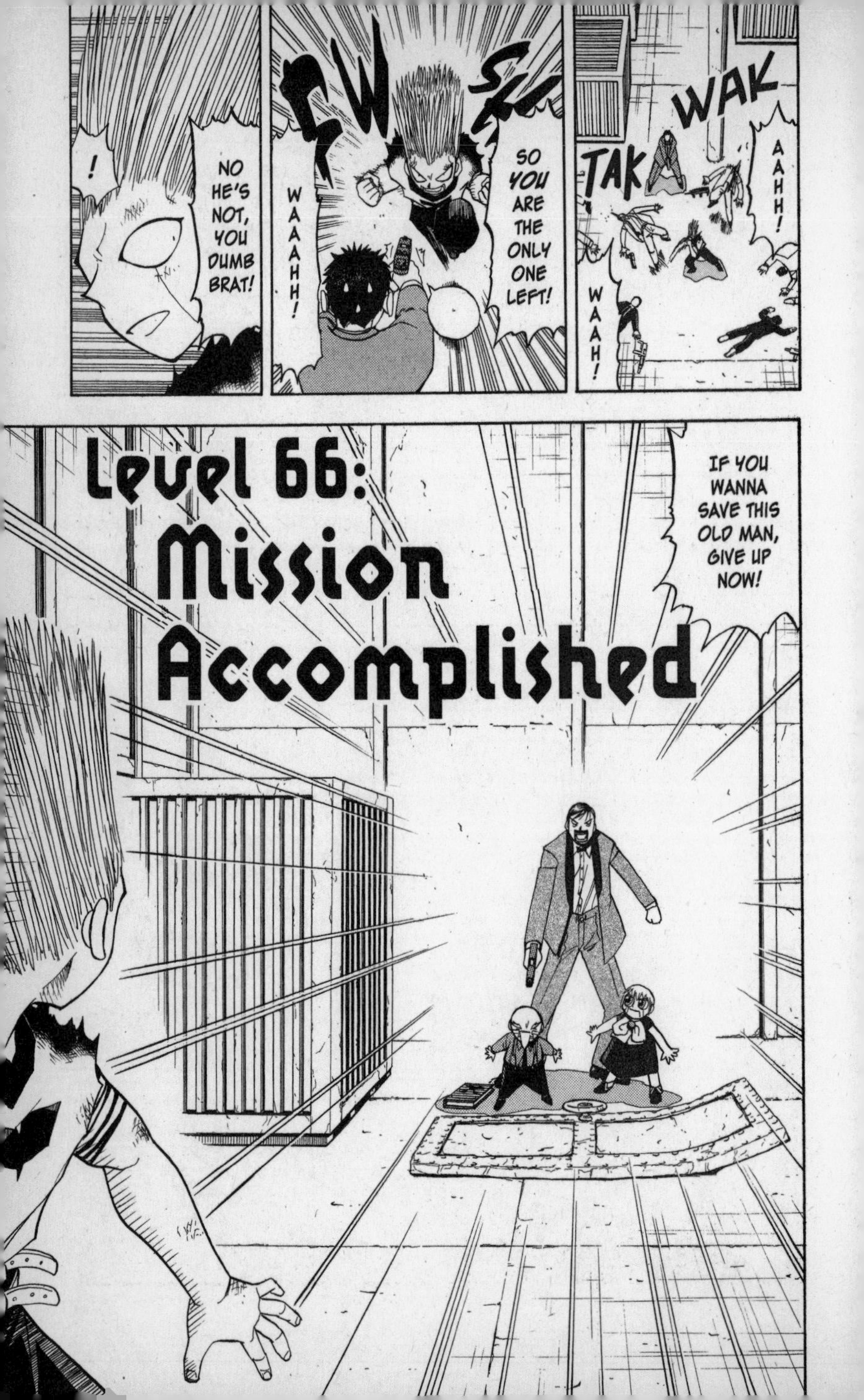
WAK
TAK
AAHH!
WAAH!
FWSH
SO YOU ARE THE ONLY ONE LEFT!
WAAAAHH!
NO HE'S NOT, YOU DUMB BRAT!
!
Level 66: Mission Accomplished
IF YOU WANNA SAVE THIS OLD MAN, GIVE UP NOW!

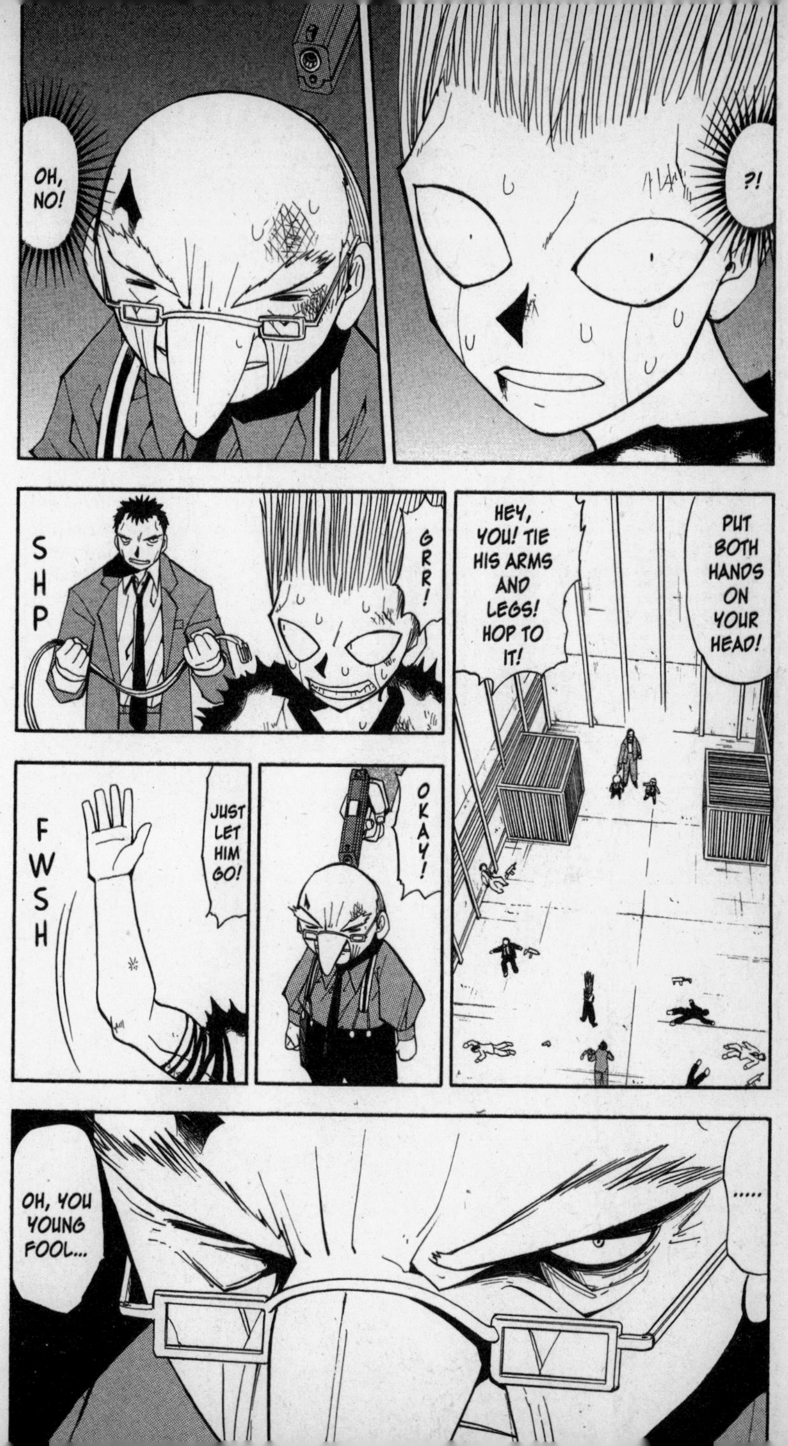
?!
OH, NO!
PUT BOTH HANDS ON YOUR HEAD!
HEY, YOU! TIE HIS ARMS AND LEGS! HOP TO IT!
GRR!
SHP
OKAY!
JUST LET HIM GO!
FWSH
.....
OH, YOU YOUNG FOOL...

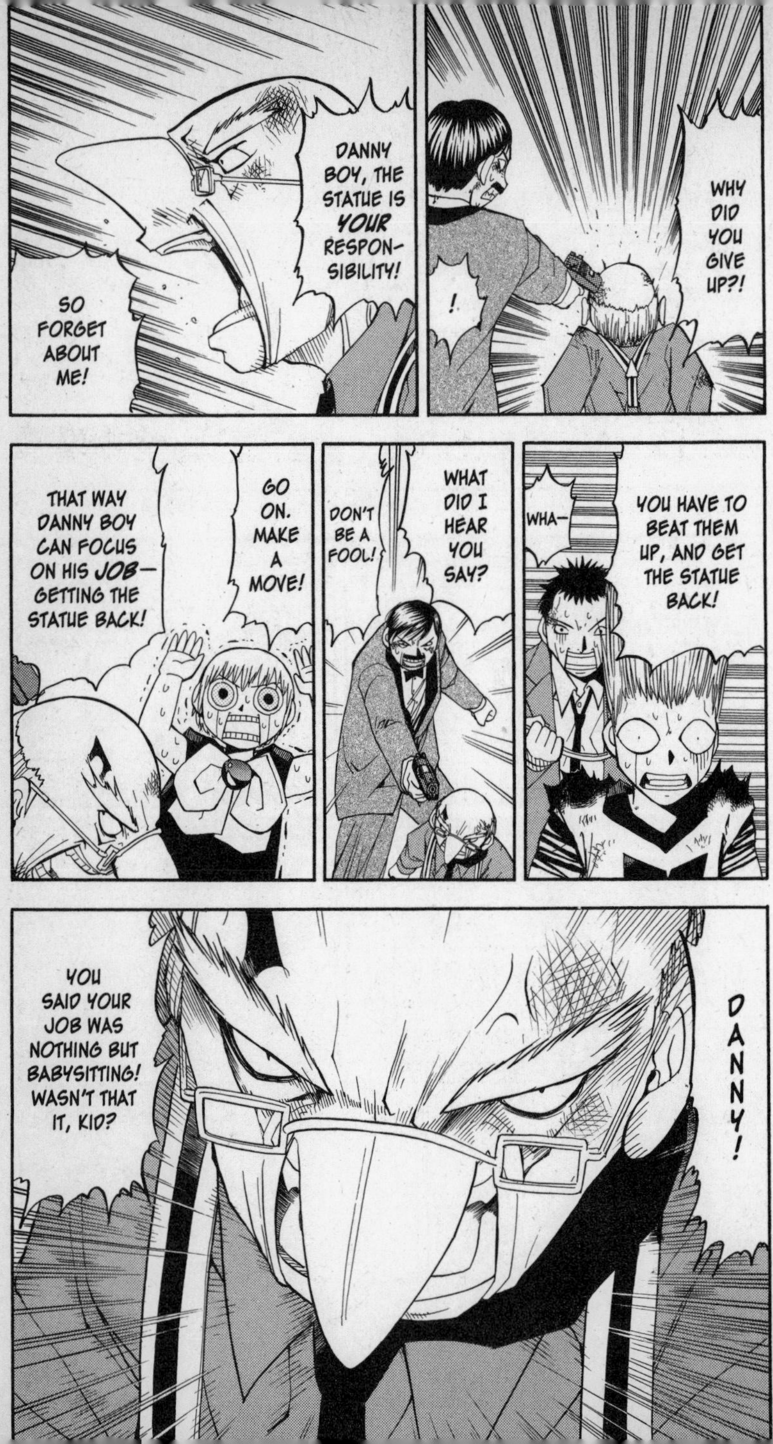
WHY DID YOU GIVE UP?!
!
DANNY BOY, THE STATUE IS YOUR RESPONSIBILITY!
SO FORGET ABOUT ME!
WHA—
YOU HAVE TO BEAT THEM UP, AND GET THE STATUE BACK!
WHAT DID I HEAR YOU SAY?
DON'T BE A FOOL!
GO ON. MAKE A MOVE!
THAT WAY DANNY BOY CAN FOCUS ON HIS JOB— GETTING THE STATUE BACK!
DANNY!
YOU SAID YOUR JOB WAS NOTHING BUT BABYSITTING! WASN'T THAT IT, KID?

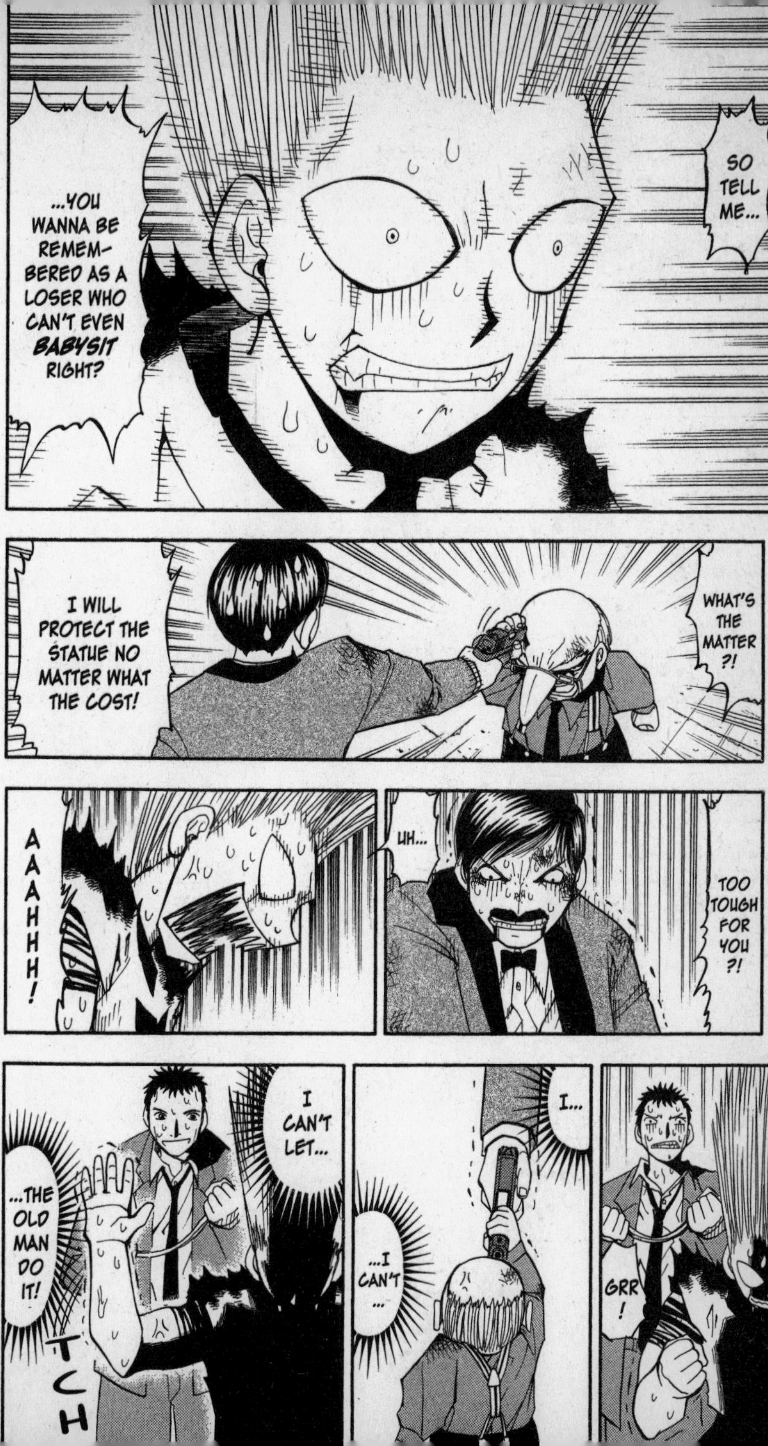
SO TELL ME...
...YOU WANNA BE REMEMBERED AS A LOSER WHO CAN'T EVEN BABYSIT RIGHT?
WHAT'S THE MATTER ?!
I WILL PROTECT THE STATUE NO MATTER WHAT THE COST!
TOO TOUGH FOR YOU ?!
UH...
AAAAHHHH!
GRR!
I...
...I CAN'T ...
I CAN'T LET...
...THE OLD MAN DO IT!
TCH

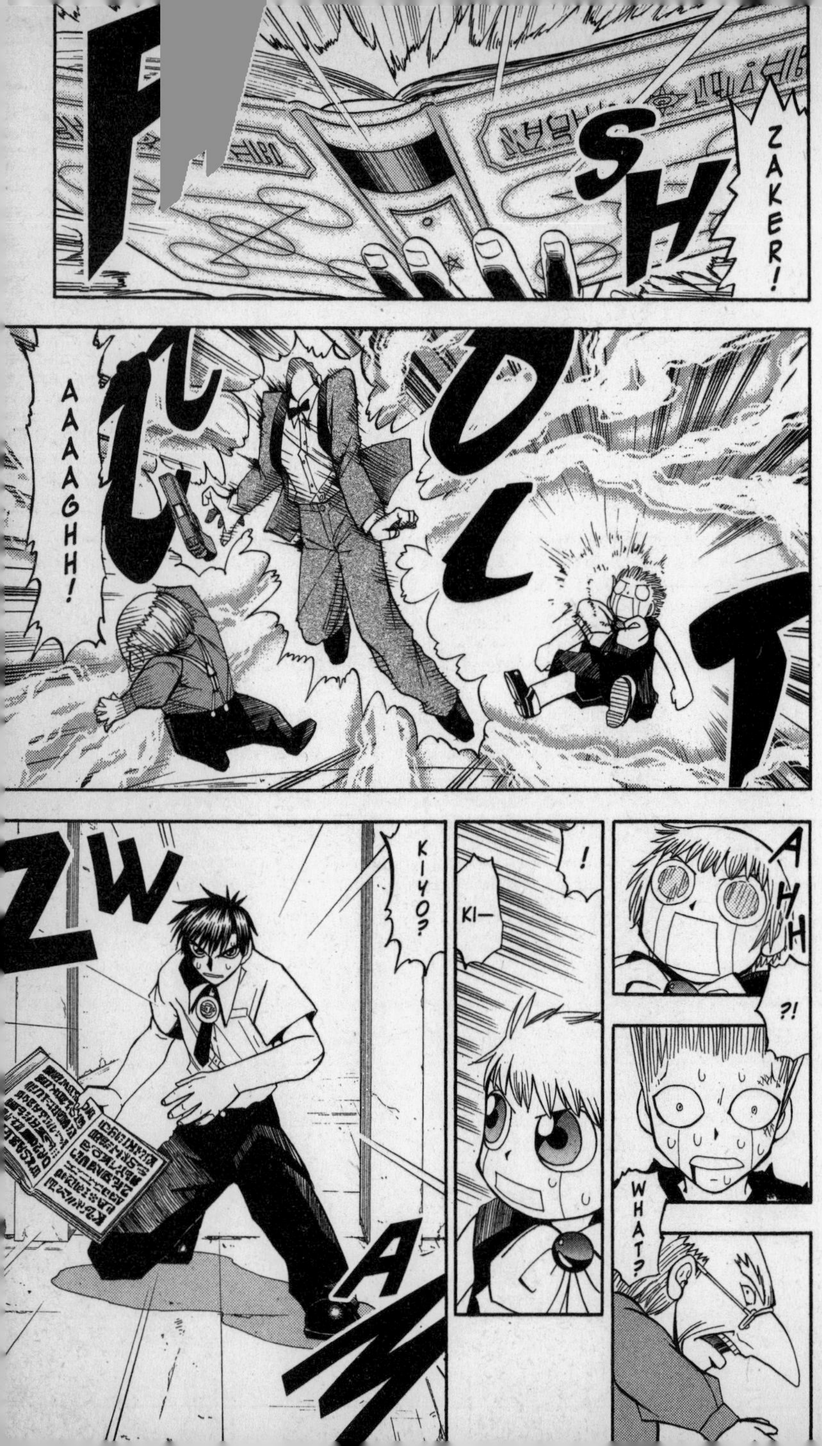
ZAKER!
AAAAAGHH!
AHH
?!
WHAT?
!
KI—
KIYO?

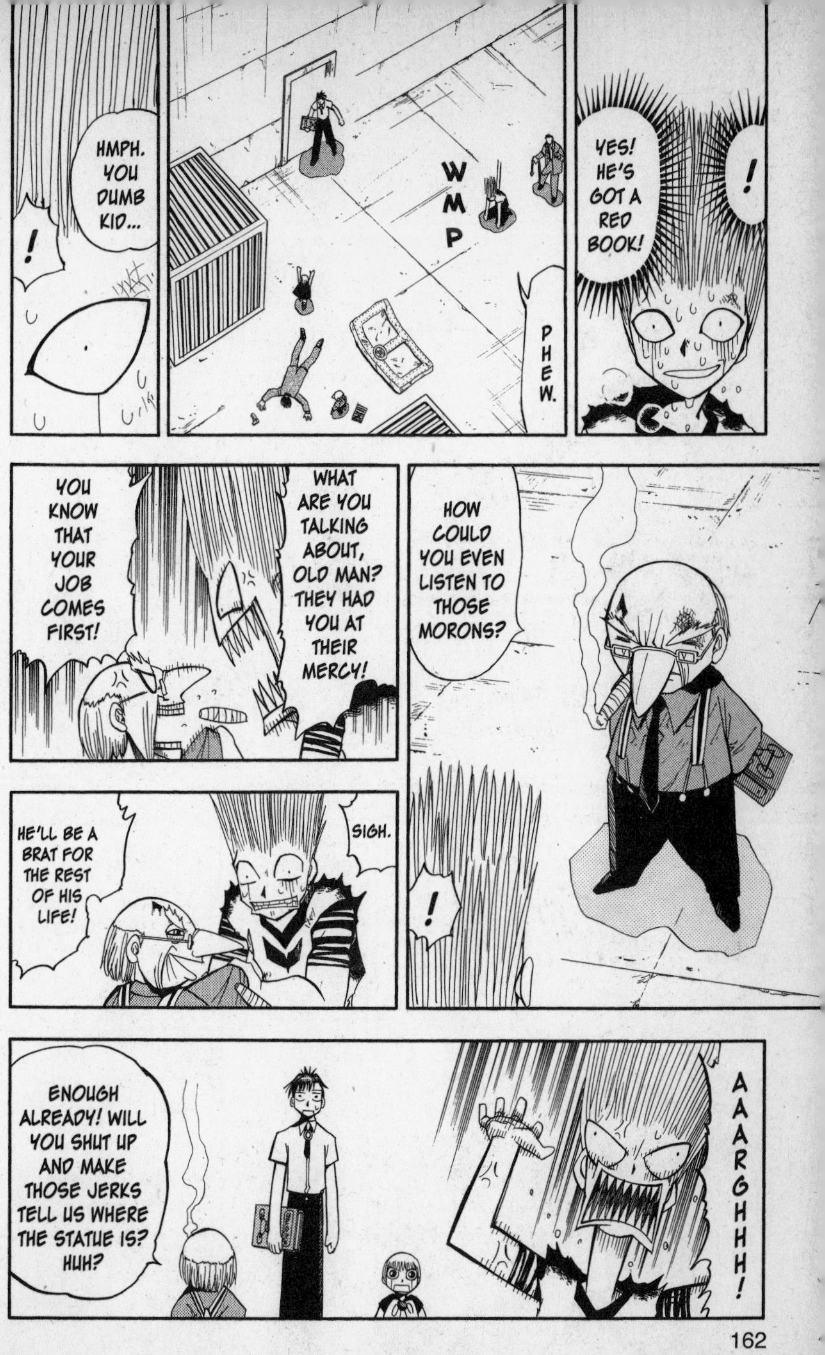
!
YES! HE'S GOT A RED BOOK!
PHEW.
WMP
HMPH. YOU DUMB KID...
!
HOW COULD YOU EVEN LISTEN TO THOSE MORONS?
!
WHAT ARE YOU TALKING ABOUT, OLD MAN? THEY HAD YOU AT THEIR MERCY!
YOU KNOW THAT YOUR JOB COMES FIRST!
SIGH.
HE'LL BE A BRAT FOR THE REST OF HIS LIFE!
AAARGHHH!
ENOUGH ALREADY! WILL YOU SHUT UP AND MAKE THOSE JERKS TELL US WHERE THE STATUE IS? HUH?

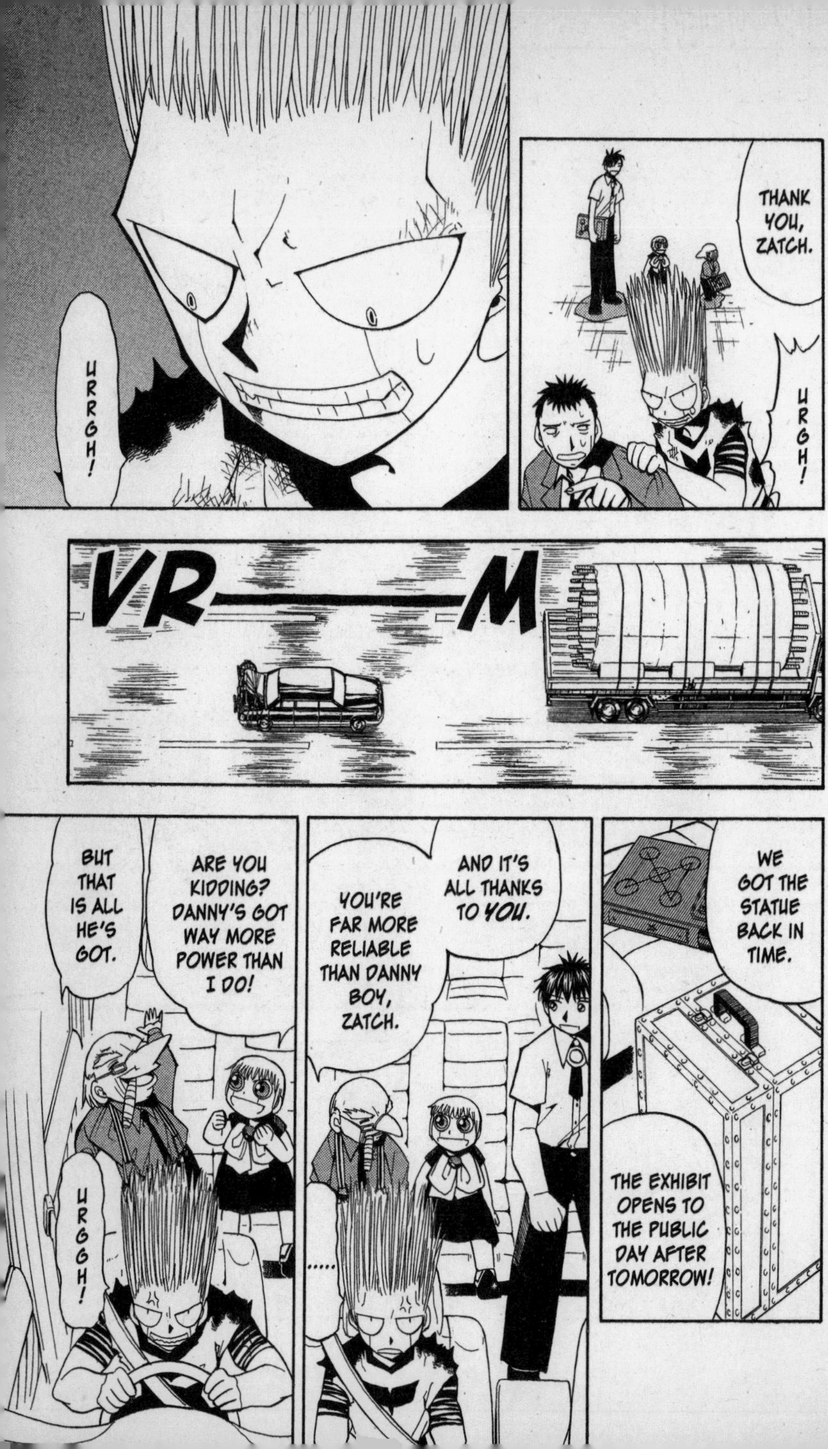
THANK YOU, ZATCH.
URGH!
URRGH!
VR——M
WE GOT THE STATUE BACK IN TIME.
THE EXHIBIT OPENS TO THE PUBLIC DAY AFTER TOMORROW!
AND IT'S ALL THANKS TO YOU.
YOU'RE FAR MORE RELIABLE THAN DANNY BOY, ZATCH.
.....
ARE YOU KIDDING? DANNY'S GOT WAY MORE POWER THAN I DO!
BUT THAT IS ALL HE'S GOT.
URGGH!

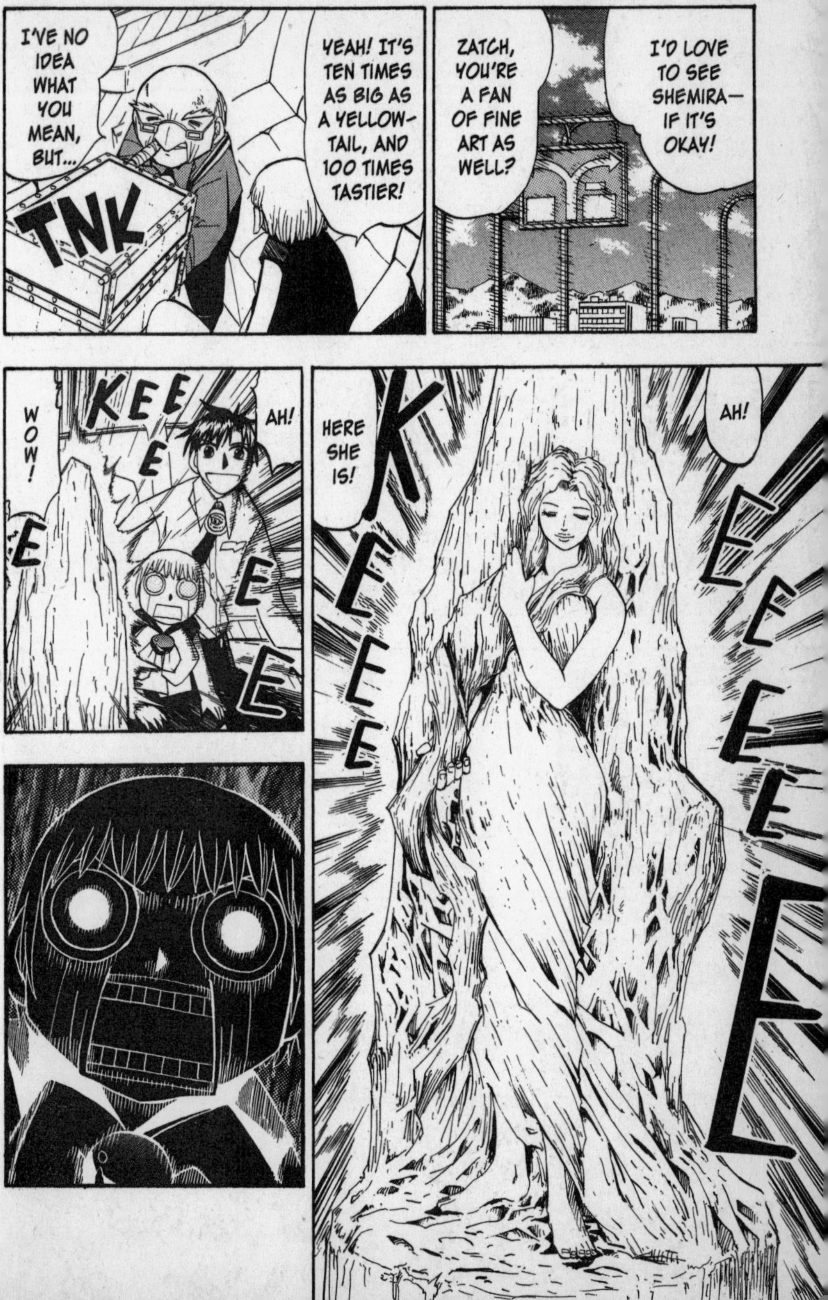
I'D LOVE TO SEE SHEMIRA— IF IT'S OKAY!
ZATCH, YOU'RE A FAN OF FINE ART AS WELL?
YEAH! IT'S TEN TIMES AS BIG AS A YELLOW-TAIL, AND 100 TIMES TASTIER!
I'VE NO IDEA WHAT YOU MEAN, BUT...
TNK
AH!
HERE SHE IS!
KEEEEEEEEEE
AH!
KEEE
WOW!
EEEE

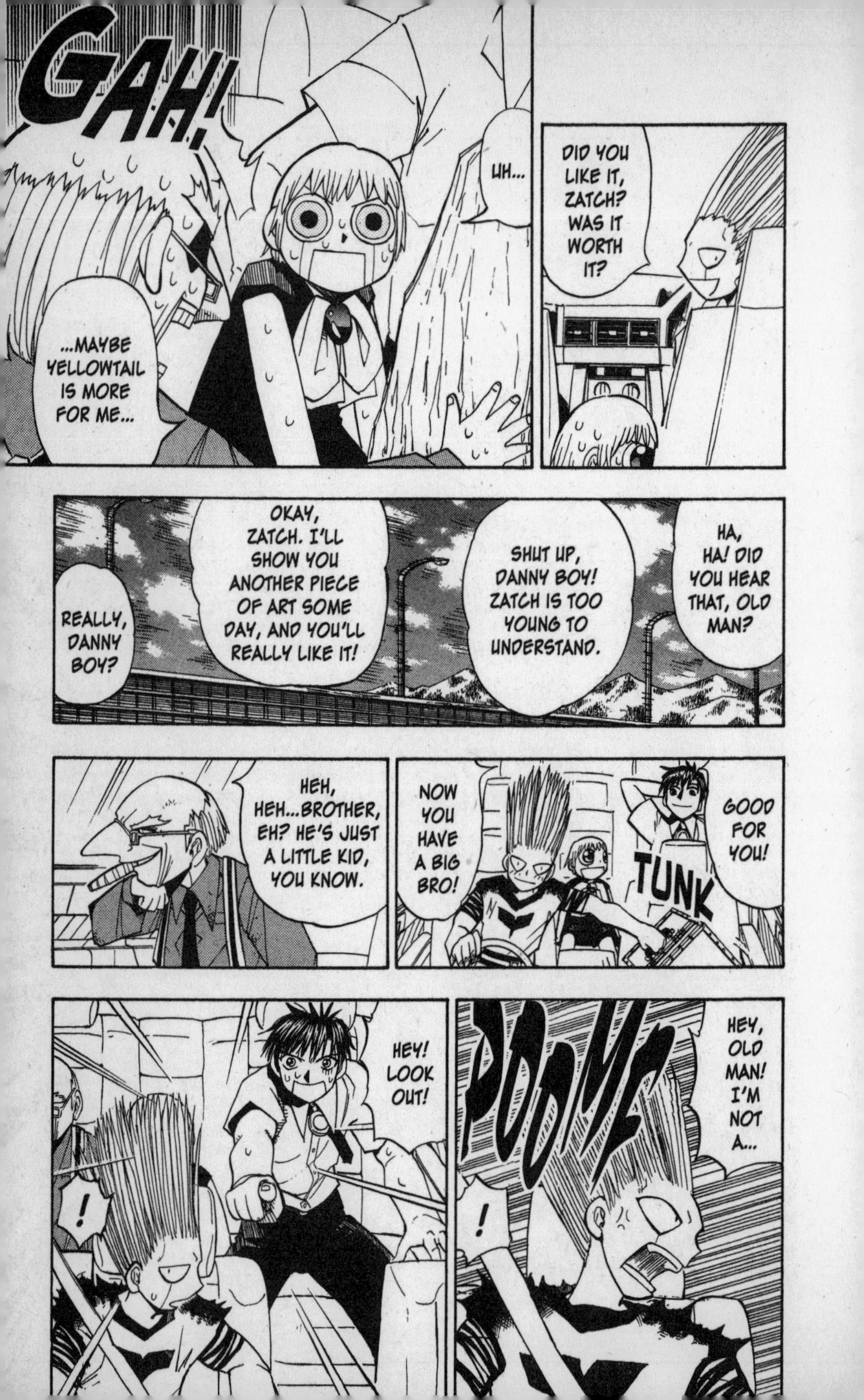
DID YOU LIKE IT, ZATCH? WAS IT WORTH IT?
UH...
GAH!
...MAYBE YELLOWTAIL IS MORE FOR ME...
HA, HA! DID YOU HEAR THAT, OLD MAN?
SHUT UP, DANNY BOY! ZATCH IS TOO YOUNG TO UNDERSTAND.
OKAY, ZATCH. I'LL SHOW YOU ANOTHER PIECE OF ART SOME DAY, AND YOU'LL REALLY LIKE IT!
REALLY, DANNY BOY?
GOOD FOR YOU!
TUNK
NOW YOU HAVE A BIG BRO!
HEH, HEH...BROTHER, EH? HE'S JUST A LITTLE KID, YOU KNOW.
HEY, OLD MAN! I'M NOT A...
!
HEY! LOOK OUT!
!

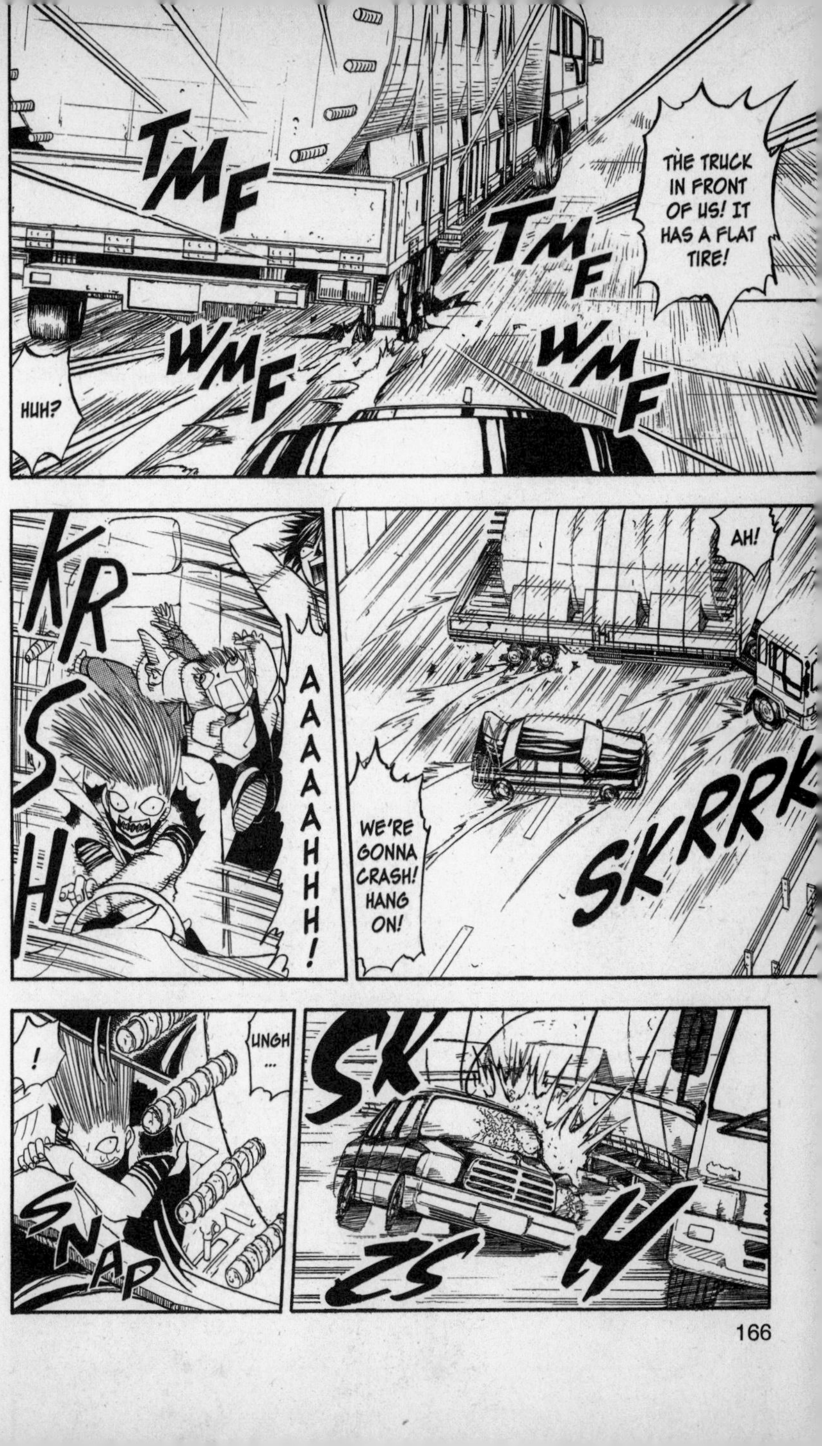
THE TRUCK IN FRONT OF US! IT HAS A FLAT TIRE!
TMF
TMF
WMF
WMF
HUH?
AH!
SKRRK
WE'RE GONNA CRASH! HANG ON!
AAAAAAHHH!
KRSSH
SK
ZS
H
UNGH ...
!
SNAP

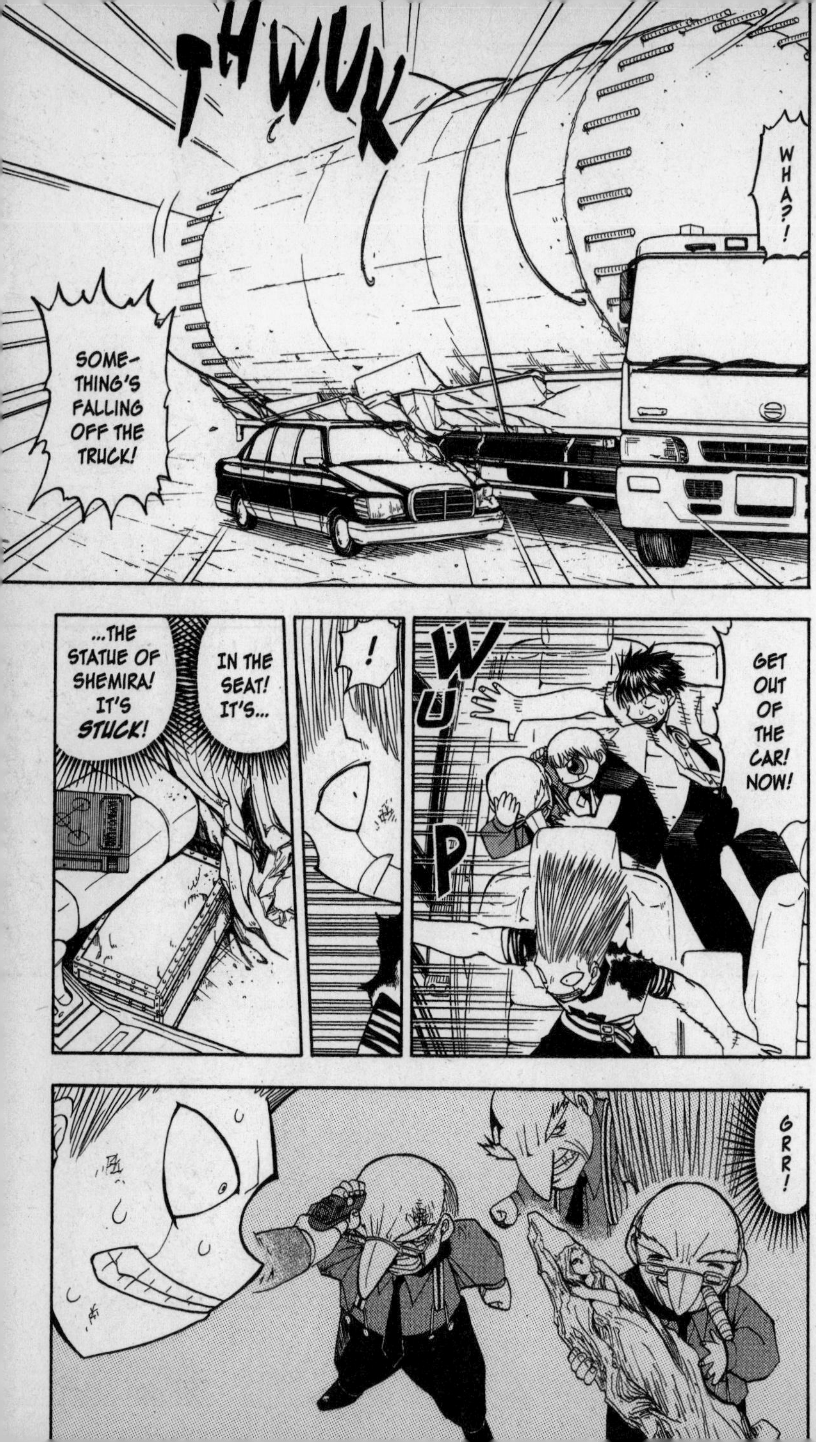
THWUK
WHA?!
SOMETHING'S FALLING OFF THE TRUCK!
GET OUT OF THE CAR! NOW!
WUP
!
IN THE SEAT! IT'S...
...THE STATUE OF SHEMIRA! IT'S STUCK!
GRR!

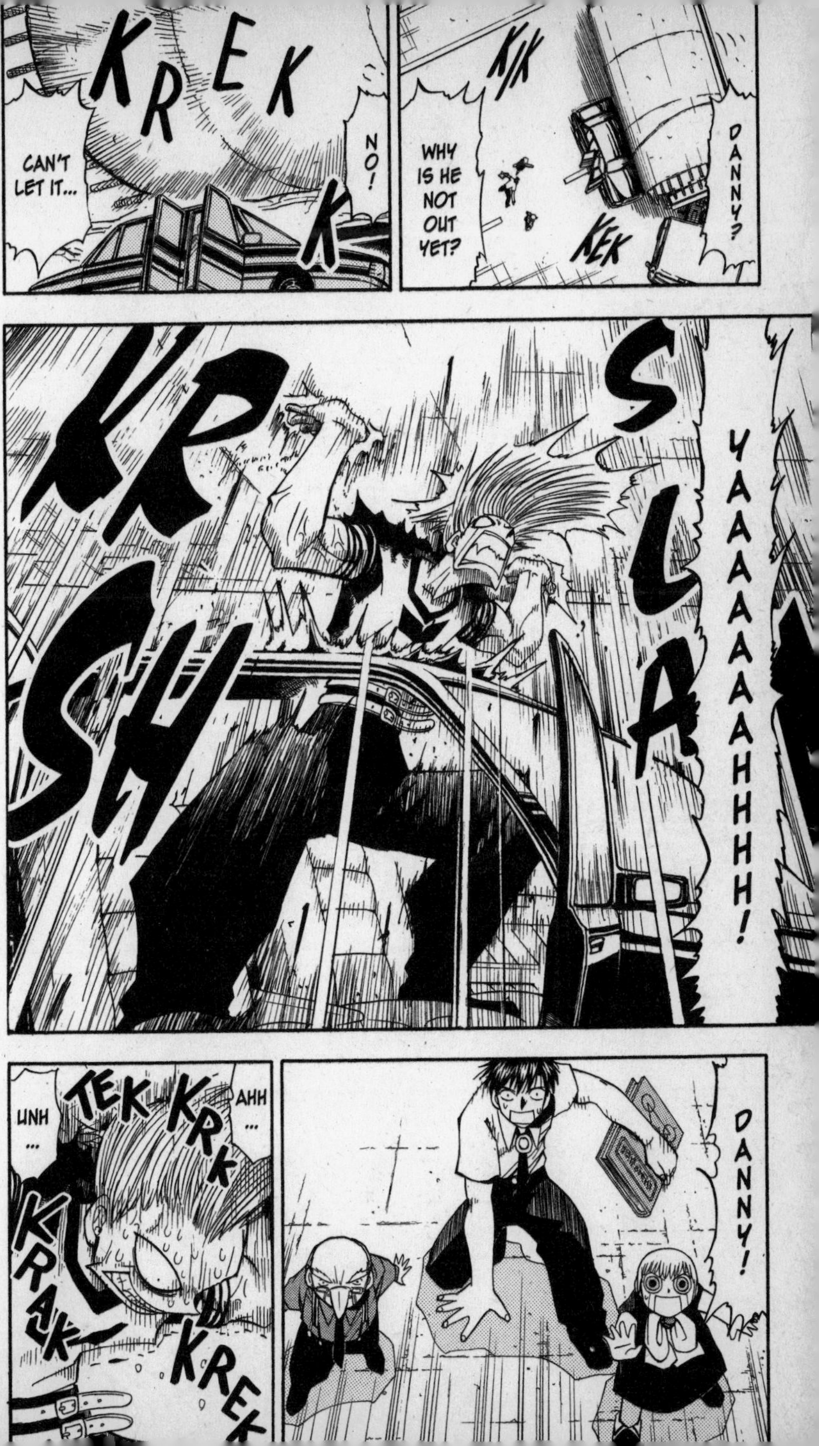
DANNY?
KIK
KEK
WHY IS HE NOT OUT YET?
NO!
KREK
K
CAN'T LET IT...
YAAAAAAAHHHH!
SLA
KR
SH
DANNY!
AHH ...
TEK KRK
KRK
UNH ...
KRAK
KREK

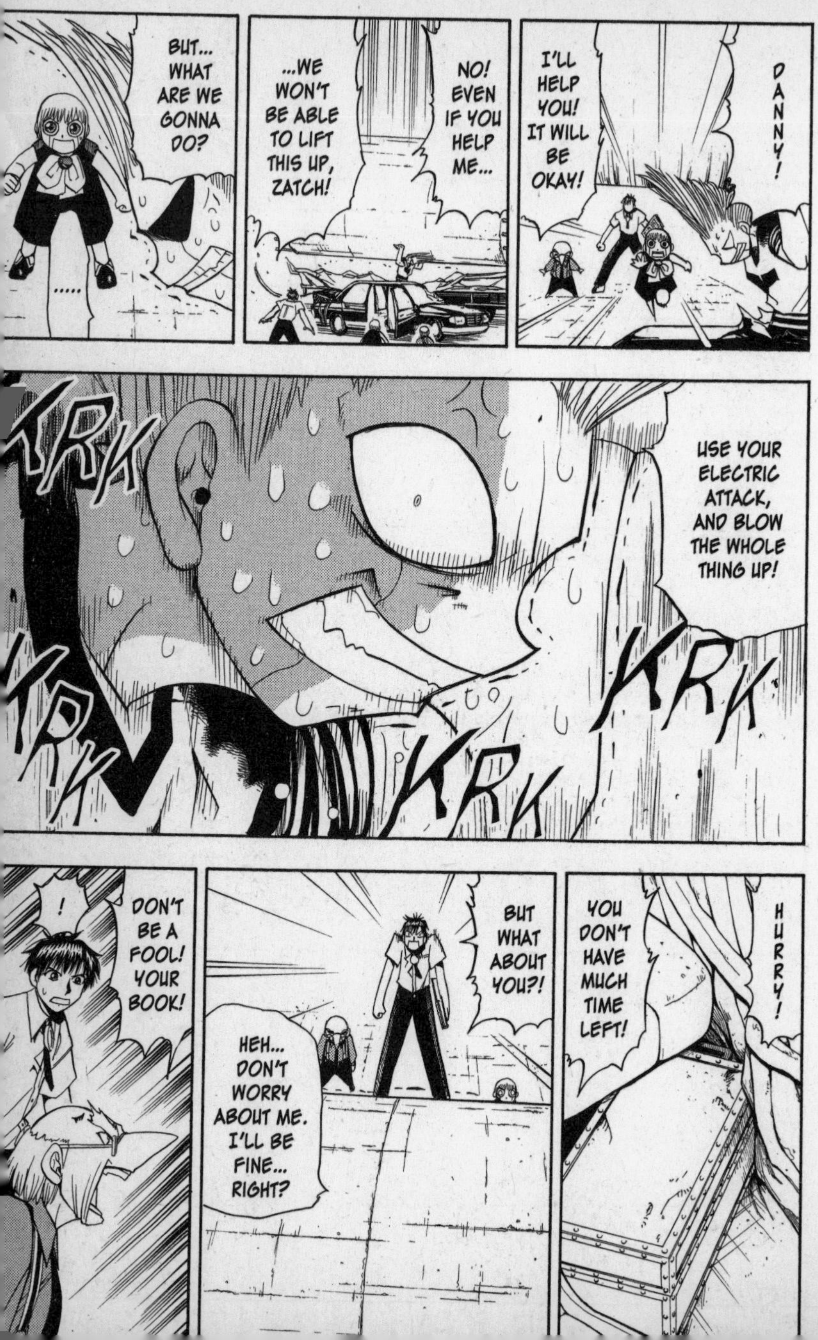
DANNY!
I'LL HELP YOU! IT WILL BE OKAY!
NO! EVEN IF YOU HELP ME...
...WE WON'T BE ABLE TO LIFT THIS UP, ZATCH!
BUT... WHAT ARE WE GONNA DO?
.....
USE YOUR ELECTRIC ATTACK, AND BLOW THE WHOLE THING UP!
KRK
KRK
KRK
KRK
KRK
HURRY!
YOU DON'T HAVE MUCH TIME LEFT!
BUT WHAT ABOUT YOU?!
HEH... DON'T WORRY ABOUT ME. I'LL BE FINE... RIGHT?
!
DON'T BE A FOOL! YOUR BOOK!

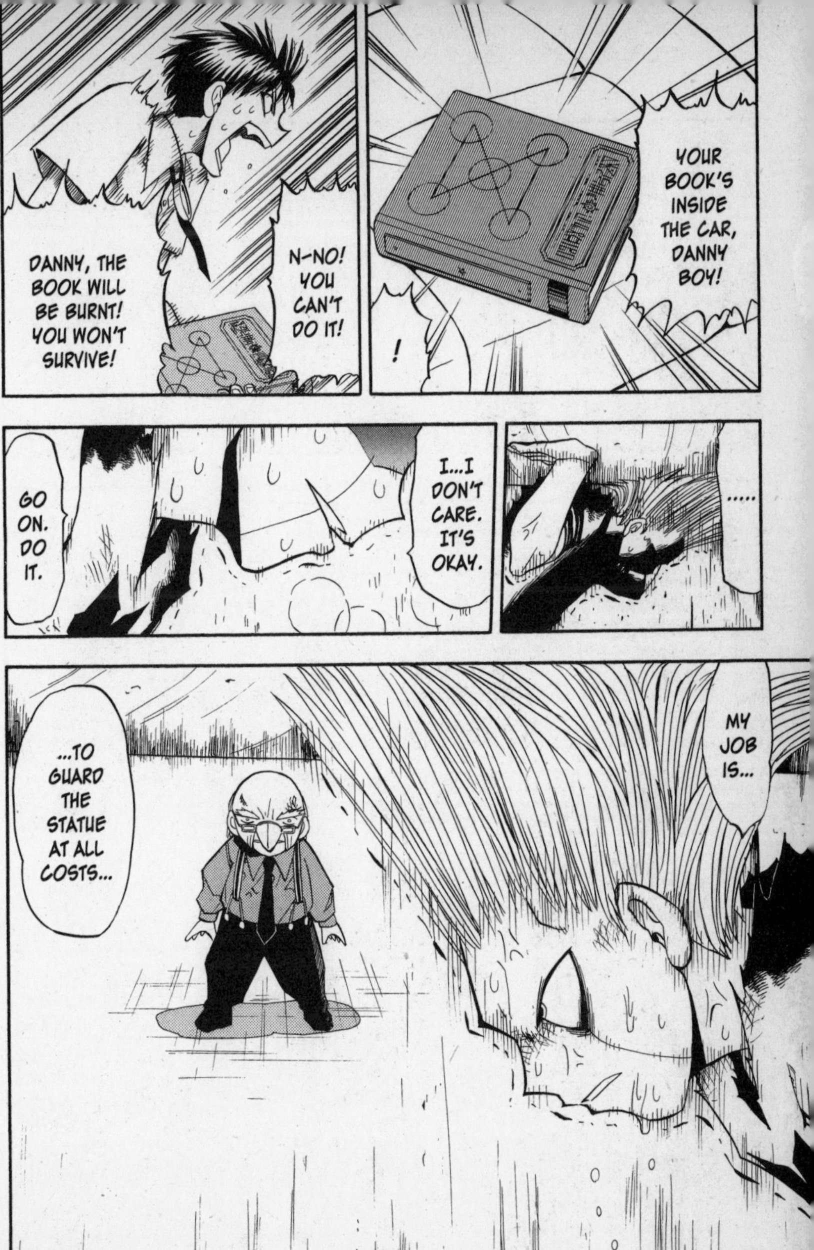
YOUR BOOK'S INSIDE THE CAR, DANNY BOY!
!
N-NO! YOU CAN'T DO IT!
DANNY, THE BOOK WILL BE BURNT! YOU WON'T SURVIVE!
.....
I...I DON'T CARE. IT'S OKAY.
GO ON. DO IT.
MY JOB IS...
...TO GUARD THE STATUE AT ALL COSTS...

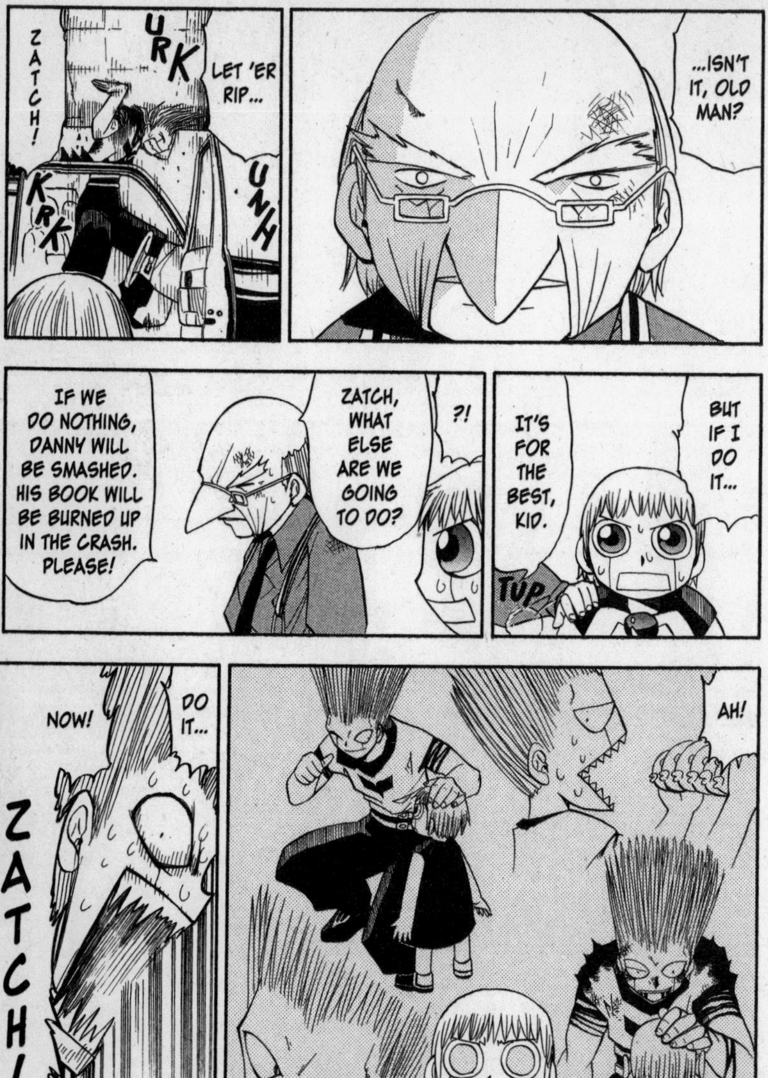

...ISN'T IT, OLD MAN?
URK
LET 'ER RIP...
ZATCH!
UNH
KRK
BUT IF I DO IT...
IT'S FOR THE BEST, KID.
TUP
?!
ZATCH, WHAT ELSE ARE WE GOING TO DO?
IF WE DO NOTHING, DANNY WILL BE SMASHED. HIS BOOK WILL BE BURNED UP IN THE CRASH. PLEASE!
AH!
DO IT...
NOW!
ZATCH!

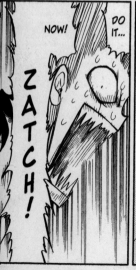

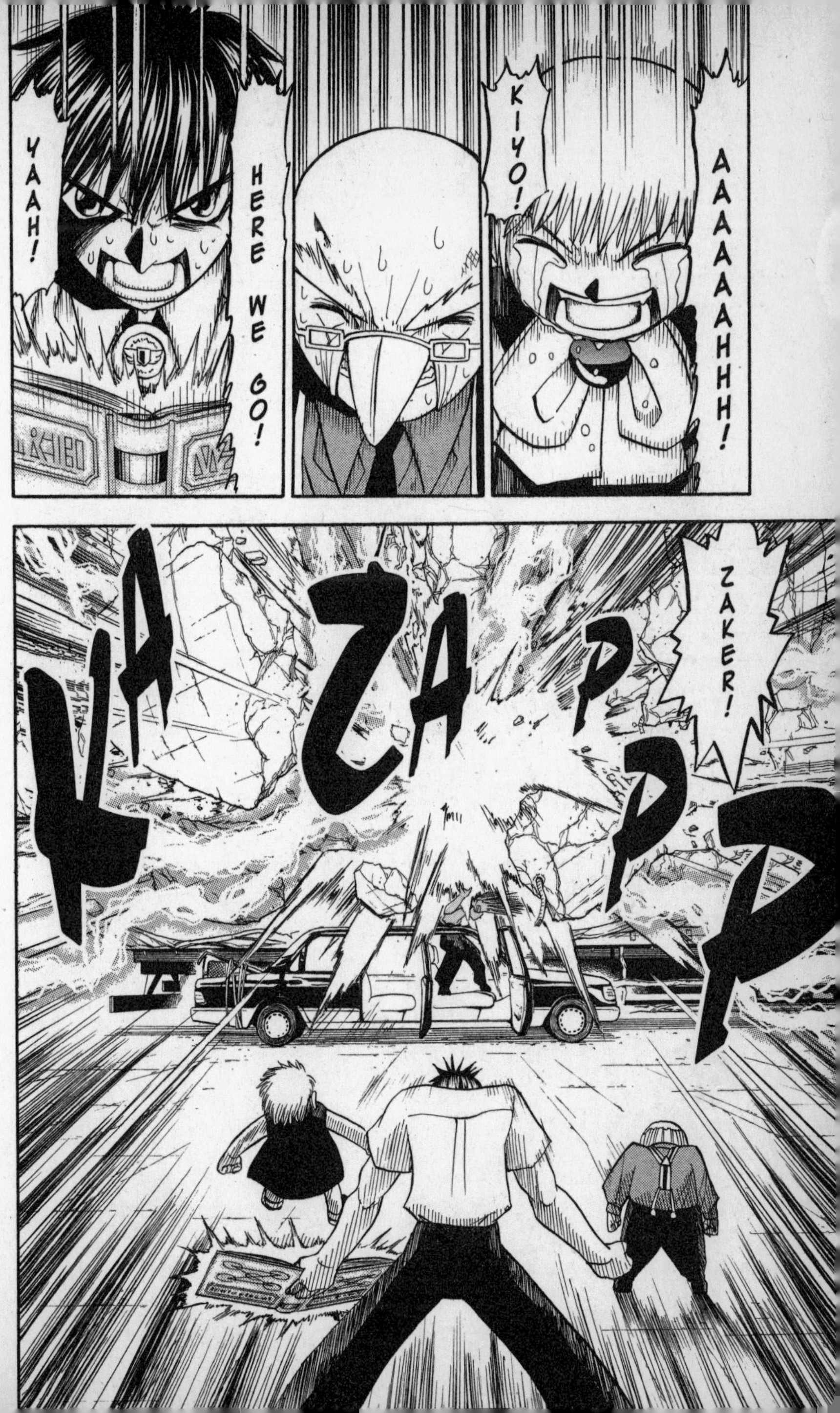

AAAAAAHHH!
KIYO!
HERE WE GO!
YAAAH!
ZAKER!
KAZAPPP

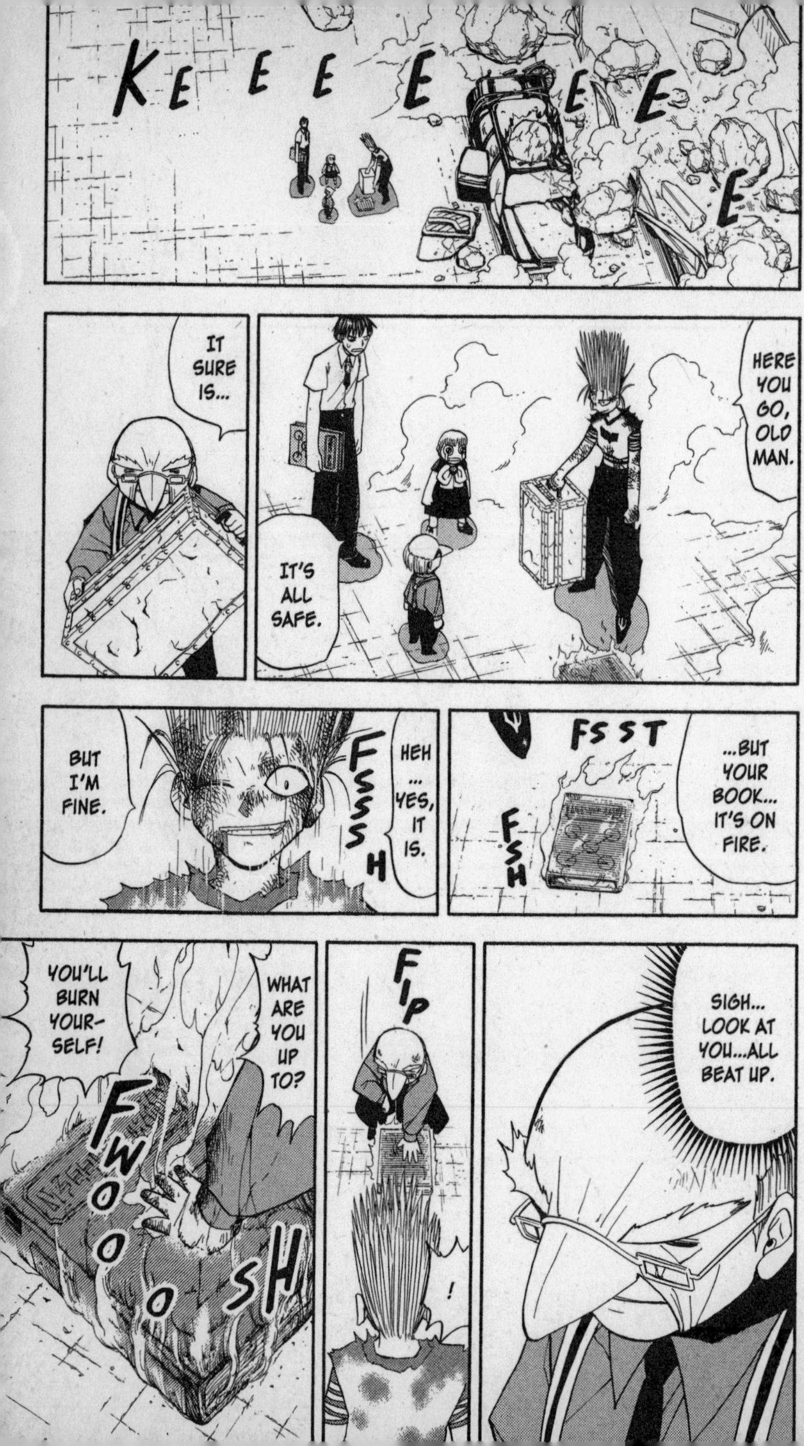
KEEEEEEE
HERE YOU GO, OLD MAN.
IT'S ALL SAFE.
IT SURE IS...
...BUT YOUR BOOK... IT'S ON FIRE.
FS ST
FSH
HEH... YES, IT IS.
FSSSH
BUT I'M FINE.
SIGH... LOOK AT YOU...ALL BEAT UP.
FIP
!
WHAT ARE YOU UP TO?
YOU'LL BURN YOUR-SELF!
FWOOOSH

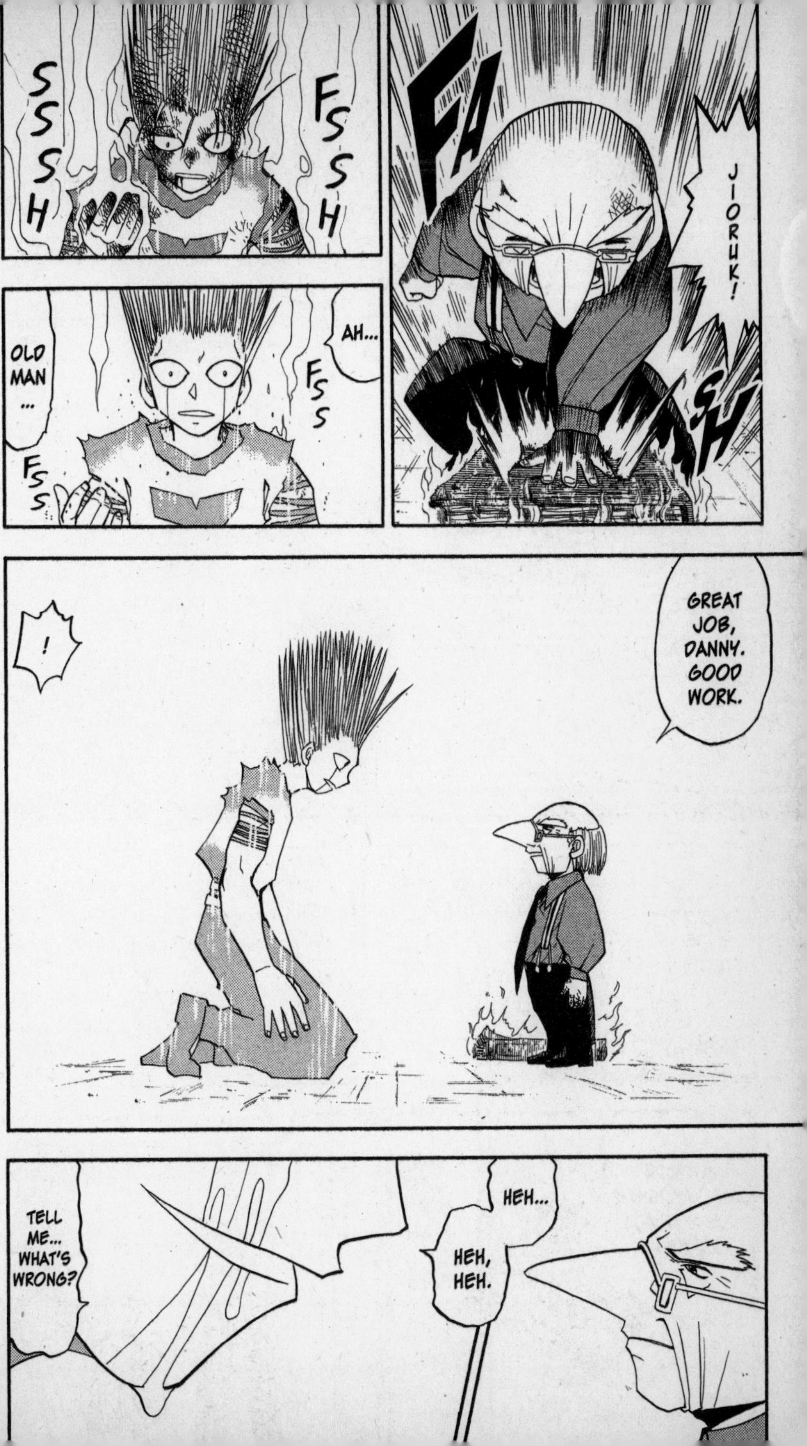
FA
JIORUK!
SH
SSSH
FSSH
AH...
OLD MAN...
FSS
FSS
GREAT JOB, DANNY. GOOD WORK.
!
HEH...
HEH, HEH.
TELL ME... WHAT'S WRONG?

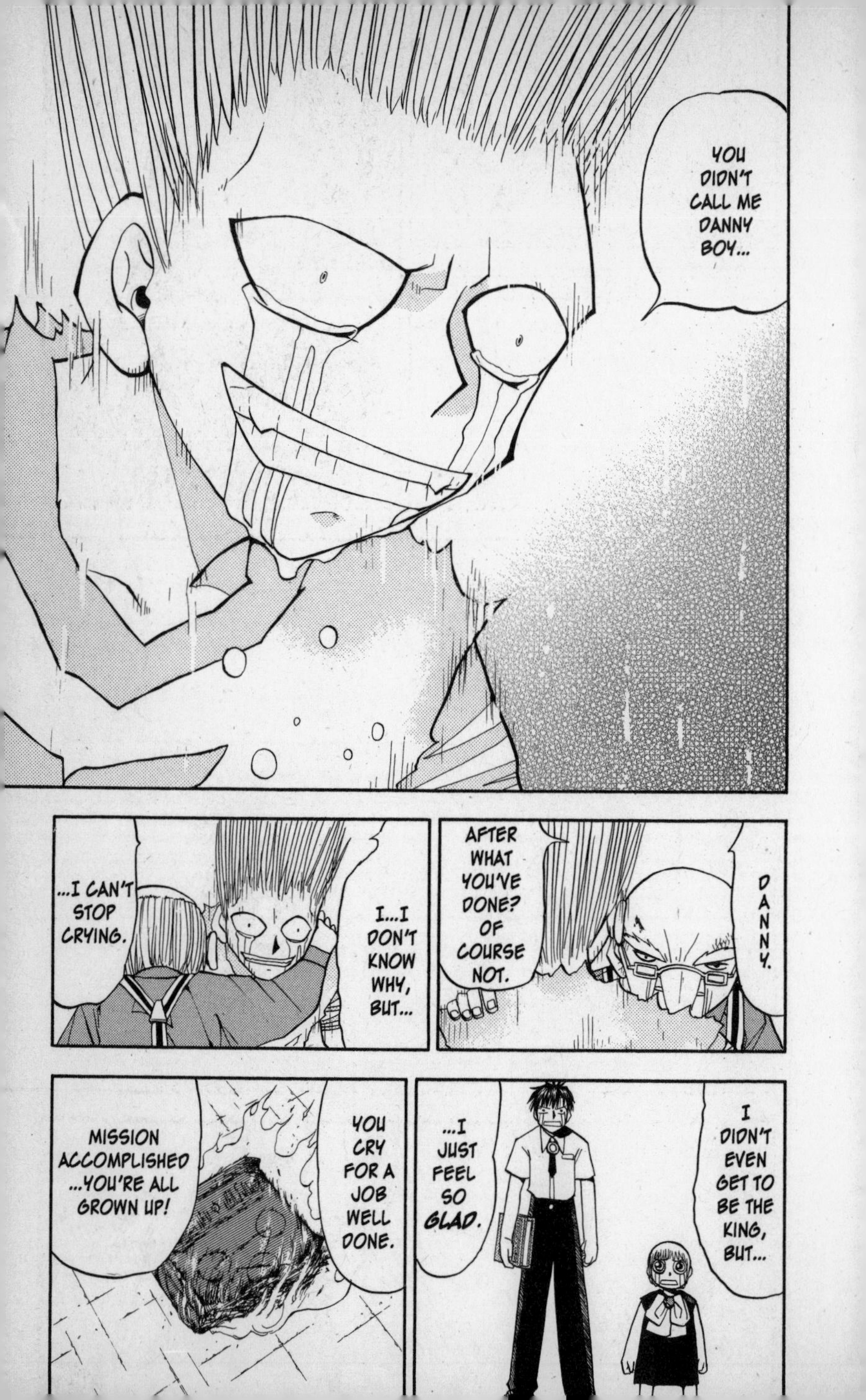
YOU DIDN'T CALL ME DANNY BOY...
DANNY.
AFTER WHAT YOU'VE DONE? OF COURSE NOT.
I...I DON'T KNOW WHY, BUT...
...I CAN'T STOP CRYING.
I DIDN'T EVEN GET TO BE THE KING, BUT...
...I JUST FEEL SO GLAD.
YOU CRY FOR A JOB WELL DONE.
MISSION ACCOMPLISHED ...YOU'RE ALL GROWN UP!

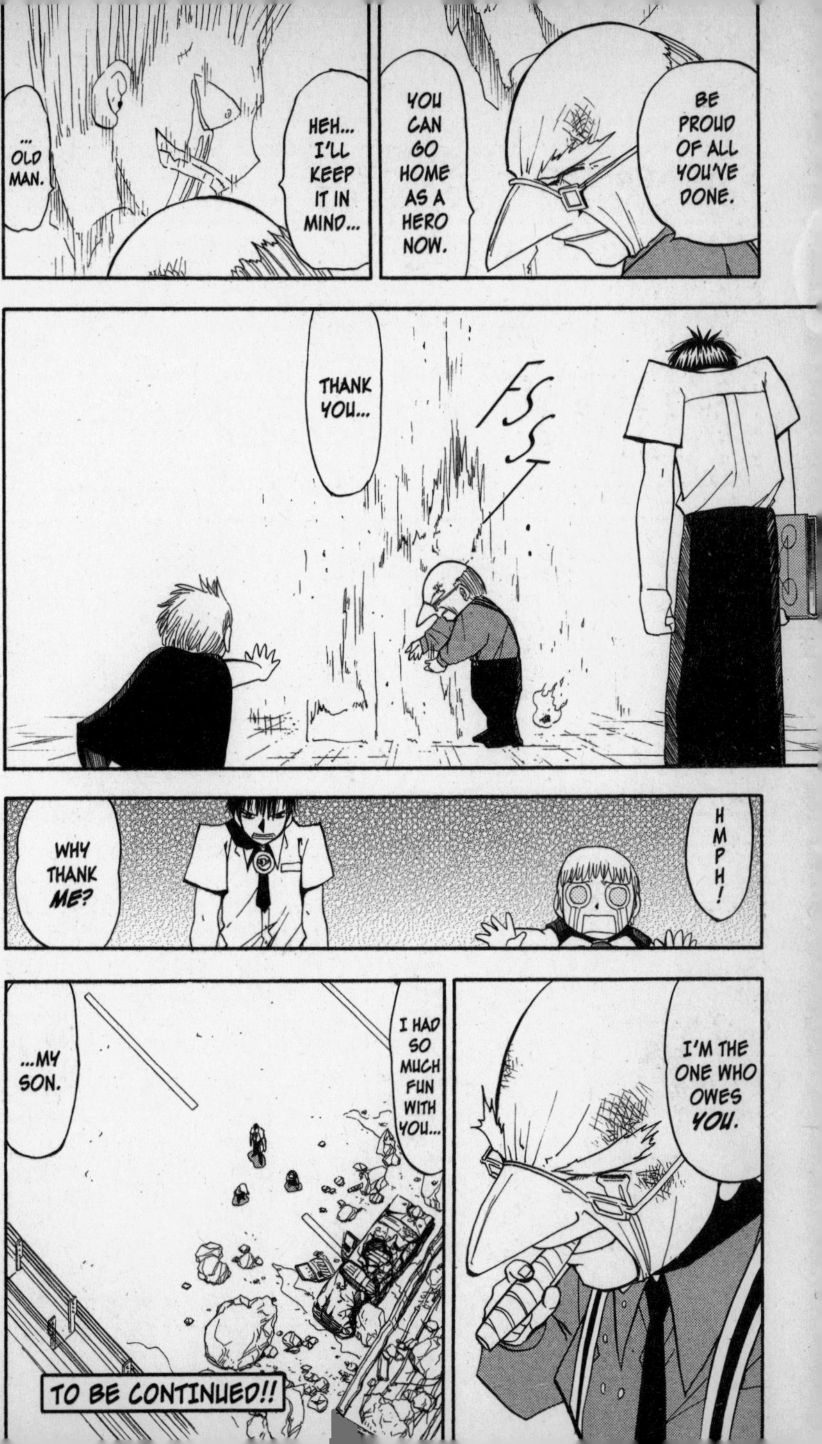
BE PROUD OF ALL YOU'VE DONE.
YOU CAN GO HOME AS A HERO NOW.
HEH... I'LL KEEP IT IN MIND...
... OLD MAN.
FSST
THANK YOU...
HMPH!
WHY THANK *ME*?
I'M THE ONE WHO OWES *YOU*.
I HAD SO MUCH FUN WITH YOU...
...MY SON.
TO BE CONTINUED!!

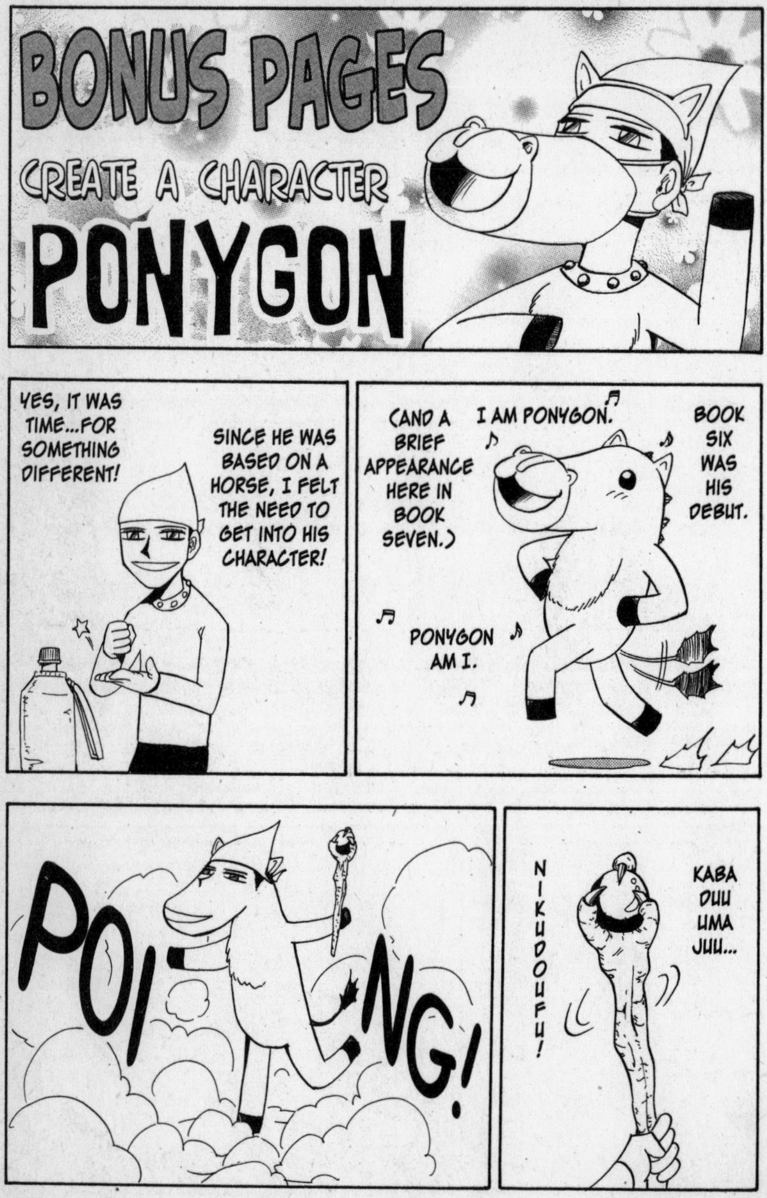
BONUS PAGES
CREATE A CHARACTER
PONYGON
BOOK SIX WAS HIS DEBUT.
I AM PONYGON.
(AND A BRIEF APPEARANCE HERE IN BOOK SEVEN.)
PONYGON AM I.
SINCE HE WAS BASED ON A HORSE, I FELT THE NEED TO GET INTO HIS CHARACTER!
YES, IT WAS TIME...FOR SOMETHING DIFFERENT!
KABA DUU UMA JUU...
NIKUDOUFU!
POING!

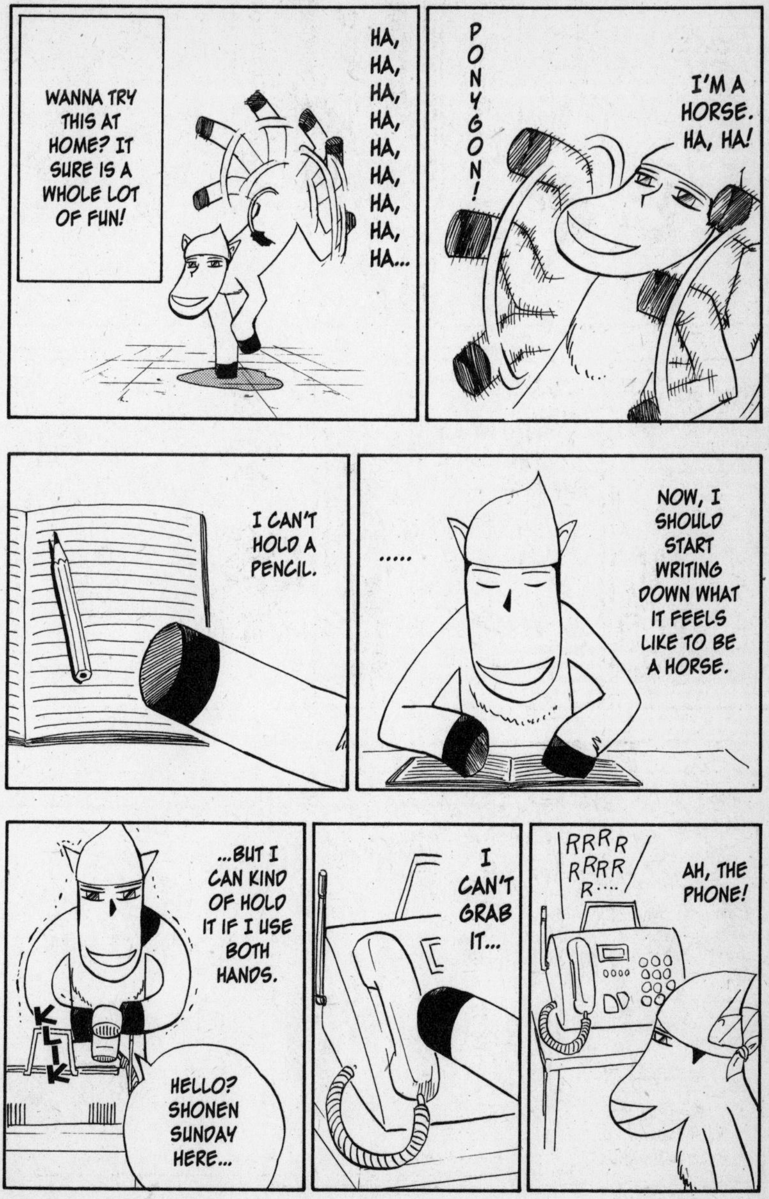
I'M A HORSE. HA, HA!
PONYGON!
HA, HA, HA, HA, HA, HA, HA, HA, HA...
WANNA TRY THIS AT HOME? IT SURE IS A WHOLE LOT OF FUN!
NOW, I SHOULD START WRITING DOWN WHAT IT FEELS LIKE TO BE A HORSE.
.....
I CAN'T HOLD A PENCIL.
RRRR RRRR R....
AH, THE PHONE!
I CAN'T GRAB IT...
...BUT I CAN KIND OF HOLD IT IF I USE BOTH HANDS.
KLIK
HELLO? SHONEN SUNDAY HERE...

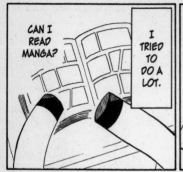

AH.
OOPS.
BEEP
BEEP
BEEP
BEEP
I TRIED TO DO A LOT.
CAN I READ MANGA?
CAN I MAKE SOME COFFEE?
HOW DO I HOLD A CUP?
THIS ISN'T RIGHT.
HORSES SHOULD BE WAY COOLER THAN THIS.
CHMP
CHMP
HA, HA, HA, HA...
OH, WELL! SO IT GOES...
AFTER ALL, A HORSE IS A HORSE, OF COURSE, OF COURSE!
HEE HEE HEE
WHY DIDN'T I PICK UP ON THAT FACT?
NOW I'M ALL SET!
I CAN DO IT!
AND THAT IS HOW PONYGON WAS CREATED!

THE END

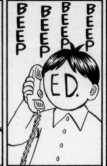

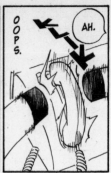

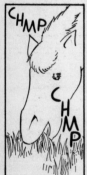

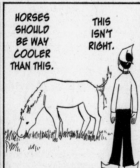

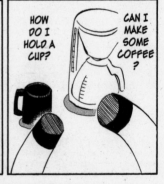

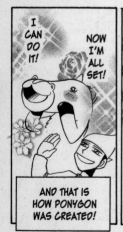

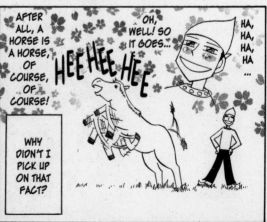

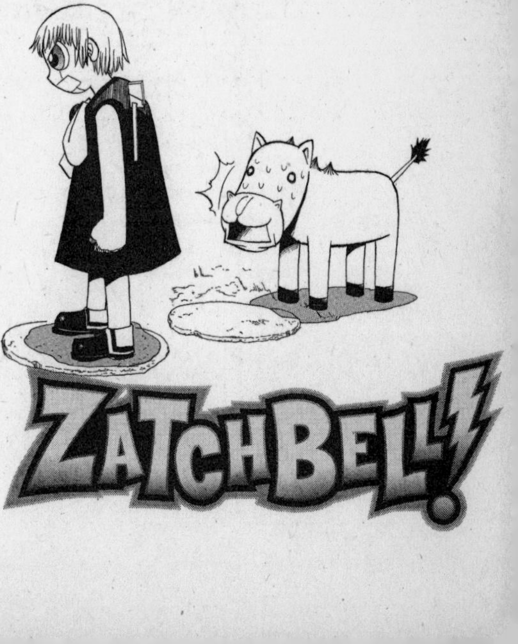

ZATCH BELL!

ZATCH & SUZY

BY MAKOTO RAIKU

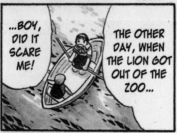

THE OTHER DAY, WHEN THE LION GOT OUT OF THE ZOO...
...BOY, DID IT SCARE ME!
RRRR
YEAH... LIONS HAVE A LOT OF TEETH.
ROWR
GRR
BUT I'M NOT AFRAID AT ALL!
WOOM
WAAHHH!
OH, I'M SORRY! ZATCH, DID I SCARE YOU? OH, NO!

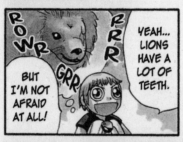

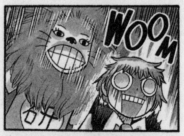

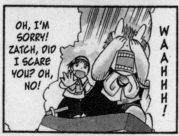

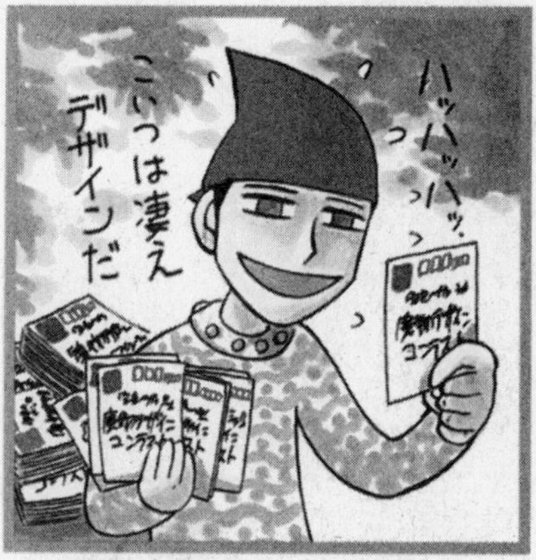
ハッハッハッ
こいつは凄え
デザインだ

MAKOTO RAIKU

Ha ha ha!

Wow, what a nice look!

The Mamodo Design Contest is going crazy. The number of postcards I received this time has doubled since the first time around. It's hard work, but it makes me happy. Thank you so much for sending your postcards. I'm still accepting submissions, so I look forward to receiving more!